HEIDEGGER AND PLATO

Topics in Historical Philosophy

General Editors David Kolb

John McCumber

Associate Editor Anthony J. Steinbock

HEIDEGGER AND PLATO

Toward Dialogue

Edited by Catalin Partenie
and Tom Rockmore

Northwestern University Press
Evanston, Illinois

Northwestern University Press
Evanston, Illinois 60208-4170

Printed in the United States of America

10   9   8   7   6   5   4   3   2   1

ISBN 0-8101-2232-4 (cloth)
ISBN 0-8101-2233-2 (paper)

Library of Congress Cataloging-in-Publication data are available from the
Library of Congress.

⊗ The paper used in this publication meets the minimum requirements of the
American National Standard for Information Sciences—Permanence of Paper
for Printed Library Materials, ANSI Z39.48-1992.

Contents

Acknowledgments

We would like to thank all our contributors for their patience and support. Thanks are also due to the three anonymous readers of the press who read the complete manuscript and offered helpful comments and criticism, and to Theodore Kisiel for his comments on the introduction. We would like to express our gratitude to Susan Bradanini Betz for her editorial support. We would also like to thank Daniela De Cecco for her translation of Enrico Berti's essay.

Abbreviations

Heidegger's Works

Throughout the volume, the following abbreviations are used for Heidegger's works. A slash separates the German edition from its English translation (if any). Unless otherwise noted, all references are to the German editions. When references to the page numbers of German editions are followed by a slash and another number, the latter refers to the English translations listed below. In a few cases, when there are two English translations listed below, references to the page numbers of German editions are followed by two slashes and two numbers, which refer to the two English translations listed below. With very rare exceptions, in all translations the German pagination is indicated; thus, the reader can easily find in a translation the page number(s) that correspond to reference(s) to the German edition. *GA* stands for Heidegger's *Gesamtausgabe,* the "complete edition" of his work published by Klostermann in Frankfurt am Main from 1975 on. Some volumes in German of Heidegger's works were published in a second and third edition; when that was the case, we have indicated the year(s) of further edition(s), but references to the page numbers of German editions are always to the first, fully cited, edition.

"ANAX"   "Der Spruch des Anaximander," in *GA* 5, 321–73/"The Anaximander Fragment," in *Early Greek Thinking,* tr. D. F. Krell and F. A. Capuzzi (New York: Harper and Row, 1984), 13–58. (Lecture of 1946.)

BT   *Sein und Zeit,* 15th ed. (Tübingen: Max Niemeyer, 1979)/*Being and Time,* tr. J. Macquarrie and E. Robinson (New York: Harper and Row, 1962). (First published in 1927.)

"ECP"   "Vom Wesen und Begriff der *Phusis:* Aristoteles, Physik, B, 1," in *GA* 9, 239–301/"On the Essence and Concept of *Phusis* in Aristotle's Physics B, 1," tr. T. Sheehan, revised by T. Sheehan and W. McNeill, in *Pathmarks,* ed. W. McNeill (Cambridge: Cambridge University Press, 1998), 183–238. (Essay of 1939.)

"EG"   "Wom Wesen des Grundes," in *GA* 9, 123–75/"On the Essence of Ground," tr. W. McNeill, in *Pathmarks,* ed. W. McNeill (Cambridge:

Cambridge University Press, 1998), 97–135. (An essay first published in 1929.)

EN   *Der europäische Nihilismus,* in *GA* 6.2, 23–229/*Nietzsche,* vol. 4, *Nihilism,* tr. F. A. Capuzzi (San Francisco: Harper and Row, 1982). (First published in 1961 on the basis of notes from 1940.)

"EP"   "Das Ende der Philosophie und die Aufgabe des Denkens," in *Zur Sache des Denkens* (Tübingen: Niemeyer, 1969), 61–80/"The End of Philosophy and the Task of Think," in *On Time and Being,* tr. J. Stambaugh (San Francisco: Harper and Row, 1972), 55–73. (Lecture of 1964 first published in a French translation in 1966.)

GA 5   *Holzwege,* ed. F.-W. von Herrmann, *Gesamtausgabe,* vol. 5 (Frankfurt am Main: V. Klostermann, 1977). (Essay of 1935–46.)

GA 6.1   *Nietzsche I,* ed. B. Schillbach, *Gesamtausgabe,* vol. 6.1 (Frankfurt am Main: V. Klostermann, 1996).

GA 6.2   *Nietzsche II,* ed. B. Schillbach, *Gesamtausgabe,* vol. 6.2 (Frankfurt am Main: V. Klostermann, 1997).

GA 7   *Vorträge und Aufsätze,* ed. F.-W. von Herrmann, *Gesamtausgabe,* vol. 7 (Frankfurt am Main: V. Klostermann, 2000).

GA 9   *Wegmarken,* ed. F.-W. von Herrmann, *Gesamtausgabe,* vol. 9 (Frankfurt am Main: V. Klostermann, 1976; 2d ed. 1996/*Pathmarks,* ed. W. McNeill (Cambridge: Cambridge University Press, 1998). (A collection of lectures and essays from 1919 to 1961; first published in 1967.)

GA 10   *Der Satz vom Grund,* ed. P. Jaeger, *Gesamtausgabe,* vol. 10 (Frankfurt am Main: V. Klostermann, 1997)/*The Principle of Reason,* tr. R. Lilly (Bloomington: Indiana University Press, 1991). (First published in 1957 on the basis of lectures of 1955–56.)

GA 15   *Seminare,* ed. C. Ochwadt, *Gesamtausgabe,* vol. 15 (Frankfurt am Main: V. Klostermann, 1986)/ partially translated in M. Heidegger and E. Fink, *Heraclitus Seminar,* tr. C. H. Seibert (Evanston: Northwestern University Press, 1993). (A collection of seminars from 1951 to 1973.)

GA 16   *Reden und anderen Zeugnisse eines Lebensweges 1910–1976,* ed. Hermann Heidegger, *Gesamtausgabe,* vol. 16 (Frankfurt am Main: V. Klostermann, 2000). (Various texts from 1910 to 1976.)

GA 17   *Einführung in die phänomenologische Forschung,* ed. F.-W. von Herr-
         mann, *Gesamtausgabe,* vol. 17 (Frankfurt am Main: V. Klostermann,
         1994). (Lectures of 1923–24.)

GA 19   *Platon: Sophistes,* ed. I. Schüßler, *Gesamtausgabe,* vol. 19 (Frankfurt
         am Main: V. Klostermann, 1992) / *Plato's Sophist,* tr. R. Rojcewicz and
         A. Schuwer (Bloomington and Indianapolis: Indiana University
         Press, 1997). (Lectures of WS 1924–25.)

GA 20   *Prolegomena zur Geschichte des Zeitbegriffs,* ed. P. Jaeger, *Gesamtausgabe,*
         vol. 20 (Frankfurt am Main: V. Klostermann, 1979; 2d ed. 1988, 3d
         ed. 1994) / *History of the Concept of Time: Prolegomena,* tr. T. Kisiel
         (Bloomington: Indiana University Press, 1985). (Lectures of SS
         1925.)

GA 21   *Logik: Die Frage nach der Wahrheit,* ed. W. Biemel, *Gesamtausgabe,* vol.
         21 (Frankfurt am Main: V. Klostermann, 1976). (Lectures of WS
         1925–26.)

GA 22   *Grundbegriffe der antiken Philosophie,* ed. F.-K. Blust, *Gesamtausgabe,*
         vol. 22 (Frankfurt am Main: V. Klostermann, 1993). (Lectures of SS
         1926.)

GA 24   *Die Grundprobleme der Phänomenologie,* ed. F.-W. von Herrmann,
         Gesamtausgabe, vol. 24 (Frankfurt am Main: V. Klostermann, 1975;
         2d ed. 1989) / *The Basic Problems of Phenomenology,* tr. A. Hofstadter
         (Bloomington: Indiana University Press, 1982). (Lectures of SS
         1927.)

GA 25   *Phänomenologische Interpretation von Kants Kritik der reinen Vernunft,*
         ed. I. Görland, *Gesamtausgabe,* vol. 25 (Frankfurt am Main: V. Kloster-
         mann, 1977; 2d ed. 1987, 3d ed. 1995) / *Phenomenological Interpreta-
         tion of Kant's Critique of Pure Reason,* tr. P. Emad and K. Maly (Bloom-
         ington: Indiana University Press, 1997). (Lectures of WS 1927–28.)

GA 26   *Metaphysische Anfangsgründe der Logik im Ausgang von Leibniz,* ed.
         K. Held, *Gesamtausgabe,* vol. 26 (Frankfurt am Main: V. Klostermann,
         1978; 2d ed. 1990) / *The Metaphysical Foundations of Logic,* tr. M. Heim
         (Bloomington: Indiana University Press, 1984). (Lectures of SS
         1928.)

GA 27   *Einleitung in die Philosophie,* ed. O. Saame and I. Saame-Speidel,
         Gesamtausgabe, vol. 27 (Frankfurt am Main: V. Klostermann, 1996).
         (Lectures of WS 1928–29.)

GA 28   *Der deutsche Idealismus (Fichte, Schelling, Hegel) und die philosophische Problemlage der Gegenwart,* ed. C. Strube, *Gesamtausgabe,* vol. 28 (Frankfurt am Main: V. Klostermann, 1997). (Lectures of SS 1929; the volume also contains, as an annex, a one-hour course delivered in the same semester entitled "Einführung in das akademische Studium.")

GA 29/30   *Die Grundbegriffe der Metaphysik: Welt-Endlichkeit-Einsamkeit,* ed. F.-W. von Herrmann, *Gesamtausgabe,* vol. 29/30 (Frankfurt am Main: V. Klostermann, 1983; 2d ed. 1992)/*Fundamental Concepts of Metaphysics: World-Finitude-Solitude,* tr. W. McNeill and N. Walker (Bloomington: Indiana University Press, 1994). (Lectures of WS 1929–30.)

GA 31   *Vom Wesen der menschlichen Freiheit: Einleitung in die Philo sophie,* ed. H. Tietjen, *Gesamtausgabe,* vol. 31 (Frankfurt am Main: V. Klostermann, 1982; 2d ed. 1994). (Lectures of SS 1930.)

GA 33   *Aristoteles: Metaphysik Θ1–3,* ed. H. Hüni, *Gesamtausgabe,* vol. 33 (Frankfurt am Main: V. Klostermann, 1981; 2d ed. 1990)/*Aristotle's Metaphysik Θ 1–3,* tr. W. Brogan and P. Warnek (Bloomington: Indiana University Press, 1996). (Lectures of SS 1931.)

GA 34   *Wom Wesen der Wahrheit: Zu Platons Höhlengleichnis und Theätet,* ed. H. Mörchen, *Gesamtausgabe,* vol. 34 (Frankfurt am Main: V. Klostermann, 1988; 2d edition 1997)/*The Essence of Truth: On Plato's Cave Allegory and* Theaetetus, tr. T. Sadler (London, New York: Continuum, 2001). (Lectures of WS 1931–32.)

GA 36/37   *Sein und Wahrheit: 1: Die Grundfrage der Philosophie, 2: Wom Wesen der Wahrheit,* ed. H. Tietjen, *Gesamtausgabe,* vol. 36/37 (Frankfurt am Main: V. Klostermann, 2001). (Two series of lectures: the first one of SS 1933, the second one of WS 1933–34.)

GA 39   *Hölderlins Hymnen "Germanien" und "Der Rhein,"* ed. S. Ziegler, *Gesamtausgabe,* vol. 39 (Frankfurt am Main: V. Klostermann, 1980; 2d ed. 1989). (Lectures of 1934–35.)

GA 40   *Einführung in die Metaphysik,* ed. P. Jaeger, *Gesamtausgabe,* vol. 40 (Frankfurt am Main: V. Klostermann, 1983)/*An Introduction to Metaphysics,* tr. R. Manheim (New York: Doubleday, 1961)/*Introduction to Metaphysics,* tr. G. Fried, R. Polt (New Haven and London: Yale University Press, 2000). (First published in 1953 on the basis of lectures of 1935.)

GA 41   *Die Frage nach dem Ding: Zu Kants Lehre von den transzendentalen Grundsätzen,* ed. P. Jaeger, *Gesamtausgabe,* vol. 41 (Frankfurt am Main: V. Klostermann, 1984). (Lectures of WS 1935–36.)

GA 45   *Grundfragen der Philosophie: Ausgewählte "Probleme" der Logik,* ed. F.-W. von Herrmann, *Gesamtausgabe,* vol. 45 (Frankfurt am Main: V. Klostermann, 1984; 2d ed. 1992) / *Basic Questions of Philosophy: Selected "Problems" of Logic,* tr. R. Rojcewicz and A. Schuwer (Bloomington: Indiana University Press, 1994). (Lectures of WS 1937–38.)

GA 52   *Hölderlins Hymne "Andenken,"* ed. C. Ochtwadt, *Gesamtausgabe,* vol. 52 (Frankfurt am Main: V. Klostermann, 1982; 2d ed. 1992). (Lectures of WS 1941–42.)

GA 53   *Hölderlins Hymne "Der Ister,"* ed. W. Biemel, *Gesamtausgabe,* vol. 53 (Frankfurt am Main: V. Klostermann, 1984; 2d ed. 1993). (Lectures of SS 1942.)

GA 54   *Parmenides,* ed. M. S. Frings, *Gesamtausgabe,* vol. 54 (Frankfurt am Main: V. Klostermann, 1982; 2d ed. 1992) / *Parmenides,* tr. R. Rojcewicz and A. Schuwer (Bloomington and Indianapolis: Indiana University Press, 1992). (Lectures of WS 1942–43.)

GA 55   *Heraklit. Der Anfang der abendländischen Denkens. Logik. Heraklits Lehre vom Logos,* ed. M. S. Frings, *Gesamtausgabe,* vol. 55 (Frankfurt am Main: V. Klostermann, 1979; 2d ed. 1987, 3d ed. 1994). (Lectures of 1943 and 1944.)

GA 56/57 *Zur Bestimmung der Philosophie,* ed. B. Heimbüchel, *Gesamtausgabe,* vol. 56/57 (Frankfurt am Main: V. Klostermann, 1987; 2d ed. 1999). (Lectures of SS 1919.)

GA 58   *Grundprobleme der Phänomenologie,* ed. H.-H. Gander, *Gesamtausgabe,* vol. 58 (Frankfurt am Main: V. Klostermann, 1992). (Lectures of WS 1919–20.)

GA 60   *Phänomenologie des religiösen Lebens,* ed. M. Jung, T. Regehly, and C. Strube, *Gesamtausgabe,* vol. 60 (Frankfurt am Main: V. Klostermann, 1995). (Lectures of 1918–19, 1920–21, 1921.)

GA 61   *Phänomenologische Interpretationen zu Aristoteles: Einführung in die phänomenologische Forschung,* ed. W. Bröcker and K. Bröcker-Oltmanns, *Gesamtausgabe,* vol. 61 (Frankfurt am Main: V. Klostermann, 1985; 2d ed. 1994) / *Phenomenological Interpretations of Aristotle:*

Initiation into Phenomenological Research, tr. R. Rojcewicz (Blooming-ton: Indiana University Press, 2001). (Lectures of WS 1921–22.)

GA 63 *Ontologie: Hermeneutik der Faktizität,* ed. K Bröcker-Oltmanns *Gesamt-ausgabe,* vol. 63 (Frankfurt am Main: V. Klostermann, 1988; 2d ed. 1995) / *Ontology (Hemeneutics of Facticity),* tr. J. van Buren (Blooming-ton: Indiana University Press, 1995). (Lectures of SS 1923).

GA 65 *Beiträge zur Philosophie (Vom Ereignis),* ed. F.-W. von Herrmann, *Gesamtausgabe,* vol. 65 (Frankfurt am Main: V. Klostermann, 1989; 2d ed. 1994) / *Contributions to Philosophy (From Enowing),* tr. P. Emad and K. Maly (Bloomington and Indianapolis: Indiana University Press, 1999). (Manuscripts of 1936–38 first published in 1989.)

GA 66 *Besinnung,* ed. F.-W. von Herrmann, *Gesamtausgabe,* vol. 66 (Frank-furt am Main: V. Klostermann, 1997). (Manuscripts of 1938–39 first published in 1997.)

"HG" "Hegel und die Griechen," in *GA* 9, 427–44/"Hegel and the Greeks," tr. R. Metcalf, ed. and rev. J. Sallis and W. McNeill, in *Path-marks,* ed. W. McNeill (Cambridge: Cambridge University Press, 1998), 323–36. (Lecture of 1958, first published in a French transla-tion in 1958.)

"LH" "Brief über den Humanismus," in *GA* 9, 313–64/"Letter on Human-ism," tr. F. A. Capuzzi, in collaboration with J. G. Gray, ed. and rev. W. McNeill and D. F. Krell, in *Pathmarks,* ed. W. McNeill (Cam-bridge: Cambridge University Press, 1998), 239–76. (Letter of 1946 to Jean Beaufret, first published in 1947.)

"PDT" "Platons Lehre von der Wahrheit," in *GA* 9, 203–38/"Plato's Doc-trine of Truth," tr. T. Sheehan, rev. T. Sheehan and W. McNeill, in *Pathmarks,* ed. W. McNeill (Cambridge: Cambridge University Press, 1998), 155–82. (An essay first published in 1942 on the basis of lec-tures of 1931–32, see *GA* 34.)

PIA *Phänomenologische Interpretationen zu Aristoteles (Anzeige der hermeutis-chen Situation),* in *Dilthey-Jahrbuch für Philosophie und Geschichte der Geisteswissenschaften* 6 (1989), 228–69/ *Phenomenological Interpretation with Respect to Aristotle: Indication of the Hermeneutical Situation,* tr. M. Baur, in *Man and World* 25 (1992), 355–93.

"QCT" "Die Frage nach der Technik," in *GA* 7, 7–36/"The Question Con-cerning Technology," in *The Question Concerning Technology and Other Essays,* tr. W. Lovitt (New York: Harper and Row, 1977). (A lecture of 1953, first published in 1954.)

"SGU"   "Die Selbstbehauptung der deutschen Universität," in *Die Selbst-behauptung der deutschen Universität: Das Rektorat 1933/34,* ed. H. Hei-degger (Frankfurt: Klostermann, 1983)/"The Self-Assertion of the German University," in *Martin Heidegger and National Socialism: Questions and Answers,* ed. G. Neske and E. Kettering (New York: Paragon House, 1990).

"THOR68" "Seminar in Le Thor 1968," in *GA* 15, 286–325.

"THOR69" "Seminar in Le Thor 1969," in *GA* 15, 326–71.

"WM"   "Was ist Metaphysik?" in *GA* 9, 103–22/"What is Metaphysics?" tr. D. F. Krell, ed. and rev. D. F. Krell and W. McNeill, in *Pathmarks,* ed. W. McNeill (Cambridge: Cambridge University Press, 1998), 82–96. (A lecture of 1929.)

WPA   *Der Wille zur Macht als Kunst,* in *GA* 6.1, 1–225/*Nietzsche,* vol. 1, *The Will to Power as Art,* tr. D. F. Krell (San Francisco: Harper and Row, 1979). (First published in 1961 on the basis of notes of 1936–37.)

"Z"   "Seminar in Zähringen 1973," in *GA* 15, 372–400.

Plato's Works

Alc. I   *Alcibiades I*

Ap.   *Apology*

Chrm.   *Charmides*

Cra.   *Cratylus*

Cri.   *Crito*

Criti.   *Critias*

Euthd.   *Euthydemus*

Euthphr.   *Euthyphro*

Grg.   *Gorgias*

Hp. Ma.   *Hippias Major*

Hp. Mi.   *Hippias Minor*

La.	*Laches*
Lg.	*Leges (Laws)*
Ly.	*Lysis*
Men.	*Meno*
Mx.	*Menexenus*
Phd.	*Phaedo*
Phdr.	*Phaedrus*
Phlb.	*Philebus*
Plt.	*Politicus*
Prt.	*Protagoras*
R.	*Republic*
Smp.	*Symposium*
Sph.	*Sophist*
Tht.	*Theaetetus*
Ti.	*Timaeus*

Other Abbreviations

SS	*Sommersemester* (Summer Semester)
WS	*Wintersemester* (Winter Semester)

Introduction

Catalin Partenie and Tom Rockmore

This is a volume of original essays on issues raised in Heidegger's treatment of Plato. Important philosophers often have interesting things to say about their predecessors and/or their contemporaries. Martin Heidegger possessed an unusually detailed grasp of the history of Western philosophy. Throughout his philosophical development he was extremely interested in the interpretation of key figures in the history of philosophy, with special attention to ancient Greek thinkers.

Heidegger's views of Plato are extremely complex. His writings on Plato provide no more than a fragmentary indication of the importance of the latter for his philosophical theories. During his life Heidegger published only one relatively short essay on Plato, "Plato's Doctrine of Truth" ("PDT"), which appeared in 1942. Yet he was deeply interested in Plato. Three of the courses given at the Universities of Marburg and Freiburg im Breisgau were exclusively devoted to his writings. They include one on the *Sophist* in 1924–25 (*GA* 19), another on the *Republic* in 1931–32 (*GA* 34) and a final one on the *Theaetetus* (*GA* 36/37, part 2). At the beginning of the course on the *Sophist,* Heidegger also announced a course on the *Philebus* (*GA* 19, 7). The latter, which was supposed to occur in the same semester, was never given. In summer semester 1929, Heidegger gave a one-hour course entitled "Introduction in Academic Studies,"[1] based on an interpretation of Plato's cave allegory that was later developed in the 1931–32 course. Also in winter semester 1930–31 and in summer semester 1931, he gave a seminar whose full title, according to Herbert Marcuse's transcript, was "Plato's *Parmenides* (On the problem of time)." No transcripts or lecture notes of this seminar have so far appeared, and it is not known if their publication is planned.

A simple way to describe Heidegger's reading of Plato might be to say that what began as an attempt to appropriate Plato (and through Plato a large portion of Western philosophy) finally ended in an estrangement from both Plato and Western philosophy. What follows is a brief sketch of this attempt to appropriate, and this estrangement from, Plato.

Heidegger's attempt to appropriate Plato for his own purposes began in the early 1920s and ended in the late 1920s. Throughout his remarks on Plato, Heidegger consistently maintains that Plato understood being as *idea*.[2] According to Heidegger, "the fundamental question of Greek philosophical research is the question of Being, the question of the meaning of Being, and characteristically, the question of truth" (*GA* 19, 190/132). The fundamental question of Heidegger's philosophy is the question of being. His deep interest in Greek philosophy arises out of his consistent claim that philosophy is nothing but a battle concerning this question.

Heidegger considers Aristotle to be the "scientific high point of ancient philosophy" (*GA* 22, 22),[3] and he straightforwardly claims that "what Aristotle said is what Plato placed at his disposal, only it is said more radically and developed more scientifically" (*GA* 19, 11–12/8). He further claims, however, that "philosophy has not made any further progress with its cardinal question [the question about being] than it had already in Plato" (*GA* 24, 399–400). Heidegger's first major work, *Being and Time* (1927), opens with a quotation from Plato's *Sophist* (244a). The quotation precedes a section of the *Sophist* usually called "the battle of the Gods and Giants," which describes a debate about what being is (see *Sph.* 245–49). The fact that Heidegger's first major work opens with a quotation from Plato indicates that at the time he composed this book Plato appeared to him to be the main hero of the philosophical battle about the meaning of being, the so-called *gigantomachia peri tês ousias,* which *Being and Time* was supposed to take up again in a way not seen since the early Greeks, and to resolve.

From the early 1920s to the late 1920s Heidegger attempted to show that the question of being takes its clues from Dasein. And his claim throughout that period that Plato understood being as *idea* was an attempt to show that Plato's philosophy also takes its clues from Dasein (see for instance his interpretation of the idea of the good in "EG," 160–62, and the recollection of ideas in *GA* 26, 184–87).

The estrangement from Plato's thought that began in the late 1920s or early 1930s—the exact chronology is unclear—appears to result from Heidegger's conviction that Plato inaugurated the distortion of the early Greek understanding of being, and that Plato's conception of being as *idea* was later responsible for the birth of so-called nihilism. Not all scholars, however, share this "developmentalist" view of Heidegger's relationship to Plato.

In *Introduction to Metaphysics* (1935), Heidegger argues that the early Greek thinkers and poets, especially Parmenides and Heraclitus, inaugurated a specific understanding of being in terms of *phusis, alêtheia,* and *logos.* Heidegger here attributes a key role to Plato in arguing that the latter "conceived of Being as idea" (*GA* 40, 207/212).[4] In Heidegger's opinion, this Platonic "distortion" of the early Greek understanding of *phusis*, *alêtheia,* and *logos* is the source of all later "distortions" of the original Greek conception of being. Heidegger's reading of these terms in the 1930s is detailed and interesting. He claims that the Platonic *idea* forces both *phusis* and *alêtheia* into a "yoke" (*zugon; R.,* 508a), "the yoke of idea." Thus in Plato, Heidegger argues, "*phusis* becomes the *idea* (*paradeigma*)" (*GA* 40, 197/201; cf. also "PDT"), and *alêtheia* becomes *phôs, Helle,* "brightness," that is, "accessibility and manifestness," as a result of which *alêtheia* loses its original meaning of "sheltering-concealing" (*Verbergung; GA* 65, 331–32/232–33; cf. also "PDT"). He finally maintains that for Plato, "that which appears, appearance, is no longer *phusis,* the emerging sway [*das aufgehende Walten*], nor the self-showing of the look, but instead it is the surfacing of the likeness. . . . The truth of *phusis*—*alêtheia* as the unconcealment that essentially unfolds in the emerging sway—now becomes *homoiôsis* and *mimêsis:* ressemblance, directedness, the correctness of seeing, the correctness of apprehending as representing" (*GA* 40, 193/197).[5] As a result, the early Greek understanding of *logos* is also distorted since "*logos* becomes the assertion, the locus of truth as correctness, the origin of the categories, the basic principle that determines the possibilities of Being."[6] This distortion is, Heidegger claims, implicitly stated by Plato in the *Republic,* in the so-called allegory of the cave (*R.,* 514–18). In this famous passage, according to Heidegger, concealment, the original sense of *alêtheia,* which is present in the distinction between the cave and the surface of the earth, becomes subordinated to the dominance of fire and sunlight, that is, to the correctness of apprehending as representing, and thus to *ideai.*

In *Introduction to Metaphysics* Heidegger's reading of Plato's role with respect to the supposed "distortion" of the original Greek view of being can be summarized as two points. First, he claims that "the interpretation of Being as *idea* in Plato is so little a departure, much less a downfall, from the so-called inception that instead it grasps this inception in a more unfolded and sharper way, and grounds it through the 'theory of ideas.' Plato is the fulfillment of the inception. In fact, it cannot be denied that the interpretation of being as *idea* results from the fundamental experience of Being as *phusis.* It is, as we say, a necessary consequence of the essence of Being as emergent shining [*Scheinen*]" (*GA* 40, 190–91/194). Second, Heidegger maintains that the interpretation of being as *idea* in Plato is a downfall. "If that which is an essential consequence is raised to the level of essence itself, and thus takes the place of the essence, then how do things stand? Then there is a fall, and it must for its part generate its own distinctive consequences. This is what happened. What remains decisive is not the fact that *phusis* was characterized as *idea*, but that the *idea* rises up as the sole and definitive interpretation of Being" (*GA* 40, 191/194).

For Heidegger, Plato's revision of the early Greek view of being is not innocent but rather fraught with consequences for all later Western philosophy and modern life itself. He detects three main consequences as concerns nihilism, specific Nietzschean doctrines of being as value and the will to power, and a so-called productionist metaphysics leading to modern technology. Heidegger specifically claims that Plato's interpretation of being as *idea* inaugurates the era of nihilism in the form of the oblivion of being that continues to this day.

Throughout the 1930s and 1940s, Heidegger studied Nietzsche intensively. He argued that at the core of Nietzsche's thought lies the following remark from his *Notebooks* of 1870–71: "My philosophy . . . an *inverted Platonism:* the farther removed from true being, the purer, the finer, the better it is. Living in semblance as goal" (*WPA,* 156/154).[7] According to Heidegger, Nietzsche rejects the world of ideas while arguing that being is nothing but becoming qua eternal return; yet Nietzsche's reversal of Platonism is essentially metaphysical, and his key ideas—the will to power, the eternal return, *Gerechtigkeit,* nihilism, and superman—stand as conclusive evidence for such a claim. On the basis of this interpretation, Heidegger concludes that the history of Western European philosophy, from Plato to Nietzsche, is nothing but the history of metaphysics (*GA* 6.2, 196).

Metaphysics, however, is nothing other than the oblivion of being: "Being itself necessarily remains unthought in metaphysics. Metaphysics is a history in which there is essentially nothing to Being itself: *metaphysics as such is nihilism proper;*" in short, metaphysics is nihilism with respect to the oblivion of being. And Plato is the first stage of this oblivion: "meta-physics begins with Plato's interpretation of Being as *idea*" (*GA* 6.2, 196/164).[8] Also, "because metaphysics begins with the interpretation of Being as *idea,* and because that interpretation sets the standard, all philosophy since Plato is 'idealism' in the strict sense of the word: Being is sought in the idea, the idea-like and the ideal" (*GA* 6.2, 196/164). According to Heidegger, the fact that Plato "conceived of Being as idea" (*GA* 40, 207/212) opened the way for thinking being (*Sein*) not in itself, but as beings (*Seiende*). This means that Plato abandoned the thinking path opened by the early Greek philosophers and poets and inaugurated the era of nihilism as the oblivion of being (*GA* 6.2, 315–17).

Heidegger further argues that Plato's interpretation of ideas in terms of *agathon* opened the way to Nietzsche's doctrines of being as value and as will to power. For Plato, Heidegger claims, "the highest of ideas is at the same time conceived as *agathon*," which is the "essence of all ideas" (*GA* 6.2, 204/173; for Plato's idea of *agathon* see *R.*, 505a). "Thought in a Greek sense, *agathon* is what *makes suitable*, what befits a being and make it possible for it to be a being. Being has the character of making possible, is the condition of possibility. To speak with Nietzsche, Being is a *value*" (*GA* 6.2, 198/165–66). Although in working out his analysis Heidegger tends to privilege similarities in suppressing differences, Plato's notion of *agathon* cannot simply be identified with Nietzsche's notion of value. Heidegger, however, claims that "the history of metaphysics proceeds on its path from Plato's interpretation of Being as *idea* and *agathon* to an interpretation of Being as will to power, which posits values and thinks everything as value" (*GA* 6.2, 198/166).

Heidegger specifically argues that Plato's interpretation of being as *idea* led to so-called productionist metaphysics resulting in the modern technological period that, he claims, is marked by the forgetfulness of being. According to Heidegger, the Platonic *ideai* are understood as products analogous to those of the craftsman (*R.*, 596–98). Heidegger claims that this amounts to asserting that "the essence of the idea, and thereby of Being" is grounded for Plato "in the initiating action of a creator whose essentiality appears to be saved only when what he creates is in each case something singular, a one" (*WPA*, 186/183). In other words, for Heidegger, Plato interprets being in terms drawn from human production. He maintains that Plato's interpretation of being as *idea* brought forth a productionist metaphysics that led to the modern technological era, in which "to be" means to be manipulable, as raw material, by the human will. "The unlimited modern hegemony of the technical in each nook and cranny of the planet is only the recent result of a very old technical approach to the world—this approach is called metaphysics. The essential origins of modern technology lie in the Platonic beginning of metaphysics" (*GA* 52, 91).

Heidegger's reading of Plato is linked to the so-called turning (*Kehre*) in his thought, which, as most observers agree, divides Heidegger's philosophical development into two main periods. At some unspecified time after the publication of *Being and Time*, but no later than the early 1930s, Heidegger claimed that a turning occurred in his thought. The concept of the turning is not well understood. Views of it range from claims that it responds to the wholly internal development of his own theories to the very different view that it is related to his political turning to National Socialism. Difficulty in understanding the turning creates additional difficulty in understanding the change in his approach to Plato and Western philosophy. In the pre-*Kehre* period, Heidegger raises the question about the meaning of being and attempts to answer that question on the basis of the assumption that human understanding of being is determined by its transcendental structure. In the post-*Kehre* period, Heidegger moves from the question about the meaning of being revealed to Dasein to the question about being in itself. It is difficult to determine to what extent the two phases of Heidegger's interpretation of Plato relate to his pre- and post-*Kehre* periods. It is clear, however, that his attempt to appropriate Plato's thought aimed inter alia at proving that Plato's philosophy takes its clues from Dasein. That initially very clear picture later seemed to dissolve as Heidegger's view of philosophy and of his relation to it changed radically. Shortly after World War II, Heidegger confessed to one of his former students that "the structure of Platonic thought is totally obscure to me."[9] That is why, perhaps, almost ten years later, in 1954, in a letter to Hannah Arendt, he expressed the wish to read Plato anew: "I would like to begin my Plato studies with the *Sophist* [lectures] (of 1924–25), to go through it again and to read Plato anew."[10] Did Heidegger read Plato anew?

In a lecture Heidegger gave in 1964, "The End of Philosophy and the Task of Thinking," there is a short and enigmatic passage which reads: "we must acknowledge the fact that *alêtheia,* unconcealment in the sense of the opening of presence, was originally only experienced as *orthotês,* as the correctness of representations and statements. But then the assertion about the essential transformation of truth, that is, from unconcealment to correctness, is also untenable [*nicht haltbar*]" ("EP," 78/70). This passage implies that Heidegger later basically changed his views about the early Greek understanding of being and its subsequent distortion by Plato. Is this an indication that he managed to read Plato anew and that his interpretation of Plato's thought entered a third phase? That the second phase of his interpretation of Plato, including his so-called estrangement from Plato and from Western philosophy in general, was followed by a third, radically new phase? These are very difficult questions if one had to judge from what has so far been published.

Heidegger's controversial interpretation of Plato is important for several reasons. One, of course, is for understanding Heidegger's own theories, which were clearly linked to how he initially sought to appropriate and then distanced himself from various Platonic theories. A second reason, which has not so far received much notice among scholars of ancient philosophy, especially those writing in English, is Heidegger's contribution to opening new approaches to Plato and early Greek philosophy. With rare exceptions, Plato scholars are not usually interested in discussing Heidegger's admittedly unorthodox views. A third reason is Heidegger's contribution to the vexed problem, about which there is still no agreement, as to how we ought or ought best to approach the history of philosophy.

It will be useful to say a brief word here about what is currently available about Heidegger's interpretation of Plato. There are at present only two books on Heidegger's views of Plato, namely those by Holz (1981) and Boutot (1987). Holz examines various similarities between the existential analytic Heidegger develops in *Being and Time* and Plato's dialogues. He argues that the *Crito, Euthyphro* and *Hippias Minor* "point to the distinction between authentic and inauthentic selfhood" (1981, 293–94). He suggests that the death scene that concludes the *Phaedo* "takes an added significance" if read with Heidegger's phenomenological analysis of "being-toward-death" in the background (Holz 1981, 198/166). Holz also comments on the *Protagoras, Lysis, Symposium, Phaedrus* and *Republic*. Boutot's book, which is available only in the original French, is more ambitious. It aims at an account of the Heideggerian interpretation of Plato in its entirety, and focuses on Heidegger's interpretation of a number of key Platonic notions.

Barnes (1990) is severely critical of Heidegger's essay, "Plato's Doctrine of Truth," in which he distinguishes four main theses. These are (1) that there are two conceptions of truth, that is, truth as unconcealment and truth as correspondence (the semantic thesis); (2) that in the history of philosophy, the conception of truth as correspondence replaced the conception of truth as unconcealment (the historical thesis); (3) that this historical transition is also present in an implicit way in Plato's allegory of the cave (the exegetical thesis); and (4) that the conception of truth as unconcealment is, "in a way, the philosophically preferable viewpoint" (the philosophical thesis; Barnes 1990, 176). Barnes argues that all these theses are false and concludes that "if there is a Platonic doctrine—or at least if there is an interesting theory—of truth . . . it is not located in the framework which Heidegger imagined" (1990, 195). Barnes's view has not gone unnoticed. Aubenque (1992, 28) argues that Barnes interprets Plato from his own point of view as well, which is that of a post-Fregean and post-Russellian logician.

Hyland contrasts Heidegger's use of myth in *Being and Time* with several of Plato's myths in arguing that they "speak to similar themes but in an even richer way" (1997, 91). Hyland also discusses "Heidegger's occasional greater sensitivity to mythological thinking" (1997, 91). Brogan (1997), Gonzales (1997 and 2002), Figal (2000), and Webb (2000) comment on various aspects of Heidegger's interpretation of Platonic dialectic. Heidegger's lectures on Plato's *Sophist* have been given special attention in Kisiel 1993b, Schüssler 1996, Brogan 1997, Gonzales 1997, Figal 2000, and Webb 2000. Rosen (1993) offers a comprehensive, especially useful account of Heidegger's thesis that European philosophy from Plato to Nietzsche is the history of metaphysics qua Platonism. Zimmerman (1990) offers detailed analysis of Heidegger's critique of productionist metaphysics. Peperzak (1997) deals with Heidegger's interpretation of the Platonic notion of truth. Beierwaltes (1992) explores Heidegger's interpretation of the idea of the good and addresses Heidegger's views on the *Platon-Rezeption*. Hyland (1995) raises many objections to Heidegger's reading of the *Republic*'s cave allegory. There are also several articles that offer a brief overall account of Heidegger's interpretation of Plato: Gadamer 1983b, Dostal 1985, Rosen 1988, and Courtine 1990. Also, there are a number of scholars who wrote extensively on Plato, as well as on Heidegger; among them are Hans-Georg Gadamer, Jacques Derrida, John Sallis, and Dorothea Frede.

After these general remarks on Heidegger and Plato, we can turn very briefly to the ten chapters of this volume.

In 1933, Heidegger delivered a speech as the newly installed rector of the University of Freiburg. In "On the Purported Platonism of Heidegger's Rectoral Address," Theodore Kisiel examines the theme of Platonism in this speech.

Heidegger's relation to Plato is also a factor in his reading of Sophocles' *Antigone*. Jacques Taminiaux distinguishes two phases in Heidegger's reading of *Antigone* (in 1935, in the context of an examination of metaphysics, and again in 1942, in the context of a discussion of Hölderlin), and relates them to Heidegger's reading of Platonic and Aristotelian views of tragedy.

Heidegger's most elaborate dialogue with Plato occurs in the lecture course on the *Sophist* which was delivered in 1924–25. In his detailed examination of Heidegger's interpretation of Platonic dialectic in this lecture course, Catalin Partenie brings out how Heidegger's interpretation, in spite of its bias, draws our attention to a genuine and important Platonic distinction between authentic and inauthentic human existence, a distinction that also lies at the core of the fundamental ontology expounded in *Being and Time*.

Heidegger's very original but controversial view of truth is taken up in four chapters. In an account of truth and untruth in Plato and Heidegger, Michael Inwood assesses the importance of Heidegger's reaction to Plato in terms of Heidegger's own view of truth as unconcealment. This topic is pursued from another angle by Enrico Berti, who shows that Heidegger's interpretation of Plato's view of truth is linked with Heidegger's interpretation of Aristotle's view of truth. María del Carmen Paredes argues that the evolution in Heidegger's view of Plato reflects changes in his view of the possibility of metaphysics. Still another approach is provided by Joseph Margolis in respect to the theme of Heidegger's view of truth and being. Margolis contends that the widespread philosophical interest in truth is invariably linked to realism, and he argues that Heidegger employs a semantic conception of truth which fails to convince.

The so-called turning (*Kehre*) in Heidegger's thought is extremely important for understanding Heidegger. In "With Plato into the *Kairos* before the *Kehre:* On Heidegger's Different Interpretations of Plato," Johannes Fritsche shows Heidegger's different approaches to Plato in the 1920s and 1930s and links them to the development of Heidegger's own thinking, with special attention to the concept of "historicality" in *Being and Time.*

In "Remarks on Heidegger's Plato," Stanley Rosen links Heidegger's own theory of being to his reading of Plato. Rosen points out that Heidegger's interpretation of Plato attributes to Plato a theory of ideas understood as an ontology of production. Rosen's essay is a criticism of the interpretation of Plato as the originator of a productionist account of being.

Heidegger's reaction to Plato presupposes a specific approach to the history of philosophy. In "Heidegger's Use of Plato and the History of Philosophy," Tom Rockmore focuses on that approach. He contends that Heidegger's effort to recover philosophy beyond the history of philosophy is intrinsically flawed.

Notes

1. "Einführung in das akademische Studium," in *GA* 28, 345–61.

2. For a list of selected Platonic loci and issues discussed or referred to by Heidegger, see Appendix 1. Except in direct quotations, where we left anything within the quotation marks intact, the word "being" is spelled throughout the volume with a lowercase initial.

3. Throughout this introduction if no page number to an English translation is given for a quotation in English, the translation is that of the editors.

4. Quotations in English from *GA* 40 are from M. Heidegger, *Introduction to Metaphysics,* tr. G. Fried and R. Polt (New Haven and London: Yale University Press, 2000).

5. *Das aufgehende Walten* is "abiding emergence," which suggests the paradoxical joining of permanence and change.

6. *GA* 40, 197/201–2 ; cf. also 201/206: "On the basis of all this, the final interpretation of Being that is secured in the word *ousia* works itself out and works itself to the fore. *Ousia* means Being in the sense of constant presence, presence at hand. Consequently, what really is is what always is, *aei on.*"

7. Nietzsche's remark from F. Nietzsche, *Sämmtliche Werke: Kritische Studien-*

ausgabe, 15 vols., ed. G. Colli and M. Montinari (Berlin: Walter de Gruyter, 1980), 7:199; its English translation by D. F. Krell, *WPA,* 154.

8. Quotations in English from GA 6.2 are from M. Heidegger, *Nietzsche,* vol. 4, *Nihilism,* tr. F. A. Capuzzi, D. F. Krell, ed. (San Francisco: Harper and Row, 1982).

9. Picht 1977, 203. In this text about Heidegger, Picht tells that "shortly after the war" he had a conversation with Heidegger about the allegory of the cave; at the end of this conversation, Heidegger confessed that the structure of Plato's thought remained for him totally obscure.

10. From a letter to Hannah Arendt dated October 10, 1954, in Arendt 1999.

HEIDEGGER AND PLATO

On the Purported Platonism of Heidegger's Rectoral Address

Theodore Kisiel

[T]he very word "political," which in all European languages still
derives from the historically unique organization of the Greek
city-state [*polis*], echoes the experiences of the community which
first discovered the essence and the realm of the political.

[T]he problematic of the *Rectoral Address* is the last avatar of
Platonism.

It should perhaps be no real surprise that Heidegger's various concepts of
the political invariably pass through the simple paradigms provided by
the Greek *polis*. His early phenomenological concept of the political,
which takes its point of departure from the equiprimordiality of Aristotle's two definitions of the living being called human, as the talking and
the political animal, develops its sense of the political arena punctuated
temporally by crisis-laden occasions of public speaking (the deliberative
future, the judicial past, and epideictic present) as they are described in
Aristotle's *Rhetoric*. His later archaic-poietic concept of the political finds
its prepolitical roots at the level of the unique human situation of communal facticity that precedes and underlies the fateful conflict between
family piety and royal dictate that Sophocles (and, by way of his German
translation and commentary, Hölderlin) portrays in *Antigone*.[1]

Our concern here is with Heidegger's middle concept of the political that emerges during his rectoral period (1933–34), where the Platonic
polis of *paideia*, the "educational state" (*Erziehungsstaat*) outlined by Plato's
Republic, is made the paradigm for the structure of the German university,
for the German university is the institution of higher learning "that,
grounded in science and by means of science, educates and disciplines

the leaders and guardians of the destiny of the German people" (*RA*, 11/6).[2] But what is the destiny of the German people among the nations of the world? Nothing less than the development of the educational state itself as the highest expression of the German community. "To cultivate the new order of such a community: that is Germany's 'world-mission,' learned from the war; it is in the name of its *culture* for which it enters the lists against the 'equalizing and leveling "civilization"' that is now spanning the globe, in order to represent it as 'world culture'" (*DWB*, 1, 2).[3] In the aftermath of the cultural propaganda wars that erupted shortly after the outbreak of World War I in 1914, Paul Natorp thus defends the superior ideals of German culture over against the materialistic, utilitarian, libertarian, and plutocratic Western civilizations being increasingly leveled by technology. "The peculiarly German goal of 'culture' . . . wants to cultivate and develop humanity out of the inner roots of its inherent growth-potential, on the ancestral, religiously preserved, and faithfully prepared ground of a people's individuality. It is out of the genuinely German and humanized state that the human state is to grow, as the state of humanity's 'culture,' where only human beings dwell upon the earth. This is what we have been seeking: the *world mission* of the Germans" (*DWB*, 2, 55f). This homegrown community cultivated into a state is thus a moral-pedagogical totality that is at once a state of economy, a state of law, a state of education (*Wirtschaftsstaat, Rechtsstaat, Erziehungsstaat*), which do not constitute three competing and conflicting goals but instead three perspectives that together define the unified single possible goal of the state as the state of human culture, the genuinely human state (*DWB*, 2, 195f). The last and highest perspective is that of education. Humans do not work in order to work, let themselves be governed in order to be governed, "but in order to live the genuine human life of the spirit and the heart, for the sake of their humanity" (*DWB*, 2, 196). In order to develop the inherent strengths of a people and to attain its common goals, one requires not merely an economic and political but a much more comprehensive and deeply grounded education, a "spiritual/intellectual, moral, artistic, religious education of the entire nation" (*DWB*, 2, 197). The communism of the upper-class aristocracy of Plato's educational state is displaced by the socialism of universal education of a national community, as the "Swiss-German" Pestalozzi developed it, beginning with the working class, "out of the depths of the philosophy and religion of German idealism" (*DWB*, 2, 131f). The idea of the state finds its high point in a social pedagogy grounded in a social economy and a social law, in a uniquely German socialism based on the Kantian categorical imperative that respects all persons as ends and resists treating them as means.[4] In this "kingdom of ends," education is the self-cultivated formation, that is, the shaping from within, of each individual and through it the internal shaping of the community itself into a genuine individuality, into a self-composed interiority (Natorp 1907, 95). In this communal individuality, the individual and the community are no longer separated "but rather condition each other in freedom" (*DWB*, 2, 180). For freedom does not mean a lack of all restraining bonds but rather internal self-binding and assumption of responsibility for the community and one's duty toward it (*DWB*, 2, 132, 130). It is the freedom that Kant finds to be correlative with obligation and duty and regards as the sole transcendental fact of pure practical reason. German freedom is binding obligation (*Bindung*), and the individual's bonds in and with a community constitute a whole (*Bindungsganzes*) which is the human world (*GA* 26, 247/192).

"And where there is freedom, there is Germanness, there is a fatherland in the German sense, an internally grounded and free community of the free" (*DWB*, 2, 110). This is the German socialism (in which "we will ourselves") that Natorp in his social pedagogy makes into an ideal and an infinite task of the Germans, years before August 1914 and the spontaneous unification of all Germans concentrated on the war effort in a solidarity that already in these war years was called a uniquely "German socialism" (Natorp, Naumann, Sombart) and even a "national socialism" (*nationaler Sozialismus;* Plenge, from a more economic perspective). In the reciprocal relation between the individual and the community, German socialism is a social personalism whose motto is "all for one and one for all and yet each is entirely himself."[5] It is precisely the opposite of Western individualism, whose commonality is regarded as a plurality of abstract atoms of equal and "private" individual persons (*DWB*, 2, 20).

Thus, the provincial minister's complaint to Heidegger immediately following his rectoral address, that he was promoting "a kind of 'private national socialism' which circumvents the perspectives of the [Nazi] party program" (*RA*, 30/23)[6] was historically not quite on the mark. Heidegger's brand of "national socialism" had been blatantly part of the German public domain, from scholarly essays to the political tracts of right-wing political parties, at least since the emergence of the "Ideas of 1914" and the wide currency given to the "pure socialism" (Naumann) of the "band of brothers" (*Kameradschaft*) being bonded together into a "combat community" (*Kampfgemeinschaft*) of service and sacrifice through the "experience of the front" (*Fronterlebnis*), in a wartime solidarity between the war front and the home front that was then projected as the model for German unification to be emulated by the forthcoming peacetime community. After Fritz Ringer,[7] Heidegger's more "private" brand might be called the "mandarin" socialism of an educational state that the social pedagogue Paul Natorp, by way of a hybridization of Plato with Pestalozzi and

German idealism, had been promoting from the 1890s into the postwar years. It is this idealistic socialism centered on the moral and mental-spiritual will of the community that Heidegger seeks to promote in the "new German reality" of 1933, in his many laudations of the national socialist "movement" and "revolution" during the rectoral period.

> The national socialist revolution is therefore not an external takeover of an existing state apparatus by a party become powerful enough to do so, but the internal re-education of an entire people to the task of willing its own unification and unity. . . . The basic character of the new spiritual and political movement which passes through the people is that of an education and *re-education of the people to becoming a people through the state.* And when it is a matter of the deepest and broadest *education,* is this not the task of the highest school in the land? . . . *Education of the people through the state to becoming a people*—that is the meaning of the national socialist movement, that is the essence of the new national education. *Such* an education in the highest knowledge is the task of the new university. (*GA* 16, 302, 304, 307)[8]

The "movement" thus becomes an educational movement, the awakening of a people to its most profound aspirations befitting its traditions. The asymptotic goal of this movement is the idealistic "socialism of universal education" structured upon Plato's educational state modified into a Kantian idea befitting the German people. This sense of Idea as a progressively realizable goal for historical humanity is for Natorp Plato's true discovery, making of Plato "a Kantian before Kant, indeed a Marburg neo-Kantian before Marburg."[9] The neo-Kantian philosophy of culture in general, from Windelband to Cassirer, has humanity progressing, through science and education and in the spirit of cosmopolitan enlightenment, toward the asymptotic transcendental horizons of the True, Good, Beautiful, and Holy.

It is commonly remarked in retrospect that this optimistic idealistic *Kulturpolitik* suffered a resounding defeat with the "end" of the First World War.[10] How is it then that vestiges of this optimism survive the deep pessimism of the Weimar years into 1933 and provide the justification for a whole spectrum of conservative German intellectuals, many of them mandarins, to lend their wholehearted and enthusiastic support to the "National Socialist Revolution"?

Exactly two months after the constitutional—and popular—transmission of political power to the German National Socialist Labor Party, its so-called *Machtergreifung*—a term that became applicable only in the ensuing months, as the new regime gradually displayed its true stripes—

thus even before the very prospect of the rectorship that would empower him to implement his own long-incubating ideas on university reform for the Third Reich, Heidegger, in a revealing letter to Elisabeth Blochmann, with whom he had been conducting an ongoing frank discussion of German party politics, expresses his enthusiasm over the sudden surge of historical events on the political front, to the point of regarding it as an onto-logical *Ereignis* full of opportunity and potential, a veritable *kairos:*

> The current events have for me—precisely because so much remains obscure and uncontrolled—an extraordinarily concentrative power. It intensifies the will and the confidence to work in the service of a grand mission and to cooperate in the building of a world grounded in the people. For some time now, I have given up on the empty, superficial, unreal, thus nihilistic talk of mere "culture" and so-called "values" and have sought this new ground in *Da-sein*. We will find this ground and at the same time the calling of the German people in the history of the West only if we expose ourselves to be-ing itself in a new way and new appropriation. I thereby experience the current events wholly out of the future. Only in this way can we develop a genuine involvement and that *in-stantiation* [*Inständigkeit*] in our history which is in fact the precondi-tion for any effective action.[11]

Heidegger is thus already busy deconstructing neo-Kantian concepts like "culture" and "value," which he regards as "unreal" and "nihilistic," and at the same time reconstructing a *Kulturpolitik* in terms of his own ontology of "Da-sein" and temporal-historical "be-ing." This is clearly evident in the Rectoral Address, where the Dasein of the German folk is described in terms of the fateful communal decision that it must make over the critical historical situation in which it finds itself in Europe's middle. A people de-ciding for the state appropriate to its being: This is the *ontological essence of the political* for Heidegger during these trying times, which he is regarding not in terms of a calculative *Realpolitik* but as a potential *Bildungspolitik* to guide the self-determination of the university community on its way to re-forming itself into and for the future "educational state," understood as a Teutonic *polis* of *paideia*.

The ontological deconstruction of the neo-Kantian concept of cul-ture (*paideia*) into the ontological categories of Dasein is in full swing in the Rectoral Address. The traditional divisions of human "culture," delib-erately listed in somewhat haphazard yet incomplete detail to exemplify the confusing variety of their division into "rigidly separate [scientific] specialties" among the university faculties, and so "their endless and aim-less dispersal into isolated fields and niches . . . such as: nature, history, language; people, custom, law, state; poetizing [art], thinking, believing; disease [medicine], madness [psychiatry], death; economy, technology," are instead reidentified as "world-shaping powers of human-historical Dasein" (*RA,* 13f./9). It is the task of the university, in its basic will to know (which Natorp likened to the Platonic *erôs*), to bring this diversity of domains together under a single will to know, traditionally called science, which in turn creates the singular spiritual world of a historical people, especially a "people of poets and thinkers." This unifying science must be understood in the original Greek sense of philosophy, "not as a 'cultural asset' but as the innermost determining center of the entire Dasein of a people and its state" (12/7). Science in this radical sense is the "passion to remain close to and pressed by beings as such," the questioning stance that holds one's ground in the midst of the ever self-concealing beings as a whole" (12/8), "the *questioning and exposed standing of one's ground in the midst of the uncertainty of beings as a whole*" (14/9, italics in original). This stormy questioning of the meaning of be-ing by and for Greek Dasein or German Dasein "will create for our people its world, a world of innermost and most extreme danger, i.e., its truly *spiritual* world. . . . And the *spiritual world* of a people is not the superstructure of a culture, no more than it is an arsenal of useful information and values; it is the power that most deeply preserves the people's strengths tied to their earth and blood; as such it is the power that most deeply arouses and most profoundly moves the Dasein of a people" (14/9, italics in original). To counter the idealistic flight into superstructures which the term "spiritual" is prone to take, Heidegger must repeatedly emphasize that we are dealing with the indigenous spirit of a native people ensconced in a unique historical infrastructure. The "spiritual world" is in fact the thoroughly historical world of an earthbound historical people which, like an individual life, comes into being and then enters into its maturity, only to decline and pass away. In coming to its maturity, the Dasein of a people, like an individual Dasein, has its moments (*kairoi*) of crisis of self-definition, in which it must contextually "size up" its holistic situation in its historical sense (*Besinnung*) and direction, becoming responsive to the directive demands exacted by that situation in order to determine an appropriate course of action-in-crisis that would be true to its historical be-ing in context and direction. Aristotle called this responsiveness to the protopractical situation of action *phronêsis,* and Heidegger, drawing on his analysis of Dasein's self-authentication in *Sein und Zeit,* calls it *Ent-schlossenheit,* resolute openness, and equates it with "spirit" in this quasi-idealistic context of promoting "The Self-Determination of the German University." "Spirit is the originarily attuned, knowing resoluteness toward the essence of be-ing" which is "empowered by the deepest vocation and broadest obligation" (*RA,*

14/9) to be found in the Dasein of a people. In other contexts at this time, Heidegger describes resolute openness, again in quasi-idealistic terms, as the will to question, will to learn, and will to know. But to offset the activistic thrust of such formulations, in keeping with the call for the "self-assertion of the university," it should be recalled that the "primal action" (*Urhandlung*), the action that underlies all actions, of the "virtue" of *phronêsis*, resolute openness, is that of letting be, *Gelassenheit*.

The Platonic-Teutonic Educational State

And what resolute openness lets be in this context is the singular historical opening and unique "leeway of freedom" granted the German people to act historically, understood as the "space of play" (*Spielraum*) in which its indigenous "spiritual" powers are granted free play and full amplitude on both the domestic and larger European scene. This "temporal playing field" (*Zeit-Spiel-Raum*) of freedom is the educational state of "national socialism," articulated "platonically" into the three levels of work service, defense service, and science service. Since this freedom that is granted to us from our historical opening is "of the essence of truth" (*Vom Wesen der Wahrheit*), Heidegger identifies such a state (and the university modeled after it) as the "place of truth" (*locus veritatis*) and the "clearing of be-ing," where the great powers of be-ing to which human being is exposed— nature, history, art, technology, economy; indeed, the state itself—are gathered into their possibilities and bound into their limits (*GA* 16, 200f, 767f).

The Rectoral Address thus begins with the question of the essence of the university, which it provisionally grounds in the essence of science and eventually traces back to the originating ground of the "essence of truth," understood as the ever unique historical unconcealment of be-ing from which errant humans, individually and communally, *must* recover their equally unique historical opening, their "spiritual world." Noteworthy in the *speech* "On the Essence of Truth," which Heidegger delivered on several occasions from 1930 through 1932, is the "German-conservative" emphasis on freedom as binding obligation, an emphasis which is muted in the first published version in 1943. In the 1930 talk, the manifestive behavior operative within and through the truth of statements, in opening the leeway of a world, at once establishes a hold in the world. Thus, freedom as the letting be of a world is sometimes described as letting oneself become bound, which in its binding obligation (*Bindung*) measures itself to the obligation (*Verbindlichkeit*) of the world. The world: a communal whole of binding obligations and playing field of freedom in the development of their possibilities, which constitutes the "cultivation of the world" (*Welt-bildung*). "The two characters of any comportive behavior, manifestive opening and letting-itself-be-bound, are not at all double but one and the same." The note of necessity invested in such a freedom is in fact the state of "turning in the need" (*Not-wendigkeit*) between ex-sisting in the mystery and in-sisting in the errancy of untruth. "Freedom is nothing but the need that must take a first and last measure and bind itself to it."

The "Ideas of 1914"—"Socialism is freedom as binding obligation"— in their contrast with the "Ideas of 1789" are especially evident in Heidegger's notorious polemic in the Rectoral Address, directed against academic freedom. Underlying the attack is the association of academic freedom with the "liberty" and "equality" of abstract individuals liberated from the old bonds of religion, natural necessities, and provincial communities, who then bind themselves artificially ("the social contract") in cosmopolitan "fraternity," the solidarity of which only thinly disguises the anarchy of "equal" individuals (*GA* 16, 290). Academic freedom is a purely negative "freedom from" abstracted from any binding context and all limitations, and thus prone to arbitrary caprice, "arbitrariness of intentions and inclinations, lack of restraint in what was done and left undone." The German student body, on the other hand, in its resoluteness to will the essence of the new university, "through the new Student Law places itself under the law of its own essence and thereby first determines and defines this essence of being-students. To give the law to themselves is the highest freedom. . . . The concept of the freedom of the German student is now brought back to its truth. Henceforth the bond and service of the German student will unfold from this truth" (*RA*, 15/10).

This freedom of the German university students, preparing themselves to become the leaders and guardians of the nation, develops a triple bond of obligation to the educational state in its articulation into three services of *equal rank* and necessity.

> 1. The bond to the community of the people is cultivated by means of Work Service. "It obligates to help support the community by active participation in the struggles, strivings, and skills of all classes and elements of the people" (*RA*, 15/10).
> 2. The bond to the honor and destiny of the nation among other nations is established through the Defense Service. It demands the readiness to give one's all, to make the ultimate sacrifice for one's nation, and to acquire the necessary military knowledge, skills, and discipline.
> 3. The bond to the spiritual mission of the German people is cultivated by the service to science, the Knowledge Service. Once again, it is the people that, especially in its various professions, wills to be a spiri-

tual/intellectual people at the vanguard of the ever renewed struggle for its spiritual world. It does so "by putting its history into the openness of the superpower of all the world-shaping powers of Dasein," thereby becoming "exposed to the most extreme questionability of its Dasein" (*RA*, 15/10). And extreme questions demand extreme answers. Therefore, such a people "demands of itself and for itself that its leaders and guardians attain the strictest clarity of the highest, broadest, and richest knowledge" (16/10). This extreme knowledge of the basic questions "is not the calm cognizance of essences and values in themselves; rather, it is the keenest threat to Dasein finding itself at the very center of the superpower of beings. The very questionability of being compels the people to work and struggle and forces it into its state, to which the professions belong" (16/11). "Because the statesman and the teacher, the doctor and the judge, the minister and the architect guide and *lead* the Dasein of a people in its state, because they *guard* and keep this Dasein keen in its fundamental relations to the world-shaping powers of human being, these professions and the education for them are the responsibility of the Knowledge Service" (16/10f, emphasis added), the service that has traditionally come to be expected from the university. But this does not mean that knowledge must serve the professions. On the contrary, "the professions [are called upon to] execute and administer this highest and essential knowledge of the people which concerns its entire Dasein" (16/11). This presumably applies especially to the statesman, who thereby assumes some of the traits and virtues of Plato's philosopher-ruler.

"These three bonds—*through* the people *to* the destiny of the state *in* its spiritual mission—are *equiprimordial* for German being. The three services that arise from it—Work Service, Defence Service, Knowledge Service—are equally necessary and of equal rank" (*RA*, 16/11; italics in original).

The Worker State

This equality of rank of the three services in the new German university is clearly brought out in Rector Heidegger's various attempts to bridge the traditional gulf between "gown" and "town," between the notoriously elitist German university and the larger folk community (*Volksgemeinschaft*). The bridge concept becomes "work," which Heidegger takes to be rooted in his fundamental-ontological concept of care. In the first wave of enthusiasm for the political revolution of 1933, he thus models the university after the *worker state* projected by the National Socialist *German Work-ers* Party (*GA* 16, 239), thereby modifying the ideality of the university to accommodate a uniquely German folk ethos, its vaunted "work ethic." The new German university student, as a future leader of the nation, is to engage in work service and defense service as well as in the main service of the university, the service of knowledge and science, which as the "work of the brain" does not differ in kind from, and so is no higher than, the two levels of the "work of the hand and fist." All work is intellectual or "spiritual," a knowledge-laden deed and action that incorporates a craft know-how and an ordered understanding of its place in the world. But work in particular involves a "capacity of resoluteness and perseverance in carrying out the undertaken task to its conclusion, in short, *freedom,* which means: *spirit*" (*GA* 16, 239); to which we might also add the prized German trait of *Gründlichkeit* (thoroughness) and even a related word then current in Nazi jargon, the "hardness" needed to overcome almost insuperable obstacles.

Contrary to the divisive Marxian concept of work that leads to class warfare, work in the indigenous German context "does not divide us into classes, but rather binds and unites fellow workers and levels of work into a single great will of the state" (*GA* 16, 236). The German people is not "an amorphous mass without will and direction in the hand of some self-serving powerholder" (302). In and through work, the people develop into a knowledgeable and self-responsible people. It is by way of this will to self-responsibility on the part of every level that work, as the unifying element of the whole of the people, is brought into movement. "On the basis of this will to self-responsibility, every work on every level small and large assumes the place and rank of its equally necessary vocation. The work of each level sustains and solidifies the vital structure of the state. Work wins back autochthony for the people, and displaces this state as the reality of the people into the operative field of all the essential powers of human being" (190).

Work is at once knowledge and resolute responsive will. "Work is every cognitive doing and acting out of care for the people in preparation for the will of the state. There is work only there, but also everywhere there, where the free human power of resolution commits itself to putting through a responsible willing. Every work is thus defined by mindfulness, determination, and an understanding of the work" (*GA* 16, 303). What is "science" in this context?

> Science is but the *more rigorous* and thus *more responsible* form of that knowledge which the entire German people must seek and demand for its own historical Dasein as a [worker] state, provided that this people

still wills to secure its continuance and its greatness and to preserve these in the future. The knowledge of genuine science is *in essence in no way* different from the knowledge of farmers, foresters, miners or gravediggers, and handworkers. . . . For knowledge means: *to know our way around* the world in which we are placed as individuals and in community. Knowledge means: in decisiveness and initiative *to be equal* to the task to which each of us is consigned, be it the task of plowing the field, felling the tree, digging the grave, interrogating nature in its laws, or expositing history in the power of its destiny. Knowledge means: *to be master* of the situation in which we are placed. (*GA* 16, 234f; italics in original)

Rector Heidegger's various expressions of the university's solidarity with the folk community, in the spirit of the "new German reality" of 1933, thus seek to effect closer ties between the handworkers involved in their respective handicrafts and the scientific laborer in his or her particular "labor-atory," between the "workers of the fist" and the "workers of the brain."

"Workers" and "scientific knowers" are not opposites. Every worker is each in his way a knower, for only as knower can he work at all. . . . And everyone acting on knowledge and deciding on a scientific basis is a worker. This will to fulfill the provision of work with the provision of the appropriate knowledge [has as its aim] . . . that the German people as a people of work may once again find its developed unity, its simple worth, and its genuine power, and secure endurance and greatness as a worker state. . . . All the workers of our people have to *know why and for what purpose* they stand where they stand. For it is only through this vital and ever current knowledge that each life is rooted in the people as a whole and its destiny. (*GA* 16, 236f, 233; italics in original)

The reciprocal action of work service, defense service, and knowledge service on the young students of the new German university will slowly but surely develop a new basic attitude toward scientific work. Like the words "work" and "worker," the words "knowledge" and "science" will develop a new, non-Platonic sound and sense and a transformed meaning. "Science" is now no longer the possession of a privileged class of elite citizens who would abuse this privilege of possession by exploiting the people who do the work. The university continues to be the institutionalized expression of the human desire to know, still akin to the Platonic *erôs.* But this desire to know now assumes a uniquely German accent, more specifically, the folk accents of German idealism concretized through Heidegger's *protopractical* and multivalent sense of Dasein as *care* and *work.* As we have seen, the will to know, learn, question, discover on the level of the university takes on the form of *Ent-schlossenheit, phronêsis,* resolute openness, at first actively strenuous in its volitional rigor in responding to the demands exacted by a time of national crisis and, on its other face, receptive in its openness to the "new German reality" of a *worker* state. This resolute openness is the very *spirit* of the German university *in its concrete ethos of work,* where its will to science is the will to *question* the various sciences in "their boundless and aimless dispersal into particular fields and niches" in order to expose them once again to the full comprehensiveness of overwhelming "world-shaping powers of the human-historical Dasein" of a people "*in the midst of the uncertainty of beings as a whole,*" in the interwoven contexts *of work* in the traditional domains of nature, history, language, art, and religion; to which Heidegger adds medicine and psychiatry, indeed statesmanship itself, as well as the law, custom, economy, and technology that thereby develop from a worker state. Such an authochthonous will to science "will create for our people its world of most intimate and extreme danger, which is its truly *spiritual* world." But the *spiritual world* of a people *of work* is not a superstructure of high culture or a depository of useful information and values; rather, "it is the power that most deeply preserves the people's earth-and-blood-bound energies and, as such, it is the power that most deeply moves and most profoundly shakes the Dasein of a people." It is this resolute power of indigenous spirit that guarantees each particular people its possibility of greatness, for it to choose in resoluteness or to allow to lapse and fall into decline (*RA,* 14/9).

After the rectorate, Heidegger from his university podium continues to pose this fateful choice as late as summer 1935 to the German people, challenging it to recover its autochthonous spirit and so reclaim the spiritual world indigenous to it. Germany, this "nation of poets and thinkers" (and workers) caught in the landlocked vicelike grip of Central Europe, now lies in the great pincers between the metaphysical twins of America and Russia, both of which are caught up in "the same hopeless frenzy of unchained technology."[12] It is thus metaphysically threatened on its Western front by the international "spirit of capitalism" (Max Weber's phrase) and on its Eastern front by the international "specter of communism" (opening line of *The Communist Manifesto*) then "haunting" Europe and the entire planet. Germany, the most metaphysical of peoples, is by the same fact best equipped spiritually to reverse the drift of the disempowerment of the spirit through scientism, positivism, materialism, utilitarianism, and other identifiable versions of nihilism incurred by the Industrial Revolution, and so to arrest "the decline of the West." For the "inner truth and greatness" of the indigenous German *movement* called "national socialism," born of the "spirit of the front" (*Frontgeist*) in the First

World War and fostered by university mandarins like Natorp, Troeltsch, and Sombart, resides in its promised autochthonous resolution, through a *völkischen* worker state, of "the encounter between global technology and modern humanity."[13] This is "the unthought of National Socialism" that Heidegger virtually alone in his time tried to think (Lacoue-Labarthe and Nancy 1997, 148).

On Misreading Plato and Heidegger

Lacoue-Labarthe's reading of the Rectoral Address likewise observes the "shadow of Plato" hanging over it, such that leadership as Heidegger conceives it, and his rerouting of the *Führerprinzip* into a "spiritual" leadership, "is not far removed from Plato's *basileia*" (*FP*, 26, 28). By his own admission, Heidegger "entered politics 'by way of the university' and limited his political engagement and his philosophical responsibility to university politics." From the vantage of asserting the university's autonomy, Heidegger "arrogates to himself the right to define leadership in its essence" as the necessary submission to a spiritual mission and "the compulsory acknowledgment of a leadership above all leadership."[14] The hegemony of the spiritual/philosophical over the political is the decisive insight of Plato's *Republic*. That philosophers must be the rulers, however, "does not mean that philosophy professors should conduct the affairs of state. It means that the basic modes of conduct that sustain and define the community must be grounded in essential knowledge, according to which the community, as an order of being, grounds itself on its own basis."[15] Heidegger as rector of the educational state that constitutes the autochthony of the German university puts himself forward not as a politician but as a political educator of the future leaders and guardians of the nation, grounding them in the *ontological Realpolitik* of the German tradition. As an ontological rather than a political concept, the "people" appears first of all not as a racial community, but as a working community bound by a common language which, like individual Dasein, discovers its national identity from its tradition become destiny; and the "state" is the gathered confluence of the world-shaping powers of human being in confrontation with the overwhelming powers of the various domains of be-ing. The relationship between a people and its state accordingly constitutes the ontological essence of the political. The political as a basic human possibility, a distinctive mode of being human, is the reason that a state comes to be and is (and not vice versa). The be-ing of the state is rooted in the political be-ing of human beings, who as a historical *people decide* for this particular state and *will to support and sustain* it in their tradition. Clarification of this essentially *phronetic* connection between the people and its state thus constitutes the political education of a people, an introduction to its political be-ing. Ratification of this historical decision by each new generation of a people; assessment of the modes and degrees of commitment of a people to its state, as manifest in its degree of dedication, service, sacrifice, and care for the state; concern for the essence and form of the state most appropriate to a particular people, as expressed in a collective deliberation on its meaning and changing historical direction (*Be-sinnung*) by a people; in short, cultivation of the various bonds between the people and its state: these are the goals of a political education. Needless to say, all such bonds are phronetic bonds, which are possible only through the self-cognizance and self-determination of a people, which the educational leaders of a nation are called upon to awaken and to enhance in their basic endeavor to "educate a people toward its state."

But in Lacoue-Labarthe's reading, *phronêsis* is displaced by *technê* in Heidegger's archepolitics. Especially after the failure of the rectorate, that is, of the project of the self-determination of the university and, through it, of Germany itself, science gives way to art, phronetic thinking yields to poietic thought (*FP,* 55). The question of the political "retreats" (and so retraces itself) into the problematic of the work of art. The discourse on *technê* becomes a discourse on art, which is defined in its essence as "putting truth into the work." "'Work' (*le travail*) has been supplanted by 'the work' (*l'oeuvre*) and in the very same process . . . National Socialism has been supplanted by what I shall call a *national aestheticism*" (*FP,* 53, 110). Heidegger's retreat to *The Origin of the Work of Art* "thus pro-duces [*sic*] the truth of National Socialism as *national aestheticism*. . . . (this monstrosity is forced upon me by a reading of Heidegger)" (Lacoue-Labarthe and Nancy 1997, 150, 119).

With this aestheticizaton of politics, we come to one of Goebbels's favorite themes, "Politics is the plastic art of the State," thus belonging to the sphere of *technê:* "Politics too is perhaps an art, if not the highest and most all-embracing there is" (*FP,* 61f). Lacoue-Labarthe thus conjures up images of Hitler, the failed artist, who takes up politics instead in order to turn the state itself into his own work of art (71n), to create in any way, shape, or form that he wills, architecturing its capitol in the Greek mode, landscaping its autobahns: "The Third Reich as total artwork of a perverted West," akin to Wagner's *Gesamtkunstwerk* fusing music, drama, and poetic text. Hitler thus becomes the supreme director of his filmmakers (e.g., Riefenstahl) and his opera composers (e.g., Wagner) as he himself conducts the Second World War as his own big-budget war film. "Hitler saw the war and its newsreel footage as his heroic epic." He identified himself with the Third Reich that he created to such a degree that he, in Nietzschean fashion, even orchestrated its final destruction, as "the horrific and total suicide of Hitler in the form of Germany" (63). Such figuring and prefiguring is the ultimate "fictioning of the political" that constitutes Lacoue-Labarthe's central point. "The political (the City) belongs to a form of plastic art, formation and information, fiction in the strict sense. This is a deep theme which derives from Plato's politico-pedagogic writings (especially the *Republic*), reappearing in the guise of such concepts as *Gestaltung* or *Bildung*" (66). The "man-made" logic of this political *technê* is the *mimêsis* of human types (heroes, models of German manhood) and antitypes (racial stereotypes, images of the enemy) in endless varieties of the fictioning or figuring of the political. From the Platonic forms to the Kantian schematisms and Nietzsche's agonistic heroes, the aesthetization of the political is based on an ontotypology and its mimetology that we have come to associate with a long tradition of Western metaphysics.

Aristotle distinguished sharply between two practical know-hows, the *technê* (art) of making, whose endpoint is in the product made, and the *phronêsis* (prudence) of acting, whose end point is the same as its starting point in its self-referential trajectory that remains within the domain of the acting self, whether this self be an individual (the ethical action) or a community (the political action). Thus, if politics is to be called an art, it must be regarded as a performative art rather than a technical art, an art of machination. Politics can be called an art or *technê* by metaphoric transfer, but "the metaphor becomes completely false if one falls into the common error of regarding the state or government as a work of art, as a kind of collective masterpiece" (Arendt 1968, 153). Political institutions are more like theatrical performances than tangible works of art. In order to maintain them in their proper existence, their essential acts must be repeatedly performed by new generations of actors and activators, the inaugural events of these institutions must be repeatedly celebrated and memorialized, the precedents of their traditions must be repeatedly reviewed and revised in active application to new settings. "Political institutions, no matter how well or how badly designed, depend for continued existence upon acting men; their conservation is achieved by the same means that brought them into being. Independent existence marks the work of art as a product of making; utter dependence upon further acts to keep it in existence marks the state as a product of action" (Arendt 1968, 153). Politics moreover manifests other significant affinities with the performing arts, "where the *accomplishment* lies in the *performance* itself" and not in any external product. "Performing artists . . . need an audience to show their virtuosity, just as acting men need the presence of others before whom they can appear; both need a publicly organized space for their 'work,' and both depend upon others for the performance itself. Such a space of appearances is not to be taken for granted wherever men live together in a community. The Greek *polis* once was precisely that 'form of government' which provided men with a space of appearances where they could act, with a kind of theater where freedom could appear" (Arendt 1968, 154).

The "common error of regarding the *polis* as a work of art" thus comes from confounding the political virtue of *phronêsis* with the machinative virtue of *technê*. It is a confusion which is repeated time and again in the long tradition of reading Plato's *Republic* (cf. *DWB*, 2, 137f, 176f).[16] For Plato was not as careful as Aristotle in distinguishing his use of the terms *technê* and *phronêsis*. Heidegger accordingly, in his reading of the *Republic*, observes that, in order to preserve Plato's *technê* from the purely "technical" interpretation of later times, its "innermost essence" must be conceived as the "acquired capacity of *performance*, know-how as the comportment of *accomplishment* . . . the care-fulness of concern. This fullness of care is more than practiced diligence; it is the mastery of a composed *resolute openness* toward beings."[17] It is the overt cultivation of the basic posture of Dasein to let beings be by opening them into their proper space of appearance. In short, Plato's *technê* in the *Republic* is by and large *phronêsis*, the political and philosophical virtue par excellence, to be cultivated by the repeated performance of the "State built from words" over which philosophers, through dialectical conversing, are to become rulers. This Platonic *polis* of *paideia* nevertheless reflects a "real educational state, the community of Plato's Academy," and, by extension, every university that models itself after it. "Its goal is to lead to a new discovery of justice in one's own soul and thus to the education of the political human being." Such an education is hardly a "total manipulation of the soul" through machination toward a predetermined goal. "This education is not authoritative instruction based on an ideal organization; rather it lives solely from questioning,"[18] the will to learn, *phronêsis*. One is reminded of the dangerous storms of the powers of be-ing to which Rector Heidegger found his own fragile "State built from words" exposed.

Notes

In the epigraph, the first exergue is but one rendering of a passage taken from an oft reworked essay by Hannah Arendt in both English and German under titles ranging from "What is Freedom?" (Arendt 1968) to "Freedom and Politics"

(Arendt 1961, esp. 193f.) The second is from Phillipe Lacoue-Labarthe (1990, 26), citing Gérard Granel. Lacoue-Labarthe's book is hereafter cited as *FP,* after its subtitle and original French subtitle, *La fiction du politique.*

1. A detailed overview of these three concepts is to be found in Kisiel 2002. As for a schematic overview:

Heidegger's Three Concepts of *Polis* and the Political Period

	Period	Basic Text	Basic Concepts
Phenomenological	1923–25	Aristotle, *Rhetorica*	pathos, ethos, logos of doxic speech situation
Metontological	1933–35	Plato, the *Republic*	leader of people, guardians of state, 3-leveled service
Archaic-Poetic	1935–43	Sophocles, *Antigone*	polemos of thinker, poet, and statesman as prepolitical

2. Martin Heidegger, *Die Selbstbehauptung der deutschen Universität* (1933; 9–19) and *Das Rektorat 1933/35: Tatsachen und Gedanken* (1945; 21–43), ed. Hermann Heidegger (Frankfurt: Klostermann, 1983; also included in *GA* 16). "The Self-Assertion of the German University" (5–13) and "The Rectorate 1933/34: Facts and Thoughts" (15–32), English translation by Lisa Harries in *Martin Heidegger and National Socialism: Questions and Answers,* ed. Gunther Neske and Emil Kettering (New York: Paragon, 1990). These sources are hereafter referred to in the text as *RA* (*Rectoral Address*), with page numbers of the German and English versions separated by a slash.

3. Natorp 1918, hereafter cited in text as *DWB* 1 and 2.

4. Natorp 1907, 23f., 36, 70, 282. The first essay in the collection is "Platos Staat und die Idee der Sozialpädagogik," 1–36.

5. Lübbe 1963, 201, citing Ottmar Dietrich's characterization of Fichtes *Urvolk,* the primal Teutonic folk.

6. Here we are citing from Heidegger's postrectorate recollection of 1945, "Facts and Thoughts" (see note 2).

7. Fritz K. Ringer defines the mandarins "as a social and cultural elite which owes its status primarily to educational qualifications, rather than to hereditary rights or wealth" (1969, 5). They include doctors, lawyers, ministers, goverment officials, gymnasium teachers, and university professors, precisely the "professions" that Heidegger identifies in the Rectoral Address as the "leaders and guardians of the State."

8. I shall cite frequently from "The German University (Two Lectures for Foreign Exchange Students at Freiburg University, August 15 and16, 1934)," *GA* 16, 285–307, where Heidegger traces a direct lineage, exactly twenty years after their emergence, from the "Ideas of 1914" and frontline "German Socialism" to the National Socialist Revolution.

9. Natorp 1921, 462; citation from the 1921 Appendix. See Mariano Campo, "Natorp, Paul," in *Encyclopedia of Philosophy,* vol. 5, ed. Paul Edwards (New York: Macmillan, 1967), 445–48.

10. Most memorable is Gadamer's retrospective assessment: "But the general

attitude of the times, its consciousness of culture and belief in the progress of the liberal age, was severely shaken by the battles of material attrition of the First World War. In the philosophy of the time, this change in the general sense of life took shape in the feeling that the reigning philosophy, which grew out of the renewal of Kant's critical idealism in the second half of the 19th century, in one blow seemed unbelievable.... Among the men who gave philosophical voice to the general critique of the liberal piety of culture and the reigning 'mandarin' philosophy [*Kathederphilosophie*] was the revolutionary genius of the young Martin Heidegger." See Gadamer's introduction to Martin Heidegger, *Vom Ursprung des Kunstwerkes* (Stuttgart: Philipp Reclam, 1960), 102f. But when one looks more closely at this revolutionary transformation, one finds both old and new in creative ferment and full voice during the entire decade of the republic, as exemplified in the 1929 Davos debate between Heidegger and Cassirer. I have therefore put "end" in quotes to suggest that the vigorous survival of the "Ideas of 1914" into 1933 was at least in part due to the lack of closure that the revanchist Versailles Treaty instilled in a defeated Germany during the Weimar years.

11. Letter dated March 30, 1933, in Martin Heidegger and Elisabeth Blochmann, *Briefwechsel 1918–1969,* ed. Joachim W. Storck (Marbach am Neckar: Deutsche Schillergesellschaft, 1989), 60. Translated by Frank W. H. Edler in "Selected Letters from the Heidegger-Blochmann Correspondence," *Graduate Faculty Philosophy Journal* 14, no. 2–15, no. 1 (1991): 557–77, esp. 570f.

12. Martin Heidegger, *Einführung in die Metaphysik* (Tübingen: Niemeyer, 1957), 28. English translation by Gregory Fried and Richart Polt, *Introduction to Metaphysics* (New Haven: Yale University Press, 2000), 40.

13. Ibid. 152/213.

14. Lacoue-Labarthe 1980, 172, 178. Citing from the last essay, "Transcendence Ends in Politics," 267–300.

15. Martin Heidegger, *Nietzsche I* (Pfullingen: Neske, 1961), 194. English translation by David Farrell Krell, *Nietzsche,* vol, 1, *The Will to Power as Art* (San Francisco: Harper and Row, 1979), 166.

16. That even Natorp falls into this confusion, regarding the state as a "living work of art" and the "artwork of all artworks" and identifying it as the "German conception of the state," suggests how prevalent this "common error" may be in the German tradition. That the French have exposed this Teutonic error in Heidegger (wrongly) is no great consolation, for it has only compounded the errors in interpretation of the Heideggerian opus: I recently encountered a paper on the Rectoral Address, in part inspired by Lacoue-Labarthe and Nancy, bearing the title, "Heidegger and Political Action: *Technê* as Collective Self-Production." I have sought in vain for a treatise on the history of this "Platonic" error, especially among political theorists; I suspect that it is a long one. More on the mark on Heidegger's "politics" is Gillispie 2000, which notes that Heidegger sought to displace the "domination of theory and technology in modern life" by the "rule of practical wisdom or *phronêsis* that is rooted in a historical understanding of the world and that puts human beings and human actions ahead of values, ideological imperatives, and the processes of production" (140).

17. Heidegger, *Nietzsche I,* 192/164, emphases added.

18. Hans-Georg Gadamer, "Plato und die Dichter" (1934), in Gadamer 1985, 187–211, esp. 197; "Plato and the Poets," in Gadamer 1980, 39–72, esp. 52. Also relevant is Gadamer's essay of 1942, "Platos Staat der Erziehung/Plato's Educational State," in Gadamer 1985, 249–62/Gadamer 1980, 73–92. Gadamer was a student of both Natorp and Heidegger.

Plato's Legacy in Heidegger's Two Readings of *Antigone*

Jacques Taminiaux

The topic "the two readings of *Antigone* by Heidegger" presupposes a historical background in German philosophy. By this I mean that time and again before Heidegger, major German philosophers have treated Greek tragedies as metaphysical documents. In Schelling, Hegel, Schopenhauer, Nietzsche, tragedy is construed to be, in one way or another, an introduction to metaphysics. However different their interpretation of the essence and the ground of Being might be—Identity between freedom and necessity, Absolute Spirit, Will—they have this in common: for all of them tragedy is the voice of Being.

I believe that such an astonishing continuity deserves close examination. It raises first a problem of genealogy which includes two questions. First question: How did the Greeks of the fifth century look at tragedy? Second question: How did Plato and Aristotle consider tragedy?

To be sure, the answer to the first question is, to a large extent, more a matter of reconstruction than of empirical evidence. However, there is evidence enough to ensure some agreement among the historians and philologists of classical Greece. Plato himself suggests in the *Laches* that tragedy was linked to Athens as the military arts were linked to Sparta. According to contemporary historians, the evidence of this link is most obviously provided by a set of institutions. Nine tragedies were performed twice a year in Dionysian festivals which were official celebrations. The person in charge of selecting the three poets whose trilogies would be presented to the public was a magistrate chosen by the drawing of lots. That magistrate, called the *epônumos archôn* because he gave his name to the year, was in charge of choosing, again by drawing lots, the wealthy citizens who during several months of rehearsal would recruit and support the members of the chorus assigned to each selected poet. During the period of rehearsal, the chorists were exempted from all military obligation. Once the nine tragedies had been performed, a special jury was in charge of electing the best poet. The members of that jury were themselves chosen by lot as representatives of all the constituencies of the City. Finally, at the end of the festival, the public Assembly of the citizens held one of its meetings in the theater itself. All of these institutions suggest that the tragic theater was indeed an intimate concern for the political regime of Athens.

Given this institutional backdrop, contemporary historians have been induced to regard as a nonissue the problem of the origin of tragedy which obsessed the nineteenth-century philologists. These contemporary scholars call attention to the fact that the blossoming of tragedy coincides with the blossoming of democracy in Athens. Hence, the real issue for them is the link between tragedy and the invention by Athens of an entirely new way of life, the *bios politikos* (political existence). In spite of very serious historical limitations such as the strictly private condition of women as well as slavery for prisoners of war, this way of life allowed all citizens to share publicly words and deeds in a spirit of agonistic parity, and to be equally entitled to any public office.

The tragedies that have come down to us represent only 3 percent of the more than a thousand works staged in Athens. But it is remarkable, as Christian Meyer notices, that none of them is a work of propaganda. Instead of celebrating the city of Athens, they highlight what is questionable in human interaction. And, as Martha Nussbaum observes, instead of reducing these questions to simple terms, they stress their complexity and ambiguity, by showing that those who simplify them and claim to be able thereby to solve them are blinded by *hubris* (overweening self-assertion) and thus doomed to failure. Moreover, the very structure of the tragic works, the distinction between stage and chorus, functions, as Jean-Pierre Vernant notices, like a distinction between the possible revival of the tyrannical inclinations of the past and the ordinary condition of a democratic citizen. Consequently, the general consensus of contemporary scholarhip runs approximately as follows: those dramas gave the citizens twice a year the opportunity to realize that in human affairs nobody but the gods is in a position of mastery and that the best attitude toward human affairs is measure, prudence. In other words, for the City, tragedies were documents about *praxis*, action as human interaction.

The second question is this: How did Plato and Aristotle look at tragedy?

Let me first recall Plato's teaching on this matter. The *Republic* condenses his views. We may accept that the trial and sentencing of Socrates played a decisive role in the articulation of the dialogue. If a democratic tribunal had been unable to understand that, by raising higher questions than those which are discussed in the *ekklêsia*, Socrates was a benefactor of the community instead of its corrupter, then indeed the democratic regime deserves suspicion and it is worth asking how the City should be organized in order to prevent in the future similar verdicts from reoccurring. The answer provided half ironically, half seriously, by the dialogue is that the harmony of the City, the justice of its regime, should be modeled on the harmony of the soul of the wise man, that is, the one who dedicates his life to a contemplative way of being, the *bios theôrêtikos*. In the justification of this principle, the dialogue again and again celebrates the excellence of the specialized activity of the artisan, by contrast to the numerous flaws of the unspecialized activity of the citizen. In a way, the dialogue also stresses some sort of kinship between the specialized activity of the craftsman and contemplative life itself. Indeed—so goes the argument—at the very outset of his productive activity, the artisan in any craft has to contemplate an ideal model. Such contemplation alone allows him to find the right equipment and the right materials in order to shape the best possible copy of the ideal form. But in order for that activity to be successful, the art or technical know-how of the artisan must be specialized. Socrates emphasizes this in book 4: "This is after all a kind of image of justice, its being right for a man who is by nature a shoemaker to practice shoemaking and do nothing else, and for the carpenter to practice carpentry and so on for the rest" (*R.*, 443c).[1] Likewise the rightness or justice of the soul of the wise person depends on this: "so far as ruling and being ruled are concerned, each of the parts of the soul minds its own business" (443c). Accordingly, the deliberative and reasoning part of his soul is entirely dedicated to the contemplation of Ideas of the highest rank, thanks to which it rules over the spirited part in such a manner that both parts are set over the desiring part which is by nature insatiable. A just City ought to correspond to that hierarchy: it should be ruled by a few wise men contemplating the order of the highest Ideas, supervising the education of the military auxiliaries, and controlling the manifold appetites of the many by compelling every one to practice a single task useful to the entire body politic. The City is just if and only if "each of the three classes in it minds its own business" (441d). "One man, one job" should be the rule of a good regime.

It is needless to demonstrate that this ironic construct is the exact opposite of the democratic regime of Athens, as we may easily realize by comparing Plato's picture of the best regime with Pericles' description of Athens in the funeral oration related by Thucydides in book 2 of his *Peloponnesian War*. Whereas Plato justifies the maxim: "One man, one job," Pericles says: "I doubt if the world can produce a man, who, where he has only himself to depend upon, is equal to so many emergencies, and graced by so happy a versatility as the Athenian."

Consequently, Plato, who understood perfectly that tragedy was linked to the democratic regime, turns it as well into a target of his mockery. Here again the excellence of specialized fabrication is the principle of his argument. Compared to the products of any serious artisan, tragedy is a fraud, never a genuine *poiêsis*. According to the *Gorgias* (*R.,* 502b), any breaker of horses improves the mounts he tames, but no dramatist improves his spectators. According to the *Apology,* when Socrates had conversations with artisans, he always learned something because their work depends on an expertise, but in his conversations with dramatists, Socrates repeatedly realized that no precise knowledge was at the root of their poetry (22a–b). According to the *Republic,* the work of a dramatist is mere dispersion: He is like an impersonator becoming himself the manifold characters he puts on the stage.

Does this mean that in Plato's mind a good tragedy is inconceivable? No. It is quite conceivable provided that, instead of being a show of sheer appearances, the drama becomes a theater of truth (cf. *R.,* 608a), that is, an imitation of models of excellence. But it would no longer have anything to do with the dramas staged in the democratic theater. Permit me to quote from the *Laws.* At a key point in the dialogue, the elderly citizen of Athens, most probably Plato himself, asks whether or not the ordinary tragic poets could be allowed to bring their poetry into the best City. The answer is:

> Best of strangers, we ourselves are poets who have to the best of our ability created a tragedy that is the most beautiful and the best; at any rate, our whole political regime is constructed as the imitation of the most beautiful and best way of life, which we at least assert to be really [*ontôs einai*] the truest tragedy. Now you are poets, and we too are poets of the same thing; we are your rivals as artists and performers of the most beautiful drama, which true law alone can by nature bring to perfection, as we hope. So don't suppose that we'll ever easily, at any rate allow you to come among us, set up your stage in the marketplace, and introduce actors whose beautiful voices speak louder than ours. (*R.,* 817b–c)

Let us recall that our question was: Did Plato consider Greek tragedy as a metaphysical document?

The answer is certainly no if we mean the tragic poetry of Aeschylus, Sophocles, and Euripides: They merely depict the miserable imprisonment of human interaction in the cave of appearances. But the answer is yes if we mean by tragedy a drama or action which is entirely based on the contemplation of the *ontôs on*. That kind of action avoids all the ambiguities of praxis. It is the highest possible *poiêsis*. In fact, the topics stressed in Plato's picture of the ideal tragedy, namely the City as an ontological drama, as an accomplished work of art, as a setting-into-work of truth— all topics by which Plato's irony gets rid of both the *bios politikos* and the tragedies performed in the democratic City, all of them were to determine paradoxically, that is without the slightest touch of irony, the metaphysical interpretations of Greek tragedy in German philosophy.

In all of them, it seems that Plato's irony is ignored. Indeed, what remained unsaid but presupposed when Plato ironically contemplated in speech the substitution for praxis of a collective production, defined in its blueprint, thoroughly predictable, and fully tangible and reliable in its product, is, of course, that human interaction is simply not reducible to these features.

Before trying to demonstrate the persistence of these themes, let me add a few words about Aristotle. His *Poetics* deals extensively with tragedy but contains no trace of Plato's disdain for the real tragic poets. Against Plato, Aristotle makes it clear that by imitating praxis as they do, the tragic poets provide for their audience a truly philosophical teaching that those who simply relate a sequence of events, as do most historians, are unable to provide. The reason is that tragic imitation, instead of being a passive reflection of particular phenomena, as Plato claims, is an active composition of a plot which reveals universal possibilities of human interaction. But the truly philosophical impact of such revelation does not depend on the contemplation by the poet of an ontological realm. There is no allusion whatsoever to metaphysical issues in Aristotle's *Poetics*. Moreover, Aristotle insists that the genuinely tragic plot, far from featuring individuals who endeavor to imitate ideal models of excellence, depicts characters who are neither better nor worse than the average spectator. In the tragic plot those characters, says Aristotle, fail to fare well and to attain *eudaimonia*, happiness in the sense of excellence in one's own individuation, because of some mistake (*hamartia*), literally because they fail to hit the right target. In other words, the philosophical worth of tragic poetry is a matter of elucidation of praxis, not a matter of contemplation of ultimate foundations beyond the realm of human affairs. And the tragic poets bring about that elucidation—or *katharsis*—by building into the plot elements of fear and compassion. A fearsome course of events teaches the spectators that what happens on the stage could happen to them as well. A pitiable event teaches them that the impact of human deeds often transcends the doer's intentions because action as interaction by contrast to *poiêsis* is unpredictable, indefinite in its beginning as well as in its effects. All this suggests that, for Aristotle, instead of being a matter of ultimate contemplation, the philosophical teaching of tragedy lies in an appeal to *phronêsis,* a prudent discernment midway between two extremes, an excess and a deficiency. Hence, we are entitled to say that Aristotle did not consider tragedy as a metaphysical document but, in agreement with the spirit of the City, as a document about praxis, or human interaction, a *praxeological* document.

We are now in a position to ask why German philosophy treated Greek tragedies as metaphysical documents. It seems clear that their metaphysical interpretation has no foundation in the history of Athens. It has no foundation either in Aristotle's *Poetics* which, as a matter of fact, is, I believe, marginalized by these interpretations. Consequently, the problem is: Could there be some sort of Platonic legacy in these metaphysical interpretations? In my opinion, the answer is definitely yes. In order to keep this essay within reasonable limits, allow me before dealing with Heidegger's readings of *Antigone* to focus primarily on a prior interpreter of the same tragedy: *Hegel.* He deals with tragedy twice in the *Phenomenology of Spirit.*

In the first instance Hegel describes the life of the Greek City in the light of Sophocles' *Antigone.* According to Hegel, the life of the Greek City was thoroughly ethical, by which he means that the individual existence of the members of the City was in spontaneous harmony with a universal, namely the City itself. By simply being who they are, the members of such a community carry out their duty. They never envisage the possibility of a higher world. For them there is no conflict between obligation and freedom, and no hesitation about what is right. In the ethical life of the City, Hegel says, reason "is conscious of itself as its own world, and of the world as itself."[2]

At first sight, this picture seems to be far removed from Plato's ironic views: Did he not criticize the actual City on behalf of a better one? But that first impression is shaken as soon as we realize that Hegel describes the actual life of the Greek City in the very terms that Plato employed to depict the ideal City. Indeed, the pattern of a workshop ruled by the principle "one man, one job" is the very fabric of Hegel's picture: The only kind of action at stake in Greek political life was a work, the collective fabrication of a product, the City itself, a work achieved by each individual accomplishing his own task. In short, Hegel transposes to the real City of Athens Plato's picture of the ideal City.

Now we have seen that in Plato's picture of the best City, the contemplation of the *ontôs on* played a decisive role. In fact, an ontolgical contemplation also plays a decisive role in Hegel's description of ethical life understood as a fabrication of a collective product. Indeed, in the City, taken as a product of a collective fabrication, a self-mirroring of Spirit is attained, or an ultimate identity between action and the highest contemplation. This is undoubtedly a retrieval of the Platonic association of *poiêsis* with *theôria*.

These convergences raise an important question: Did Hegel really believe that Plato's picture of the ideal City was in fact a picture of the real City? A brief investigation is sufficient. The answer is yes indeed. From his early teaching at the University of Jena all the way to his professorship in Berlin, Hegel never stopped repeating: "Plato's Republic which passes proverbially as an empty ideal, is in essence nothing but an interpretation of the nature of Greek ethical life" (1942, 10). This means, of course, that in principle, Hegel's interpretation of the Greek City overlooks praxis as a sharing of words and deeds among individuals who are all alike but different as well and takes *poiêsis* (or production) to be the ultimate criterion for the right description of political life.

But this suggests another question: Why does Hegel refer to Sophocles' *Antigone* in his phenomenology of Greek ethical life? How can *Antigone* overlap with the *Republic?* As a matter of fact, we can grasp the overlapping "fit" between the two works as soon as we realize that Sophocles' tragedy is meant to demonstrate, in Hegel's mind, both the historical justification of Plato's views and the historical necessity for their being overcome. Hegel claims that Plato's notion of the City in the *Republic* was rigorously in keeping with what the real City attempted to be, that is, the embodiment of a total fusion between the individual and the universal. But the same notion also testifies to the historical necessity of an overcoming of Greek ethical life. Indeed, Hegel claims, in his *Phenomenology of Spirit*, that the intrinsic limitation of such a life lies in its immediate character: "The basic flaw of an immediate unity between the individual and the universal is that it is more natural than reflective or fully self-conscious" (*PS,* 205). Hegel's extensive use of *Antigone* is precisely meant to demonstrate the intrinsic deficiency of an immediate ethical life and therefore the necessity for Spirit to move beyond it. In other words, for Hegel, the *Republic* and *Antigone* are two works which confirm one another.

According to Hegel's lectures on Plato, when the *Republic* recommends the abolition of private property and of monogamy, the dialogue simply vindicates the immediate fusion between individual and universal by trying to prevent individuals from becoming independent or from proclaiming their personal inclinations. The reason for this prevention is that an independent individuality, recognized as such, has no place whatsoever in the ancient ethical order. But for Hegel, that is precisely what Sophocles' tragedy stresses in its own way. The tragedy depicts the ethical order as ruled by two laws. According to the human law of the City, which Creon incarnates, an independent individuality makes no sense because the individual belongs to the City. According to the divine law of the family, which Antigone incarnates, there is something sacred in the individual qua individual but only after death. Plato had the premonition that the principle of independent individuality would ruin the ethical order. Sophocles demonstrates that the ethical order reveals its internal deficiency in the way of a contradiction, as soon as it is confronted with the emergence of that very principle. The ethical order turns out to be contradictory because in principle both Creon and Antigone are entitled to find in their deeds the evidence of a harmony between their consciousness and their world, but in fact the outcome of their action proves the contrary. In the final analysis, the reason for this contradiction lies, according to Hegel, in the immediate or natural foundation of the ethical order, that is, the natural difference between men and women, the former in charge of enforcing the City law, the latter the family law.

There is a second analysis further on in the *Phenomenology of Spirit,* the issue of which is no longer the ethical content of tragedy but the assessment of its spiritual accomplishment as a work of art. Here again a Platonic pattern governs the analysis, which is part of a description of what Hegel calls "the Religion of Art." At the outset the very definition by Hegel of the Religion of Art obviously repeats the Platonic association *theôria-poiêsis:* "Spirit has raised the shape in which it is present to its own consciousness into the form of consciousness itself and it produces such a form before itself" (*PS,* 424). This definition straightaway suggests that Hegel approaches tragic poetry in terms of its speculative or metaphysical function. To be sure, whereas the privilege of an ontological contemplation allowed Plato to discard tragedy inasmuch as it disrupts the ethical order, it allows Hegel to celebrate tragedy as a metaphysical document which demontrates the necessity for the world Spirit to progress beyond the level attained by Greek ethical life. But the replacement of a static speculation by a historical one is precisely what allows him to project upon tragic poetry a new version of Plato's parable of the cave. Indeed, he insists that there are two levels of awareness in tragic poetry: the lower level of the chorus and the higher level of the stage. The chorus alone remains trapped in the cave of appearances. But the stage corresponds to the theater of truth. What happens on the stage is a manifestation of what Hegel calls the Concept or the Idea now understood in a properly Hegelian manner as an ontological process of overcoming opposites through a synthesis which is higher than both. This of course represents a tremendous metamorphosis of Plato's Idea, but in the final analysis, Hegel, like Plato, claims that the only competent spectator of Greek tragedy is the philosopher himself.

———

Let me turn briefly to Nietzsche, who is often believed to have nothing in common with Hegel, at least as far as his interpretation of tragedy is concerned.

In keeping with what I just said, allow me a few words about *The Birth of Tragedy*. There is a text written by Nietzsche immediately after the publication of the book, though never published by him, which opens the way to the demonstration of a Platonic legacy in *The Birth of Tragedy*. At the time, Nietzsche was still full of admiration for Richard Wagner and even more perhaps for his young wife Cosima. In a reply to questions raised by Cosima after reading *The Birth of Tragedy*, Nietzsche sent her a short essay on "The Greek City-State," which in fact is a feverish celebration of Plato's *Republic*. Let me quote from the last page of that essay:

> The ideal City of Plato (is) something evidently greater than even its most fervent admirers believe, let alone the arrogance of our scholars when they refuse such a beautiful fruit of Antiquity. A poetic insight and a forceful brush reveal the real purpose of the State, i.e., Olympian existence, the ever renewed creation and formation of geniuses, with regard to which all other beings are auxiliary instruments. . . . To be sure, the only genius that Plato puts at the top of his perfect City is a genius of wisdom and science, and he excluded from his State the artistic genius. This is the harsh consequence of Socrates' judgment about art, and Plato made that judgment his own, though not without struggling with himself. But this is a superficial and almost contingent deficiency which should not prevent us from recognizing in Plato's overall notion of the State the extraordinary hieroglyph of an esoteric doctrine on the relationship between State and genius, a profound doctrine which forever deserves to be deciphered. (Nietzsche 1988, 776)

In the light of an ontological contemplation, Plato ironically denigrated both the political life of Athens and its tragedies. We have just seen that in his ontological rehabilitation of the political life of the Greek City, Hegel claims that the latter was in fact the embodiment of Plato's ideal City. And his ontological interpretation of tragedy as a work of art amounted to considering it somehow as another version of the parable of the cave. Now this is precisely what Nietzsche does as well in his own way, but with a major difference: He is not at all interested in ethical life but in aesthetics or, in his own words, in "an artist's metaphysics." In his view, Plato was above all an artist who, in order to please Socrates, had to conceal his dedication to fine arts. Hence when Plato puts philosophers at the summit of the City's hierarchy, we should understand that in fact he meant the artists.

Likewise when Plato stresses the will to truth, he means in fact the will to art. Once it is deciphered, the hierarchical structure of the *Republic* means that the function of the state is to enslave the many in order to allow the happy few to become artists.

As soon as we realize that Nietzsche's secret intention was to decipher in artistic terms the supposedly esoteric doctrine of the *Republic,* we realize as well that for him, Greek tragedy was an artistic version of the parable of the cave, which itself, of course, is deciphered as an esoteric document. From this it comes as no surprise that everything in Nietzsche's interpretation of the Greek fine arts is a matter of levels of vision. The many in everyday life are trapped within the world as representation: They only see the outcomes of the principles of individuation and sufficient reason. By contrast, the Apollinian artist sees the principles which rule the phenomenal world: individuation and sufficient reason. On a still higher level, the Dionysian artist sees the ontological power of the will in its inexhaustible productivity and destructiveness. And finally the tragic poem makes visible the link between the world as a reasonable individuation and the world as an inexhaustible will. In Plato's esoteric language, it makes visible the link between the appearances and the *ontôs on.* The vision of the *ontôs on* is embodied in the chorus which celebrates the power of the will whereas the vision of the individuated appearances is symbolized by the stage. Tragedy as a whole—chorus and stage—reveals the link between individual appearances and the will. The Platonic background of *The Birth of Tragedy* is made manifest by Nietzsche himself when, immediately after stressing that "the celebrated figures of the Greek stage—Prometheus, Oedipus, etc.—are mere masks of the original hero, Dionysus," he adds the following: "[T]he Platonic distinction and evaluation of the 'Idea' and the 'idol', the mere image, is very deeply rooted in the Hellenic character. Using Plato's terms we should have to speak of the tragic figures of the Hellenic stage somewhat as follows: the only truly real Dionysus appears in a variety of shapes, in the mask of a fighting hero, and entangled, as it were, in the net of the individual will" (1988, 71–72).

It seems to me significant that the earliest allusion to tragedy in Heidegger's itinerary occurs in a lecture course of 1931–32, *The Essence of Truth: On Plato's Cave Allegory and Theaetetus.* The allusion is a brief quotation and translation without commentary of the first verse of Antigone's famous chorus *polla ta deina.* The translation runs:

> There is much that is strange, but nothing
> That surpasses man in strangeness.

This is the first symptom of an encroachment of the tragic text upon the text of Plato. In the context of the lecture course of 1931–32, the verse of Sophocles is quoted by Heidegger in order to illustrate Plato's notion of man as a being who has the discursive capacity to disclose the Being of beings. What Plato calls *kalôs legein* consists, Heidegger says, in that capacity which is "the authentic beauty of human existence" (*GA* 34, 198). Heidegger claims that the verse of Sophocles expresses nothing else than that capacity.

The next allusion occurs two years later. It is a quotation and translation by Heidegger of a single verse of Aeschylus's *Prometheus*. The translation runs:

Knowledge is by far weaker than necessity.

This second allusion appears in the framework of the infamous rectoral address which, after all, is a bad remake of Plato's *Republic*. The discourse is a celebration of the normative position of metaphysics as the queen of sciences, more specifically of *theôria*, defined as "the passion of remaining close to beings as such, under their constraint" ("SGU," 11). Heidegger insists that such *theôria* is not a detached contemplation but an extreme possibility of Dasein, including both "the supreme modality of *energeia*, proper to man's being-at-work," and "the highest accomplishment of *praxis*" ("SGU," 11). The verse of Aeschylus's *Prometheus* which in Greek runs *Technê d'anankês asthenestera makrô* (514) is meant to point out that the ontological *theôria* is at once the highest praxis, and the highest know-how in the sense of a mode of disclosing adjusted to a specific *poiêsis* or production, a putting into work of truth. In this context, the Prometheus of Aeschylus turns out to be the philosopher himself. Thanks to this conflation of *theôria*, praxis, and *poiêsis*, Heidegger, in agreement with Plato, describes the body politic as a huge workshop wherein each has a defined role. There is an obvious echo of Plato's *Republic* in Heidegger's image of a corporatist state wherein each of the estates (*Stände*—a favorite word in Hegel's political philosophy) provides a distinct service: service of work, service of defense, and, at the top, service of knowledge, above all service of metaphysics, because it is taken for granted that the state should be ruled by philosophers.

This is a second form of evidence of an encroachment of the tragic text upon the text of Plato.

The third allusion occurs in the winter semester of 1934–35, in Heidegger's first lecture course on Hölderlin. His interpretation of the poems *The Rhine* and *Germania* is still ruled by a major topic of *Being and Time* and of his fundamental ontology as a whole, that is, the contrast between falling everydayness and resolute authenticity. What is new, however, is that what is at stake in the contrast no longer is the *who* of an individual Dasein at each time as mine, but the Dasein of the German people. Very rarely, Heidegger says, are the human beings able to be up to the truth of the Dasein of a people. They are the poet who founds (*Stift*) that truth, the thinker who articulates and makes understandable the Being of beings disclosed by the poet, and the political founder of a state which is in tune with the essence of his people. Only these three creators qualify to be in charge of the Promethean *technê* mentioned in the Rectoral Address. Among Heidegger's many references to the Greeks in this lecture course, we find: "The poem of Sophocles called *Antigone* is, as a poem [*Dichtung*], a foundation of the Greek Dasein as a whole" (*GA* 39, 216). Since the lecture course on Hölderlin obviously develops the theme of the Rectoral Address, which was itself somehow a paraphrase of Plato's *Republic*, we may presume, on the basis of the three allusions mentioned so far, that in a next step, Heidegger's first explicit analysis of *Antigone* is going to be carried out against the backdrop of Plato's legacy, and perhaps with a further implicit kinship with Hegel as well.

The first comprehensive interpretation of Greek tragedy by Heidegger is found in the lecture course of 1935 on the *Introduction to Metaphysics*. This framework already suggests that Heidegger, like Hegel and Nietzsche, for that matter, considers tragedy as a metaphysical "document." Moreover, the immediate context in which Heidegger's lecture course explicitly deals for the first time with a tragic drama quite obviously points toward Plato's legacy. The drama is Sophocles' *Oedipus King*, the context is the *polemos* between Being and appearance (*Schein*). To be sure, when it comes to the ontological *polemos*, Heidegger's pays more attention to Heraclitus and Parmenides than he does to Plato. But on close inspection, it turns out that his handling of the topic is pervaded by Platonic schemes. The *polemos* is inherent to *alêtheia* itself as the disclosive process which defines the pre-Socratic *phusis*. *Alêtheia* is innerly conflictual not only because it is a tension between concealment and unconcealment, but also because there is a tension in unconcealment itself which can be a genuine appearing and can decline as well into mere appearance or semblance. Heidegger insists that *Schein* basically has three meanings: radiance, appearing, and semblance. "Appearing" means being present as unconcealed. The tension at stake takes place between the possibility for unconcealment to be either the radiance of presence or its concealment by semblance. It seems to me highly significant of the Platonic reminiscence in Heidegger's analysis that his favorite example of such a radiance is the sun. No less significant of this reminiscence is his definition of *doxa*, the

Greek word for *Schein*. I quote: "*Doxa* is the regard in which a man stands, in a broader sense the regard [*Ansehen*] which every being conceals and discloses in its appearance [*Aussehen*] [*eidos, idea*]" (*EM*, 88).[3] The sun, *eidos*, these words are the very words of Plato in the parable of the cave. And the Platonic sense of hierarchy is obvious in the following sequence introducing the many meanings of *doxa*: "(1) regard as glory; (2) regard as sheer vision that offers something; (3) regard as mere looking-so: . . . mere semblance; (4) view that a man forms, opinion" (89). To be sure, Platonism is criticized by Heidegger for having obliterated the tension at stake by imposing an ontic duality between a lower realm of mere appearances and a higher realm of real beings. But Heidegger insists that Platonism is not Plato's position but a later Christian misinterpretation of the Greek thinker; and consequently it is in the very language of Plato that he attempts to restore what he takes to be the presocratic *polemos*.

At any rate, it is in the context of an interpretation of the pre-Socratic *polemos* between Being and appearance that Heidegger introduces tragedy. He writes: "Solely in the enduring struggle between being and appearance did the Greeks wrest Being from the being, did they carry beings to permanence and unconcealment: the gods and the State, the temples and the tragedy, the games and philosophy; all this in the midst of appearance, beset by appearance, but also taking it seriously, knowing of its power." All this points toward some sort of reminiscence of the Hegelian connection between ethical life and the religion of art. It also points toward an interpretation of tragedy which, as it was the case in Hegel, ties tragedy to an ontological *theôria*. This is what comes to the fore in Heidegger's reading of *Oedipus*. Allow me to quote: "At the beginning Oedipus is the savior and lord of the State, living in an aura of glory and divine favor. He is hurled out of his appearance which is not merely his subjective view of himself but the medium in which his *Dasein* appears; his being as murderer of his father and desecrator of his mother is raised to unconcealment. The way from the radiant beginning to the gruesome end is one of struggle between appearance (concealment and distortion) and unconcealment (Being)" (*EM*, 90). Since what is at stake in Sophocles' tragedy is taken to be the ontological *polemos* of *Alêtheia*, Heidegger insists that beyond the downfall of a powerful individual, "we must see him as the embodiment of Greek *Dasein*, who most radically and wildly asserts its fundamental passion, the passion for the disclosure of Being." It is significant, I believe, that the passion mentioned here was what Heidegger, some twelve years before, in his lecture course on the *Sophist*, was already discovering in Plato's deliberate dedication to the *bios theôrêtikos* against sophistry and rhetoric. And this is precisely how he now interprets Hölderlin's verse "Perhaps King Oedipus has an eye too many." "This eye too many," Heidegger says, "is the fundamental condition for all great questioning and knowledge and also their only metaphysical ground. The knowledge and the science of the Greeks were this passion" (90–91). This of course has nothing to do with the poem of Hölderlin, who simply means in the late poem quoted by Heidegger that in *Oedipus at Colonus* the old and blind Oedipus was still a seer. Not unlike Hegel, Heidegger lets the text of Plato encroach upon the tragic text. Like his predecessor in the *Phenomenology of Spirit,* he treats tragedy not as a document about praxis as interaction and interlocution between mortals, but as an expression of the *bios theôrêtikos* itself. It is significant, I believe, of his obsession for *theôria* and of his disdain for interactive praxis and plurality, that he does not even pay attention to the original title of Sophocles' tragedy, *Oedipos Tyrannos,* a title which clearly indicates that Oedipus the king was in fact a tyrant. This is precisely what was recognized by Hölderlin, who is not quoted by Heidegger on this point. Hölderlin was the first to translate correctly the title of Sophocles' masterpiece and to show with intensity in his "Remarks" about the drama that Oedipus, instead of acting as a prudent statesman, wrongly claimed to be a confidant of the divine powers. In other words, Hölderlin clearly suggests and deplores that there is a Promethean hubris in Oedipus. By contrast, Heidegger in 1935 celebrates the Promethean character of Oedipus.

What about *Antigone?*

Again it is significant, I believe, of a disdain for interactive praxis, and therefore for Aristotle's definition of tragedy as *mimêsis praxeôs,* that Heidegger entirely overlooks the plot of *Antigone.* He focuses exclusively on the chorus *polla ta deina.* And he does so in the context of a discussion of another mode of the ontological *polemos,* that is, the conflictual relationship between Being and Thinking, obviously not a key topic for those who are primarily interested in human affairs, though a central issue for the few who dedicate their life to the *bios theôretikos.* Heidegger approaches the topic in the light of Heraclitus and Parmenides. According to the modern views, he says, thinking is the subject matter of logic, and it is an activity of a subject opposed to an object. In contrast to that modern concept of the logical, Heraclitus teaches that *logos* is another name for Being understood in terms of the unconcealing process of *phusis.* More precisely, he teaches that *logos* is a gathering of what in Being itself is conflictual, concealment and unconcealment, appearing and semblance. He also teaches that only the few can be open to this conflictual gathering whereas the *polloi* are blind to it. Heidegger's emphasis on that contrast between the few and the many again betrays a Platonic scheme.

———

But—so goes the argument—if Logos, which is a name for thinking as well, is primarily a name for Being itself, how can there be a conflict between thinking and Being? At this point Heidegger turns to Parmenides. At first sight his poem on Nature only emphasizes a belonging-together of Being and thinking. But Heidegger claims that on closer inspection it turns out that, in the Parmenidian *noein*, or apprehension, a resistance as well as a receptive welcoming are *involved*. And since apprehension is understood by Parmenides as "a process in which man first . . . comes into being," his teaching means that a "separation between Being and being-human comes to light in their togetherness" (*EM*, 119).

At this juncture, Heidegger decides to consult Greek tragedy, more specifically *Antigone*'s famous chorus *polla ta deina*, "for a better understanding of Greek poetic philosophy" (*EM*, 122), in other words, for a better understanding of Parmenides and Heraclitus.

There are three phases in Heidegger's reading of the chorus of *Antigone* in 1935. In the first phase the emphasis is put on the word *deinon*, which is indeed repeatedly used by the chorus. But it is noteworthy that Heidegger deliberately overlooks the use of the word elsewhere in the drama, for example, to qualify the burial of her brother by Antigone or to describe the blasphemous stubbornness of Creon. By overlooking in his reading of the chorus what in it is an echo to the drama itself, Heidegger discards all the connotations of the word *deinon* which do not fit with his strictly ontological perspective. The Greek word has three basic meanings: (1) frightening, (2) gifted of a wondrous power, and (3) skillful. Its meaning oscillates, so to speak, between the terrible and the terrific. Apart from the chorus, when the word is used in the dialogues of the drama, it designates most of the time a hubris or excess. For instance, there is something *deinon*, or frightening, in Antigone's antilegalism as well as in Creon's stubborn legalism. Once again this was clearly perceived and underscored by Hölderlin in his *Remarks*. But all this has no place whatsoever in Heidegger's analysis. Indeed, by translating *deinon* as *unheimlich* and by focusing on the line: "nothing surpasses man in *Unheimlichkeit*," he channels as it were the meaning of the chorus into a strictly ontological issue, that is, the ontology of Dasein as a being whose condition is a tension between an authentic relationship to Being and a falling away from Being into the mere appearances which make everydayness familiar and secure. This, of course, is in continuity with *Being and Time*. What is new is the element of violence introduced in the definition of *Unheimlichkeit*. Indeed, Heidegger insists that the word *deinon* translated as *unheimlich* qualifies both the overpower of Being as a whole and Dasein's relation to this overpower. Not only is man *deinon* because he belongs to Being, but he is also *deinon* as the fundamentally violent one, who "uses violence [*Gewalt*] against the overpowering" (*EM,* 126) in order to hold in check the power of appearance. It turns out that there is a necessary link between this ontological violence and a high kind of *technê* open to a creative production, a production which is at stake in the life of the *polis.* Like Hegel, Heidegger interprets the *polis* as a setting into work of a historical truth. Like Hegel, he interprets the City as a huge workshop, the members of which are dedicated to a specific task. The political, he says, is "at the site of history, provided there be (for example) poets *alone,* but then really poets, priests *alone,* but then really priests, rulers *alone,* but then really rulers" (152). Like Hegel when he was dealing with the great individuals who are supposedly the real agents of the historical process, Heidegger claims that the truly efficacious agents of the setting into work of *alêtheia* are creative "men of action." They are, at the same time, he says, high above the *polis,* and without *polis,* "without place, lonely, strange and alien, without issue amid being as a whole, without statute and limit, without structure and order, because they themselves *as* creators must first create all this" (152–53).

The second phase in Heidegger's reading of the chorus provides further remarks about the high *technê* which rules over that creation. And here the legacy of the Platonic association of *poiêsis* and *theôria,* already retrieved by Hegel, becomes obvious. Indeed, Heidegger insists that *technê* in its authentic sense is a form of knowledge consisting in "the initial and persistent looking out beyond what is present-at-hand at any time" (*EM,* 159). Such knowledge is therefore "the ability to put into work Being itself within what is" (159). The Sophoclean *technê,* in other words, is taken to mean a strictly ontological form of knowledge.

But that interpretation overlooks the fact that the use of the word *technê* in the drama itself, instead of indicating an ontological insight, is meant to evoke the dangerous temptation to approach human interaction, as Creon does, in strictly technical terms.

Another sign of Plato's legacy is to be found in Heidegger's interpretation of *dikê,* which, in his view, "loses its fundamental metaphysical meaning" in being translated as "justice" in the juridical and ethical sense. Like Plato in the *Republic,* he understands *dikê* as an ontological adjustment. *Dikê* is another name for the governing order or harmony of an ontological realm. Plato referred *dikê* to the *ontôs on;* Heidegger likewise claims that it is another name for Being.

In the third phase, Heidegger, after insisting on the risk involved in the confrontation between *technê* and *dikê,* claims that such a risk is the highest feature of Dasein because it is necessitated by Being itself. "The Dasein of historical man means: to be posited as the breach into which the preponderant power of Being bursts in its appearing" (*EM,* 163).

Therefore the song of the chorus is supposed to be essentially a celebration of an ontological necessity. To be sure, the last verses of the chorus seem to suggest a reservation. They tell:

> May such a man never frequent my hearth
> May my mind never share the presumption
> of him who does this.

But Heidegger, because his approach is exclusively ruled by the primacy of the contemplative way of life, does not suspect in these words any call for moderation, measure, or prudence. In his interpretation, one paragraph suffices to express the meaning of those last verses: "Insofar as the chorus turns against the strangest of all, it merely says that this manner of Being is *not* that of every day. Such *Dasein*, Heidegger says, is not to be found in the usual bustle and activity" (*EM*, 165). Translated in ontological terms, the last verses of the chorus merely express the unavoidable blindness of everydayness.

There is no doubt that this reading of *Antigone* by Heidegger also demonstrates several points of agreement with Hegel in the wake of Plato. They are the privilege of an ontological *theôria*, the reduction of action to *work*, the definition of the City in terms of an ontological production, the emphasis on an ontological necessity—condensed in the notion of *dikê*—understood as the historical movement of the Concept in Hegel, and as the urgent request of Being in Heidegger. The emphasis on these points is even stronger in Heidegger than in Hegel insofar as the former, unlike the latter, does not pay any attention to the plot of the tragedy and argues as though it had nothing to do with human interaction but everything with the disclosure of Being. At any rate, in both cases, the tragic themes related to praxis—*phronêsis, sophrosunê, hubris, hamartia*—are thoroughly overlooked. Incidentally, it is important to notice in this context that Heidegger, who lectured extensively on Aristotle's work, never lectured on his *Poetics*.

There is a second reading of *Antigone* by Heidegger. It occurs in the summer semester of 1942 in the context of a lecture course on Hölderlin's poem *Der Ister* (*GA* 53). Again the interpretation of *Antigone* is focused on the chorus *polla ta deina*. The translation of the chorus by Heidegger remains unchanged, but his reading is different. The Promethean proclamations of 1935 have vanished in 1942. There is no longer any allusion to the confrontation between the overwhelming power of *technê* and the overpowering order of *dikê*. Moreover, there is another striking difference: Whereas in 1935 the last verses of the chorus were almost overlooked because they allegedly expressed everydayness, in 1942 the same verses now deserve many pages of commentary.

Finally, instead of violence, the basic tonality in Heidegger's second reading of the chorus of *Antigone* has been altered into expectation, an expectation which is presented by him as the only relevant attitude toward Being.

Do these changes mean that Plato's legacy is now overcome?

Quite the contrary. In fact, what occurs in the new reading is a shift toward a sort of hyper-Platonism, by which I mean that this reading is exclusively ruled by the pathos of wonder (*thaumazein*) before Being.

Let me focus on a few symptoms of this shift.

The words *pantoporos-aporos* ("inexperienced" and "without issue"), which formerly meant the risk involved in being cast out of every relation to the familiar everydayness, now merely mean that it belongs to the human nature simultaneously to understand Being and to forget Being.

Likewise, the words *hupsipolis-apolis,* which formerly meant the strangeness of the condition of the political creator, now almost lose all political connotation. Heidegger insists that "*polis* is in no way a political concept" (*GA* 53, 99). It is just another name for what he calls *das Offene,* the open clearing in which all beings and all relations to them gather or are gathering. This new meaning gives Heidegger the opportunity to reaffirm the Platonic dignity of *theôria.* Indeed, the word *polis* now designates what the thinker alone—with the help of the poet but without reference to the dictator—is able to "see" (113) and what remains questionable for both.

Accordingly, the word *tolma* (risk) no longer means the fragility of the human *technê* compared to the overpowering nature of Being. It rather designates a destiny of erring which is necessitated by Being itself defined in terms of an unconcealment which again and again preserves its secret. In this context, the very distinction between success and failure, excellence and vileness, which, in the previous interpretation, preserved a quasi-ethical connotation, no longer makes sense. The only distinction at stake in the new reading is the strictly ontological contrast between Being and non-Being. Consequently, Plato more than ever remains at the background of the new reading. He is explicitly referred to, once again, when Heidegger justifies his translation of the words *to mê kalon,* the "not beautiful," into "not-being" (*GA* 53, 109). He writes: "Insofar as Western metaphysics begins in Plato's thought, Plato also prepares the subsequent aesthetic interpretation of the beautiful and of art. Yet to the extent that Plato simultaneously stands in the tradition of the Greek thinking of the 'commencement' and is a transition, he also still thinks *to kalon* nonaesthetically. This can be seen in his equating of *kalon* with the *on.*" In other words, Plato's equating of the beautiful with the truly being retrospectively justifies Heidegger's own equating of Sophocles' *kalon* with the *on.*

As I said, the last verses of the chorus, which deserved merely a short

JACQUES TAMINIAUX

paragraph of commentary in 1935, are now given thirty pages of very intense analysis. In 1935 the "hearth" mentioned in these verses was supposed to designate the cozy shelter of everydayness. Instead, in 1942, it means Being itself as the only authentic home for the uncanny essence of human beings. And once again Plato, more specifically the *Phaedrus*, is in charge of providing the justification for Heidegger's ontological interpretation of the Greek word *Hestia*—the "hearth." On the basis of an overlapping of the text of Sophocles with the text of Plato, Heidegger recalls how, in his second speech concerning *erôs*, Socrates in the *Phaedrus* describes the place of abode of the gods that lies beyond the heavenly firmament. According to the description, *Hestia* is the deity who alone always remains steadfastly behind in the homestead of the gods. The description is given the following commentary by Heidegger: "Here in Plato's recollection of the poetizing telling of beings as a whole and the way they are governed and constituted, the following essential point is clearly brought to light: If the gods, dwelling in an inaccessible location beyond the heavens, are indeed those who remain, then among them the one who most remains and is most steadfast is *Hestia*. She is the middle of all steadfast constancy and presence—that which essentially prevails in being, that which the Greeks experience in the sense of constant presence" (*GA* 53, 141–42). In other words, Heidegger finds in Plato what he calls "the insight into the essential connection between *Hestia* and Being" (143). Consequently, instead of expressing everydayness and its fleeing away before the uncanniness of human Dasein in general and of the Dasein of a people in particular, the last verses of the chorus are now supposed to introduce a distinction between an inauthentic exile and an authentic one, the latter consisting in becoming homely in being unhomely.

In this context, Heidegger seems to pay attention, for the first time, to the plot of *Antigone*. He quotes and analyzes the dialogue between Ismene and her sister at the beginning of Sophocles' tragedy; as well as the dialogue between Creon and Antigone that follows the choral ode *polla ta deina*. But on close inspection, it turns out that the plot is of no interest to him. Right after mentioning Hölderlin's *Remarks on Antigone,* he makes it clear that they do not reach the ontological center of the tragic work: "Because those who seek to explain that tragedy are always eager to find in Antigone's words an explanation of her actions, that is, a statement about whatever it is that causes her deeds, they are concerned only with finding some reference to beings, whether the prevailing or ancient cult of the dead, or the familial blood-relatedness. They fail to recognize that in her words, Antigone speaks of neither of these. One is still unable to see that she is not speaking of a being at all" (*GA* 53, 144). In other words, the tension between family law and city law upon which both Hölderlin in his *Re-*

marks and Hegel in his *Phenomenology of Spirit* were focusing, the former in terms of hubris and the latter in terms of an inadequate development of the world spirit, is no longer relevant, because in both cases human in teraction prevails upon the requirements of the vision of Being. Heidegger accordingly insists that nothing happens in the poem and that there is no action in it in the usual sense of interaction. The only action of the character called Antigone is a matter of seeing: enduring knowingly the destiny which is offered to her by Being itself. And that is why, once again, Plato is the guide of Heidegger's translations of the dialogues. Plato's ontological *theôria* as it is evoked in the *Phaedrus* is what justifies Heidegger's translation of the reply of Antigone to her sister at the outset of the drama. In the usual translations, the reply runs approximately like this: "Even if I must die, at least my death will not be vile." With the help of Plato's conflation of *to kalon* with Being, Heidegger translates without hesitation: "I shall not endure a death which does not belong to Being." Likewise, when Antigone replies to Creon that her decision comes from beyond Zeus and beyond the lower gods, it is Plato's description of the *huperouranios topos* in the *Phaedrus* which allows Heidegger to claim that Antigone's determination springs from Being itself. Antigone therefore is simply the emblem of enduring the *deinon* as the only abode. Antigone's determination means that she is "taking it upon herself to become homely within Being" (146).

Needless to say that under these conditions, the tension between *phronêsis* and *hubris* is no more an issue in 1942 than it was in 1935. In both cases an ontological *theôria* is the only ground of tragedy, and the poem called *Antigone* is a speculative hymn to destiny, to the advent of Being, whatever the differences might be between a Promethean and a meditative approach of the *Seinsgeschichte*. In other words, in both readings it turns out that only the sage, the one who is entirely dedicated to the *bios theôrêtikos*, and in no way the ordinary spectator in the theater, is a competent judge of what tragedy is all about. And the reason for this is that in both readings what is at stake is what Plato would call the "theater of truth."

Notes

1. Unless otherwise noted, all translations in this essay are mine.

2. G. W. F. Hegel, *The Phenomenology of Spirit*, tr. A. V. Miller (Oxford: Oxford University Press, 1977), 263 [hereafter cited in text as *PS*].

3. All references to *Introduction to Metaphysics* are to M. Heidegger, *Enführung in die Metaphysik* (Tübingen: Niemeyer, 1953) [hereafter cited in text as *EM*].

Imprint: Heidegger's Interpretation of Platonic Dialectic in the *Sophist* Lectures (1924–25)

Catalin Partenie

In a letter to Karl Jaspers dated December 20, 1931, Heidegger describes himself as a simple "attendant" (*Aufseher*) in the great museum of philosophy. As such an attendant, he goes on, his sole duty is to make sure "that the blinds over the windows are raised and lowered correctly, so that the few great works of tradition receive a more or less adequate illumination for the chance observer."[1]

Heidegger, however, knew very well that he was being misleading when he described himself in that letter to Jaspers as a simple attendant in the great museum of philosophy. Just one year before he wrote that letter, in a lecture he gave at the University of Freiburg, he described himself in completely different terms: as a murderer with a noble alibi. The interpretation of a philosophical work, he said there, should be a *Destruktion*, a "destruction" of that work (*GA* 31, 292). In such a "destruction," during which one should attempt to bring the questions raised in that work to their ultimate transparency, one will metaphorically murder that work's author. Thus, he claims, "it is—in the history of everything essential—the privilege and also the responsibility of all descendants to become the murderers of their forebears" (*GA* 31, 37).[2]

Heidegger's interpretation of Plato (all along its significant transformations) is a complex *Destruktion* of Plato. Can we call this interpretation murder? Perhaps not. Perhaps he was just being melodramatic, as he often was, when he claimed that *Destruktion* amounts to murder. But in his interpretation of Plato he is definitely not just a simple attendant who merely takes care of the blinds so that the right light will be cast on Plato's masterpieces. Most of the time he actually modifies these masterpieces, and he does so intentionally. And while he modifies them and leaves his mark on them, they too trespass on his thinking and leave their mark on it. My essay will follow one episode of this Platonico-Heideggerian interplay. The episode has at its core four theses centered upon the Platonic dialectic that Heidegger advances in his lectures on Plato's *Sophist*. I shall argue that these theses, although they reveal a biased reading of Plato, manage to draw our attention to a genuine and important Platonic distinction, usually overlooked, between authentic and inauthentic human existence, and that this distinction also lies at the core of the fundamental ontology expounded in *Being and Time*. At the close of the essay I shall address, but only in a preliminary way, the question of why Heidegger did not acknowledge this Platonic imprint on his *Being and Time*.

The lectures on Plato's *Sophist* were delivered at the University of Marburg during the winter semester 1924–25. They contain a running commentary of the *Sophist* completed by extensive analyses of book Z of the *Nicomachean Ethics*, book A (chapters 1 and 2) of the *Metaphysics*, and the *Phaedrus*. Of the many theses Heidegger advances in these lectures (whose published text counts 653 pages), I shall focus here on four, centered upon the Platonic dialectic.

The first thesis (T1) states that for Plato man always exists *miteinander,* with other men (*GA* 19, 135–36).[3] This view, Heidegger argues, according to which communality is a fundamental feature of human existence, was also envisaged by Aristotle when he determined man as a *zôon politikon* (*GA* 19, 135, 140), and by the Greeks in general, for whom "existence" (*Existenz*) was "existence in the *polis*" (*GA* 19, 231/159), that is, communal existence. This thesis, however, is not further developed.

For the Greeks in general, and also for Plato, Heidegger claims, man is not only a *zôon politikon;* for them man is also, to use another famous Aristotelian phrase, a *zôon logon echon* (cf. *GA* 19, 17; cf. also 340, 585), an "animal that speaks" (*"[ein] Lebewesen, das reden kann"; GA* 22, 310). The second thesis (T2) comes in two parts: one about speaking in general, the other about speaking as *Miteinandersprechen,* as speaking with others. Speaking is mostly a mere speaking about things "carried out *in isolation*" (emphasis in original) from them (*GA* 19, 339/235). As such, speaking is "free-floating" (*freischwebend*); thus, "in itself, insofar as it is free-floating, *logos* has precisely the property of disseminating presumed knowledge in a repetition that has no relation to the things spoken of" (*GA* 19, 339–40/ 235). Speaking is then, according to its "original facticity" (*ursprüngliche Faktizität*), not "unconcealing" (*aufdeckend*), but precisely "concealing" (*verdeckend*). So, "insofar as speech is the basic mode of access to the world and of commerce with it . . . , the emptiness of the speech is equivalent to an ungenuineness [*Unechtheit*] and uprootedness [*Entwurzelung*] of human existence" (*GA* 19, 231/159). The spoken word dominates "in single individuals as well as in the community" (*GA* 19, 230/159). The communal existence of men was for the Greeks determined by speaking (cf. *GA* 19, 577). In this communal existence, speaking is at first speaking with others: "[I]n its very first aspect, *legein* is understood as utterance and is genuinely and primarily understood as a speaking with others about something" (*GA* 19, 584/404). Speaking with others, however, is "at first mere prattle," or "idle talk" (*Gerede*) (*GA* 19, 197/136), and as such it promotes an "unconcern with substantive content" (*GA* 19, 230/159), that is, with disclosing beings (*GA* 19, 231).[4] That is why human existence, as "it expresses itself in communal spiritual life," is uprooted, and it is not "genuine existence" (*GA* 19, 231/159–60); in other words, human communal existence is inauthentic existence. To conclude, T2 states that (1) according to its original facticity, speaking conceals the things it approaches, and (2) human communal existence, being determined by speaking, which promotes an unconcern with substantive content, is not genuine existence.

In his comments on the *Phaedrus*, Heidegger claims that Plato's attack on writing (*Phdr.*, 274ff.) is in fact an attack on public speaking (cf. *GA* 19, 342) as a "free-floating" speaking that does not relate to the things spoken of (*GA* 19, 339–40). The opposite of this public speaking is, according to the *Phaedrus*, the "living *logos*" (*Phdr.*, 276a8f.), the one embodied in the dialectical dialogue. For Plato only *logos* as a proper *dialogos*, that is, as dialectical dialogue, "takes its life from a relation to the matters themselves" (*GA* 19, 345/239), and that makes dialectic a concern with "substantive content," that is, with "disclosing beings," in which "genuine existence" resides (*GA* 19, 231/160). Dialectic is a "'speaking-through' ['*Durchsprechen*'] [that] begins with what people first say about the matter, passes through this, and is directed to and finds its end in a speaking which genuinely expresses something about the theme, i.e., in a genuine assertion, genuine *logos*" (*GA* 19, 196/135). This "impetus . . . to pass from *logos* as prattle, from what is said idly and hastily about all things, through genuine speaking, to a *logos* which, as *logos alêthês*, actually says something about that of which it speaks" is "an inner need of philosophizing itself" (*GA* 19, 196/135). The third thesis (T3) comes in two parts, and it states that (1) dialectic is a *Durch-brechen des Geredes*, a breaking through the concealing strata of idle talk that surround all things (*GA* 19, 195) and (2) in it resides a concern with "substantive content," that is, with "disclosing beings," which represents "genuine," authentic human existence (*GA* 19, 231/159–60).[5]

Yet dialectic, Heidegger argues, although it may transcend idle talk, is bound to fail in its attempt to disclose the things it approaches. Speaking "has precisely the meaning of *apophainesthai*, letting be seen" (*GA* 19, 200/138; cf. also 339, 343, and 569). Speaking then, as well as dialectic as a form of speaking, "possesses an intrinsic tendency toward seeing [*Sehen*], disclosing [*Aufdecken*]" (*GA* 19, 198/137). Speaking, however, is (as Aristotle showed) *legein ti kata tinos*, "saying something about something"; thus, "insofar as *logos* addresses something as something [*etwas als etwas*], it is in principle unfit to grasp that which by its very sense cannot be addressed as something else but can only be grasped for itself. Here, in this primary and predominating structure, *logos*, as it were, fails" (*GA* 19, 206/ 142). Dialectic cannot transcend the linguistic medium in which it takes place; it "still remains in *legein*," and so it cannot but remain an "attempt" (*Versuch*) to disclose the thing under discussion (*GA* 19, 197/136). In other words:

> Although *dialegesthai* [i.e., dialectic] does not reach its goal and does not purely and simply disclose beings, as long as it remains in *legein*, it need not be a mere game but has a proper function insofar as it cuts through the idle talk, checks the prattle, and in the speeches lays its finger, as it were, on what is at issue. In this way, *dialegesthai* presents the things spoken of in a first intimation and in their immediate outward look. That is the fundamental sense of Platonic dialectic. (*GA* 19, 197/136–37)

The fourth thesis (T4), which comes in three parts, states that (1) speaking has an inner tendency toward seeing, that (2) this tendency is sabotaged by the fact that speaking has an *etwas als etwas* structure, and that (3) dialectic, which cannot transcend its own linguistic medium, fails to disclose the things it approaches. Dialectic does offer a grasp of the thing under discussion, unlike idle talk, which conceals everything it approaches. But dialectic gives us only an elusive indication of what a thing really is. The thing itself can be disclosed only in a direct apprehension, *theôria*, of it. Such a pure *theôria*, however, we have to assume, can only be experienced individually, not collectively, through dialogue. I need the other only to break through the idle talk; then, I am on my own.

To sum up, the picture depicted by T1–T4, which Heidegger claims is a Platonic one, is this: Human existence is communal and is determined by speaking; speaking, however, conceals the things spoken of, and so the communal existence of men is not genuine existence; genuine existence, the one aimed at disclosing the world, is (partially) embodied by dialectic, which manages to break through the concealing idle talk that permeates human communal existence, but fails nonetheless to disclose the world as it is, because it cannot transcend its linguistic medium and attain a direct apprehension of things.

Heidegger gave his lectures on the *Sophist* in 1924–25. The first drafts of *Being and Time* (published in 1927) were composed in 1924 (the

"Dilthey draft"), 1925 (the "Husserl draft"), and 1926 (the "Kantian draft").[6] In fact, as various scholars have now established, the entire period of 1919–27 was marked by the emergence of the fundamental ontology that was fully articulated in *Being and Time*.[7]

In the *Sophist* lectures various fundamental notions of *Being and Time* are already there—"Dasein," "being-in," "being-in-the-world"—and they are used to describe the most intimate recesses of Plato's thought (see, e.g., *GA* 19, sec. 80). As far as the four theses (T1–T4) are concerned, they do not seem to be supported by strong textual evidence. Rather, they seem to be derived in a fairly loose way from various sections of the *Sophist* and the *Phaedrus;* they also obviously contain, in nuce, several fundamental notions of *Being and Time:* "being-with," "fallenness," and "idle talk." At first sight, then, Heidegger seems to read back into Plato parts of his own emerging fundamental ontology. Let us see, however, if some stronger support may be found for these four theses.

In Plato's late dialogues the ideas are claimed to form a *koinônia,* "communion" (cf. *Sph.,* 252a–e, 259e–60a; cf. also *Ti.,* 30c, where he claims that the forms of all things that exist in our universe are all parts of a totality). For Plato, man is able to grasp, as much as his limited intellectual powers allows him to, this communion of ideas. Man himself, however, is also a being whose existence is communal.

Politeia gar trophê anthrôpôn estin, "political constitution," *politeia,* that is, life organized commonly in a *polis,* "is the nurture of men."[8] This is what Plato says in the *Menexenus* (238c). *Polis,* as the human community par excellence, is a central notion in Plato and is amply discussed in many dialogues. In the one that has it at its core, the *Republic,* Plato claims that human community was caused by need (369b–c). Men are not self-sufficient: They have many varied needs, and these needs can be met only if they live in a community. This amounts to saying that men cannot but live *miteinander,* in common (a thought stated again in *Lg.,* 676b–c). This down-to-earth explanation of human communal life, however, has a more subtle addendum, which lies in the "immanent tendencies" (if I may use this Heideggerian expression, *GA* 19, 228/158) of some other Platonic texts.

In the *Protagoras,* we are told, men "lived at first in scattered groups" (322a). The need to defend themselves from wild beasts forced men to come together and form a bigger community, a *polis.* But they could not live in a *polis* "for want of political skill, and so scattered again" (*Prt.,* 322b). Then, Zeus sent Hermes to impart to all men "justice [*dikê*] and respect [*aidôs*] for their fellows" (*Prt.,* 322d); for if only a few shared in these "virtues," "there could never be cities" (*Prt.,* 322c–d). The idea behind the myth is that in order for men to be able to form a *polis*, a unifying element must be equally distributed to all of them, and this is a shared understanding of justice and respect. Need may be the cause of the *polis*, the human community par excellence; but a given, equally distributed understanding of justice and respect, we may venture to say, is the condition for the possibility of communal life. This idea is, obliquely, pointed at in the *Republic*. Here *polis* is again said to be caused by need: "[W]e, being in need of many things, gather together into one place of abode as associates and helpers, and to this dwelling together we give the name city [*polis*]" (*R.,* 369c). Plato does not explicitly say here, as in the *Protagoras*, that this dwelling together presupposes that a unifying element be equally distributed to all souls. But he claims that the human soul has a particular tripartite structure; and each soul, it is implied—be it of a cave dweller or of one who managed to have a glimpse at the real world outside the cave— has the same tripartite structure. So, one may argue, it is this basic structure, equally distributed to all souls, that, in a way, makes any dwelling together possible. This idea, explicitly claimed in the myth of the *Protagoras*, might seem difficult to read back into the *Republic*. In a late dialogue, however, which a long and reputable tradition considered to be the hub of Platonic philosophy, it resurfaces with vigor. That dialogue is the *Timaeus*.

At the end of the *Republic*, Socrates suggests that there could be a Demiurge able to produce "all plants and animals, including himself, and thereto earth and heaven and the gods and all things in heaven and in Hades under the earth" (596c). In the *Republic* Plato is still hesitant to pronounce the existence of such a Demiurge. In the period in which he wrote the *Timaeus*, however, this hesitation disappeared altogether. In this period, he came to believe that every thing that exists in our world of becoming, every *gignomenon*, is actually a *poioumenon*, that is, a "product" of some sort.[9] Thus, he imagined in this dialogue that the whole universe is a "product" framed from a primordial given matter (*Ti.,* 52d) by a Demiurge and other gods (*Ti.,* 28a–29e; 31b), in the likeness of an ideal model (*Ti.,* 30c; 38b–c; 39e).

The universe has both a soul and a body (*Ti.,* 31b–34a; 34c–36e), and they are both framed by the Demiurge.[10] After framing the world soul, the Demiurge turns to the task of making the human souls. He pours the remains of the three ingredients he used for framing the world soul (being, sameness, and otherness, 35a) "into the cup in which he had previously mingled the world-soul" (41d). He divides the whole mixture into as many souls as there will be (41d–e). And then, using the same pattern he used for framing the world soul, he makes two rings from the mixture (the ring of sameness and the ring of otherness), divides them in certain proportions, and sets them in motion (so that the rational human life be carried out by the revolutions of the two rings) (cf. 43d–e, 44d; cf. also 35a–36e).[11]

The many details about the ratios used for framing the two rings of the soul cause one main idea in this passage to be easily overlooked. It is the idea that human reason is multiplied and distributed equally to all human beings. There is something that pervades us all. It is our rationality, symbolized by the two rings that we all have. And this rationality that pervades us all unifies us, brings us together. This idea announces the motif of "being-with," which is at the core of the next passage.

The Demiurge has now framed the human souls. Some other, inferior deities are to frame the human bodies. The souls will then be embodied and "thrown" into their earthly life.[12] The Demiurge, however, postpones their embodiment and shows them "the nature of the universe" and declares to them the "the laws of destiny" (*nomous tous heimarmenous*— *Ti.*, 41e), their destiny. The human souls listen and learn this about their fate:

> 1. Their first birth will be "one and the same for all," so that "no one should suffer a disadvantage" (*Ti.*, 41e);
> 2. they will be embodied in the same kind of body (42e–43a);
> 3. they will "all have in them one and the same faculty of sensation" (42a);
> 4. they will be the most god-fearing of animals (41e–42a);
> 5. the human nature (*hê tês anthrôpinês phusis*) being twofold (*diplês*, 42a1–2), they will be born as men and women, and men will be "the superior race" (42a);
> 6. they will have love, fear, anger, and "the feelings which are akin or opposite to them" (42b);
> 7. and each one of them will be responsible in its earthly life for the life it will live (42c): If one masters his own desires and emotions (such as fear and anger), one will live justly and return to his native star, where one will live a happy and congenial life (42b); if not, one will reincarnate as a woman or as a different creature, according to "the character of his depravation" (42c; translation from Cornford 1937).

The main motif that runs through all these laws of destiny is "communion," "being-with." The laws announce to men a common destiny. First, there is the communion between man and woman: The souls are to be born as men and women and be attracted to each other by the Eros of begetting (*Ti.*, 91b). Second, the text implies, there is the religious communion into which the fear of gods will bring men (religion, in any of its known forms, is a social phenomenon; and so it is for Plato: both popular and philosophical religiousness is commonly experienced; see, e.g., the *Republic* and the *Laws*). Finally, the text obliquely points out there is the communion with others within a *polis*. If one masters his de sires and emotions, states the law, one "would live justly," *dikê biôsointo*, that is, according to *dikê*, "justice" (*Ti.*, 42b). For Plato, however, living according to justice, living rightly, does not refer, in the first instance, to the way one behaves toward oneself, but to the way one behaves toward others. In two earlier accounts of reincarnation, those from the *Phaedo* (113e–14b) and the *Republic* (448c, 615a-b), we are told that a life rightly lived, upon which future reincarnations depend, implies that one behaved in a right way toward others. We do not have any reason to doubt that in the *Timaeus* this communal dimension of a life rightly lived has been abandoned; and so the law of destiny that makes the reincarnation process depend on "living according to justice" seems to point out, obliquely, that human beings are destined to a political existence, i.e., an existence in *polis* as the main locus in which a life can be justly or unjustly lived.

The laws of destiny, however, are not only about the communions destined to men: familial, religious, and political. They also state what may be called the very conditions for the possibility of a communal existence. The very fact that the Demiurge reveals the laws to all souls collectively, unites them. Each soul becomes aware of the laws, and this awareness becomes a unifying element. But this is not the only unifying element at work here. The rational framework that is equally distributed to us, that is, the rational part of our souls, is to be complemented with equally distributed sensible features: The same birth, the same kind of body, the same faculty of sensation. "No one should suffer a disadvantage" (*Ti.*, 41e), so that we will all be equal as far as our rational and sensible frameworks are concerned. Why would Plato insist upon all this at this point in his cosmology, just before stating, more or less obliquely, that a communal existence is destined to men? The idea behind the myth of the *Protagoras* comes to mind. There Plato says that in order for men to be able to form a *polis*, a unifying element must be equally distributed to all, and this is a shared understanding of justice and respect. Here, in the *Timaeus*, the same idea seems to lie in the subtext. We are destined to live in a *polis*; but in order to be able to do so, a unifying element has to be equally distributed to us. Here, however, Plato does not say what he has said in the *Protagoras*, namely that this must be a shared understanding of justice and respect (although here, too, that unifying element is given to us by divinity, which amounts to saying that our communal existence has a divine ground, just as the erotic community, in the *Symposium* is said to have a divine ground—namely Eros, the god of love). Here he moves to a deeper level. We will understand the world and our own selves differently, but the laws of destiny state our very cognitive apparatus will be the same, for we are given the same type of mind and senses. And this cognitive apparatus given to all of us, the text invites us to assume, is what allows us to belong to a community—the human community.

Let us go back to T1, Heidegger's first thesis. This thesis, which states that for Plato communality is a fundamental feature of human existence, is in fact supported by textual evidence: The idea is explicitly expressed in the *Republic* and the *Laws,* pointed out obliquely in the *Timaeus,* and given a subtle explanation in both the *Protagoras* and the *Timaeus.*

Let us now turn to T2–T4. The Socratic dialogues, down to and including the *Protagoras,* seem to have the same main narrative pattern. Socrates, the central character, while he is in a public place of his *polis,* encounters someone, A, who believes he knows what something, *x,* is. Usually, *x* is a serious thing, something considered to belong to *ta megista,* "the most vital" things in our life (*Grg.,* 527e1), such as courage or virtue. About these "most vital" things men hold an opinion (*Euthphr.,* 7d; cf. also *Grg.,* 506c–9c). And so it is with A: He holds an opinion about *x;* at first sight, his opinion looks rather acceptable, for it is endorsed by the many, hoi polloi. *Hoi polloi nomizousin houtôs,* "the many think so" (*Grg.,* 489a), and so A cannot but do the same: "What else am I to do?" (*La.,* 184d). The many believe and agree upon many things. Yet, Socrates claims, their agreement is not to be taken as an indication of truth; their agreement, on the contrary, is more likely an indication of falsity (*Cri.,* 44c, 47c, 48a; *La.,* 184d; *Hp. Ma.,* 284e, 299b). Thus, Socrates engages A in an examination of *x*—a *skepsis* (*Chrm.,* 158e6; *La.,* 198a1–2, c9; *Euthd.,* 282c7; *Grg.,* 487e8; *Prt.,* 347c2, 348c7, 349a5, 361c7), a *zêtêsis* (*Grg.,* 457d4, 506a4), or an *exeuresis* (*Prt.,* 353b1). Socrates and A form now a "communion," a *sunousia* (*La.,* 196b; *Ly.,* 223b; *Grg.,* 457d and *Prt.,* 335b, 336b, 337b, 338c, 347e), which is a *koinônia tou logou,* a "communion of language" (*La.,* 197e7): Socrates and A pursue in common, through speaking, an examination of *x.* They undertake a *koinê skepsis,* a "common search" that aims at revealing what *x* is (*Chrm.,* 158d8; cf. also *Cri.,* 46d, 48d; *La.,* 187d, 189c; *Grg.,* 453c, 472b–c, 495a; *Prt.,* 343c, 347c, etc.). To A, such an examination may sometimes appear to be mere "idle talk" (*huthlos, Ly.,* 221d5) about *x.* But it is not: It is, unlike idle talk, a "strict form of dialogue" (*to akribes eidos tôn dialogôn; Prt.,* 338a1–2), in which Socrates asks A what exactly *x* is and then refutes all A's answers by the procedure of the so-called Socratic elenchus. With those who are bound to break the rules of the Socratic dialogue (*Prt.,* 335c, 353b) and with hoi polloi (*Cri.,* 49d, *Grg.,* 474b), Socrates is not willing to undertake an examination of *x.* Socrates "hunts" (*thêreutikê;* cf. *Ly.,* 218c and *Euthd.,* 290b–d) the essence of *x.* But his hunting turns into a "wandering" (*planê;* cf. *Hp. Mi.*, 376c and *Hp. Ma.*, 304c) and the sought-after values run away from him and his interlocutor as if they were Daedalus's statues (*Euthphr,* 11c) Eventually, Socrates' examination of *x* ends in an aporia, that is, before a firm answer is found, and so *x* remains, as it were, concealed.

The picture that emerges from this narrative pattern is supported by what Socrates himself claims in Plato's only writing that is a real monologue: the *Apology*. In the *Apology* Socrates claims that there are three kinds of wisdom: the real (cf. *tô onti,* 23a5) wisdom, which only gods have (23a); the real (cf. *tô onti,* 20d7) human wisdom, which, according to the Delphic god, is Socrates' wisdom (20d); and the inauthentic human wisdom, which Socrates does not know how to name (20e1–2) and which belongs to all those men who believe they know something without actually knowing it (21b–22e). When the Delphic god uttered his oracle, says Socrates, he "is not referring literally to Socrates; he has merely taken my name as a *paradeigma*" (23a8–b1). Socrates appears then as a paradigmatic possibility within the *polis*. But he is, nonetheless, alone. No one in the *polis*— be he a politician, a poet, or a skilled craftsman (cf. 21c–22d)—knows that he does not know. No one in the *polis,* except Socrates, is aware that what he believes he knows is just public, untested knowledge.

According to the picture that emerges from the main narrative pattern of Plato's early dialogues the human community, the *polis,* is composed of men who speak between them about various things. Socrates' *polis* is not silent. On the contrary, everyone is ready to speak to someone else. But no one realizes that their public speaking does not lead to any firm knowledge about the things spoken of, especially about those considered to be *ta megista,* "the most vital" things in our life. Socrates is the one, the only one, who confronts this public speaking. He is the paradigm of the real, authentic human wisdom, and as such he opposes his entire community, which embodies the public, pseudowisdom, the inauthentic wisdom out there in the *polis*. He engages his fellow citizen in a dialogue, which aims at disclosing what the matter under discussion really is. But the dialogue remains only an attempt: Each time it ends in an aporia, failing thus to disclose the matter in question. Throughout the dialogues, however, Socrates is presented as the paradigm not only of real human wisdom but also of the most positive features of human being: "[H]e was, we may fairly say, of all those whom we knew in our time, the bravest and also the wisest and most upright man" (*Phd.*, 118a); which makes him appear as a lonely voice amid a public hubbub, a call addressed to his community to turn to a more valuable existence.

Going back to Heidegger's theses T2–T4, we must ask if they are supported by the early dialogues. First, there is hardly any evidence for T4.

The early dialogues fail to disclose the matter under discussion. But there is nothing in them to suggest that this failure has been caused by the inability of the Socratic dialogue to transcend its own linguistic medium, and that this medium is that which blocks access toward a proper apprehension of the matter in question. One given reason for this failure is that words are polysemantic (*Euthd.*, 277e–78a). This may somehow support Heidegger's vision of speaking as a "free-floating," unreliable medium. But for Plato this is not, in fact, the real reason; for, says Socrates, even if one knew all the meanings of words, "one would be no nearer knowing what the things really are" (*Euthd.*, 278b). The real reason is that "the real wisdom is the property of God" (*Ap.*, 23a). Socrates and his interlocutor fail to attain firm knowledge about *x* because they fail to inscribe a definition of *x* into a set of consistent propositions, and this is due to their being just human beings, that is, their having just a human, not divine, intelligence.

Let us now go to T2 and T3. Their "mechanics," as it were, do not seem to be supported by the early dialogues, and they cannot be *inferred* from the texts. Speaking per se is not said to be the origin of the pseudoknowledge that permeates Socrates' *polis*. And yet, if we leave Heidegger's jargon aside, T2 and T3 manage to draw our attention to a background opposition that is to be found in the texture of the early dialogues. On the one hand is the vast community, the *polis*. The *polis* speaks, but it cannot disclose the things spoken of, and it is not aware of this; thus, human communal life, as it is first encountered, is permeated by the illusion of knowledge. On the other hand, opposing the entire *polis*, is the Socratic *koinê skepsis*, common search, which is carried out through dialogue: the only authentic human gesture amid a public, concealing speaking. The Socratic dialogue attempts to break through this pseudoknowledge and attain true, reliable knowledge, but its attempt eventually fails.

The picture emerging from the narrative pattern of the early dialogues is, in its great lines, to be found in the middle and late dialogues as well. Everything in these dialogues happens against the background of a divided *polis*. On the one hand, there are the many, the hoi polloi, who are like a "great strong beast" in the *polis*, a beast almost devoid of reason (*R.*, 493a; cf. also *Phd.*, 64b, *R.*, 493e–94a, *Phdr.*, 249c–e), and the allies of this "beast": the sophists, the politicians, and the poets; those aim at pleasing the many and thus situate themselves within the unreliable realm of opinion (cf. *R.*, 493a; *Ti.*, 19d–e). On the other hand, there are the philosophers. They are the only ones in the *polis* to rely solely on their reason, and in doing so, they attain the "divine nature" (*Phd.*, 82c), become "truly perfect" (*Phdr.*, 249c), live the best life (*Ti.*, 90b–c), and thus they situate themselves opposite all the other members of the *polis*.

In the *polis* portrayed by the middle and late dialogues, however, the many and their allies are not opposed by a single character, namely, Socrates. There are now several others, who are Socrates' equals: the Stranger from Elea, Timaeus, Critias, Hermogenes or the Athenian. Socrates, as well as each one of his equals, is undertaking a *koinê skepsis*, a "common search" whose aim is true knowledge (*Phlb.* 26e2–3; cf. also *Men.*, 80d, 81; *Tht.*, 150a–51e, 181c; *Sph.*, 218b-d; *Plt.*, 258bf.; and *Phlb.* 19a–c). True knowledge, which is often contrasted with true opinion (*Men.*, 71c, 85cff., 97aff; *Phd.*, 66aff.; *R.*, 477b, 478b; *Tht.*, 200d–1c, *Ti.*, 51d), is said to be reached through a methodical inquiry. In Plato there are three main methods for achieving true knowledge, and all of them are called "dialectic": The method of hypothesis (cf. *Phd.*, 101e; cf. also 99dff. and 67a–b), the method of the so-called upward path (cf. *R.*, 511b–c, 532a, 533c), and the method of synthesis and division (cf. *Sph.*, 231c, 253d–e). As Robinson put it in his classical study, "the word 'dialectic' had a strong tendency in Plato to mean 'the ideal method, *whatever that may be.*'" (1953, 70, emphasis in original; cf. also 145). The word *dialektikê*, which seems to be Plato's coinage, contains an explicit reference to "dialogue" (*dialegein*), and in various writings he explicitly relates dialectic to dialogue. In the *Republic,* for instance, he claims that dialectic is the supreme method of achieving true knowledge (533b, 534c–e), that its technique consists of asking and answering questions (534d; cf. also *Phd.*, 75d, 78d and *Cra.*, 390c, 398d–e), and that the dialectician is eager to test his knowledge by elenchus (534b–c; cf. also *Men.*, 75d). Thus, to quote Robinson again, "Plato was so absolutely certain, throughout his life, that the supreme method has its being in conversation, that he could name it from this fact" (*PED,* 77; cf. also 81).[13]

In the middle and late dialogues something firm is usually achieved. The *Sophist,* for instance, ends with a firm definition of the sophist that is not questioned any further, and the *Timaeus* contains a positive cosmological account whose excellence no "man in his sound senses could venture to dispute" (*Criti.*, 107a). But the idea that the things approached remain, to a certain extent, concealed is also there. In some dialogues— such as the *Parmenides* and the *Theatetus,* which end before a firm solution is found—it is explicitly expressed. In some others, it is only alluded to by more subtle devices. The *Sophist,* for instance, although it ends with a firm definition of the sophist, belongs to a tetralogy (*Theaetetus, Sophist, Politicus, Philosopher*) that ends before its essential part is achieved: the *Philosopher* was never written. And the cosmological account of the *Timaeus* is said to be only a "likely story" (30b, 48d, 53d, etc.), which, besides, is also just the first part of another unfinished project (*Timaeus, Critias, Hermocrates*).

According to the picture that emerges from the middle and late dialogues, the search for truth is pursued by a community of minds: It is the community of philosophers. The community of philosophers, which embodies the human reason at its best, aims at attaining knowledge about forms. The forms are the purest and most beautiful realities, and the life of those who aim at knowing them is also the purest and most beautiful human existence. But the philosophers' quest for knowledge always occurs within a larger community, a *polis*, which represents the realm of opinion; to this realm belong the hoi polloi (the "great strong beast" almost devoid of reason) and those who aim at pleasing them: the sophists, the politicians, and the poets. The community of philosophers, however, does not always achieve firm knowledge.

Now to go back to Heidegger's theses T2–T4. T4, again, seems to be the most problematic. Why, for Plato, do philosophers fail, when they do, to disclose the things they approach? The *Timaeus* suggests that they fail because of an inbuilt cognitive deficiency. The revolutions of our souls "were corrupted at our birth" (*Ti.*, 90d1–2). When the souls are newly incarnated, the revolutions which constitute human rational life are perturbed by various things, such as the flow of nourishment (43aff., 44bf., 89e–90a). So, when embodied souls "meet with something outside . . . they show themselves mistaken and foolish" (43c–d) by not discerning what is the same and what is different in the things they deal with (44a). Some of the perturbations that occur in early infancy are partly remedied by the time physical maturity is reached. Then, the revolutions are corrected and the human souls "call the same and the other by their names and make the possessor of them to become a rational [*emphrôn*] being" (44b). But, even if the revolutions are in adulthood more regular than they were in infancy, one will still not escape the worst of maladies, which is ignorance (cf. *amathia* at 88b5); and one's life will only be imperfect (*atelos*) and without understanding (*anoêtos*) if one's revolutions are not further corrected (44c). This means that according to Plato, human beings have an inborn tendency toward pseudoknowledge. This tendency can be fought back: If the human soul is provided with the right nurture (*orthê trophê*, 44b, 90c), education (*paideia*, 44b–c, 52e, 86e and 87b), and philosophy (*philosophia*, 47b), then it can escape the worst of maladies, that is, ignorance, and attain, as much as human nature permits, truth (*alêtheia*) (90c). But, even if I were fed the right nurture, were given the right education, and devoted my life to philosophy, I could not attain the ultimate truth and be omniscient, as is the model of my mind, the world soul. The very ingredients from which the human soul was framed, although they were the same ingredients from which the omniscient world soul was framed, are said to be less pure: They were "diluted to the second and third degree" (41d). Which means that according to the *Timaeus,* the inborn tendency toward pseudoknowledge cannot be completely overcome. An inborn cognitive deficiency does not allow us to be the equals of the world soul. I cannot fully grasp the rationality of the world because of this inbuilt cognitive deficiency, not because I attempt to grasp the rationality of the world through a "free-floating," unreliable medium, i.e., speaking, which blocks access toward a proper, non-linguistic apprehension of things. There is nothing wrong with speaking. In fact, the omniscience of the world soul manifests itself in speaking:

> [W]henever it [the world soul] comes into contact with something whose being is scatterable or else with something whose being is indivisible, it is stirred throughout its whole self. It then declares [*legei*] what exactly that thing is the same as, or what it is different from. . . . And when this contact gives rise to an account [*logos*] that is equally true whether it is about what is different or about what is the same . . . , then, whenever the account concerns anything that is perceptible, the circle of the Different goes straight and proclaims [*diangeilê*] it throughout its whole soul. This is how firm and true opinions and convictions come about. Whenever, on the other hand, the account concerns any object of reasoning [*to logistikon*], and the circle of the Same runs well and reveals it, the necessary result is understanding [*nous*] and knowledge [*epistêmê*]. And if anyone should ever call that in which these two arise, not soul but something else, what he says will be anything but true. (37a–b; translation from Zeyl 1997)

It would be difficult to argue that here *nous* has to be taken as a nonlinguistic apprehension of things (see also note 10). The stress in this passage is on *logos,* and *theôria* is not even hinted at.

In two of his writings (if we count the *Seventh Letter* among his writings) Plato does speak, however, about a nonlinguistic apprehension of things. In the *Symposium,* he claims that one may grasp the form of beauty by a sort of sight (*katopsis,* 210e4; cf. also 211b6, e1), and that the form of beauty grasped in this way will not take "the form of a face, or of hands, or of anything that is of the flesh. It will be neither words, nor knowledge, nor something that exists in something else . . . —but [something] subsisting in itself and by itself in an eternal oneness" (211a). But grasping the form of beauty requires an initiation, which consists in an ascent in love: It starts with loving physical beauty, and then moves up to loving intellectual beauty. The study of philosophy is, in fact, the penultimate phase of the ascent (210d), and philosophy is, throughout the dialogues, carried out in speaking, through dialectic.

In the *Seventh Letter,* in an attack against language as such, be it written or spoken, Plato claims that the ultimate kind of knowledge is a sort of incommunicable insight (343a–d), implying thus that words can only imperfectly depict the reality of forms. But he also claims that such an insight is actually sparked, not blocked, by dialectical speaking: The insight occurs "after a long period of attendance on instruction in the subject itself and of close companionship" (the *Seventh Letter,* 341c), and this close companionship consists in practicing the technique of question and answer and the elenchus (the *Seventh Letter,* 344b; cf. also *Prm.* 136d: truth may be attained only after lengthy dialectical dialogues).

Let us go back to Heidegger. In the *Sophist* lectures, Heidegger does not discuss the two passages from the *Symposium* and the *Seventh Letter.* But even if he did, one may argue, he could not find in them a solid ground for T4. It is true that in these passages truth is grasped by a nonlinguistic apprehension of things that is beyond dialectic; but this apprehension is said to be triggered, not blocked, by dialectic. T4, however, is also marred by an inconsistency. Later on in the lectures, Heidegger claims that according to the *Phaedrus,* a "seeing of truth is [after all] carried out in dialectic" (*GA* 19, 319/221).[14] The theme of a pure beholding as the locus of truth occurs in several early courses, such as *Basic Problems of Phenomenology* (WS 1919–20; *GA* 58) and *Ontology (Hemeneutics of Facticity* (SS 1923; *GA* 63), and it culminates in *Being and Time.* There Heidegger claims that the "primordial and genuine truth lies in pure beholding [*reine Anschauung*]" (*BT,* 171/215; see also 33–34) and that the Platonic dialectic, since it fails to attain such a beholding, is no more than "a genuine philosophical embarrassment" (*eine echte philosophische Verlegenheit; BT,* 25/47). This view, as various commentators have argued, is a Husserlian heritage.[15] So, one may assume, in claiming that Platonic dialectic fails to reach a pure beholding of the things it approaches because it "remains in *legein*" (*GA* 19, 197/136), Heidegger was in fact reading back into Plato his own Husserlian influence.

As far as T2 and T3 are concerned, their "mechanics," once again, do not seem to be supported by the middle and late dialogues, and they cannot be *inferred* from the texts. Speaking per se is not said in these dialogues to be the origin of the pseudoknowledge that permeates the *polis.* For Plato, the origin of this pseudoknowledge seems to be the feebleness of our human nature, which hinders our rational part to take the lead and guide us all. And yet, if we leave Heidegger's jargon aside, T2 and T3 manage to draw our attention to a background opposition that is to be found in the texture of the middle and late dialogues as well. On the one hand is the vast community, the *polis*, in which the things that are spoken of are not disclosed: Human communal life, as it is first encountered, is permeated by the illusion of knowledge. On the other hand, opposing the entire *polis*, is the community of philosophers, which attempts to disclose things through dialectic. Taking part in such a community is the only authentic human gesture amid a *polis* almost devoid of reason. Such a community attempts to break through the pseudoknowledge and reach the truth; but its attempt is not always successful.

From the four main theses advanced by Heidegger in his interpretation of Platonic dialectic, one (T1) can be backed by strong textual evidence, one (T4) remains extremely problematic, while two (T2 and T3) seem to be rather difficult to defend in their details. And yet, on the whole, Heidegger manages to draw our attention toward a background opposition that is a genuine and important one in Plato: the opposition between authentic and inauthentic human life.

At first sight, this opposition seems extremely banal, for it is as old as the human race and belongs to our everyday life. From 1919 on, Heidegger became more and more convinced that philosophy should attempt to penetrate precisely human everyday life and start its investigations from there. Now, everyday life pervades Plato's dialogues. In them particular characters meet in particular circumstances in a particular *polis* and begin their philosophical thinking because a particular (and puzzling) event in their lives triggers it. For Heidegger the everyday life that pervades Plato's dialogues embodies the real *archê* of philosophy, and it should not be ignored but treasured as a rare indication that philosophy should start out of the concrete texture of our lives. Heidegger's attempt to ground a philosophical program on what is given to our everyday life, first referred to as "the hermeneutics of facticity" in 1922, was brought to its fullest development in the fundamental ontology of *Being and Time*. *Being and Time* is a polyphonic, baroque piece. At its core, however, there is an opposition that is extremely similar to the one revealed by T2 and T3: the opposition that occurs in everyday life between authentic and inauthentic.

Heidegger claims that the ontological constitution of Dasein is determined by some given elements called "existentialia" (*die Existenzialien*), such as "being alongside" (*Sein bei*), "being-one's-self" (*Selbstsein*), "understanding" (*Verstehen*), "interpretation" (*Auslegung*), "language" (*Sprache*), and "being-with-one-another" (*Mitsein;* cf. *BT*, sec. 25–34). The idea that these existentialia are given to Dasein's existence is of Kantian extraction.

Kant's transcendental argument comes in two main parts. First, he makes a distinction between the phenomenal world (the world as human beings experience it) and the noumenal world (the world as it really is);

and then he argues that the phenomenal world is constituted by the transcendental subject, because the transcendental subject adds to its perception of the noumenal world various elements of its own, such as space and time. For Kant, then, the world as we experience it depends ontologically upon the transcendental subject (a position often called transcendental idealism). Heidegger's transcendentalism is of a more complex variety. On the one hand, he does not make a distinction between a phenomenal and a noumenal world, and he claims that the transcendental subject (Dasein) and the world are equiprimordial. On the other hand, he argues that a specific understanding of being (*Seinsverständnis*)—as a global framework of existentialia—is projected by Dasein onto the world, and that this projection determines the mode of being in which external entities appear to us.[16] *Mitsein*, then, is for Heidegger part of a transcendental framework that is projected by Dasein onto the world ("the 'they' is an existentiale; and as a primordial phenomenon, it belongs to Dasein's positive constitution," *BT,* 129/167). As such, *Mitsein* is what makes a human being exist in a communion with other human beings, even when it is alone (*BT,* 129). We are not *Mitsein* because we live a communal life; we live a communal life because we are *Mitsein*.

Dasein is "in each case mine," it "has in each case mineness" (*Jemeinigkeit*) (*BT,* 42/68). And yet Dasein is, "at first and for the most part" (*zunächst und zumeist*), not an individual self, but a "they-self" (*BT,* 129/167). Each human being exists, at first and for the most part, in an average, public sphere, the sphere of *das Man*, where one thinks and says what "one" does. In this public sphere, speaking becomes idle talk (*Gerede*), understanding becomes curiosity (*Neugier*), and things around me get obscured, while my self starts loosing its authenticity ("by publicness [*Öffentlichkeit*] everything gets obscured"; *BT,* 127/165). This public sphere is Dasein's "everydayness" (*Alltäglichkeit*), which is also its "falling" (*Verfallen;* cf. *BT,* 175/219) and "inauthenticity" (*Uneigentlichkeit; BT,* 179/223). Dasein exists, then, at first and for the most part, in a public sphere, where it becomes inauthentic and where everything hides its true essence behind the misleading shadows of uniformity.

In *Being and Time,* at section 34, Heidegger introduces the notion of hearing, *Hören,* and claims that hearing is constitutive for discourse (*Rede*) and that discourse is constitutive for understanding (*Verstehen*). Hearing, he goes on, "constitutes the primary and authentic way in which Dasein is open for its ownmost potentiality-for-Being [*sein eigenstes Seinkönnen*]—as in hearing the voice of the friend whom every Dasein carries with it" (*BT,* 163/206).[17] Dasein listens. "Listen to . . . is Dasein's existential way of Being-open as Being-with for Others" (*BT,* 163/206). Dasein listens to both the other, whose paradigm seems to be the "friend," and to itself (*BT,* 163/206). But the escape from inauthenticity is triggered by an inner, individual gesture: Dasein can be saved "from its lostness in the 'they'" (*BT,* 274/319) only if it is able to hear the call of its own conscience (cf. *BT,* sec. 56–57). The escape from inauthenticity does not involve hearing the voice of the other as friend, nor an *Auseinandersetzung* with another. It does not even involve an inner dialogue: "The call itself [the call of conscience] is a primordial kind of discourse [*Rede*] for Dasein; but there is no corresponding counter-discourse [*Gegenrede*] in which, let us say, one talks about what the conscience has said, and pleads one's cause. In hearing the call understandingly, one denies oneself any counter-discourse" (*BT,* 296/342). In hearing the call of conscience, however, and in understanding it, one discloses one's self and the world and thus reaches the realm of authenticity (*BT,* 296–97).

To sum up: communal existence is, for Heidegger, a transcendental element that Dasein projects onto the world, which means that Dasein cannot but exist "with-others." Dasein exists, at first and for the most part, in a public sphere, where it lives inauthentically and where everything hides from it behind the shadows of uniformity. The escape from this public and inauthentic existence, however, is an inner, individual act (the hearing of one's own inner conscience), which does not require the presence of another. Is this picture similar to the one emerging from Plato's dialogues? One of the main axes of *Being and Time,* the opposition between authenticity and fallenness, makes one wonder along with Derrida: "[I]s not the opposition of the primordial to the derivative still metaphysical? Is not the quest for an *archia* in general, no matter with what precautions one surrounds the concept, still the 'essential' operation of metaphysics? Supposing, despite powerful presumptions, that one may eliminate it from any other provenance, is there not at least some Platonism in the *Verfallen*?" (1982, 63).

The picture emerging from Plato's dialogues and the one emerging from Heidegger's *Being and Time* seem to differ in three main respects.

First, the communality of human existence is given different grounds in Plato and Heidegger. For Heidegger *Mitsein* is part of a transcendental framework that is projected by Dasein onto the world; whereas for Plato the communality of human existence (or at least its condition of possibility) is destined to humans by the divinity. In the *Timaeus* the laws of human common destiny are declared to human souls by the Demiurge before they are embodied and sown into their earthly life. They are "impressed" on them before their actual birth as embodied souls. At the beginning of the cosmological discourse, the Demiurge is said to be the maker and the father of the universe (*Ti.,* 28c). Now he is said to be a sower: He sows in human souls the seed of their divine part, that is, the seed of human reason (41d); and then he sows the human souls in the earth and other planets where they will exist as embodied souls. But, by declaring to human souls the laws of their common destiny, he also sows in them, as it were, the knowledge of their common destiny. This knowledge, one may speculate, would then be forgotten and possibly recollected in the earthly life. But the laws are out there, governing our destiny: They are given by an entity that is beyond the human realm, and so the laws themselves are transcendent. It is true, they are also deposited in us: They were declared to us, and thus impressed in our most intimate memory. But they are not "projected" onto our earthly existence by us. We live a communal life not because we "project" the laws of our common destiny onto our existence but because the divinity ordained for us a communal existence. Just as the divinity made the world soul and the human souls from being, sameness, and otherness because soul, in order to know reality, must correspond to the ultimate ontological elements, which are being, sameness, and otherness (see note 11); obviously the ultimate ontological elements are not being, sameness, and otherness because the world soul or human soul "projects" its "ingredients" onto reality.

Second, for Heidegger the escape from the public and inauthentic existence is triggered by an individual act—the hearing of my own conscience—whereas for Plato the escape is triggered by a collective one— the *koinê skepsis,* the common search for truth through dialectical dialogue. For Plato the great community of hoi polloi is opposed by the small community of philosophers; for him the escape from the realm of opinion does require the presence of another, just as in the allegory of the cave a prisoner cannot free himself from his bonds but needs the help of another.

Third, the cleavage between authentic and inauthentic human existence is not of the same kind in Heidegger and in Plato.

The very hub of Plato's philosophy, the so-called theory of ideas, splits reality in two: a "here" that contains its physical, visible realm, and a "there" that contains the intelligible forms, which are beyond the physical "here" and ground it. This ontological cleavage, however, is complemented in Plato by a symmetrical social cleavage: that between the communion of philosophers and the communion of the many and their allies. And behind this social cleavage lies another one: a cleavage between nature and society.

In the *Timaeus,* the cosmological account is prefaced by Socrates' summary of a discourse he gave "yesterday" (17a–19b) about a utopian community (which seems to be a brief summary of the *Republic*), and is followed by a discourse on how a pseudohistorical embodiment of that utopian community imagined by Socrates, a mythical city of Athens, fights the evil city of Atlantis (27a–b). This scenario brings forth an originary imperfection of the human community. The Demiurge "was good, and the good can never have any jealousy of anything. And being free of jealousy, he desired that all things should be as like himself as they could be" (*Ti.*, 29e–30a). Thus, the universe, the Demiurge's creation, is declared at the end of the cosmological discourse to be "an image of the intelligible, a perceptible god, supreme in greatness and excellence, in beauty and perfection" (*Ti.*, 92c; translation from Cornford 1937). Nowhere was Plato more favorable to the world of becoming. The universe framed by the Demiurge is the best possible physical world. That is why, as the tone of the cosmological discourse implies, it would not make any sense to imagine a better universe, or a better part of it, say, a better world soul, or a better human soul, or a better human body. But it makes perfect sense to imagine a better *politeia,* as Socrates did "yesterday," and as Critias will do "today," when he will recount the story of the mythical city of Athens. That suggests that the human community does not have the same onto-logical status as the Demiurge's creation.[18] The Demiurge, we may as-sume, allotted humans a communal earthly life; but he is not involved in framing, as it were, the *politeia,* the structure of their communal life. In the *Republic,* ruling is said to be like the craft (*technê*) of navigating a ship (388d–e). In the *Timaeus,* however, the Demiurge, the consummate crafts-man whose *technai* enabled him to frame a most wonderful universe, does not wish to try his craftmanship on human communal life. This one ap-pears to be left to humans to frame. In the *Timaeus,* there is not an arche-typal, demiurgic *technê* of ruling human beings. The Demiurge and the other gods, after they gave us a most wonderful soul and body, provided us with a most wonderful world to live in, and allotted us a communal ex-istence, left the shaping of this communal existence to us. Each one of us will be responsible in his earthly life for the life he will live, states one of the laws of human destiny (cf. *Ti.*, 42e; cf. also *Lg.*, 904c). But we will also be responsible for the way we order our community, in which each one will live his earthly life.

"When a community [*polis*] is ruled not by God, but by man, its members have no refuge from evil and misery"—says Plato in the *Laws* (713e). The God, however, deserted us. In the *Timaeus,* the Demiurge and the other gods do not rule our communal existence, in spite of Plato's claiming, in the *Critias,* that the traditional Greek gods were at first the herdsmen of men (cf. 109b). The allegory of the cave, in the *Republic,* sug-gests the same thing: Those prisoners in the cave, who symbolize the human community as a whole, seem to be abandoned by gods, and no di-vinity is mentioned in the allegory. The myth of *Politicus* says the same, only this time explicitly. There the universe is said to have two alternating cosmic eras: the reign of Kronus and the reign of Zeus (269a–70e). In the reign of Kronus fruits "sprang up of themselves out of the ground without man's toil" (*Plt.,* 272a), and men had no *politeia* (271e), for God, "the maker and father [of the universe]" (273b), was their shepherd (272a). In the reign of Zeus, which is our era, the metaphor changes: God is now said to be the "divine pilot" of the universe (*Plt.,* 273c). But in this era he abandons the "ship of the universe"; he "let go the handle of its rudder and retires to his conning tower in a place apart" (*Plt.,* 272e). The human community is also abandoned, so that men have to rule themselves by means of a *politeia,* which they have to devise themselves: "[T]he divine guardianship of men ceased . . . and men had to manage their lives and fend for themselves the same way as the whole universe was forced to do" (*Plt.,* 274d). Man falls from a sort of Garden of Eden, and the human community is abandoned by God. But this abandonment is not because of men's sins; it is because God abandons the entire universe, including man. Here in the *Politicus,* unlike in the *Timaeus,* the fallenness of human communal existence is part of a universal fallenness caused by the flight of gods. Regardless of its particular form, however, there is in Plato a refusal of the gods to rule our communal existence, and this refusal points out the idea that the human community has an originary imperfection: The human community was caused by need, but its proper functioning is always in need of a divine hand, for it is imperfect. Its imperfection could be overcome if we would "order our private households and our public societies alike in obedience to the immortal element in us" (*Lg.,* 714a), that is, our reason. Our reason is the divine element in us, the one framed by the Demiurge himself, and it is the only thing that could make our *politeia* get closer to a divine ruling. That is why everything in the attempt to devise a better *politeia* is centered upon reason. Everything, however, that happens in Plato's middle and late dialogues happens against the background of a *polis* deserted by gods, a *polis* which makes possible the idea of a utopian *polis,* grounded solely on reason, the only divine element in us.

Thus, the cleavage between authentic and inauthentic human existence is not of the same kind in Heidegger and in Plato. In Heidegger, it is a cleavage of the self: The inner cleavage between authentic and inauthentic temporality that characterizes Dasein, a cleavage which is not said to be the effect of a divine will. In Plato, it is a cleavage caused by a divine gesture: God's will to create a cleavage between nature and society.

In spite of these three main differences, however, both Plato and Heidegger believed that there is an originary cleavage between authentic and inauthentic human life. For both Plato and Heidegger, we live at first and for the most part in a public sphere, in which we do not have a proper understanding of ourselves and the world we live in. For both of them, we live as prisoners in a public cave: There, not only our legs and necks are fettered, we all are fettered together by our being thrown into this public cave, in which we cannot but look in one direction and believe that the shadows we see on the facing wall are real things. And for both Plato and Heidegger, an escape from this inauthentic mode of existence is possible. *Being and Time* bears, then, a Platonic pattern on its very crest, the pattern of the originary cleavage between authentic and inauthentic human life as it unfolds in a given communal existence.

One may argue that various existentialia of the fundamental ontology of Dasein in *Being and Time,* such as "care" (*Sorge*), "anxiety" (*Angst*), and even the cleavage between authentic and inauthentic human existence can be traced back to various Christian sources that the early Heidegger studied vigorously, such as St. Paul, St. Augustine, Eckhart, and Luther.[19] I do not deny this argument. One might also argue that Heidegger's view according to which the escape from the public and inauthentic existence is triggered by an individual act (namely, the hearing of my own conscience) can be traced back to Luther's claim that one's relation to God is a private one and that one does not need the presence of another (required, for instance, in the communal sacraments performed by the Roman Catholic Church) in order to reach God. But the backdrop against which Heidegger's fundamental ontology, with its arsenal of existentialia and its authentic-inauthentic axis, took shape was, mainly, his *Destruktion* of Greek philosophers, especially Plato and Aristotle. And *Being and Time* does not open with a fragment from St. Paul, St. Augustine, or Luther; it opens with one from Plato.

Being and Time opens with a short, untitled fragment, which opens in its turn with a quotation from Plato's *Sophist* (244a). The quotation precedes a section of the *Sophist* usually called "the battle of the Gods and Giants" (245–49), which refers to a *gigantomachia peri tês ousias,* an immemorial quest for the sense of being. *Being and Time,* Heidegger seems to suggest by opening it with this quotation from Plato, is to be taken as a continuation of this *gigantomachia,* fought by many heroes, among which Plato deserves a special place. *Being and Time,* however, was supposed to expose the philosophical tradition to a fatal destruction and offer a new, a radical new approach to the question of being. And yet, despite its undisputed originality, *Being and Time* has not come out uncontaminated from the destruction it envisaged: Its victims managed to leave on it their imprints. One such imprint is, in my view, the Platonic cleavage between authentic and inauthentic human life.

Relatively few scholars have explored the Platonic side of Heidegger's *Being and Time.*[20] Many more have attempted to reveal its Aristotelian one;[21] one of the most fervent of them, Franco Volpi, has even claimed that *Being and Time* might be read as a sort of "translation" of Aristotle's *Nicomachean Ethics*.[22] All these attempts to reveal the Aristotelian side of *Being and Time* seem to have Heidegger's blessing: In "My Way to Phenomenology" he confesses that it was Aristotle who led him to develop his phenomenological approach that was fully articulated in *Being and Time*.[23] He never confessed a Platonic influence.

Heidegger's appropriation of Aristotle can be traced back to the Natorp essay. There Heidegger argues that the object of philosophy is factical human life[24] and claims that the same view, which led him to the fundamental ontology of *Being and Time,* is to be found at the core of Aristotle's thinking. Relying mainly on book Z of the *Nicomachean Ethics* and book A (chapters 1 and 2) of the *Metaphysics,* Heidegger argues that Aristotle's notion of first philosophy (*sophia*) originated from human concerns (*PIA,* 263) and that the main Aristotelian ontological concepts (such as *ousia, dunamis, energeia,* etc.) were drawn from the sphere of production (cf. *PIA,* 253, 260, 268). This, according to Heidegger, reveals that at the core of Aristotelism lies the same view that he, Heidegger, has, namely, that what genuine philosophy ultimately addresses is factical human life.

Much of this interpretation of Aristotle is to be found, in an extended form, in the *Sophist* lectures, where Heidegger discusses at length book Z of the *Nicomachean Ethics* and book A (chapters 1 and 2) of the *Metaphysics.* In the *Sophist* lectures, however, he claims that, according to what he called "the old principle of hermeneutics" (proceeding from what is clear back to what is obscure), we should interpret the more obscure Plato by way of a "guiding line" (*Leitfaden*), namely, the clearer Aristotle (*GA* 19, 11–12/8). For "what Aristotle said is what Plato placed at his disposal, only it is said more radically and developed more scientifically" (*GA* 19, 11–12/8; cf. also 189–90). But then, Aristotle's basic idea that what genuine philosophy ultimately addresses is factical human life, which, Heidegger claims, led him to the fundamental ontology of *Being and Time,* has (pace Heidegger) a Platonic origin. If so, then behind the Aristotelian mark of *Being and Time* there must be, according to Heidegger's own view, a Platonic one. Yet, if Aristotle is nothing but a more radical and scientifically developed version of Plato, why did Heidegger not acknowledge the originary source of his influence? Why did he mention only Aristotle's influence in developing the philosophical program of *Being and Time?*

Heidegger's own philosophy, as both Heidegger himself and his exegetes admit, is divided by an important "turn" (*Kehre*) that occurred in his thinking somewhere between the late 1920s and the early 1930s. In the pre-*Kehre* period, whose essence, as it were, is to be found in *Being and*

Time, Heidegger attempts to argue that the sense of being is determined by Dasein's transcendental framework of existentialia. This, however, is not the only *gigantomachia* Heidegger fights in the pre-*Kehre* period. There is another one, which, if won, will prove that the radical transcendentalism advocated by Heidegger has been constantly and discreetly swept under the carpet by the entire philosophical tradition. The entire philosophical tradition should undergo a massive "destruction" in order to extract from it its most intimate essence, which, if distilled correctly, will turn into a raw version of Heidegger's transcedentalism. "The Problematic of Greek ontology," Heidegger claims in *Being and Time,* "like that of any other, must take its clues from Dasein itself" (*BT,* 25/47). But this is not evident: This is something that has to be brought to light, and Heidegger is willing to do the job. In the pre-*Kehre* period, Heidegger takes great effort to prove that "the original [Greek] sense of *ousia*" is "to be produced" (*Her-gestelltsein; GA* 19, 270/186); in other words, that the original Greek understanding of being is derived from the sphere of human production, that is, from Dasein's productive mode of comportment. This original sense of being, Heidegger argues, is both brought forward and developed by Plato. In the *Sophist* lectures, for instance, he claims that in the *Sophist* (cf. 219b and 233d) the "fundamental connection between the meaning of *ousia* and that of *poièsis*" (*GA* 19, 271/187) resurfaces vigorously. A few years later, in *The Basic Problems of Phenomenology,* a lecture course given at the University of Marburg in the summer semester 1927, he reiterates the idea that the ancient Greek understanding of being is derived from human production; and he suggests that this understanding makes its way right into the heart of Plato's philosophy: The idea of the good, which is at the core of Plato's *Republic,* is to be understood as the "condition of possibility of the understanding of being," and as such it is nothing but "the *dêmiourgos,* the producer pure and simple," and "this lets us see already how the *idea agathou* is connected with *poiein, praxis, technê* in the broadest sense" (*GA* 24, 405/286).

In the *Sophist* lectures, Heidegger states explicitly that his interpretation of Aristotle, as well as his entire course on Plato's *Sophist,* "is grounded on a phenomenology of Dasein" (cf. *GA* 19, 62). As far as Plato is concerned, however, Heidegger goes beyond the attempt to prove that Plato's ontology takes its clues from the sphere of production. In a lecture course of summer semester 1928, he argues that Plato's so-called theory of recollection, which states that being as *idea* is a priori, brings forward the temporal horizon in which Dasein understands being (see *GA* 26, 184–87). And in "Vom Wesen des Grundes," an essay first published in 1929, he argues that Plato's idea of the good is to be taken as pointing toward the transcendence of Dasein (see *GA* 9, 159–61). In the pre-*Kehre* period,

Heidegger does indeed attempt to appropriate Plato's thought by arguing that Plato's fundamental philosophical notions emerged in Dasein's horizon. And yet, by explicitly acknowledging only Aristotle as his main ally in the battle about being that he undertakes in the 1920s, he seems to imply that his transcendentalism is somehow better accommodated by Aristotle than by Plato. Why would he think so?

Heidegger grew up in a Catholic milieu, and his father, Friedrich Heidegger, served as a sacristan. Martin Heidegger first wanted to become a Jesuit (1909), then a theologian (1911), then, after writing his habilitation on a scholastic topic (1916), a Catholic philosopher. But each time something happened and hindered his way into a religious career. Heidegger, however, continued to be interested in Christian theology. Between 1918 and 1921, he gave a series of lectures at Freiburg on the phenomenology of religion, St. Paul's letters, and Augustine (*GA* 60); and in 1921, in a letter to Karl Löwith, then his student, he claimed to be a "Christian theo*logian*."[25] At the time, Heidegger was deeply immersed in the works of Luther. In the course on the phenomenology of religion (1920–21) he seemed to share Luther's view that Greek metaphysics had distorted the spirit of early Christianity and aim at retrieving the authentic Christian religiosity from the Scholastic tradition. In 1921 Heidegger turned to Aristotle, and this turn, as Philipse (1998, 175) put it, "was originally motivated by the Lutheran thesis that Aristotelian philosophy had perverted the Christian experience of life." So, when Heidegger began to write the Natorp essay (1922), one of his main goals was to deconstruct Aristotle's legacy "in order to restore religious life to its original meaning and intensity" (Philipse 1998, 175).[26] But the Natorp essay did not turn out as planned. In it Heidegger came to the conclusion that genuine philosophy is fundamentally self-centered, not God-centered, and that Aristotle, instead of being blamed for perverting the authentic Christian experience of life, should rather be praised for bringing forth the idea that what genuine philosophy ultimately addresses is factical human life (from which the complex notion of Dasein, the main topic of *Being and Time*, will emerge). In Aristotle, however, first philosophy does not deal with human life: It deals with first principles and divinity (cf. *Metaphysics*, 983a6–9), and they do not envisage human life. But, Heidegger argued, "for Aristotle the idea of the divine did not derive from an explication of something that became accessible in a religious fundamental experience" (*PIA*, 263; translation from Philipse 1998, 81). Only that this origin remains hidden, for Aristotle construed the divine in terms of the physical analysis of movement, namely, as an unmoved mover. In Heidegger's view, as Philipse put it, "both Aristotle's notion of (first) philosophy and his notion of Deity . . . disguise the fact that they originated from human concerns, . . . [for]

Aristotle derived their content from the physical analysis of movement"
(1998, 81).[27]

To go back to Plato. The narrative of his dialogues suggests that philosophy is indeed triggered by factical human life: In almost all of them,
philosophy emerges from a particular concern with a particular, "factical,"
aspect of human life. Even the complex cosmology of the *Timaeus* is said
to be somehow triggered by a factical element: "[H]ad we never seen the
stars and the sun and the heaven, none of the words which we have spoken about the universe would ever have been uttered" (*Ti.*, 47a2–3). But
in the *Timaeus*, philosophy deals with the divine. And here divine (*theion*)
is both the eternal Demiurge, who framed the entire universe (34a; cf.
also 28aff., 29d–e, 31b, etc.), the universe itself (34b), human immortal
soul (90eff.), and the eternal model of the universe, "the fairest and most
perfect of intelligible beings" (30d; cf. also *Smp.*, 208a-b: that which is always the same, *to auto aei einai*, is divine, *theion*). Plato's idea of the divine
is then embedded in a creationist scenario, drawn from the sphere of
artifacts production. And, since artifacts production is a fundamental feature of human life, one may argue, in Plato the notion of the divine clearly
originated from human concerns. Thus, one may conclude, what Plato's
philosophy actually addresses—even in its most elevated episode, the cosmological account of the *Timaeus*—is factical human life. Yet Heidegger,
in spite of attempting to argue that Plato's ontology takes its clues from the
sphere of production, does not discuss the creationist cosmology of the
Timaeus, and, as I said, acknowledges only Aristotle's influence on his view
that factical human life is the main object of philosophy. What might have
inhibited him to find in Plato an ally at least as strong as Aristotle?

In the *Sophist*, Plato claims that there are two kinds of creation (*poiêsis*): the divine (*theion*) and the human (*anthropinon*) kind (265b). As I argued elsewhere (Partenie 1998), Plato believed that the human creation
is solely a copy of the divine creation.[28] For him, that is, when a human
craftsman puts each of his materials in an order (*taxis*) and combines them
into a "product," a *kekosmemenon pragma* (cf. *Grg.*, 504a1, *Smp.*, 186dff.,
187a–c, *Cra.*, 389d–e, *Lg.*, 626c, 628a), that craftsman is actually repeating
the archetypal gesture of the divine Demiurge, gesture by which the whole
world was brought from disorder into order (cf. *Ti.*, 30a5: *eis taxin auto
egamen ek tes ataxias*).

The figure of this all-embracing, divine, and eternal Creator, which
dominates one of Plato's most influential writings, namely the *Timaeus*,
might have inhibited Heidegger, I speculate, to find in Plato a better ally
than Aristotle in his attempt to make man, Dasein, the ultimate ground of
being. It is difficult to say if *Being and Time* is or not religious at a deeper
level.[29] It is clear, however, that in it Heidegger dismisses the creationist

conception of God. In *Being and Time* man is not the creature of God, and so the Christian notion of God as a creator is, although indirectly, discarded.[30] The Platonic creationist metaphysics, which revolves around an all-embracing, divine, and eternal Creator who has an eternal model and frames a sempiternal universe, could hardly accommodate Heidegger's self-centered ontology, which at the time gravitated toward temporal, changeable human life rather than toward eternal being.[31]

Notes

I am grateful to Tom Rockmore, Herman Philipse, Michael Inwood, Theodore Kisiel, and Matthias Fritsch for their helpful comments on earlier drafts of this essay.

1. Martin Heidegger and Karl Jaspers, *Briefwechsel,* ed. W. Biemel and H. Saner (Frankfurt am Main: V. Klostermann, 1990), 144; the quoted fragment is in E. Osers's translation, as it appears in Safranski 1998, 215.

2. Translation taken from Inwood 1999b, 183.

3. All references to Heidegger's works are to the German editions. For quotations in English, page numbers to the English translations are keyed to the list of abbreviations. In all the English translations I use, the German pagination is indicated.

4. The sophist—who, according to Heidegger, is at the core of the *Sophist* in its entirety—represents a particular case of unconcern with substantive content (*GA* 19, 230).

5. In his analysis of book Z of the *Nichomachean Ethics,* Heidegger calls *sophia* "the genuine possibility of Dasein," which "is carried out in pure knowledge, pure seeing, *theôrein*—in the *bios theôrêtikos*" (*GA* 19, 61–62/44).

6. Cf. Kisiel 1996, 33. Herman Philipse (1998, 79) argues that the earliest draft of *Being and Time* is a manuscript from 1922, often referred to as the "Natorp essay," published posthumously as *Phänomenologische Interpretationen zu Aristoteles (Anzeige der hermeutischen Situation) (PIA).*

7. See, for instance, Kisiel 1993a and Van Buren 1994b.

8. Unless otherwise noted, the translations of Plato's texts I quote here are those collected in Hamilton and Cairns 1989. Sometimes I slightly modify the translations I quote.

9. Cf. also *Phlb.* 26 e–27 a: between "that which is made [*poioumenon*] and that which comes to be [*gignomenon*]" there is only a "mere verbal difference."

10. This assertion may seem strange to a modern reader of the *Timaeus.* But Plato has a reason for thinking that it must be so. He believed that the motions of the sun and the stars, as well as everything we see around us, compel us to say that the entire universe is an ordered universe (cf. *Ti.,* 47a; cf. also *Sph.,* 265c–d, *Phlb.* 28e, *Lg.,* 966e). And he claimed that that which is "the king of heaven and earth" (*Phlb.* 28c) and which is responsible for the "ordered array" of the universe (*Lg.,*

967b) is *nous*—a word that we may translate in this context as "reason." For him, however, reason could only exist within a soul (*Sph.*, 249a, *Phlb.* 30c, *Ti.*, 30b, 46d). So he made the Demiurge in the *Timaeus* frame a world soul and spread it throughout the body of the world (36d–e), to host, as it were, the rationality of the world.

11. The model of the universe contains in itself all the intelligible beings (*Ti.*, 31d), that is, all forms. And all forms, as we are told in the *Sophist* (cf. 259a), are "pervaded" by three ultimate ontological elements: being, sameness, and otherness. The world soul was framed from being, sameness, and otherness in order to correspond to these ultimate ontological elements of the model (and so of reality in general); which reflects, as various scholars have claimed, Plato's belief that "like knows like"—cf., e.g., Cornford 1937, 94, 96–97 (see also 59–66).

12. I will call the life lived by embodied human souls "earthly" although the Demiurge sows "some of them [human souls] in the earth, and some in the moon, and some in the other instruments of time [i.e., in some other planets]" (*Ti.*, 42d).

13. Robinson 1953, 77; cf. also 81. For a similar view, see also Kahn 1998, 301.

14. T4 is also weakened by a related inconsistency. Heidegger presents Aristotle as the one who understood that the Platonic dialectic "is being underway toward *theôrein*," and so, understanding it more radically, focused instead on the act of *noein* (*GA* 19, 199/138). Yet, Heidegger claims, Aristotle admits eventually that a pure *nous*, a pure apprehension of things, remains only an unfulfilled possibility for us; the only apprehension that man can reach is called by Aristotle a "so-called *nous*" (*De Anima* 3.4, 429 a 22ff.), and "this *nous* in the human soul is not a *noein*, a straightforward seeing, but is a *dianoein*, because the human soul is determined by *logos*" (*GA* 19, 59/41; cf. also 196). What Heidegger claims here, as Figal put it, is that for Aristotle a human being cannot see a thing as it really is because for human beings seeing "is structured according to the structure of language" (see Figal 2000, 102). In which case, Figal remarks, it seems that, "from Heidegger's perspective, Plato's dialectic and Aristotle's theoretical philosophy are virtually identical" (103).

15. See, for instance, Taminiaux 1994; 1997, 56–79. (Taminiaux's readings, however, are open to various objections).

16. For an overview of Heidegger's transcendentalism, see Philipse 1998, 121–44, 322–30.

17. For the occurrence of this enigmatic "friend" (and its ramifications in Heidegger's work), see Derrida 1994.

18. Another indication that the universe and human community have different ontological statuses is the dynamic between their rational and nonrational elements. In the creation of the universe, there has been a cooperation between the rational and nonrational element—*nous*, that is, the Demiurge, persuaded *anankê*, most likely the inherent forces of the given matter from which the universe was framed, to obey (*Ti.*, 47e–48a); whereas in the human community there is a confrontation between the two—the disobedient citizens obey by force the rule of the guardians (17d–18a) and Atlantis has to be conquered by the mythical city of Athens (25a-c). In the human community, unlike in the universe, the nonrational element cannot be persuaded to cooperate. After summing up his account of a

utopian community expounded "yesterday," Socrates tells his interlocutors that he would like to watch his ideal *polis* in motion, that is, in going to war and "achieving results befitting her training and education, both in feats of arms and in negotiation with various other states" (19c; translation from Cornford 1937). And yet the ancient city of Athens depicted in Critias's speech, which embodies the utopian *polis* of Socrates, is not depicted (in Critias's summary of his story) as having any negotiations with other states. The ancient city of Athens is depicted only as conquering its nonrational counterpart.

19. For a detailed account on Heidegger's Christian background, see Philipse 1998, 172–89; and Kisiel 1994, 187.

20. J.-F. Courtine (1990, 129–58), for instance, has discussed how various key Platonic notions, such as *epistêmê*, the *anamnêsis* of forms, and the transcendence of the idea of good have some correspondences to various issues developed in *Being and Time:* the science of being (*Wissenschaft des Seins*), the originary temporality of being (*Temporalität des Seins*), and the transcendence of being. G. Figal (2000, 105) has argued that the hermeneutics of facticity developed by Heidegger in the early 1920s (mostly in connection with his interpretation of the Aristotelian notion of *phronêsis*) is not actually very different from the Platonic dialectic as he, Heidegger, understands it in his lectures on the *Sophist*. H. G. Holz (1981) examines various similarities between *Being and Time*'s existential analytic and Plato's dialogues, arguing inter alia that the *Crito, Euthyphro,* and *Hippias Minor* point to the Heideggerian distinction between authentic and inauthentic selfhood (cf. 293–94).

21. See, for instance, Bernasconi 1989; Brogan 1994; Philipse 1998, 77–98; and Taminiaux 1989.

22. Volpi 1994. See also Volpi 1984, 90–116. In a related paper, Volpi argues that the notions of *Vorhandenheit, Zuhandenheit,* and Dasein correspond to the Aristotelian notions of *thêoria, poiêsis,* and *praxis* (1988, cf. 15).

23. In M. Heidegger, *Zur Sache des Denkens* (Tübingen: Niemeyer, 1976), 81–90; cf. 86.

24. Cf. *PIA* 238/359: "The object of philosophical research is human Dasein as it is interrogated with respect to its Being-character. This basic direction of philosophical questioning is not added on and attached to the questioned object, factical life, externally; rather it is to be understood as the explicit grasping of a basic movement of factical life."

25. The letter, dated August 19, 1921, was published in Pappenfuss and Pöggeler 1990, 29.

26. For Luther's influence on Heidegger, see Courtine 1992; Van Buren 1994a; and Philipse 1998, 180–89.

27. Cf. also Philipse 1998, 95: "According to Heidegger this implies, however, that Aristotle analyzes human existence in terms that are alien to Dasein [i.e., in terms of the physical analysis of movement], so that Aristotelian ontology is an alienation that has to be destroyed if we want to be able to grasp the movement of our life as it really is" (see *PIA*, 248–54, 260).

28. The evidence is plentiful. Cf. *Smp.*, 197a: "in every *technê*, the [human] craftsman who achieves the brightest fame is the one whose teacher is the god,

while those that lack his influence grow old in the shadow of oblivion"; *R.*, 597c–d: when a carpenter makes a couch having in his mind the *eidos* of couch, which was made by God, he is actually copying what the God did; *Lg.*, 902e: "we are never, then, to fancy god the inferior of human workmen"; cf. also *Lg.*, 907a. In general, for Plato the humans copy in their activities the gestures of that which is divine; our soul, for instance, in its revolutions, is actually trying to copy the revolutions of the divine soul of the world (cf. *Ti.*, 47c); cf. also *Mx.*, 238a4–5: "[T]he woman on her conception and generation is but the imitation of the [divine] earth, and not the earth of the woman."

29. Cf. Philipse 1998, 178: "One cannot deny that there is a strong religious impetus in Heidegger's early works. . . . But the text of *Sein und Zeit* does not (yet) enable us to decide whether Heidegger's intentions in writing the book were purely ontological, as they seem to be, or rather ontological and religious. Even if Heidegger in 1927 still had the religious objectives that he adopted in 1922, these objectives were not stated in the text. This fact explains that *Sein und Zeit* could be interpreted both as a preparation for the jump to religion (Bultmann) and as an atheist ontology (Sartre)."

30. Cf. Philipse 1998, 185: "We saw that *Sein und Zeit* implies at least one possible reason for discarding the traditional Christian conception of God: if human existence cannot be understood in terms of a created entity, then God cannot be conceived of as a creator"; cf. also 178.

31. It is only ironic, however, that in the post-*Kehre* period—while perceiving himself as estranging from Plato, now seen as the key perpetrator of nihilism—Heidegger gets closer to Plato by placing at the center of his thinking the Platonic (in my view) theme of the "flight of the gods" (although Heidegger links this theme to Hölderlin, not Plato). It should also be noted that in the post-*Kehre* period Heidegger's thinking gets closer to what one may call traditional monotheist thought. Although not an equivalent of God, being is now understood as a transcendent event that sends humans beings their fate, that is, their historical epochs, and gives being to entities. For references to the texts in which Heidegger makes these claims, and for a detailed commentary on these texts, see Philipse 1998, 189–201. For his part, Philipse believes that "Heidegger's postmonotheology admits of an analogue of the creation myth" (191). In the post-*Kehre* period, Philipse concludes, "Heidegger's message seems to be that we should reject the traditional notion of God as creator. . . . Instead, we should accept the notion of Being as the wonderful process of revealing entities to us. We might be inclined to identify Heidegger's Being with the mere fact or event that entities are, and sometimes Heidegger seems to do so. But mostly Heidegger's later grammar of Being suggests that Being is an agent, the agent that inaugurates and sustains the fact that beings are. In other words, there is postcreationism in Heidegger's postmonotheism" (191–92).

Truth and Untruth in Plato and Heidegger

Michael Inwood

> Alas! They had been friends in youth;
> But whispering toungues can poison truth.
> S. T. Coleridge, *Christabel*

Plato's Two Truths

In the *Meno* and *Theaetetus* Plato discusses true "belief" (*doxa*) and in the *Sophist* true "statement" (*logos*): the belief that Larissa is this way (*Men.*, 97b1f.), the belief that the man in the distance is Socrates (*Tht.*, 188a1ff.), the statement "Theaetetus is sitting" (*Sph.*, 263a2). Truth of this type is coordinate with falsity. Such beliefs and statements can be false: that Larissa is that way, that the man in the distance is Theaetetus, and "Theaetetus is flying." A true belief of this sort may, if an appropriate Logos (in a different sense of *logos*, "rational account") is added, become knowledge (*Men.*, 98a4: *aitias logismoi*; *Tht.*, 201c9f.). The *Republic* (written after the *Meno* and before the *Theaetetus*) presents a different conception of truth. This type of truth belongs not primarily to statements or beliefs but to nonlinguistic, nonmental entities: forms or Ideas, such as "the beautiful itself."[1] Things that "participate" in the forms, the "many beautifuls," for example, are not exactly false, but they have a lower grade of truth than the forms. This type of truth combines the notions of reality and of knowability or luminosity (*R.*, 508d4f.). The perfect circle, for example, is a real or "true" circle. It is also precisely knowable. The definition of a circle fits it exactly. Imperfect circles, by contrast—the circles we draw—are not real circles. They do not correspond exactly to the definition of a circle or to any other precise formula. This does not mean that forms are more accessible to everyone than perceptible individuals are. To those of defective intellectual equipment or training, perceptible individuals are more accessible than forms. Even nascent philosophers start from the consideration of perceptible individuals and ascend to knowledge of forms only with time and effort. But (in Aristotle's terminology) while individuals may be "more knowable" *to us,* forms are "more knowable" *simpliciter.*[2] ("Knowable" here is used loosely and does not imply that perceptible individuals are strictly known. Knowledge [*gnôsis, epistêmê*] and belief [*doxa*]—do not, as they do in the *Meno, Theaetetus,* and *Sophist,* have the same type of object. We have knowledge of forms, not belief; we have beliefs, not knowledge, of or about perceptible individuals. To differences between types of object correspond differences between cognitive states or attitudes.) When a prisoner in the cave is released and looks at the artifacts casting the shadows, he finds the artifacts less accessible than their shadows, but he is told that "now that he is somewhat nearer to being and turned toward things that more fully are, he will see more rightly [*orthoteron blepoi*]."[3] Heidegger takes this as a sign of the "agreement" (*Übereinstimmung*) or correspondence theory of truth—that truth consists in "correctness" of vision.[4] But for Plato the higher being and truth of the object is crucial, whereas it does not matter to the correspondence theory. Plato has in mind the clarity and distinctness of the vision as much as its accuracy.[5]

Plato does not specify the connection between these two types of truth, but it is presumably this: When we consider objects of low-grade reality and truth, we may nevertheless make true statements and have true beliefs about them and, conversely, make mistakes. The prisoners predict what shadows will appear later and in what order (*R.,* 7.516c8ff.). Some predictions turn out to be true, some false. A true prediction may even be supported by good inductive reasons, a sort of Logos. But it cannot amount to knowledge in the *Republic* sense, since its object is not "true" in the *Republic* sense. To acquire knowledge, the prisoner must turn to objects of a higher type.

Similarly, when we consider objects of a higher grade of truth, we can presumably make mistakes about them as well as get them right. Plato does not explicitly consider mistakes about forms. (None of his examples of false belief or statement concerns forms as such.) Implicitly he supplies two answers to the problem "Does someone who makes mistakes about forms nevertheless have knowledge?" One solution is: The forms are so luminously knowable that any mistake about them shows that we are not fully operating at the level of knowledge but still encumbered by remnants of belief and its objects. The other is: As we ascend the hierarchy of forms by dialectic, we make mistakes, but our mistakes are an intrinsic part of the dialectical movement—stepping-stones rather than stumbling blocks—

and are thus integrated into the overarching process of knowledge.[6] (Analogously, talk of the "advance of scientific knowledge" does not mean that scientists make no mistakes or that their mistakes are irrelevant to science.) Errors at the lower level do not admit of a similar integration into an overall truth, since belief is piecemeal rather than systematic. We cannot use false beliefs as stepping-stones to true beliefs without rising to the level of knowledge.

Does "truth" have a single meaning in these two conceptions of it? The first type of truth contrasts with falsehood. It does not readily admit of degrees. The second type of truth admits of degrees. It does not contrast so obviously and readily with falsity. The shadows may be false, but Plato does not say that they are. He does not use *pseudês* or *pseudos* in this context.

True Gold and True Logoi

Heidegger insisted (correctly) that *alêtheia* comes from the privative *a* and the verb *lêthô*, "escape notice, be unseen, unnoticed." He inferred (controversially) that *alêtheia*, in its "original" meaning, should be translated as *Unverborgenheit*, "unhiddenness."[7] *Alêthês*, "true," is to be translated as *unverborgen*, "unhidden," but also by related words, such as *aufdeckend*, "uncovering," when it applies to a Logos or an assertion.[8] In his lectures on Plato's *Sophist* (1924–25), he notices two apparently different senses, or uses, of "true." We ascribe truth and falsity, on the one hand, to things ("true gold," "false gold") and, on the other hand, to assertions and beliefs. These two senses are comparable to Plato's two types of truth. The truth of forms, in contrast to the relative falsity of perceptible individuals, is not far removed from the truth of true gold. (The similarity is enhanced if we take an example that reproduces the uniqueness of truth and the plurality of falsity: the true, or "original," *Mona Lisa,* in contrast to the many false ones or "copies.") Heidegger's treatment of these two types of truth illustrates his use of the notion of *Unverborgenheit* but also its inadequacy and instability. In 1924–25 he says that "false gold" is gold that "looks genuine, but is not so [*so aussieht wie echtes, es aber nicht ist*]," while false speaking, "*legein* that disguises [*verstellt*] something, presents itself [*gibt sich*] as what it is not: the *legein* disguises itself [*verstellt sich*], it is intrinsically [*in sich*] false" (*GA* 19, 602–3). Heidegger is right about false gold. It may be an "obvious fake," so manifestly false that it deceives only the inexpert eye. But it must look something like gold to be false *gold*. False speech is not parallel, however. Unlike false gold, it disguises something other than itself: It says, for example, "Theaetetus is flying" when he is sitting (*Sph.*, 263a8). Does false speech disguise itself? It does not disguise itself as *speech*. Whereas false gold is not really gold, false speech really is speech. Typically it disguises itself as *true* speaking, when it is not. False statements are not usually blatantly false. If they were, no one would believe them, and therefore none of us, or at least few of us, would make them. "Theaetetus is flying" is, however, blatantly false, but no less false for that.

In 1931–32 Heidegger returns to this case:

1. . . . A being is true if it shows up [*sich zeigt*] as what it is and in what it is: true gold. By contrast, fake gold [*Scheingold*] shows up as something that it is not. It covers, conceals [*verdeckt, verbirgt*] its what-being [*Wassein*], it conceals itself as the being that it really [*eigentlich*] is . . .

2. The assertion is true, *so* far as it *measures up* [*sich anmisst*] *to* something that is already true [an ein schon Wahres], that is, to the being as what is unhidden in its being [*an das Seiende als das in seinem Sein Unverborgene*].

Sense 1 is the primary sense of "true," "unhidden" applied to a "being" such as gold. Sense 2 is secondary: "correctness," *Richtigkeit*, which "presupposes," *unhiddenness* (GA 34, 118). (Heidegger derives this sense of *Richtigkeit* from the expression *sich richten nach*, "conform to," which is close in meaning to *sich anmessen an; GA* 34, 2f.)

Again, the account of false or "fake" gold is unexceptionable. But why must true gold look like true gold or even like gold? ("Everything about you, Minister, is phoney; even your hair, which looks like a wig, is really your own!")[9] False gold would not be false *gold* if it did not look somewhat like gold. But gold may be true gold even if it does not look it. It may, unusually, be disguised as false gold. If unhiddenness has a role here, it must be a more subtle role. We might say that true gold, having a definite atomic weight, molecular structure, and so on, is intrinsically knowable, unhidden, whereas false gold has no unique determinate nature. Similarly, I know where I am with a true friend, or indeed a true enemy; but a false friend keeps me guessing.

Heidegger's account of the assertion differs entirely from his 1924–25 account. He does not mean that we can only make true assertions about such entities as true gold, true friends, and the true *Mona Lisa*. Rather, if I make an assertion about something, it must already show up, be unhidden, in some way or other, and if my assertion is true (except by sheer luck), then what it is about must show up as what it is. It need not show up very obviously. If it does, my assertion may be superfluous, since everyone knows it already. But it must show up to me at least, and, if my assertion is to serve its purpose, it must show up to others once I have pointed it out to them.

As this discussion indicates, Heidegger, too, has two types of truth: first, the truth of Logos, primarily assertion, and also the truth of *doxa,* "belief," or *Ansicht,* "view" (*GA* 34, 256), and second, the truth of things— not especially of things such as true gold, but of things in general and indeed of the world and of oneself.

Heidegger on True Assertion

Not every Logos need, or can, be true or false, only what Aristotle called the *apophantikos logos* (*De Interpretatione,* 17a2ff.), an assertion, a Logos that affirms or denies something of something. Heidegger is adverse to the doctrine that truth consists in the "correctness" (*Richtigkeit*) of an assertion or in its "agreement" (*Übereinstimmung*) with or correspondence to "things" (*Sache;* e.g., *GA* 34,2), and/or he is adverse to the type of assertion whose truth is accurately described by the doctrine (e.g., *GA* 34, 118). His objections to this doctrine are of two types. First, he argues that truth is not *exclusively* or *primarily* correctness or correspondence, for truth as correctness or correspondence presupposes truth as unhiddenness. The things about which we make true assertions, or even false assertions, must be unhidden to us in advance. I cannot say that Theaetetus is sitting, or that Theaetetus is flying, unless Theaetetus is already somehow accessible to me. So the truth (or falsity) of assertions presupposes truth as unhiddenness.[10] Another argument of this type is that the unhiddenness theory of truth is self-reflexive in ways that the correspondence theory is not. First, its own historical emergence and its later displacement by rival theories can be described in terms of its emergence from and consignment to hiddenness. The correspondence theory, by contrast, cannot account for its own ups and downs, and those of its rivals, in terms of truth itself. The correspondence theory has no special bearing on the history of conceptions of truth. Second, the correspondence theory cannot easily ascribe truth to itself. If the theory is true, it agrees with the facts. What facts? Itself? Our ordinary uses of the word "true"? The unhiddenness theory does better on this score. The theory itself can be as unhidden as anything else. As a corollary of the theory, we can say that the theory that truth is unconcealing or revealing is itself unconcealing or revealing. Of course, given the haziness of the concept of unhiddenness, it is hard to deny that the correspondence theory reveals. It reveals, for instance, the instability of truth as unhiddenness. But despite its being (in Heidegger's later view) only one in a historical sequence of conceptions of truth, the unhiddenness theory has for Heidegger a certain priority over the others. However, none of these arguments entails that the truth of assertions does not consist in correspondence. In response to the first, we might say that whereas the unhiddenness of things enables us to make any assertions about them at all, the *truth* of an assertion depends not on unhiddenness alone but on the assertion's correctness or its correspondence to the unhidden entity. In response to the second, we might say that even if the truth of the correspondence theory does not itself consist in its correspondence to anything, the truth of other assertions does consist in correspondence. Nevertheless, Heidegger tends to reject such a compromise and to present the relationship between unhiddenness and correctness as a conflict (e.g., *GA* 36/37, 127f.). Unhiddenness, he argues, accounts not only for our ability to make assertions about things but also for the truth of our assertions about them. Hence he offers a number of objections to the doctrine that the truth of an assertion consists in correspondence.

First, the doctrine gives no clear account of the relation of correspondence (*GA* 34, 3ff.; *GA* 36/37, 122).

Second, it requires the detachment of a chunk of reality, the chunk with which the assertion agrees (or disagrees), from its worldly context. This means that equipment and, even worse, Dasein itself are conceived as "present-at-hand" (*vorhanden*).

Third, it requires us to focus on the assertion itself, the words uttered or the idea expressed, rather than (as we usually do) on the things the assertion is about. Thus one of the supposed relata of the relation of correspondence is not normally available to speakers or hearers (e.g., *GA* 19, 416f.).

Fourth, if correspondence is a genuine relation, the assertion and the thing with which it agrees must be independent of each other, two distinct entities agreeing with each other. If so, then the assertion acts as a sort of screen between ourselves and the reality with which it agrees. It does so, because to be a meaningful assertion, it must derive its meaning from ideas in our minds, ideas to which we have primary access and which mediate our access to things. Hence the correspondence theory of truth is open to the same objection as the representative theory of perception: It cuts us off from reality (*BT,* 217f.). Assertions (and beliefs), Heidegger argues, do not work in this way. An assertion about Theaetetus latches directly onto Theaetetus, Theaetetus, for example, sitting (*GA* 19, 598: *ein logos ist logos tinos*). An assertion is not a self-contained entity, independent of what it is about and what it says about it. It essentially points to something outside the assertion itself. Heidegger rejects the view that the name

"Theaetetus" is really a disguised description, so that the assertion "Theae-tetus is sitting" retains its sense regardless not only of whether Theaetetus is sitting or not, but of whether there is or was any such person at all. On this view, Theaetetus's nonexistence would affect the truth-value of the assertion, but not its meaning. Heidegger disagrees.

Finally, the doctrine situates truth not in things but in the intellect, *en dianoiai*,[11] in *intellectu humano vel divino*.[12] This is a consequence not of the correspondence theory of truth as such—a relation is not essentially situated in one of its relata at the expense of the other—but of the fact that truths are generated by the intellect's endeavor to "conform to" (*sich richten nach*) things. Often Heidegger implies that Dasein is the primary seat of truth.[13] But Dasein is not a self-contained entity. It is "eccentric."[14] It goes out to things, "ex-sists," in something like the way assertions do. Truth is not in Dasein, Dasein is in the truth. Heidegger often assimilates Plato's concept of *psuchê* (soul) to his own concept of Dasein (*GA* 19, 22f., 348, 617; *GA* 34, 175, 201ff.). But his charity is not indiscriminate, and he does not extend it to Aquinas's *intellectus*.[15]

For such reasons as these, Heidegger resists the correspondence theory. Or at least the early Heidegger does so. The later Heidegger is more inclined to say that the truth of an assertion consists in agreement, or *homoiôsis*, but that this results from a change in the "essence of truth" (e.g., *GA* 34, 323f.)—a change, he implies, for the worse. What the earlier Heidegger regards as a philosophical error becomes, for the later Heidegger, a stage in our historic decline.

In the 1920s, however, Heidegger interprets the truth of assertions in terms of *Unverborgenheit*. Like any *apophantic logos*, a true Logos is *sehendlassend*, "letting [us] see" or "letting [things] be seen" (e.g., *GA* 19, 407). But in contrast to a false Logos, a true Logos "uncovers" (*aufdeckt; GA* 19, 510), "discovers" (*entdeckt; GA* 19, 510), or "opens up" (*erschliesst; GA* 19, 488) beings; it lets beings be seen as they are. Heidegger does not explain very explicitly or clearly the connection between the uncovering of Logos and the unhiddenness of beings. Are beings unhidden before I make an assertion about them? Was the sitting Theaetetus unhidden before I said "Theaetetus is sitting"? Presumably he was. How else could I know whom to talk about and what to say about him?[16] Moreover, some things are said by many people. The loveliness of the day must be un-hidden before I or anyone else in particular says, "It's a lovely day today." The truth of beings and the truth of Logoi go together:

> *alêthês:* das Seiende als Unverborgenes—daraufhin vermeint und vernom-men und als solches verwahrt. Die nächste Art des Verwahrens: *logos* als legomenon. Das in einem apophantikos *logos* Gesagte: ein Seiendes als Aufgedecktes. Das legomenon ist alethes—der *logos alêthês*. (*GA* 19, 616)

True: beings as what is unhidden—thereupon supposed and perceived and kept as such. The immediate mode of this keeping: *logos* as what is said. What is said in an *apophantic logos:* a being as what is uncovered. What is said is true—the *logos* true.

This seems to mean: Beings are unhidden, and that is why we have beliefs about them, perceive them, and keep them in a state of unhiddenness; the immediate way in which they are kept unhidden is the Logoi that uncover them.[17] Verbal uncovering, the general practice of Logos utterance, sustains the general unhiddenness of beings. In 1925–26 Heidegger believed that the Greek view of being is "oriented to the *logos*" (*GA* 19, 448f., 512, 638f.). He also believes that for the Greeks, being is "presence," *Anwesenheit* (*GA* 19, 466f.; cf. *PLW,* 46). Beings emerge from hiddenness (*Verborgenheit*) into presence or unhiddenness. They are wrested from hiddenness by Logos, not just assertions, but all *logos, Rede,* "talk." (Questions too uncover: "*Questioning itself* is thus, by its sense, *already a determinate uncovering opening up [aufdeckendes Erschliessen]*"; *GA* 19, 448.) But it does not follow that a particular being, for example, Theaetetus, awaits my assertion before it is unhidden.

False Assertions

Assertions can be false. Plato had problems with false statement and false belief:

> 1. If I believe that the man in the distance (who is in fact Theaetetus) is Socrates, I must know both Theaetetus and Socrates. But if I know them both, I cannot mistake one for the other (*Tht.,* 188a1–c7, discussed in *GA* 34, 265–71).
> 2. To believe falsely is to believe what is not, that is, to believe nothing, that is, not to believe at all. As one can only see what is, not what is not, so one can only believe what is, that is, believe truly (*Tht.,* 188c9–89b5; cf. *GA* 34, 271–77).
> 3. If false belief is "mistaking one thing for another," *allodoxia,* it is impossible. No one can believe that the ugly is beautiful or the ox is a horse (*Tht.,* 189b11–90e3; cf. *GA* 34, 277–85). (This is a generalization of problem 1.)

Since a belief is a Logos one says to oneself (*Tht.,* 189e6–90a6; *Sph.,* 263e3–64a2), these problems about false belief are also problems about false Logos: A false Logos can be turned into a false belief by saying it to oneself. Hence the *Sophist* examines the question of false Logos, though primarily with regard to problem 2 (esp. *Sph.*, 236e1–37b3, 263a4–63d4).

Heidegger, too, has a problem with false Logos. It is not obviously the same as those raised by Plato but is perhaps related to Plato's first problem. A false (i.e., hiding or concealing) statement about Theaetetus, first, presupposes that Theaetetus is already unhidden, and second, must somehow reveal Theaetetus in order to be a statement *about* him. This problem appears in Heidegger's paradoxical descriptions of false Logos. A false Logos "lets something be seen, but not in its uncoveredness" (*GA* 19, 406). It is a *verdeckendes Sehenlassen*, a "covering letting see," or a *versperrendes Öffnen*, a "blocking opening" (*GA* 19, 407, 410). Sometimes *Sehenlassen* is restricted to *alêtheuein*, "truth-telling," while the "counter-phenomenon" is *Verstellen*, "distorting, disguising" (*GA* 19, 505). A transparently false statement cannot cover up. So Heidegger diverts the inquiry away from the subject of falsity. He translates *pseudês* and *pseudos* not as "false" and "falsity," but as "deceptive," "deceiving," *täuschend,* and "deception," *Täuschung* (*GA* 19, 504f., 580). This strategy does not fit Plato's example well. "Theaetetus is flying" is false. But who would be deceived by it? Who, that is, would believe it? I can say it to myself as often as I like, but that does not amount to believing it. Conversely, I can deceive someone by making true statements, for example, to distract attention from something else. Heidegger says: "*pseudesthai* ['to lie, etc'] . . . —so to talk that what is believed [*das Gemeinte*] is covered and hidden by what is said" (*GA* 34, 137). One can clearly talk in this way without saying anything false: "No mask like open truth to cover lies, / As to go naked is the best disguise."[18] Heidegger is not just trying to facilitate Plato's questionable transition from the possibility of false statement to the possibility of false belief.[19] He is also expressing his aversion to timeless propositions. "Falsity" is most at home in that "ideal" realm. An assertion is false if, and only if, it expresses a false proposition. "Deception" is more appropriate to assertions in a context. Assertions deceive, propositions do not.

A deceptive assertion reveals something, lets something be seen. That is involved in its being apophantic. I have to assert something if I am to deceive at all in the relevant way, and I have to purport to present the truth (*GA* 19, 636). But a deceptive assertion also covers up or disguises. Heidegger's best account is this: "In speaking I as it were push something else in front of what is there and pass it off—what is there—as something that it is not or that is not there" (*GA* 19, 504). A mistaken opinion similarly requires: "1. it itself as somehow there—present; the being of that which itself gives rise to supposition [*Vermeinen*], founds the possibility of passing off [*Ausgebbarkeit*], 2. that for which it passes itself off, as what is, what is supposed; the being of that which stands in supposedness."[20]

Item 1 is Theaetetus as he really is, sitting; item 2 is the misleading appearance of Theaetetus, as flying. The Logos lets us see Theaetetus as flying, thus disguising Theaetetus sitting. Later, Heidegger gives a more elaborate account. My belief that the man in the distance is Theaetetus (when in fact it is Socrates) is a fork with two prongs. One prong is *Gegenwärtigung*, "presentation." This prong enables me to perceive things present, such as the man in the distance. The other prong, *Vergegenwärtigung*, "representation," ranges beyond what is perceptibly present, involving my prior knowledge of Theaetetus, of his appearance and of his likely arrival at this time; it leads me to identify the man with Theaetetus.[21]

Unhiddenness and the Site of Truth

Assertions may be true, but: "The *logos* is not the site [*Stätte*] in which *alêtheuein* is at home, indigenous" (*GA* 19, 182). Later, Heidegger speaks of a "change in the place [*Ort*] of truth" (*PLW,* 42) so that, with the change from truth as unhiddenness to truth as *homoiôsis,* "likeness," the "mental asserting of the intellect is the site of truth and falsity and the difference between them" (*PLW,* 44). But this does not alter the fact that: "What is originally true, i.e., unhidden, is precisely not the assertion about a being, but the being itself" (*GA* 34, 118).

If assertions are to be true, the beings they are about must be unhidden. So must the world. And so must Dasein itself, whose self-revealing is the source of the unhiddenness of everything else. Logos helps generate this unhiddenness, not just assertions, but *Rede,* the often elliptical, nonassertive "talk" that accompanies our *Verhalten* to the significant world. This is the open space, the *Spielraum,* within which we make assertions and denials. It is not constituted by assertions and cannot be fully captured by them; it precedes and is presupposed by assertions. Heidegger sometimes calls it the "realm of perceivability" (*Bereich der Vernehmbarkeit; GA* 34, 195), generated by our *Seinserstrebnis,* "striving for being."[22]

This is truth, *alêtheia.* But it does not readily contrast with *pseudos,* falsity, even if *pseudos* is "deception" or *Verkehrung,* "perversion" (*GA* 34, 257). It contrasts with "untruth," *Unwahrheit,* and more specifically *Verborgenheit,* "hiddenness." Animals have no such realm of unhiddenness, but we do not ascribe falsity to them.[23] Humans are more or less blinkered, but that is not falsity: "we take 'untruth' in the sense of *nontruth*—which need not necessarily be falsehood; it can and must mean much else besides" (*GA* 34, 127; cf. *GA* 34, 92f.; *GA* 36/37, 188).

This, Heidegger's second conception of truth, is comparable to the truth involved in the cave simile. Implicitly, Plato probably regards the shadows as "false," in comparison to the artifacts that cast them, and, still more, to the things outside the cave. But he does not say so explicitly. Heidegger more or less eliminates falsity—but not *Verborgenheit* (*GA* 34, 26f.)—from his account of the cave in favor of "grades and stages" of unhiddenness (*GA* 34, 32; *PLW,* 34). The prisoners, in Heidegger's view, represent ourselves in "everydayness," *Alltäglichkeit* (*GA* 34, 28; *PLW,* 15: "was sich alltäglich zurträgt"; cf. *GA* 36/37, 133, 135, 148, 153). There is a hint of inauthenticity and *das Man.* Prisoners award each other praise, honors, and prizes for their skill in discerning, remembering, and predicting shadows. But an escaped prisoner is above all that (*R.,* 516c8–d7; cf. *R.,* 492b5–c8). Imprisonment is collective; escape is individual and solitary, assisted at most by a philosopher, a returned escapee.[24] In everydayness there is unhiddenness. Hammer, nails, workshop—all this is unhidden. They are real beings, not shadows or fakes. Socrates says of the prisoners: "Undoubtedly then . . . such people would not consider what is true to be anything other [*ouk an allo ti nomizoien to alêthês*] than the shadows of the artifacts" (*R.,* 7.515c1f.). They would regard (what we know to be) shadows as the true, and they would regard nothing else as true. Heidegger translates this passage literally, except that *to alêthês* becomes *das Unverborgene* (*GA* 34, 24) or *das Unverborgene* (*PLW,* 9). But then he goes on to assume that "man already has, even in this situation, the true, the unhidden."[25] Plato simply says that the prisoners would think that the shadows are the true. He leaves open the possibility, perhaps even implies, that they are not the true, but untrue, even false. Heidegger says that the shadows are (or would be) the true, the unhidden.

Heidegger does so for two reasons. First, the shadows obviously are, in a way, unhidden, more so in fact than genuine things, since they have no three-dimensional depth for us to make mistakes about. Second, Heidegger is asking a question that Plato does not ask. "To being-human belongs . . . standing in the unhidden—as we say: in the true, in truth" (*GA* 34, 25). Whether in chains or out, in the cave or outside, people relate to the unhidden. They are aware of their surroundings, of themselves and the things they encounter in a way that stones, plants, and animals are not. Plato would no doubt agree. But in the *Republic* he just takes that for granted. What primarily interests Plato is the fact that most people are engrossed in low-grade objects—perceptible things or even copies and imitations of them—rather than Ideas; and how they, or the best of them, might be elevated from the lower to the higher condition. That also interests Heidegger. Why do we sometimes ascend from everydayness to authenticity, in particular to philosophy? But he also asks: Why are things invariably unhidden for us? Hence Plato cannot mean by *alêtheia* what

Heidegger means by *Unverborgenheit*. The concepts belong to different problem-contexts. The shadows are *unverborgen;* they are not really *to alêthês*.

This is not to say that Plato makes no move in Heidegger's direction. In the cave simile, the sun, that is, the Idea of the good, is "in some way the cause of those things that they saw [inside the cave]" (*R.*, 7.517c1–4), even though in the simile, the interior of the cave seems entirely cut off from the outside. Plato also argues that cognitive access to a range of objects requires not only the objects but a corresponding mental power and a source of light (*R.*, 6.507d8ff.). More promising in this respect is a markedly Kantian passage in the *Theaetetus* (185a8–86c6, discussed in *GA* 34, 182ff. and *GA* 36/37, 242ff.), where Socrates argues that our unitary consciousness (in contrast to a "Trojan horse," in which each sense is a separate center of consciousness; *Tht.*, 184d1f.) and our knowledge of beings require not only the physical sensations that we share with animals (*Tht.*, 186c1) but also general concepts such as being, likeness, sameness, and number.[26] Here Plato is dealing with the equipment common to all humans, not with different stages in their development.

Why Leave the Cave?

Plato's prisoners have no intrinsic incentive to escape. They need to be forced by an ex-prisoner, though such force includes in reality indicating intellectual difficulties within the shadow world, such as the fact that a finger is both big and small.[27] The benefits of escape become apparent only afterward. The *Phaedo* stressed the affinity of the human soul to forms, in contrast to perceptible individuals.[28] But in the *Republic*, although rationality is in some sense the core of the soul (more especially in *R.*, 10 than in *R.*, 4), the soul belongs to no specific level in the cave complex; it ranges through them all. Nevertheless, the levels are not simply different, with the higher level being found, once we reach it, more pleasurable than the lower. At the lower level the soul has a desire for truth and being, a desire that it thinks is satisfied[29] but which can only really be satisfied at a higher level. There it will see that its desire was not satisfied at the lower level.

Why does Heidegger think that we should leave the cave? He speaks (with some license from Plato) of grades of unhiddenness and of being. Some things are *unverborgener* than others, some (usually the same things) are *seiender* than others. He gives three examples of departure from the cave, showing how "such freedom, as prefiguring projection of being [*vorbildende Seinsentwurf*], first makes possible a nearer approach to beings":[30]

(1) Galilean and Newtonian science, a "project that leaps ahead and *cir-cumscribes* what in general is to be understood by nature and natural pro-cess from now on" (though he doubts whether this made beings *seiender*); (2) Jacob Burkhardt's "history" (*Historie*), with its "anticipatory under-standing of the *happening* [*Geschehens*] of what we call history [*Geschichte*], that is, of the *being* of this being" (*GA* 34, 62); and (3) art, which "reveals the inner power of man's understanding of being, of the light-look"[31] and "puts to work the hidden possibilities of beings and thereby first gives men sight for the actual beings in which they roam about," while poetry in par-ticular "makes beings *seiender*" (*GA* 34, 64). Each of these projections is a type of freedom, of "binding oneself to the being [*Sein*] (the 'Idea,' the es-sential constitution of beings) prefigured in the anticipatory projection," and it "first of all makes possible a relationship to beings."

How do Heidegger's examples (which, apart from the first, are somewhat un-Platonic) fit the stages of the cave simile? They clarify how, in the simile, "the light-look, the looking-into-the-light, first opens and frees the look for the things."[32] Analogously, the scientist, historian, and artist look at "being" (the Idea or light) and this improves their, and our, vision for beings: nature, history, and the possibilities revealed by art. What are the "things" for which our look is liberated? In Plato's simile the "things" outside the cave do not represent the beings revealed by scien-tists, historians, and artists. They stand for the Ideas. Ideas are not them-selves a source of light (as Heidegger implies at, e.g., *GA* 34, 64 and *GA* 36/37, 153, 156, 158f.), except for the Idea of the good (the sun), which il-luminates the other Ideas and enables us to see them. (It does not follow that looking directly at the Idea of the good improves our vision of the other Ideas. In Plato's view, it enables us to analyze them dialectically, but that is not conveyed by the simile.) Scientists, historians, and artists do not primarily study Ideas, essences, or being; they look at, or project, them in order to expand our vision for beings, to extend the range of what is acces-sible to us inside the cave. Plato conceives the "things" outside the cave, the Ideas, as a distinct realm of entities, higher in their truth and reality than ordinary things (shadows and the artifacts that cast them). The philosopher would by preference stay outside forever, contemplating these objects.[33] Descent into the cave is a painful interruption of sabbati-cal leave to return to teaching and administration. For Heidegger by con-trast, Ideas, essences, being, are not self-sufficient objects of study. We look at them in order to enrich our understanding of beings. Hence for Heidegger, return to the cave is an essential phase of the philosophical en-terprise. Plato postulates different levels of beings (*Seiendes*), perceptible things, Ideas, and so on. Heidegger acknowledges only one level of be-ings, and they are all within the cave. Outside the cave is being (*Sein*), and our glimpse of this enables us to relate to what is inside the cave. A longer, clearer look at being extends and deepens our vision for the beings inside the cave. Unlike Plato, Heidegger is not primarily trying to get us outside the cave. He is trying to explain our situation in the cave, how things, even shadows, are unhidden for us there. To see what they see inside the cave, even the prisoners need an implicit glimpse of what is outside. To be in-the-world at all we must be in some way outside the cave. However, someone who is far enough outside the cave to have things unhidden inside the cave may, nevertheless, not understand his situation. In everydayness we cannot understand everydayness: "such a prisoner could never describe his situation. . . . In fact, he is not yet even aware that he is in a 'situation.' When questioned, he only ever talks about the shadows—which of course he does not know *as* shadows."[34] To find out about that, the prisoners need to go further outside the cave—but to *being*, not to *beings*. Beings remain inside the cave, but the being (*Sein*) seen by science, history, art, and philosophy extends and clarifies them.

The question addressed to Plato—"Why leave the cave?"—is not appropriate for Heidegger. To be in the cave and see shadows, we must be some way out of the cave, with access to being as well as to beings. Heidegger compares this scenario to the fork or bifurcation by which he explained false belief. But now one prong represents our striving for being, while the other aims at beings (*GA* 34, 321f.). We can, however, ask: Why do we go further out of the cave than everydayness requires? Why science, history, art, and philosophy? Heidegger replies: "Truth is not a static possession [*ruhender Besitz*], in the enjoyment of which we retire to rest . . ." (*GA* 34, 91). It requires constant striving for being,[35] even to have the level of unhiddenness granted to the prisoners or to remain in everydayness. The general thoughts required for any objective experience invite, though they do not in every case necessitate, philosophical conceptualization (*GA* 34, 208, 229f.). Thus what we have to do to stay in the cave (and not sink beneath it) tends to impel us out of the cave, or further out than we already are. Unless we, or some of us at least, rise above everydayness, we shall all sink below the level even of everyday humanity: "That man, by his essence, has ventured forth out of himself into the unhiddenness of beings is only possible so far as he has entered the danger zone of philosophy. Man outside philosophy is something entirely different" (*GA* 34, 77).

Hiddenness

Unhiddenness contrasts with hiddenness. Heidegger gives a "schematic formal indication" of the varieties of "the non-unhidden" (*das Nicht-Unverborgene*). It is (1) what is not yet unconcealed (*das Noch-nicht-*

Entborgene) and (2) what is no longer unconcealed (*das Nicht-mehr-Entborgene*). The latter divides into (2a) what has entirely sunk back into hiddenness and (2b) "something hidden [*ein Verborgenes*], which is nevertheless unconcealed [*entborgen*] in a certain way and shows itself: what is disguised [*das Verstellte*]" (*GA* 34, 145; cf. *GA* 34, 127 and *GA* 36.37, 224ff.), the subject of a false or deceptive assertion. "The Greeks understood what we call the true as the Un-hidden, no longer hidden; what is without hiddenness, therefore wrested from hiddenness, as it were stolen from it. Thus the true is, for the Greeks, something that no longer has an other, namely, hiddenness, in it, is liberated from it."[36] For the Greeks, the true is primarily what is wrested from hiddenness of type 1, though it must not have lapsed into hiddenness of type 2a. This unhiddenness is a presupposition of anything's being hidden, or unhidden, in sense 2b.

Does Plato speak of hiddenness? Not enough, according to Heidegger. He does not ask about *Verborgenheit*, and this is a sign that the "question about unhiddenness *as such* is not a vital one" for him.[37] It is nevertheless important for Heidegger's interpretation that hiddenness should play some part in the cave simile, and he does his best to find it there. "The things themselves present in a certain way, namely, in the light of the artificial cave-fire, their appearance [*Aussehen*] and are no longer hidden by their shadowings [*Abschattungen*]."[38] "The enclosure of the cave, open within itself, and what is surrounded and thus hidden, at the same time refer to an outside, the unhidden, which stretches into the light above ground" (*PLW*, 33). What the prisoners see, the shadows, is the unhidden; what they do not see—things, fire, etc.—is the hidden: "Being human thus means here, among other things, *also:* standing in the *hidden*, being surrounded by the hidden" (*GA* 34, 26f.). For Heidegger, hiddenness thus plays a variety of roles. What the prisoners see is unhidden but also hidden in its essence. What they do not see is hidden. Everything inside the cave, whether seen by the prisoners or not, is hidden; the unhidden is outside the cave.

Plato does not speak of hiddenness, but he might assign it two roles. First, what the prisoners see is, though not exactly hidden, dimly lit. Second, what they do not see is hidden from them (though it is not hidden *by* what they *do* see). As the escapee ascends, he is wresting from hiddenness the new objects that he encounters. Would Plato agree that being human means standing in the hidden? In one sense, he would. Everyone begins as a prisoner, and most people remain prisoners for life. In another sense, he would not. Once the philosopher has left the cave and seen the sun (the Idea of the good), nothing is hidden from him. He is surrounded by no area of obscurity, as the prisoners are, and there is no realm beyond the sun to ascend to. It is perhaps impossible to explain the Idea of the good in literal terms, but this is because of its simplicity, not because it conceals depths or heights inaccessible to us. Not even the contents of the cave are hidden from the philosopher: "As you become used to it, you will see far better than the people there and will know what each of the images is and what it is of, since you have seen the truth about things beautiful and just and good."[39]

Implicitly Heidegger rejects Plato's view that, to the philosopher at least, everything is unhidden.[40] Unhiddenness is overcoming a concealing (*GA* 34, 90), wresting things from concealment, *Entbergen* or *Entbergsamkeit* (*GA* 34, 73). "Unhiddenness of beings is just *wrested* from hiddenness, won in *conflict* against it" (*GA* 34, 125; cf. *GA* 34, 145). The conflict is unending. There is never unhiddenness free of the threatening encroachment of hiddenness. Why does Heidegger believe this? He appeals to the privative *alpha* in *alêtheia*, which "expresses a removal, a wrenching from, an advance against . . . hence an *attack*" (*GA* 34, 126; cf. *GA* 36/37, 188). But he also stresses the limitations of etymology (*GA* 34, 12, 117)—which is just as well, since the privative *alpha* need not have the force of "removal."[41] A better argument is this: "*What* unhiddenness is shows up in its determinacy only from *hiddenness*" (*GA* 34, 327; emphasis in original). If we have unalloyed unhiddenness, we will not recognize it as unhiddenness and it will in that respect remain hidden from us.

History and Plato's Story

The main reason for Heidegger's disagreement with Plato here is that "unhiddenness *happens* [*geschieht*] only in the *history* [*Geschichte*] of constant liberation" (*GA* 34, 91). *Geschichte* has a wide range of meaning, even when the sense of "study of history" (*Historie*) is excluded (*GA* 34, 62, 121f.). It is a "story," a "happening" or "occurrence" (*Geschehen*) in contrast to a thing or a state, and "history," what happens to, and is done by, humans over long periods of time.[42] "The *Geschichte* narrated in the cave simile gives the view [*Anblick*] of what now and in the future is still the real happening [*das eigentlich Geschehende*] in the *Geschichte* of humanity of the Western stamp."[43] Here, *Geschichte* in its first occurrence is something like "story," in its second occurrence "history." "The cave simile means to convey: the essential history [*Wesensgeschichte*] of man, and that means: to comprehend ourselves in our ownmost *Geschichte*."[44] Here *Geschichte*'s uncertain meaning is not clarified by the context.

Geschichte and *Geschehen*, always closely linked, have for Heidegger five applications.

First, even in everydayness, truth is a happening, *Geschehnis*. Heidegger has "hit upon a fundamental happening in the Dasein of man: *Entbergsamkeit* and *Seinserstrebnis*" (*GA* 34, 246). Plato implies that the prisoners' condition is static, that they might in principle eternally and effortlessly look at shadows. This is not so. If they are human, they are wresting what they see from hiddenness and striving for being.

Second, this happening impels some of them beyond everydayness to science, history, (*Historie*) and art, in which new swaths of beings are wrested from hiddenness.

Third, our general way of looking at things was established by the Greeks before Plato's time: "Impulse and unrest of this *Geschichte* is the liberation of man to the essence of being: spirit, world-projection, worldview, a fundamental actuality in which there is light and space for epic, development of the state, tragedy, cultic building, plastic art, philosophy. With the beginning of this *Geschichte* truth begins . . ." (*GA* 34, 327; cf. *GA* 34, 121). In this beginning, *alêtheia* (along with other basic words such as *ousia*) was formed on the basis of a "fundamental experience" of unhiddenness, an experience that is disappearing by Plato's time (*GA* 34, 123). This is the most significant way in which things are wrested from hiddenness—including the conception of truth as wresting from hiddenness.

Fourth, as history moves on from this momentous beginning, our conceptions of truth, being, knowledge, and so on change, in part at least because of philosophical reflection on them. When Socrates asks what knowledge is, he is not simply describing knowledge; he is deciding "*how* man *takes* himself from now on *as* a knower; . . . what from now on is for him the knowable and the nonknowable. That is neither self-evident nor simply given to man like nose and ears or suggested to him in his sleep, nor is it always the same" (*GA* 34, 157). Similarly, when Socrates asks about untruth, we are "propelled into the course of the essential history of man" (*GA* 34, 158; cf. *GA* 34, 323f.). For the "familiarity of beings in the Dasein of man always has its own *Geschichte*. It is never simply just there, indifferent and uniform throughout the history of humanity." It takes root in the *Bodenständigkeit* of man, in his native soil, "in what for him, at any given time [*jeweils*], nature and history and beings, as a whole and in their ground, *are* and *how* they are what they are."[45] This history too involves wresting things from hiddenness—and returning them to it. A new conception of truth, for example, the correspondence doctrine, emerges from hiddenness, while the unhiddenness view returns to hiddenness. (It may be retrieved from hiddenness by a philosopher; *GA* 34, 122.) History requires that not everything be on show at once.

Fifth, philosophy is itself a mode of *Entbergsamkeit*. For the early Heidegger, philosophy is essentially phenomenology, and this involves not the discovery of new facts or entities, nor the inference of conclusions from premises, but "purely from the *logos* itself something is uncovered which lay hidden in what preceded. . . . [W]hat is still there and already there is uncovered, seen *afterward* [*nachgesehen*]" (*GA* 19, 599; cf. 543). Plato inspects the Logoi he produced earlier to extract from them the "greatest kinds" implicit in them. What is hidden is squeezed out into unhiddenness. The *Republic,* too, advocates a quasi-phenomenological method of teaching. The pupil is not crammed with knowledge; his eyes are "turned round" in the right direction, in a *periagôgê* that is an ancestor of Heidegger's *Kehre* (*R.,* 518d3–7; cf. 515c7). Heidegger perhaps attributes a similar procedure to Plato in the *Theaetetus* (*GA* 34, 229f., in connection with *Tht.,* 186b210). But by now Heidegger was less interested in phenomenology than he was in 1925 and more inclined to stress that a philosophical question calls for a decision, a decision about, for instance, what is to count as truth or knowledge. Such a decision can only be taken in view of human needs, interests, and the like, since, if it could be validated by appeal to some more specific and more objective standard, it would not really be a decision, at least not a fundamental decision. So the question is really about man himself and, since the answer is a decision, it changes man; it does not simply describe him. The question is about "man" and requires a decision about "man" (cf. *GA* 36/37, 120, 147, 165, 176, 233). Man sets the standard (*Mass*), is the standard, and is changed by acceptance of the standard. If we lament the loss of objectivity, the reply is: "Only the *Bodenständigkeit* and force of the Dasein of man decides about the sense of the objectivity of objects" (*GA* 34, 210). That is, objectivity is itself one of the concepts whose nature and application depends on our decision.

This "decisionist" account of philosophy is distinct from, if not incompatible with, the phenomenological account of *GA* 19. We might think of phenomenological findings, enticed from their hiding place in our Logoi, not as decisions but as objective discoveries, about, say, what we mean by knowledge, or what knowledge really is. Conversely, a decisionist need not claim to reach his decisions phenomenologically. Hiddenness thus plays a different role in the decisionist account. In deciding for one view of, for example, knowledge, the philosopher brings it into unhiddenness; in deciding against another, he casts it—not necessarily irretrievably—into hiddenness.

From Plato to Protagoras

Plato is not a decisionist. He acknowledges that there are decisions. We decide whether or not to do philosophy, that is, whether or not to leave the cave and how far to ascend. We decide whether to ask questions and what questions to ask. But we do not decide, in Heidegger's way, what the answers are. The answers are objectively fixed and to be reached by unalterable rational procedures. The questions I ask and the answers I give will affect myself, and not only in this life. They will also affect my pupils, and an even wider group if I obtain political power. But they will not radically alter mankind or man as such. They will not change the human condition, the cave complex. People will always start off in the cave. Those who leave the cave will always find there the same things as Plato did. If they ask Plato's questions, they will, if they are sufficiently intelligent and persistent, arrive at Plato's answers.

The types of *Geschichte* involved in Heidegger's third, fourth, and fifth applications are foreign to Plato. The cave complex and its stages were not, in Plato's view, established by humans at some time in the past, nor do they change over time. Heidegger says that "the true (the unhidden) is different according to the situation and position of man," and adds in a note, "thus man is authoritative [*massgebend*]" (*GA* 34, 42). Officially he is speaking of the levels of the cave complex: What is true for, unhidden from, someone, depends on the level he has reached. Taken in this sense, Heidegger is not entitled to claim that man is authoritative: The levels and their contents do not depend on the people who occupy them. But Heidegger also means that what we find outside the cave depends on our historical situation. Plato finds a geocentric astronomy, Galileo finds a heliocentric system. Plato finds one conception of knowledge, we find another. There is no objective, history-transcendent answer to the question: What is outside the cave? This is why Heidegger says: "Idea . . . *is* itself the being [*Seiende*] that it is in a looking-out [*Er-blicken*], a formative self-prefiguring [*einem bildenden Sich-vorbilden*]. The Idea is essentially bound to the looking out [*Erblicken*] and *is* nothing *outside* this looking out [*Erblickens*]."[46] In Heidegger's view, our looking constitutes what it looks at. There are no objective Ideas independent of our vision of them. But that is not Plato. It is not supported by Plato's analogy of thought with sight. The light of the sun yokes together sight and visible objects, enabling sight to see and objects to be seen (*R.*, 6.507e6–8a2, discussed in *GA* 34, 101ff.; cf. *PLW*, 51). But objects, though they are generated by the sun, can exist unseen; they are not generated by sight or by being seen. Analogously, Ideas are not constituted by our apprehension of them, nor are they altered by the historical variations of our thinking. Heidegger disagrees and reads his own view into Plato. For example, in the winter of 1933–34, in a replay of his lectures of 1931–32, he gives two accounts of the relationship between the Idea of the good and the other Ideas. In the first account, the good radiates *ousia* or *alêtheia*, which yokes together *noein*, "thinking," with *nooumena*, the objects of thought. This linkage is parallel to the yoking of sight and its objects by the light of the sun, and it implies that the Ideas are entities in their own right. It is also more or less what Plato says (*GA* 36/37, 196). In the second account, the good yokes being or "understanding of being" (*Seinsverständnis*), now glossed as *Idee* or *Subjekt*, together with "truth as unhiddenness," now glossed as *Objekt*. This yoking is no longer parallel to the yoking of sight and its objects by light, so it is now omitted. The Ideas have switched sides. Ideas are no longer objects of thought. They are constituents of our *Seinsverständnis*, our ways of looking at things, not things in their own right. The Idea of a book, for example, is our prior understanding of what a book is, and it enables us to interpret colors as a book.[47] On this account, Plato is a proto-Heideggerian. But since Plato also tends to regard the Ideas as entities distinct from ordinary things, and as entities that belong, Heidegger argues, to the "subject" rather than the "object," Plato is also the founder of the correspondence theory of truth, the view that our access to things is mediated by ideas in the mind.[48]

Heidegger himself is closer to Protagoras, whose cryptic pronouncement—"Man is the measure [*metron*] of all things"[49]—is echoed, no doubt intentionally, in his frequent use of the term *Mass*, "measure," "standard" (e.g., *GA* 34, 74: "Our questioning attempts to take a measure"). This suggestion provokes Heidegger to ask: "What is man, that he could become the measure of *everything*?" (*GA* 34, 74; cf. *GA* 36/37, 173, 175). He argues, first, that unhiddenness is essential to man (*GA* 34, 75) and second, that what is unhidden to him, especially by philosophy, changes man from the bottom up (*GA* 34, 116). Nevertheless, it remains the case that, in Heidegger's view, what we, at any given time, find *outside* the cave depends on what we *are*, at that time, *inside* the cave. It does not depend on what is there, objectively, outside the cave—not because our historical situation determines what we select from a prearranged display of articles outside the cave, but because there really is nothing outside the cave unless we put it there. From this view Plato would heartily dissent. Plato and Heidegger are entirely at odds over philosophical truth. If their disagreement has anything to do with the correspondence theory of truth, it is that Plato believes that there is something objective outside the cave for our most fundamental thoughts to correspond to, whereas Heidegger does not.

Notes

I am grateful to Lesley Brown for reading a draft of this essay and for suggesting some improvements.

1. *R.*, 479e1. I capitalize the initial letter to distinguish a Platonic "Idea" (nor-

mally translated as *Idee* in German) from a mental, more or less Lockean, "idea" (usually translated as *Vorstellung* in German).

2. Aristotle, *Posterior Analytics* 1.2.71b33–72a8. Cf. *Nicomachean Ethics* 1.4.1095b2f.; *Physics* 1.1.184a16–b14.

3. *R.,* 5.515d2–4; all translations from Plato and Heidegger are my own.

4. *Platons Lehre von der Wahrheit* [hereafter cited as *PLW*], 2d ed. (Bern: Francke, 1952), 41f. Cf. *GA* 34, 34: "Truth as correctness [*Richtigkeit*] is grounded in truth as unhiddenness"; and *GA* 36/37, 138, 150.

5. Cf. *R.,* 6.508c4–d2, and 511e2–4, where the *sapheneia* of a faculty corresponds to the *alêtheia* of its objects.

6. Cf. *R.,* 6.511b5–6 on the use of "hypotheses" as *ekbaseis te kai hormas.*

7. Or a similar word, such as *Unverdecktheit,* "uncoveredness" (*GA* 19, 213).

8. *GA* 19, 603. At *BT,* 220, Heidegger postulates two senses of "truth": *Entdeckend-sein* (or *Entdeckung*) and *Entdeckt-sein* (or *Entdecktheit*).

9. Kingsley Martin, *Editor* (Penguin: Harmondsworth, 1969), 279. The Minister in question was Brendan Bracken, Churchill's wartime Minister of Information.

10. E.g., *GA* 36/37, 138 ("Die Wahrheit als Richtigkeit ist unmöglich ohne Wahrheit als Unverborgenheit") and 223 ("Die Aussage setzt also schon Offenbarkeit der Dinge voraus").

11. Aristotle, *Metaphysics* E.4.1027b26, quoted in *PLW,* 44, and *GA* 19, 616. Elsewhere, e.g., *GA* 36/37, 123, the doctrine is said to put truth in the "sentence" or "proposition" (*Satz*).

12. Aquinas, *Quaestiones de veritate,* qu.1, art. 4, resp., quoted in *PLW,* 44f.

13. *BT,* 220: "Primär 'wahr', das heisst entdeckend ist das Dasein."

14. "Vom Wesen des Grundes," in *Wegmarken,* 2d ed. (Frankfurt am Main: V. Klostermann, 1978), 123–73, see 160 n. 59; cf. also *GA* 27, 11.

15. He is in any case unfair to Aquinas. To locate truth in the divine intellect is quite different from locating it in the human intellect.

16. At *GA* 19, 599f., Heidegger distinguishes between the *Worüber* or *peri hou* of the assertion—Theaetetus sitting, where Theaetetus and the sitting are not distinguished from each other—and the *Wovon* or *hotou*—Theaetetus himself explicitly distinguished from his sitting and picked out as the subject of an assertion that presents him *as* sitting. The *Worüber* is presumably unhidden prior to the assertion. (The distinction is Heidegger's, not Plato's: at *Sph.,* 263a4, etc.; *peri hou* and *hotou* are used interchangeably.)

17. Cf. *GA* 19, 276: "Zugeeignet wird im Erkennen und Sprechen die Wahrheit des Seienden, seine Unverborgenheit." Also *GA* 19, 409: "Alles in diesem logos ist orientiert auf die Aneignung des Gesehenen in seiner Unverborgenheit, die Aneignung dessen, was gesichtet ist." Both claims imply that the *Unverborgenheit* of beings precedes its "appropriation" in the Logos.

18. William Congreve, *The Double Dealer,* 5.iv.

19. *Sph.,* 260c6: *Ontos de ge pseudous estin apatê,* "Since there is falsity [Heidegger: *Täuschung*], there is deception [Heidegger: *Trug*]." *Trug* excludes deliberate deception; *Täuschung* can be deliberate or otherwise. See R. B. Farrell, *Dictionary of German Synonyms,* 3d ed. (Cambridge: Cambridge University Press, 1977), 89.

20. *GA* 19, 637. Cf. Paul Natorp's account of false judgment in *Platos Ideenlehre: Eine Einführung in den Idealismus,* 2nd ed. (1921; repr. Hamburg: Meiner, 1994), 311f. But Natorp presents his account as an amendment of Plato rather than an interpretation.

21. *GA* 34, 309–14. This is an elaboration of Socrates's aviary analogy, *Tht.,* 197b8ff., discussed in *GA* 34, 302–6. Cf. *GA* 34, 135f. and *GA* 36/37, 227 on the way in which a pseudonym disguises the author's real name.

22. *GA* 34, 200ff. At *GA* 19, 552, Heidegger says that in Plato's view the soul is "yearning [*Sehnsucht*] and nothing else," yearning, that is, for "the eternal," *das aei.* Cf.*GA* 19, 641, 489.

23. See Inwood 1999a. Cf. *GA* 36/37, 242ff. on the difference between a man and a dog.

24. Cf. *BT,* 163, on the "voice of the friend that every Dasein carries with it."

25. *GA* 34, 25. Cf. *GA* 34, 27; *GA* 36/37, 131, 134, 137, 143. *PLW* is more ambiguous. It speaks of *das Wirkliche,* "the actual," without specifying whether this is *to alêthês* or *to on.* Thus *PLW,* 19: "What surrounds and gets to [*an-geht*] them there, is for them 'the actual', i.e., what is [*das Seiende*]." *Das Wirkliche* looks like a crutch that Heidegger keeps handy in case *das Unverborgene* gives out as a translation of *to alêthês.*

26. Cf. the *megista genê* of *Sph.,* 254b6ff.

27. *R.,* 7.523e2ff. Cf. *GA* 36/37, 144: *Befreiung ist kein Spaziergang,* "Liberation is no walk-over."

28. *Phd.,* 78b4–84b8.This near identification of the soul with a form is disputed at *Sph.,* 248a4ff.

29. The prisoners are "like us [*homoious hêmin*], I said; for do you think that such people would have seen anything else, in the first place of themselves and each other, except the shadows cast by the fire onto the wall of the cave facing them?" (*R.,* 515a4–7). The second part of the sentence supplies a reason for the first ("like us"). If it supplies a good reason, Plato cannot mean that the objective situation of the prisoners is like ours, or even that their subjective experience is like ours. He probably means that their experience is no less coherent than ours. Since they have only ever seen shadows of themselves, and so on, they, like us, assume that they see themselves, and so on, having nothing more substantial to compare their experience with. Analogously, people who have only lower pleasures do not have the same experience as those who have higher pleasures; but they do not notice this deficiency, since they know nothing better (583c10ff.). It does not follow that Plato does not claim that the prisoners are objectively like us or that their experience is like ours. But he does not, or at least should not, say it here.

30. *GA* 34, 61. Cf. *GA* 36/37, 160–64 for a similar account of science, history, art ("the *free, creative projection* of what is *possible for human being,*" 164), and poetry.

31. *GA* 34, 63. *Lichtblick* usually means "bright spot," but Heidegger uses it more literally to mean the ex-prisoner's "look at the light," the fire in the cave or the sun outside, and hence at being.

32. *GA* 34, 64: "im Gleichnis: wie der Lichtblick, das Ins-Licht-sehen, erst den Blick für die Dinge öffnet und befreit." *GA* 36/37, 206f. associates our "light-look for the essence of things" with the prenatal vision of "*das Unverborgene* of things"

required, according to Plato's *Phaedrus* 249 b 5, for our entry into the human form.

33. Contrast *GA* 34, 90f: "Someone who ascended from the cave only to lose themselves in the 'shining' of the ideas . . . would make the ideas themselves only into a being, into a higher stratum of beings." But the view Heidegger condemns is in fact Plato's: "[W]ho have come here do not want to engage in human affairs; their souls always long to spend time above" (*R.*, 7.517c8f.).

34. *GA* 34, 29. That liberation involves knowledge of the difference between hiddenness and unhiddenness is implied at *GA* 36/37, 140, 143, 183f., 187.

35. Socrates asks whether *ousia*, "being," is discerned by the soul itself or by a bodily sense. Theaetetus replies: "Myself I place it among the things the soul aims at [*eporegetai*] by itself" (*Tht.*, 186a4). Heidegger sees here the idea of *Seinserstrebnis*—probably wrongly: first, being is only one of the things aimed at by the soul; second, the notion of striving is not very explicit in *eporegetai*, which is more like the "intending" involved in intentionality.

36. *GA* 34, 10f. Cf. *PLW*, 32: "Truth means originally what is wrested from a hiddenness."

37. *GA* 34, 124. Cf. *GA* 34, 93: Plato considers *alêtheia* in its conflict with "semblance," *Schein*, but not in its struggle with hiddenness.

38. *PLW*, 27. (The things were never in fact hidden *by* their shadows.) At *PLW*, 39, by contrast, the shadows are "still hidden in their essence" (*die in ihrem Wesen noch verborgenen Schatten*). Cf. *GA* 34, 89.

39. *R.*, 7.520c3–6. Cf. *GA* 34, 89: With his *Wesensblick* ("essential look, look at essences") outside the cave the philosopher knows about what is inside it.

40. He criticizes it explicitly in *GA* 65, 339.

41. Can *atuchia*, "misfortune," really be the overcoming of good fortune, the wresting of bad fortune from good?

42. At this stage, a *Geschehen* is distinguished from, and more significant than, an *Ereignis*, "event": "Not any old *Ereignis*, but a *Geshehen* that now involves the *essence of men*" (*GA* 36/37, 136).

43. *PLW*, 50f. Cf. *GA* 36/37, 217: "in dieser Geschichte [story] um die Geschichte [history] des Menschen."

44. *GA* 34, 77. *Wesensgeschichte* also means "history of the essence" of man. The essence of man changes in the course of his essential history.

45. *GA* 34, 208f. On the temporalization of truth, cf. *GA* 36/37 138: "Jede Wahrheit hat ihre Zeit. Gewisse Wahrheiten, gewisse Menschen zu gewissen Zeiten verzeitigt." Cf. *GA* 36/37, 143.

46. *GA* 34, 104. Cf. *GA* 34,.70f. The force of *Erblicken* is that the looking brings "out" or "forth" what it looks at. Cf. *GA* 36/37, 171, 174, 191, 193.

47. *GA* 36/37, 152f. In the *Republic*, Plato's examples of Ideas are such things as justice, equality, and beauty. Heidegger's examples are, by contrast, such things as a book, a table, a window, a house, and a mountain (*GA* 36/37, 156, 169f., 221). Heidegger's examples enable us to interpret ordinary things, but they are not very appropriate objects of contemplation in their own right.

48. *GA* 36/37, 221f., 294. Heidegger's words also suggest another "agree-

ment" or correspondence theory, namely, that a thing (e.g., a beautiful person) is true to the extent that it conforms to a form (e.g., the form of beauty), where the form is a nonmental entity. This theory can be plausibly attributed to Plato, but it is quite different from the correspondence theory that is the primary target of Heidegger's attack.

49. *Tht.*,152a2f. Heidegger does not mention Protagoras in *GA* 34, despite his prominent role in the *Theaetetus*. His implicit interpretation of him differs widely from Plato's and also from anything that Protagoras himself is likely to have had in mind. He discusses Protagoras at length in *Nietzsche,* 2:168ff., and mentions him in passing at *GA* 36/37, 240.

Heidegger and the Platonic Concept of Truth

Enrico Berti

Heidegger's philosophical training was based on the study of Aristotle, and his interpretation of the Platonic concept of truth was deeply influenced, as I shall argue, by his interpretation of the Aristotelian notion of truth. Accordingly, it is worth starting by outlining the main points of this interpretation, for it enables us to understand and better evaluate Heidegger's analogous discourse with regard to Plato.[1]

In his published works, Heidegger devotes only a few pages to the Aristotelian notion of truth—in *Being and Time, Plato's Doctrine of Truth,* and *Letter on Humanism.* In *Being and Time* he expounds his conception of truth as "un-concealment," as opposed to the traditional concept of truth as correspondence. He also denies that Aristotle indicated that truth originated in judgment and attributes to him instead the position that the disclosure originated in the "vision" of ideas that belongs to *noêsis;* this position, Heidegger claims, was developed by Aristotle in *Metaphysics* book 9, chapter 10 (*BT,* 225–26). In *Plato's Doctrine of Truth,* on the contrary, Heidegger attributes to Aristotle an ambiguity in determining the essence of truth, given the fact that in *Metaphysics* 9.10—considered by Heidegger the place where Aristotelian thought on being reaches its apex—unconcealment is the fundamental trait of reality, although the conception of truth as correspondence is also present ("PDT," 232). Finally, in *Letter on Humanism,* Heidegger attributes to *Metaphysics* 9.10 the doctrine that only in the act of apprehension (*Vernehmen, noein*) can man touch (*thigein*) being ("LH," 332).

The reason for this change in Heidegger's position, from approval to criticism of the Aristotelian position, can be understood by examining what he claimed about this matter in some of his university lecture courses that were published posthumously.

Particularly important among these is the course given at Marburg in the winter term 1925–26, namely *Logic: The Question of Truth*. Its first part is almost wholly devoted to the concept of truth in Aristotle and contains a translation with commentary of all the relative Aristotelian texts, among which the most important is *Metaphysics* 9.10. This volume, as several others that were published later, confirms what H.-G. Gadamer said in Padua in January 1979, namely, that Heidegger, prior to his famous *Kehre*, did nothing other than to comment Aristotle, almost giving the impression that he completely identified with him.[2] In the course he gave at Marburg, however, Heidegger denies Heinrich Maier's assertion that for Aristotle the judgment is the place of truth and therefore the fundamental concept of truth for Aristotle is the agreement between thought and reality (Maier 1896). Heidegger shows that for Aristotle the *logos apophantikos* is essentially a showing, a disclosure, and only secondarily a determining, that is, a predicating (*GA* 21, 127–35). Consequently, albeit recognizing the almost exclusive presence of truth as correspondence in *De interpretatione, Metaphysics* 4.7 and 6.4, Heidegger shows that in *Metaphysics* 9.10, alongside this concept, there is also present a further concept of truth as "un-concealment" which constitutes the peak of Aristotle's account of fundamental ontology. In this regard, Heidegger (1) contests the position taken by Werner Jaeger (1912), who, following Schwegler and Christ, claims that *Metaphysics* 9.10 was totally extraneous to book 9 of the *Metaphysics;* and (2) supports Bonitz (praised for his greater intuition in having taken up the interpretations of Thomas Aquinas and Suarez), according to whom the chapter in question is an integral part of the book in which it is found. Heidegger goes on to criticize the position taken by Ross in his then very recent comment to *Metaphysics,* because he was not able to decide between the two previous interpretations, and observes that Jaeger himself (1923) is practically a convert to Bonitz's opinion, for he admits that the chapter had been added by Aristotle himself (*GA* 21, 170–74).

This interpretation of *Metaphysics* 9.10 was possible only by manipulating the Aristotelian text, under the influence of the Neoplatonic commentator known as pseudo-Alexander and of the aforementioned Hermann Bonitz. In chapter 10 of book 9 there is a particularly important passage, namely 1051b30–33, where Aristotle states:

> About the things, then, which are essences and exist in actuality, it is not possible to be in error, but only to think them or not to think them [*ê noein ê mê*]. Inquiry about their "what" takes the form of asking whether they are of such and such a nature or not [*ei toiauta estin ê mê*]. (Ross 1924)

Aristotle is speaking here of the essences of determinate realities, such as man. He reaffirms the alternative between knowledge and ignorance, expressed as "to think or not to think," excluding the possibility of error, that is, of falsehood. He then speaks of a real and proper search for their definition ("inquiry about their 'what'"), and he conceives the outcome of this search as an answer to the question "whether they are of such and such a nature or not," which is an answer to a real and proper dilemma (or dialectical problem). This means that (1) what is involved here is not the question of immobile substances, as had been believed, but that of the essence of material substances; (2) the knowledge of essence is not based on an intuition, that is, an immediate act, but the conclusion to a cognitive process, or to a discussion; and, finally, (3) this knowledge is expressed in a judgment, which says whether the thing in question is or is not of a certain nature, that is a definite judgment.

Heidegger translates the lines in question in the following way:

> Alles offenbar, was Sein an ihm selbst ist und schlechtin immer schon Vorhandenes—über dieses keine Täuschung, sondern nur entweder ein Vernehmen oder Nichtvernehmen. Es wird vielmehr in diesem Felde nach dem, *Was* je etwas ist, gesucht, nicht aber, ob es so beschaffen ist oder nicht [ob es ein solches ist oder nicht]. (*GA* 21, 176–77)

Leaving aside the typical Heideggerian terminology, which renders, for instance, *noein* as "perceive" (*Vernehmen*), what is striking in his translation is the rendering of *alla* in line 32 as a simple "rather" (*vielmehr*) and, above all, the introduction of "but not" (*nicht aber*) before "if it is made so or not" (*ei toiauta estin ê mê*), which completely overturns the sense of the text. Heidegger's translation presupposes that there is an *ouk* before *ei*, which is not to be found in any manuscript, not even in the edition of Christ used by Heidegger, rather it was a reading construed by Bonitz on the basis of the interpretation of the text given by pseudo-Alexander.[3] The fact that Heidegger should have adopted it shows that he felt there was a contrast between the text passed down by all the manuscripts and the interpretation he proposed, that is, he identified in the last sentence of the passage a clear denial of his interpretation and attempted to eliminate it, relying on the comments of an interpreter praised for his loyalty to the schools, namely, Bonitz, and of a Neoplatonic pseudo-Alexander, both of whom tended to attribute to Aristotle an intuitional conception of the knowledge of the essences.

Heidegger comments on the passage by observing that, in the case of essence, looking itself is pure discovering. It follows that it not only does not need any determination but cannot have any need for it. Consequently he opposes this thinking (*noein*) without determinations to thinking via determinations (*dia-noein*), that is, in propositions (the former corresponding to *phanai*, the latter to *dialegesthai*). Finally, he takes as example of the superiority of the first over the second the perception of a color, for which a "dialectic" that highlights the relations between the different colors is useless, whereas direct vision is essential (*GA* 21, 181–85). Noteworthy, in this comment, is the interpretation of the knowledge of the essence as knowledge completely void of discourse, that is, pure intuitive knowledge. Discourse is considered equivalent to dialectic and condemned as inadequate.

The importance attributed by Heidegger to the Aristotelian doctrine of truth, which he interpreted as fundamentally antepredicative truth, is confirmed by a further course, held at Marburg in the summer term of 1926, namely, *Fundamental Concepts of Ancient Philosophy*, where he again juxtaposes the conception of book 6, chapter 4 (truth of proposition) against that of book 9, chapter 10 (antepredicative truth), in affirming that the latter is the base of the former and that, accordingly, truth is known via a "simple and direct apprehension," as a "simple discovery by simply looking."[4]

Heidegger deals with the Aristotelian concept of truth in two other lecture courses held at Freiburg, namely *Fundamental Concepts of Metaphysics: World—Finitude—Solitude* (WS 1929–30) and *On the Essence of Human Freedom: Introduction to Philosophy* (SS 1930). In the first of these two lecture courses, Heidegger returns to, and develops, what he had said in the course on truth given in Marburg. He claims that *logos apophantikos* is disclosing discourse, and he comments again on the passages of *De interpretatione, Metaphysics* 4.7 and 6.4, adding the analysis of *De anima* 3.6 on the discernment of the indivisibles (*GA* 29/30, 441–507).

In the second one, he develops more widely the thesis he touched on in the course given in Marburg, that is, the primacy of being as true among the four more general meanings of being listed by Aristotle in *Metaphysics* 5.7. In *Metaphysics* 6.4 Aristotle excludes being as true from the framework of investigation of philosophy because it does not belong to things but to thought (*dianoia*). In *Metaphysics* 9.10, however, he describes, as we have seen, being as true through the adverb *kuriôtata* (1051b1) and states that it exists also in things and distinguishes two forms, one relating to "composite realities," expressed by judgment, and one relating to "noncomposite realities," expressed by the *noein*, which, according to Heidegger, is not a judgment. For these reasons, Heidegger claims, the chapter in question was excluded from *Metaphysics* by Schwegler, then by Jaeger (who, however, later contradicted himself by saying that it had been reinserted by Aristotle himself). What particularly disturbed these interpreters, according to Heidegger, is the adverb *kuriôtata* said of being as true: It was indeed neglected by Schwegler, excised by Ross, and interpreted by Jaeger as expressing not the most proper way of intending being but simply the way most often used in the language. Heidegger objects to this latter interpretation by saying that, even if it were true that the adjective *kurios* could have for Aristotle the meaning of "dominant" in terms of use, this meaning would certainly not be applicable to being as true, which is by no means the most widespread linguistic use, but is only one of the four meanings of being, alongside being in itself, that is, said according to the categories, alongside being by accident and being according to potentiality and actuality (*GA* 31, 75–83). Being as true, according to Heidegger, is instead really the most proper of the meanings of being, and it is above all the truth of things, that is, the constant presence, on which the truth of thought, that is, of judgment, is founded. This more proper meaning of being as true belongs especially to the "indivisible" realities in *De anima* 3.6, or "non-composite" and "simple" realities in *Metaphysics* 9.10, whose truth, or disclosure, is the simple presence. The knowledge of this truth, Heidegger goes on, is a "touching" (*thigein*), as Aristotle says, that is, a "grasping" (*Greifen*), not a "conceiving" (*Begreifen*). Aristotle alludes to this knowledge also in *Metaphysics* 7.17.1041b9–11, where he states that there is no search or teaching of simple realities but "a different type of search" (*heteros tropos tês zêtêseôs*); this different type of search, according to Heidegger, is the work of the *nous,* juxtaposed to that of the *dianoia.* Being as truth, that is, as constant presence, is no other than being as *energeia,* which book 9 of the *Metaphysics* indicates as the principal meaning of being, therefore chapter 10 is the cornerstone of the entire book 9 (*GA* 31, 92–107).

Finally, Heidegger returns to the Aristotelian conception of truth in the lecture course held at Freiburg during the winter term 1937–38, after his famous *Kehre,* namely, *Basic Questions of Philosophy: Selected "Problems" of "Logic,"* in which he attributes to Aristotle almost exclusively the concept of truth as correspondence, or correctness, or adequacy between thought and being. Yet at the same, he also notes that in *Metaphysics* 9.10 this concept of truth merges with that of truth as disclosure (truth as disclosure being the equivalent of *phusis,* the "last echo of the original essence of truth," which, however, although still present in Plato and in Aristotle, was unable to pass any further into the history of philosophy; cf. *GA* 45, 15, 97, 139, 205).

We are now at the stage of *Plato's Doctrine of Truth,* in which the Platonic-Aristotelian doctrine of truth, under the influence of Heidegger's reading of Nietzsche, is essentially criticized, and Aristotle's greatest contribution is reviewed and now reconsidered as being that of having maintained a trace of the pre-Socratic concept of *phusis*.[5]

Heidegger pursues an analogous path in his interpretation of the Platonic concept of truth. He first deals with the subject in the lecture course on Plato's *Sophist* (WS 1924–25). Here Heidegger expounds his conception of truth as "unconcealment," and he does not hesitate to attribute it to the Greeks, in particular to Socrates, Plato, and Aristotle (*GA* 19, 15–17). He then continues with a detailed analysis of book 6 of Aristotle's *Nicomachean Ethics* (which confirms that he approaches Plato from Aristotle). And he then returns to the *Sophist,* where Plato expresses for the first time the predicative conception of truth, which will later be taken up by Aristotle.

The *Sophist* introduces the concept of truth with reference to the analysis of discourse (*logos*) intended as a union between a name and a verb. Discourse—states Plato—may be true or false: It is true when it says what is, for example, "Theaetetus sits," and false when it says what is not, for example, "Theaetetus flies." As nonbeing (as it has been demonstrated in this very dialogue) is for Plato "different from being," the false discourse will be the one which says something differently from what is, that is, that says things differently from what they are, while the true discourse will be the one which says the things exactly as they are, that is, describes the being as identical to itself (*Sph.,* 261c–63d).

Heidegger explains this doctrine stating that discourse, which is a synthesis of name and verb, may be "disclosing" (*aufdeckend*) or "counterfeit" (*verstellend*): In the first case, which is that of true discourse, what is said is apprehended as it really is, that is, as identical to itself, whereas in the second case, that of false discourse, what is said is presented as different from itself. In every *deloun,* in every *legein ti,* the *legomenon* is either "identified" as itself or represented as other than itself; in this way the Logos has become false (*GA* 19, 606). In all this, Heidegger sees no abandoning of the conception of truth as unconcealment, because true discourse is one way to show (*deloun*) being.

A year later, in the lecture course *Fundamental Concepts of Ancient Philosophy,* Heidegger turns his attention to the *Republic,* to the famous allegory of the cave, seeing in it a theory of the different degrees of truth intended as "degrees of disclosure" (*Entdeckheitsstufen*). And there is no doubt, claims Heidegger, that truth is here, as in the *Sophist,* the truth of Logos understood as "assertion" (*GA* 22, 102–7).

Heidegger returns to the same subject a few years later, in the winter term of 1931–32, devoting a whole course to the allegory of the cave, entitled *On the Essence of Truth.* Here he repeats that the different degrees of truth, described in the different stages of the allegory (vision of the shadows in the cave, vision of the things inside the cave, vision of the external reality, and vision of the sun), correspond to the same number of degrees of being, which become manifest one after the other. Equally, there are degrees of disclosure; yet this does not mean abandoning the conception of truth as disclosure. Heidegger indeed underlines the Platonic claim that the higher level of being makes a "more correct" (*richtiger; R.*, 515d) vision possible, observing that here truth is conceived also as "correctness" (*Richtigkeit*). But he adds that truth as correctness is founded on truth as disclosure (*GA* 34, 34).

The conception of truth as disclosure, therefore, is not even here abandoned by Plato. This conception constitutes the foundation which makes possible a second conception of truth, that of correctness of the affirmation, which would not be possible without the first. This second conception of truth—states Heidegger—is a form of derived truth, therefore it is not in opposition to the first. Indeed, it is a decisive step toward solving the problem of the relationship between the two concepts of truth (*GA* 34, 35).

In short, until 1931–32, Heidegger considers the Platonic conception of truth as implying that truth is essentially disclosure. Yet in his famous book *Plato's Doctrine of Truth*, things are put in completely different terms. During 1931–32, Heidegger claims that the Platonic *idea* enables us to see what a thing is, that is, it enables us to see its *Was-sein* (*GA* 34, 50–51). In this regard too, as we shall see, Heidegger will say exactly the opposite in *Plato's Doctrine of Truth*.

The interpretation of Plato proposed by Heidegger in *Plato's Doctrine of Truth* is so well known that it hardly needs to be summed up here. I shall only underline a number of particular points. First and foremost, Heidegger identifies the meaning of Plato's allegory of the cave in book 7 of the *Republic*, or what it really refers to, as the process of "formation" (*Bildung*) of Man, interpreting in this way *paideia*, and sees in this the birth of humanism, that is, placing man at the center of reality ("PDT," 217–18). This, however, is only the "said" of Plato, below which the "unsaid" lies hidden, that is, the change in the truth in which the real doctrine of Plato on truth consists.

Prior to Plato, Heidegger claims, truth was conceived as disclosure, but traces of this conception remain in the allegory of the cave, where Plato identifies degrees of truth with degrees of being, affirming, for example, that the objects seen by the prisoner freed of his chains but still inside the cave are "nearer to reality" (*mallon ti enguterô tou ontos*) and therefore "truer" (*alêthestera; R.*, 515d) than the shadows he had previously seen. Here "truer," according to Heidegger, means "what is more disclosed," therefore Plato is still moving within the ancient conception of truth ("PDT," 220–22).

For the same reason it must be assumed, even if Plato does not say so, that the objects seen by the prisoner on leaving the cave are even truer than the previous ones, that is, they are "the truest realities" (*ta alêthestata*). This expression can be found elsewhere in Plato, but in the *Republic* it always refers to ideas (cf. *R.*, 484c–d). The ideas, according to Heidegger, are the appearance with which things present themselves to thought, that is, they are the essence of things, their *Was-sein*. In this way, in place of disclosure, another essence of truth springs to the forefront. Disclosure, even if it is named in its different degrees, is thought only in relation to the way in which it renders what appears accessible in its showing (*Aussehen, eidos*). Here, as we can see, Heidegger evaluates the position of Plato in exactly the opposite way as what he had done in his courses in the 1920s and early 1930s.

The aspect under which the entity makes itself present in the idea is the essence, the *Was-sein*. For Plato, being has its authentic essence in what it is. Therefore the Platonic idea is no longer true being, as Heidegger had affirmed in the course of 1931–32. Here Heidegger grasps the Platonic thought perfectly: The ideas about which Plato speaks are the essences of things, their "what is." Indeed, Plato's doctrine of the ideas responded to the Socratic question "What is *x*?" We find ourselves in exactly the same situation described by Aristotle in the last part of *Metaphysics* 9.10: Here, as there, truth is conceived as apprehension of the essences, of what it is. Hence it is impossible to understand why Heidegger interprets this conception of Plato as a loss of the original meaning of truth, when previously he had interpreted it, as that of Aristotle, as the most genuine expression of the latter.

Also in the case of Plato, as in the case of Aristotle, it might be observed that the *noein* in question is not an immediate apprehension, a *Vernehmen*, because Plato, with regard to the idea of good, will say that it can be defined only by he who takes a long walk (the so-called uphill path), "passing through all the counterarguments" (*dia pantôn elenchôn diexiôn*), "as in war," and countering "not according to opinion, but according to reality" (*ou kata doxan, to the kat'ousian; R.*, 534c). And the same is true, as we have seen, for Aristotle.

Besides, Heidegger expressed perfectly the function carried out in this process by the idea of good, illustrated in the allegory of the cave by the sun. This is "the essence of the idea" and therefore the origin, that is, the cause of the fact that ideas are ideas essences, intelligible realities ("PDT," 228–29). In Aristotelian terms, it could be said that the idea of the good is the formal cause of the other ideas, as they are the formal cause of sensible things. In this way, indeed, Aristotle characterized the One placed by Plato, in his unwritten doctrines, as the beginning of ideas and, through these, of all things, identifying it also with good and with being itself (*auto to on;* cf. *Metaphysics* 2.6, 3.4, etc.).

For Heidegger, however, this leads to "the *idea* becoming master over the *alêtheia*," for which "*alêtheia* falls under the yoke of the *idea*"; from now on, Heidegger claims, the essence of truth abandons the fundamental trait of disclosure ("PDT," 234–35). That may be true in the sense that the idea is not a process of disclosure, but it is the reality already fully disclosed, that is, fully intelligible; but it should also be noted that it is, as Aristotle will say of the essence, intelligible in itself, not yet for us, which implies our gradually adapting to it. That is what Heidegger does not like. He sees an allusion to this process of adapting, in which we must engage toward the idea without the idea disclosing itself to us, in the Platonic expression, according to which, he who is turned toward more real things sees more truly (*pros mallon onta tetrammenos orthoteron blepoi; R.,* 515d).

This passage, the only one in which Plato uses the term *orthos,* with regard to truth, is commented on by Heidegger: The transition from one condition to the other consists in looking every time in a more correct mode (*Richtigerwerden des Blickens*). Everything depends on the *orthotês,* the correctness of sight, hence the notion of *homoiôsis,* concordance of knowing with the thing known. Thus truth becomes *orthotês,* correctness (*Richtigkeit*) of the apprehension and of the assertion ("PDT," 230–31). We are at the opposite extremes of what Heidegger himself had said, with regard to *Richtigkeit,* in the course of 1931–32.

It may be observed that the *orthotês* of which Plato speaks is always an adaptation of the intellect to the idea, that is, the ability to see the true reality rather than mere appearance; it is not an exactness exclusively within knowing, that is, a form of coherency, for example, in mathematics, which starts out from simple hypotheses, exchanging them for true principles, and deducing the consequences perfectly coherently, and for this reason not considered by Plato to be authentic sciences (*R.,* 511c–e). In any case, it is not the *orthotês* that transforms perceiving into enunciation but the need to gather the essence, to say "what it is" and therefore to define. Indeed, the *orthotês* of which Plato speaks does not refer to any kind of judgment but to a precise type of judgment that is the definition of the essence, in which there is a perfect identity between subject and predicate. All this is also true for the perception of essences of which Aristotle speaks in *Metaphysics* 9.10.

Heidegger also realizes that the aforementioned passage is not enough to attest a complete abandoning by Plato of the conception of truth as disclosure. Indeed, he observes that Plato in a way still insists on "truth" as characteristic of the essence, but at the same time he transfers the problem of disclosing to the correctness and exactness of the vision. There is in Plato, Heidegger claims, an ambiguity ("PDT," 231). As proof of this ambiguity, Heidegger cites a passage from the *Republic*, where it is said that the idea of good is "the original cause of all that is correct and of all that is beautiful," interpreting it in the sense that it is the cause of correct things, since it is the origin of the *orthotês,* and cause of beautiful things insomuch as truth ("PDT," 231; cf. *R.*, 517b-c).

However, it is in *Plato's Doctrine of Truth,* which appeared at the end the 1930s, that the new interpretation of Aristotle is fully accomplished. The same ambiguity that Heidegger found in Plato, he now finds also in Aristotle. Indeed, he cites *Metaphysics* 9.10, where in his opinion there predominates, as a fundamental characteristic of the essence, disclosure, as the place in which Aristotelian thought reaches its apex, but immediately sets by its side *Metaphysics* 6.4, where instead it is stated that true and false are not in things but in the intellect. Hence Heidegger may conclude that the same ambiguity in the determination of the essence of truth also reigns in Aristotle. The asserting which expresses the judgment of the intellect is the place of truth and of falsehood and of their difference. The assertion is said to be true if it conforms to the state of facts, therefore if it is *homoiôsis.* This determination of the essence of truth no longer comprises any reference to the *alêtheia* in the sense of disclosure. Rather, it is the *alêtheia,* intended as the opposite of the *pseudos,* that is false in the sense of not correct, which vice versa is thought of as correctness. From this second conception there will stem all the representative thought, from Thomas Aquinas via Descartes to Nietzsche ("PDT," 231–33).

It might, however, be pointed out that all this was always evident: Not only did Aristotle express the concept of truth as adequacy of judgment to being in *Metaphysics* 6.4 and in other texts such as *De interpretatione* and *Metaphysics* 4.7, but in *Metaphysics* 9.10 he presents both concepts of truth, that of judgment and that of definition of the essence, without the one excluding the other. If Aristotle's thought has not changed, perhaps something has changed in the attitude of Heidegger toward the texts. The only difference between Plato and Aristotle is, if anything, that in Plato, or at least in the *Republic,* where the two concepts of truth are present, they would certainly overlap—the second, that is, the truth of judgment, will only explicitly appear in the *Sophist*—in Aristotle they are not only copresent but also clearly distinguished, and they refer one to the truth of the attributive judgment in general and the other to the particular judgment, or enunciation, that is, the definition.

This had been seen in great clarity by a philologist and historian of philosophy who was a contemporary of Heidegger, Paul Wilpert (1940), who, departing from the historical-genetic hypothesis of Jaeger, had observed that the "ontological" concept of truth (truth as being) and that the "logical" concept (the truth of judgment) are both present in Plato and Aristotle alike. However, in Plato the former is fundamental and plays a role in the mature dialogues (e.g, in the *Republic*), and the latter appears only later in the *Sophist*. But in Aristotle the contrary is true: the ontological concept is especially present in the younger, Platonized works, such as the *Protrepticus*, the first book of *Physics*, and book 2 of the *Metaphysics*, and the logical concept is present in the more mature works, such as books 6 and 4 of the *Metaphysics*, the *De anima*, and the *De interpretatione*. According to Wilpert, there is no contradiction between *Metaphysics* 6.4 and *Metaphysics* 9.10. As Jaeger had already shown, in 6.4.1027b27–29 there is a reference to 9.10; and the latter does not represent a return to the ontological concept of truth but only an analogous application of the logical concept to the objects of *Metaphysics*, highlighted by the books on substance in general, that is, books 7, 8, and 9.

In conclusion, in equal measure for Plato and for Aristotle, truth is first and foremost the correctness of the definition, which, as such, is the knowledge of causes and therefore is science (*epistêmê*). This truth does not have error as its alternative but only ignorance. Second, truth is also that of attributive judgment which can be demonstrated by departing from principles, and in this case, it is always true, or it cannot be demonstrated, and in this case, it is opinion (*doxa*), which may be equally true or false. In any case, truth is never immediacy, that is, intuition, but always mediation, either in the sense of definition (which is mediation because it is always a causal explanation) or in the sense of demonstration of an affirmative or negative judgment. As such, truth is always expressed in an enunciation, that is in a *logos apophantikos*.[6]

Notes

This essay was translated from the Italian by Daniela De Cecco.

1. I dealt with this interpretation in Berti 1990, 1997, and 2000.

2. Gadamer 1983a (from English translation by Stanley), 140: "[T]o be aware of the extent to which Aristotle was present in Heidegger's thought in those early Marburg years, one must have sat in on Heidegger's lectures during that period"; see also 141: "Aristotle was forced on us in such a way that we temporarily lost all distance from him—never realizing that Heidegger was not identifying himself with Aristotle, but was ultimately aiming at developing his own agenda against

metaphysics." Gadamer writes that in 1922, before going to Marburg, Heidegger told him that his extensive phenomenological interpretations of Aristotle were soon to be published. The first part alone took fifteen big sheets, and the second also concerned books 7, 8, and 9 of the *Metphysics;* however, at that time only the introduction was published (1983a, 7). According to R. Brague (1988, 55), who reports an information contained in a study by T. Sheehan, instead of this work, Heidegger published *Being and Time,* which, therefore, is in some sense a substitute of the book on Aristotle. In the meantime, the lecture course delivered in the winter semester 1921–22, which probably should have constituted the basis of that book, has been published as *GA* 61; despite the title, this volume showed to be less important, with regard to the interpretation of Aristotle, than the lecture course on logic. The whole question was also discussed by F. Volpi (1984, 72–73), who then took it up again in Volpi 1988.

3. Cf. Alexander of Aphrodisias, *In Aristotelis Metaphysica* 600, 24–39 (Hayduck edition); Bonitz 1849, 411.

4. Cf. *GA* 22, 302–6. These passages, however, are not contained in the notes left by Heidegger, but in H. Mörchen's transcript of the lecture course.

5. Cf. Heidegger, "ECP." Volpi has already pointed out Heidegger's change from an initial attempt of positive appropriation of the ontological potential of Aristotle's concept of truth (an attempt which characterizes the lecture course delivered in Marburg in 1925–26) to a critical position, which was consequent upon the fact that—in the lecture course delivered in Freiburg in 1937–38—he attributed to Aristotle the concept of truth as correctness; cf. Volpi 1989, esp. 72 n. 8.

6. *Phanai* in *Metaphysics* 9.10.1051b24 means "to enunciate"; thus, it has the sense of a manifesting and defining, which is neither an affirmation nor a negation.

Amicus Plato magis amica veritas: Reading Heidegger in Plato's Cave

María del Carmen Paredes

> From the way in which Plato employed the expression idea we can read-
> ily see that he meant by it something that not only is never borrowed
> from the senses, but that far surpasses even the concepts of understand-
> ing—with which Aristotle dealt—inasmuch as nothing congruent with it
> is ever found in experience. . . . I do not here want to enter into any liter-
> ary inquiry seeking to establish what meaning the august philosopher
> linked with his expression. I shall point out only that there is nothing at
> all unusual in finding, whether in ordinary conversation or in writings,
> that by comparing the thoughts uttered by an author on his topic we
> understand him even better than he understood himself.[1]

We can find this passage partially transcribed by Heidegger in his *Phänomenologische Interpretation von Kants Kritik der reiner Vernunft* (WS 1927–28).[2]
The same idea is expressed in *Grundprobleme der Phänomenologie* (1927):
"We not only want to, but also must understand the Greeks better than
they understood themselves" (*GA* 24, 157; my translation). Through his
career, Heidegger retained a strong interest in the Greeks. In fact, his in-
sistence on the need to overcome metaphysics never meant to overcome
the Greeks but rather capture the roots of their deepest insights.

Being and Time (1927) starts with the question which had been in
Heidegger's mind for several years, also raised by Plato in the *Sophist,* the
question of being as such. The Eleatic Stranger raises this radical question
in order to understand what is really meant by "being." The passage offers
a clue about the beginning of *Being and Time* which continues the lecture
course on the *Sophist* that Heidegger delivered in 1924–25. The Platonic
text suggests a possibility, which Heidegger reinforces in asking whether
we in our time have an answer to that question, or whether we are perhaps
still perplexed about how are we to understand the meaning of being. His

answer that it is first of all necessary to reawaken an understanding for the meaning of this question points to the basis of his own venture. As for those listening to the Eleatic Stranger, Heidegger's approach to the question of the meaning of being is apparently determined by the aporetic character underlined in Plato's dialogue.

In *Being and Time* Heidegger begins his ontological investigation in a Platonic manner. According to Heidegger, the question which interests him has been long abandoned by the history of Western philosophy. He refers to a forgetfulness, a silence that comes after Plato and Aristotle, "only to subside from then on as a theme for actual investigation."[3] Heidegger might mean—as he puts it more explicitly elsewhere—that this subsidence encompasses the long path of Western philosophy, from Plato to Husserl. Certainly Heidegger poses the question of the meaning of being in a way pointing to the special importance of Plato. Heidegger held courses and seminars on Plato and Aristotle over a period of several years. His exegetical work with the texts had a significant influence on the development of his philosophy. It follows that we cannot understand Heidegger merely in terms of his intention to overcome metaphysics. For it is precisely this beginning that made his path of thought so fruitful (Figal 1988, 18–19). It is reasonable to assume that his intended destruction of the Western ontological tradition has its limits in these sources. This assumption allows us to mention briefly the question of the possibility of constructing a philosophy understood as fundamental ontology without raising the main questions raised by Plato.

The Meaning of Philosophy

The theoretical discourse initiated by Plato is central for the kind of intellectual activity called "philosophy." It further defines a type of philosophy that has long been influential on Western thought. In favor of this interpretation, two reasons can be cited. First, the philosophical experience proposed by Plato perhaps requires a new way of living but by no means imposes a rupture with everyday experience. Philosophy appeals to ordinary experience from within, as it were, as cave-dwellers reflecting on the true meaning of shadows and sensible figures. The second reason is that Plato does not invoke extraordinary experience of any kind. He merely opens the way toward reflection and independence. We see this in Plato's struggle against sophistry.

Philosophy has a double task. It must not only overcome (initial) ignorance. It must also do battle with the reduction of human existence to empirical utility, which can be rendered negative by the exercise of thinking. From this perspective, Plato's philosophy might be considered as the figure of Western philosophy in its original sense. This should not be taken as implying that only Greek philosophy is authentic philosophy: philosophical thought existed before the Greeks. But if we understand philosophy as the type of reflection that is intrinsically connected with the intellectual history of Europe—as Husserl claims in *Krisis* (1954, sec. 5, 10f.)—then we can identify it as a historical work of thinking that had a long nascent phase and perhaps, as Heidegger often asserts, carries within itself the date and place of its own dissolution.

Heidegger's thought very clearly belongs to this same history of thinking. The question of being consists in a thesis about the meaning of being that the question merely explores in a way which not surprisingly corresponds to the manner in which the question is posed. Heidegger's thesis points toward a view of being as an original uncovering of itself in a mode of being that is not simply man but the inherent being in human existence. If Heidegger's thesis remains at this level without further explanation, then it necessarily remains indeterminate and almost unintelligible. But the thesis of being as an original uncovering affects each and every dimension of factical life and the sheer existence of Dasein. In the history of Western thought, the original names given to the being of beings were *phusis,* and *alêtheia. Phusis,* which is often translated as "nature," signifies not simply biological processes but also the upsurgence of all beings as they come to presence. *Alêtheia,* often translated as "truth," likewise refers to an unconcealment. For Parmenides and Heraclitus, being is that which fosters the disclosure of beings; being, therefore, is truth itself. What gives unity and wholeness to the universe of beings is that they come to presence.

According to Heidegger, the original thought of the ancient Greeks soon underwent a change. This change marked the beginning of Western metaphysics and, to the extent that the terms are used as synonymous for Heidegger, the beginning of Western philosophy. The shift of ancient thought happened when, with the rise of sophism, the focus on being as unconcealment was lost. The focus, in other words, shifted from a questioning relationship to truth as an ongoing disclosiveness to the conception of truth as the underlying reality of beings as a whole. Concern was transferred from presence as such to that which became manifest through presence, more precisely the stable feature (or features) of a universal set of enduring things. As Heidegger explains, the new orientation toward consciousness in modern philosophy since Descartes is not a radically new beginning against antiquity but only its extension and transference to the subject. Truth, for Descartes, is derivative of a clear and distinct mental representation of the self-conscious human subject. In other words, in the seventeenth century, truth became the supposed correctness of human perception, or more precisely its correspondence to a mind-independent objective reality. But, as Heidegger notes, the understanding of truth as objectivity necessitates a reliance on the notion of subjectivity. The modern subject becomes the arbiter of what is true and conversely what is false. This is a far cry from Plato's attempt to place truth beyond the perverting effects of our worldly sense and appetites in a transcendent realm of Forms. But the point is that the uneven and tortuous road leading from Plato to Descartes and Nietzsche requires only time to traverse.[4]

Heidegger and Phenomenology

It is an essential point in Heidegger's approach that it arose in a philosophical situation permeated by phenomenology. Husserl gave an original formulation to the philosophical task in the well-known claim to go back "to things themselves." One of the declared purposes of phenomenology was a critical revision of objectivity without appealing to a reductionist conception of experience. Heidegger desired to avoid some central features of Husserlian phenomenology—especially in regard to the transcendental phenomenology exposed in *Ideen I*—and in general to distance himself from Husserl's conception of the task of phenomenology as such. Heidegger clearly stated in 1924 that Husserl's conception of what is present (*das Gegenwärtige*) in an intentional presence (*Anwesen*) presupposes a certain ontological thesis about the sense of being (*GA* 17, 260ff.).

Nevertheless, for Heidegger a major achievement of Husserl's *Logische Untersuchungen* was the determination of truth as *Evidenz* and fulfillment (Husserl 1984; see also *GA* 20, 34). Husserl's phenomenological elucidation of truth is nonpropositional; it depends on the intentional character of knowing. Yet Heidegger's criticism of Husserl is intended to transform and deepen phenomenology in order to radicalize it.[5] The need to radicalize phenomenology derives from the idea that, rightly understood as a foundational discipline, it is not different from the fundamental question posed by Plato and Aristotle (*GA* 20, 184). In Heidegger's view, phenomenological investigation is *the* method of philosophy understood as an investigation that moves within the horizon of ancient ontology and the task of philosophy ever since Plato.[6] We are convinced that Heidegger's interpretation of Plato is not disconnected from his comprehension of phenomenological investigation as a repetition of what phenomenological appearing means. Understanding and constituting phenomenology as "possibility" should make it possible to understand Greek thinking in a more genuine manner (cf. Brague 1984, 250). Phenomenological appearing, which must be uncovered, leads to the original, or even to the originary, locus of philosophy. For this reason, to maintain the principle of the possibility of phenomenology in order to grasp phenomenology as a possibility of Greek thought can be said to liberate it from any concrete historical context. In Heidegger's reading of Husserlian phenomenology, Plato is in the center of this task. For it is not so necessary to renew the philosophical tradition as it is to renew ourselves (*GA* 24, 142).

The Phenomenological Access to Plato

Heidegger recollects in "Mein Weg in die Phänomenologie" the impact of Brentano's book on Aristotle, which he was already reading as early as 1907.[7] Gadamer, Heidegger's student, calls attention to the importance of Aristotle (Gadamer 1983b, 71). Heidegger was apparently especially interested in Aristotle's critique of Plato's view of the relation of particular things to the forms, universals, or ideas. It has been well said that Heidegger never recovered from the impact of the Aristotelian opus. This encounter with Aristotle has implications that not only take us to the hidden background of *Being and Time*; they also point beyond this book toward the "turn" and his later, perhaps excessive, preoccupation with the problem of truth (cf. Kisiel 1993a, 227, 251). In our view, Heidegger's approach to the question of being and its intrinsic relation to the question of truth is clearly indebted to both Plato and Aristotle. For a long time Heidegger believed that the way toward Plato necessarily ran through Aristotle.

In his lectures on the *Sophist,* delivered in Marburg in 1924–25, Heidegger explains the need for a double approach in the interpretation of the Platonic dialogues. In his opinion, an adequate approach must be philosophical-phenomenological and historical-hermeneutical. To justify his selection of the texts—the *Sophist* and the *Philebus* (at the beginning of the *Sophist* lectures another course on the *Philebus* was announced, though it was never delivered)—he claims that in them we can find the meaning of such notions as "truth" and "appearance," "knowledge" and "opinion," "assertion" and "concept," "value" and "nonvalue." These notions must be considered in the light of the two basic concepts of being and non-being. Following the philosophical-phenomenological approach, Heidegger attemps to work out an appropriate orientation toward being and non-being, as well as toward truth and appearance. According to Heidegger, the task of phenomenology is "to make clear" any topic it handles (*GA* 19,

7). The principle of the historical-hermeneutical is to go "from the clear to the obscure." Its aim lies in appropriately grasping the past that faces us with Plato. For Heidegger, Plato is not someone alien to us, since "we are the past itself" (*GA* 19, 10, 8). As Heidegger understands it, the hermeneutical way from the clear to the obscure reverses the way from Aristotle to Plato. With Kant's famous comment in mind, Heidegger contends that Aristotle understood Plato better than he, Plato, understood himself and so well, indeed, as to justify this assumption as a philosophical presupposition.[8]

From this working premise, Heidegger uses the Aristotelian interpretation as a methodological guide toward the Platonic dialogues. His basic claim is that "there is *a continuity of radical questioning and searching*" (*GA* 19, 229) in the background of the history of philosophy. He states, moreover, that in interpreting Plato we need to analyze not only what the text says but also what it does not say, which also belongs to the task of letting the text itself speak from itself (*GA* 19, 228). Some years later, when he composed his essay on *Platos Lehre von der Wahrheit*, Heidegger gave up explicit use of his earlier Aristotelian interpretation of Plato. Or to put the same point in another way, he no longer felt compelled to follow the inverse road leading from Aristotle as the essential clue to Plato in order to let Plato's texts speak to us. But he continued to maintain and to make use of the methodological principle of emphasizing what is not said by the text as the main key to his discussion. The central problem for Heidegger is: Why did the Greeks name the truth as *a-lêtheia* as if something were lacking in it? Did the Greeks understand that unconcealment of the world had to be reached? According to Heidegger, the world is first disclosed and then is at once later covered up by speech. Philosophy therefore has the double task of unconcealment: not only to overcome the initial condition of ignorance but also to abolish the supposed concealment of language. That is the reason that it is only after the long, careful interpretation of Aristotle that Heidegger undertakes, in the second part of the *Sophist* lectures, the interpretation of Plato.

Heidegger's Elucidation of Truth

Heidegger's most basic claim is that truth has a primordial connection with being, hence the question about truth comes within the range of problems belonging to fundamental ontology. He notes that in the history of philosophy, being and truth "have been brought together, if not entirely identified" (*BT,* 183/228; cf. Pöggeler 1963, 88f.). In Platonic language, we could add that being is the light of the intelligible, and truth and goodness of being are no more than the appearing character of this light. Or, as Heidegger also stated in 1923, being precedes or grounds the *ratio veri et boni,* as properties that are immediately consecutive to the notion of being (*GA* 17, ch. 4, sec. 29–33). In *Being and Time* he mentions this theory with regard to the ontico-ontological priority of Dasein, which Heidegger finds anticipated in the Aristotelian thesis that "soul is, in a certain way, entities" (*BT,* 14/34). Roughly speaking, this general outline derives from the Platonic-Aristotelian tradition and makes Heidegger's approach an exception in theories of truth of contemporary philosophy (cf. Tugendhat 1969, 286).

To be more specific, Heidegger's question about truth is part of his project to reappropiate the originary experiences supposedly hidden in this question and, as he wrote some years later, to bring about "a change in the questioning" (*Wandel des Fragens;* cf. *Von Wesen der Wahrheit,* in *GA* 9, 202) that belongs to the overcoming of metaphysics. So we must go back to these originary experiences, the original Greek *logos* of the phenomenon and the essence of truth, which, according to Heidegger, was thought in the sense of *alêtheia,* more precisely "as a pre-philosophical way of understanding it" (*BT,* 219/262).

If that is correct, then the question about being could be briefly stated as follows: Is being a posited-being (*gesetzt-Sein*) as an intentional object, or is being *epekeina tês ousias,* as Plato suggests?[9] Heidegger's critical ambivalence toward Husserl leads him to redefine the crucial phenomenological conception of phenomenon. For Heidegger, it is a question of going back to being as being and, at the same time, going back to being as phenomenon (cf. Marion 1989, 91ff.). It is then a question of starting a way of thinking toward the truth of being, in which being and appearing must coincide (cf. Tugendhat 1970, 277). Fundamental ontology is directed toward recapturing the original sense of being, which is supposedly covered up or concealed by phenomenology. In other words, the question of being emerges precisely in what might be called the "hollow" of what, according to Heidegger, Husserlian phenomenology left unthought. Herein lies the fundamental task of drawing back behind the usual phenomenological theorizing (*GA* 17, 269): to recover that which relapses and gets covered up again.

Heidegger speaks about the character of being in these terms, since, in his opinion, it remains hidden, or shows itself only "in disguise" (*BT,* 35/59). The peculiar feature of phenomenality as Heidegger understands it is this entwining (or interweaving) of concealedness and unconcealment. The potential discoveredness of being is truth. As Heidegger puts it in his famous 1927 lecture course, the problem of the connection between being and truth is included within the problem of the truth-character of being (*Wahrheitscharakter des Seins; GA* 24, 25). One cannot overestimate the importance of this approach, which differs basically from more standard concepts of truth and knowledge. In Heidegger's ontological approach, the problem of truth is simply disconnected from the theory of knowledge as well as from the theory of judgment. In Heideger's opinion, the problem of truth belongs instead to metaphysics and the task of its destruction.

The need for this destruction points again methodologically to the task of going back to the primary sources of being's experience, where metaphysics emerged. And here Heidegger's interpretation of the problem of truth forges a close connection with Plato's approach to the main ontological problem, that is, going beyond the beings of experience to their essential cause(s) and source(s). In "Platons Lehre von der Wahrheit," Heidegger's methodological principle of directing his analysis to what remains unsaid by Plato acquires a hermeneutical meaning, which includes a displacement of the Kantian principle of understanding an author better than he understood himself. The question that arises here is: What does it mean to deal with what was left unsaid by Plato? Different answers are possible. One possible answer is that to deal with what Plato did not say means to take up what has not become "objectified" by predicative language. For this reason, the supposedly "unsaid" constitutes a primary source of truth, that is, truth before its unconcealment renders it object of a propositional content. To give attention only to what Plato said could amount to going back along the way covered since *Being and Time* or going back to the apophantic Logos ruling the theory of judgment, which had been definitively disassembled in previous writings. What is unsaid is as much true as the fact that the truth does not belong to the apophantic Logos but to metaphysics, as Aristotle himself explained, in spite of so many traditional interpretations (*GA* 31, 73–109; cf. also Berti 1997, 91f.). What is unsaid might even be truer since it remains free from the tension between appearance and appearing in a concrete linguistic formulation. If the essence of appearance (*Schein*) lies in the appearing (*erscheinen*), as Heidegger writes in *Einführung in die Metaphysik*,[10] then unconcealing is not just the innocent operation of unveiling what was hidden and expressing it in a philosophical language. It is rather the struggle against appearance in the domain of the appearing. Heidegger earlier claimed that an assertion can only be true in general or can only discover (*entdecken*), because it can also cover up (*verdecken; GA* 21, 135). In our view, the interpretation of what was unsaid by Plato is an ambivalent task, as ambivalent as it can be to think in a more originally Greek manner than the Greeks thought. Nevertheless, this aim is consistent with the increasing importance granted by Heidegger to "concealment" (*Verbergung;* Tugendhat 1970, 389f.).

Heidegger's Speleology of the Cave

As Heidegger ceases to understand Plato through Aristotle and, above all, as he changes his initial interpretation of *alêtheia* in relation to the disclosing comportment of Dasein and its understanding of being (*Seinsverständnis*), his interpretation of Plato gradually changes as well. When Heidegger again takes up the problem of truth in 1930 in "Vom Wesen der Wahrheit," his changing terminology points to a new position with regard to his previous approach. In fact, the traces of modern transcendental philosophy can still be found in the analytic of Dasein. More precisely, reading *Being and Time* now from the later perspective, we can appreciate in a certain sense an implicit epistemological character of truth inasmuch as it was referred to the disclosedness (*Erschlossenheit*) of Dasein. But it is evident that Heidegger had already sketched the project of a regress from truth to its ontological possibility. The new development of Heidegger's thought can be traced, as far as the question of truth is concerned, in the years between the lecture of 1930 and its final revised version published in 1943. This reorientation in no way constitutes an abandonment of his initial concerns (Gadamer 1987). But it marks a certain development of his original thinking about the general question of making the transition from *homoiôsis* to *alêtheia*. His essay on Plato is written with a similar orientation, with a view to rendering the accessibility to ontological truth explicit, a truth that in no sense could be described in terms of knowledge.

Once more Heidegger stresses the supposedly original privative meaning, that is, as truth that needs to be or has in fact actually been wrested from concealment. His interpretation of the cave analogy depends on the negative sense of the privative alpha of *a-lêtheia*. The passage from one domain to another as well as the differences between all of them are based on the various degrees of *alêthês* and the normative character attached to it ("PDT," in *GA* 9, 215–19). Heidegger seems to disregard the mythical context in which Plato poses the *lêthê/alêtheia* dichotomy, as well as the fact that it is typical for Plato to put forward philosophical theses by means of a mythical story. That happens in *Phaedrus*, when Plato explains how nondivine souls struggle in their circular journey finally to reach the plane of truth (*Phdr.*, 246a–48b6). Heidegger was surely aware of this explanation. He referred to the mythical narrative of *Phaedrus* some years earlier, when he called Plato "the discoverer of the a priori" (*Entdecker des Apriori; GA* 24, 463f.). He was thinking of the metaphysical import of the Platonic *anamnêsis* in relation to the contemplation of truth. Stress is placed on the link between *paideia* and truth at a time when Heidegger was much concerned about eliminating any trace of anthropologism in his conception of being. In the relationship of *paideia* to truth, nothing is said about the innermost temporality of being, a theme which in 1927 had been interpreted in the line of the *anamnêsis.* Instead, Heidegger insists upon the gradual and changing process of acquiring the ability to get accustomed to each stage. For in the development of this relationship through the four moments of the analogy, we understand Heidegger to mean that the movement only belongs to, or unfolds from, the process of getting free that enables the consummation of each transition. Yet the ultimate sense of this movement does not really express the internal structure of Platonic *paideia.* For the sense of the entire passage depends upon relations evoked by Heidegger between the words conveying the adjustment to each domain (*Umwendung* and *Zuwendung*).

If truth appears only at the end of the fourth moment, then Heidegger's interpretation divides truth from the dialectical acquisition of freedom throughout the successive moments of Plato's analogy. Truth is not compatible with the coming to presence of new realms of objects. It is also not compatible with becoming as such. It is perhaps worth noting that in the *Brief über den Humanismus* Heidegger refers to the new development of his thought in the decade of the 1930s as a "turn from Being and Time to Time and Being."[11] Perhaps we should say that it is within this conceptual framework that for Heidegger the allegory of the cave only has an essential relationship to truth as unconcealment with reference to the concealed ("PDT," in *GA* 9, 224). The phenomenological destruction imposed on Plato's text can explain, to a certain extent, that if the essence of truth were understood (by Heidegger) differently, then the cave metaphor could not be applied to it.

In our view, the Platonic theory of truth in *Republic* book 7 not only offers a certain conception of truth but contains as well a cluster of presuppositions giving support to the connection between being, truth, and good. Among these presuppositions is the awareness of the limits in gaining access to truth and the correlative need to pose hypotheses. Plato made clear in the image of the Line that the intelligible realm, which is the realm of knowledge, starts with hypotheses, some of which can be "destroyed" or "confirmed" as knowledge advances (*R.,* 510b–11e, 533b-d). The concept of hypothesis is linked to the purpose of giving a positive answer to the problem of the beginning, or the "real" philosophical problem, as Hegel said. In Plato, the fundamental hypothesis is the initial presupposition of the Idea, which could eventually lead to genuine knowledge, that is, *noêsis.* Thus, speaking about Ideas entails confirmation of *some* hypotheses, but only by way of analogy.

Heidegger's approach is different from Plato's. He seems to leave aside the implicit skepticism involved in the need for posing hypotheses and opts instead for something like a metaphysical approach when he offers the following metanarrative: "Truth no longer is, as unhiddenness, the basic feature of being itself, but it is, in consequence of having become correctness by being yoked under the Idea, from this time forth the label for recognizing of beings . . ."[12] Herein lies an example of the interrelation between philosophical discourse and rhetoric in Heidegger's essay on Plato. The hypothesis of the highest Idea enables Plato to give meaning to the existence of an ultimate source of truth, which can be no more than Good, and in a sense to traverse the road toward it. Certainly, Plato does not explain what he has in mind in writing that "it is Good which gives the things we know their truth and makes it possible for people to have knowledge" (*R., 508e1f.*) either within the allegory of the cave or elsewhere in the *Republic*. On the contrary, he proposes rather "that we forget about trying to define Good itself for the time being" (*R., 506d8f.*). It follows that the question remains unanswered or at least not explicitly answered in Plato's dialogue. Heidegger's main concern seems to be, by contrast, the thinking of Good within the frame of a fundamental ontology, hence Good not as a value or as an Idea.

For Heidegger, Good cannot be a value inasmuch as that would fall within the anthropological interpretations he rejects. But, then, Good can also not function as what gives value or validity to things. For pragmatism is not a possible solution to anthropocentrism to the extent that both belong to the same context of interpretation. In Plato, nevertheless, Good only functions as a possible ethical model because it is above all an ontological model. It stands as model for the universe or cosmos, so it can also function within the moral and political life of men. Ontologically considered, Good is the cause and source of truth and of the enduring reality of Forms. In other words, the solutions to the problem of morality and to the problem of knowledge go together. Wisdom does not consist only in knowing what it is but in acting in accordance with the ultimate validity of the order which encompasses man, the community and the cosmos. Heidegger's analysis seems to follow a different path when he points to the problem of how an ontological conception of truth related to an axiological interpretation of the Good can supposedly open the road to the conformity between objects which possess the property of being good and the mind that determines or discovers it.

Conclusion: Heidegger and the Sense of Metaphysics

The changes over time in Heidegger's different interpretations of Plato can perhaps be attributed to variations in his understanding of the originary experience of truth in the early Greeks as well as the meaning attached to *alêtheia*. Between 1930 and 1946, he undertook the task of recovering a new approach to the philosophical past, in what would later result as his own highly original, idiosyncratic, and, if we remember that his own theories derive from it, his very fruitful understanding of "metaphysics." The main features of this endeavor are outlined in the lecture course of 1935, *Introduction to Metaphysics,* which in part marks the high point of the initial program of *Being and Time* but also continues the historical research started before his major work of 1927. One of the consequences of his later historical research is "Platonslehre von der Wahrheit," where Heidegger puts in practice a specific reduction of philosophy to metaphysics. His particular way of understanding Plato is only partially expounded in this essay. It is further expounded in other courses and writings in the following years, some of them published as *Nietzsche I* and *Nietzsche II.* These two volumes open a new way toward a conception of metaphysics that has little resemblance with any past historical figure. It is a figure of metaphysics that includes on one and the same level Nietzsche and Plato, Descartes and Hegel.

The ambiguity of Heidegger's conceptions of phenomenological method and fundamental ontology becomes evident in his "Platonslehre." In this essay, his view of the outermost possibility of phenomenology is clearly visible. And, since opposite extremes sometimes overlap, it can be appreciated how efficient the principle that meaning is use can be in Heidegger's language. The possibility of knowledge is an intrinsic part of Plato's allegory of the cave. It is introduced in a concrete context of the dialogue and is meant to fit in with the preceding image of the Line. The emphasis on reorienting the mind in principle allows not only for gradual liberation from one domain to another but also for grasping the paradigmatic role of Forms. Plato suggests that the capacity for knowledge is realized in a direct grasp of reality, more precisely ultimately in a grasp of the reality of the supreme Idea. For Heidegger, on the contrary, the possibility of knowledge is not explicitly taken into account within the scope of his analysis. He rather puts into question the tautological bond between truth and knowledge. In this way, he marks that bond as one that even Nietzsche has in common with Plato and the history of Platonism (cf. Sallis 1994). On the other hand, unconcealment is never defined in a way which allows us to distinguish between truth and untruth. The unconcealed does not establish the conditions for a concrete phenomenon to be seen as true. It rather establishes the conditions for a phenomenon to be either true or nontrue. But the possibility of phenomenology leaves open the way for a *retractatio* and for a change of metaphysical language. Thus, in the process of developing a nonrepresentational model of truth—which is intended as neither Aristotelian nor Platonic—Heidegger reshapes his thinking of the cave metaphor. His peculiar relationship to the history of philosophy and the epistemological tradition belonging to it are made clear in his evolving position toward Plato. For neither is independent of the evolution of, and both depend on, Heidegger's interpretation of thinking (*Denken*) as distinct from philosophizing.

Notes

The phrase *Amicus Plato magis amica veritas* is taken from Husserl's handwritten note under the title of his copy of *Being and Time*. Cf. Husserl 1989, 11.

1. I. Kant, *Kritik der reinen Vernunft*, A314/B370; translation taken from Kant 1996, 362.

2. *GA* 25, 3: "Ich merke nur an, dass es gar nichts Ungewöhnliches sei, sowohl im gemeinen Gespräche, als in Schriften, durch die Vergleichung der Gedanken, welche ein Verfasser über seinen Gegenstand äussert, ihn sogar besser zu verstehen, als er sich selbst verstand . . ."

3. *BT*, sec. 1, 2; translations from *BT* in this essay are from M. Heidegger, *Being and Time*, trans. J. Macquire and E. Robinson (Oxford: Blackwell, 1992).

4. Cf. *GA* 6.1, 447f., 486f. A different interpretation of Descartes occurs in *GA* 17, 114ff., 254ff.

5. Cf. Marion 1989; Courtine 1990; Dahlstrom 1994, 231–44.

6. "Es gibt keine Ontologie *neben* einer Phänomenologie, sondern *wissenschaftliche Ontologie ist nichts anderes als Phänomenologie*" (*GA* 20, 98; cf. 109, 179, 186, 190).

7. M. Heidegger, "Mein Weg in die Phänomenologie," in *Zur Sache des Denkens* (Tübingen, 1969), 81.

8. *GA* 19, 11: "Wir machen die Voraussetzung, dass Aristoteles Plato verstanden hat." For the changes in Heidegger's interpretation of Aristotle, see Van Buren 1994b, 220ff.

9. Cf. *R.*, 509b9. In *Grundprobleme der Phänomenologie* (1927), Heidegger meant to find in Plato's *epekeina tês ousias* Dasein's transcendance (cf. *GA* 24, 436).

10. M. Heidegger, *Einführung in die Metaphysik* (Tübingen: Niemeyer, 1953), 76.

11. M. Heidegger, *Über den Humanismus* (Frankfurt am Main: V. Klostermann, 1991), 19. The expression of this change, as "work in progress," is *Vom Wesen der Wahrheit*.

12. M. Heidegger, "Plato's Doctrine of Truth," in *Philosophy in the Twentieth Century*, ed. W. Barret and H. Aiken (New York: Random House, 1962), 265.

Heidegger on Truth and Being

Joseph Margolis

There is hardly a topic on which philosophers have spawned more non-sense than the analysis of the nature and meaning of truth. Indeed, the twentieth century has spent an inordinate amount of capital on the ques-tion, much of it tendentious and utterly pointless. It literally lost its way among both analytic and continental theorists, who of course implacably opposed one another's answers.[1] Analysts, on the whole, favor a semantic account of the use of "true" confined to propositional contexts, notably with regard to the work of the natural sciences; nevertheless, they do not usually examine the relationship between, say, language and praxis (or action) where the deeper issues seem to lie.[2] Continental thinkers, by con-trast, fault the propositional doctrine as misguided and superficial, pos-sibly even dangerous to the well-being of humanity! Certainly, Heidegger was obsessed with the latter prospect.

The propositional orientation of the analysts has always been and still is overwhelmingly supported by mainstream Western philosophy run-ning, in great profusion, from Plato and Aristotle down the centuries to the deliberately thin views of figures like Russell and Carnap and Wittgen-stein and Tarski and Quine and Davidson. By contrast, daunting though it may be, the most sustained challenge in our time to the entire proposi-tional account is to be found in the work of very nearly one figure, Martin Heidegger, who claims that Western philosophy has wandered (indeed, has "erred") from the original vision of the pre-Socratics! Yet, what, mo-mentously, the pre-Socratics discerned twenty-five hundred years ago—which Heidegger seems to have "rescued" from complete "oblivion"—re-mains as murky as before.

Both lines of theorizing have captured a disjoint strand of the entire analysis wanted, and each has pursued its exclusionary inquiry in such a way as to have finally arrived at a preposterous cul-de-sac.

Heidegger managed to convince an immense cohort of loyal professionals, who, in a matter of a few generations, made it well-nigh impossible to avoid comparing his claims with those that still dominate the mainstream tendency. There is a distinctly Hesiodic archaism in Heidegger's opposition to the modern or modernist commitments of the world, which, without invoking questionable genealogies, worrisomely recalls Heidegger's dreadful mistakes linking the political and the ontological. Fear of the *Gestell* and the "new age" are perhaps still palpable, but can they rightly account for the persistence of Heidegger's claims beyond his own lifetime?[3] I think not.

I confine myself, therefore, to assessing Heidegger's essential argument, though not solely by textual means. The reason is a triple one: first, because Heidegger's principal texts bearing on Parmenides and Plato feature certain provocative readings of *their* texts which cannot, by themselves, sustain *Heidegger's* theory of truth; second, because the opposed theories of truth that Heidegger distinguishes (roughly) as the "propositional" (or "orthotic") and the "alethic" cannot stand as independent theories, though as far as I know, Heidegger nowhere addresses the need to bring them into accord; and, third, because, strange to say, there is as yet *no* well-formed line of reasoning that yields a compelling and unified account.

The corrective I have in mind is modest enough. I argue that the central use of "true" fitted in an undistorted way to the whole of the Western tradition is surely its *realist* intent. Needless to say, both Heidegger and the analysts attempt to escape that particular stricture: the analysts, by falling back to "semantic analysis"; Heidegger, by probing more deeply in the direction of the "truth of Being." To be perfectly candid, both maneuvers fail for the same reason. I don't deny that "realist" is a disputed notion; I also have no wish to trade on my own metaphysical bias in advancing the point. But I have no doubt at all that the "realist intent" of "true" *can* be specified in a perfectly straightforward way that leaves entirely open the full space of philosophical quarrel regarding what, finally, to adopt as the "best" possible realist formula. I will come to that formulation shortly. For the moment, I emphasize only the constraint and the dearth of suitably ramified answers.

The analysts, for instance, have tended to restrict their accounts to very narrow semantic concerns, so that the epistemological and metaphysical aspects of a realist account of truth, even when narrowly addressed to the propositional issue, are shortsightedly subverted.[4] For the record, though I am concerned here primarily with Heidegger's analysis, let me mention the analytic and postmodernist theories, respectively, of Donald Davidson and Richard Rorty to clinch the point. The analysts wrongly suppose they need not provide a robust account of epistemology or metaphysics—or, indeed, the human condition itself—however skewed their view of the functional adequacy of propositional practices may be. What, by contrast, is meant by the right analysis of "Being and thought"—viewed from the side of those who, like Heidegger, favor what, for the time being, I am loosely calling the alethic account of truth as opposed to the propositional—will include cognitive and ontological questions very different from whatever analytic epistemologies and metaphysics may dictate to the propositionalists. That is certainly Heidegger's conviction, which I am prepared to honor (though not, finally, to support) in what follows. One might even construe Heidegger's corrective as something other than the epistemological: possibly, for instance, the insertion of the "ethical" in a sense not altogether distant from the line of reasoning Emmanuel Levinas features—in which the ethical somehow precedes the epistemological and metaphysical. I shall not argue the point, but Levinas's view is demonstrably incoherent. I would not say that Heidegger's thesis is incoherent; but, finally, it may prove illegible.

Heideggereans will remind us that "realism" is itself a code word for the dangerous "calculative" or "technological" orientation of the propositionalists who oppose the partisans of *alêtheia*. But they do not reckon, say, with the textual evidence that confirms the reasonableness of reading Parmenides himself—Heidegger's principal pre-Socratic ally—as a realist about Being! (I shall return to that quarrel.)

In any case, *if* the theory of truth cannot fail to convey a realist intent, then it also cannot fail to admit the inextricable union of any pertinent *non*propositional ingredient with whatever contributions the propositional side of truth requires. Contemporary analysts almost never do justice to the kind of nonpropositional features Heidegger has in mind or, more surprisingly, to what the classic tradition has always favored—running from Plato and Aristotle to, say, Descartes, Kant, and Hegel, down to the extreme views of late twentieth-century analytic philosophy—which of course Heidegger condemns almost as an unsorted heap as more than dangerously one-sided. In short, I deny that Heidegger could possibly be right in insisting on the conceptual *priority* of the alethic over the propositional, *for the same reason* I reject the priority of the propositionalist approach. They are both seriously mistaken and one-sided, though for very different reasons. That is the brief I am prepared to defend: a plague (I say) on both sides.

Nearly all discussions of Heidegger's theory of truth regard his account of the supposed "transformation" in Plato's theory of truth—centered in the "myth of the cave" in book 7 of the *Republic*—as one of the decisive foci (if not the supporting rationale) for his own theory: also, indeed, for his attack on the tradition of "metaphysics" itself beginning with Plato and extending to Nietzsche's seeming subversion of the whole of Western metaphysics, down to his attack on the "technological" or "cybernetic" or "calculative" character of the entire modern world. I must say that Heidegger's little essay, "Plato's Doctrine of Truth," is an astonishing tour de force, surely one of the most brilliant and arresting of all his brief papers, without which, as far as I can see, nearly everything else he has written on the question of truth may simply lack a commanding sense of the grounding argument he champions. For example, the text of the lecture course from 1942 to 1943, published as *Parmenides,* seems, when *not* read in close accord with the essay on Plato, hardly more than bombast. Recovered within the terms of the Plato essay, however, the *Parmenides* text begins to soften into some semblance of hermeneutical plausibility (more, to my mind, regarding Heidegger's purpose than Parmenides's). Frankly, Heidegger has shown us how to read Parmenides as a precocious Heideggerean. But it cannot persuade us unless Heidegger himself can be read as a stalwart Parmenidean!

There remains a palpable philosophical gap, nevertheless, between what Heidegger "recovers" from Parmenides' poem and what he owes us in the way of *a validating argument* for his own doctrine, *not* merely the dictum he advances or advocates in Parmenides' name. "Dictum," you realize, is Heidegger's careful term for the inclusive, authoritative pronouncements of the "pre-Socratics" which he reclaims. "Pre-Socratic" remains a misnomer of sorts, since its general use implicitly concedes the improvement of the pre-Socratics' discoveries through Plato's "transformation"; whereas Heidegger's intention is to reverse utterly any such judgment:

> We will therefore [Heidegger warns, in the Parmenides seminar,] henceforth call the primordial word of Anaximander, of Parmenides, and of Heraclitus the dictum of these thinkers. We mean by their "dictum" the whole of their utterances, not just single propositions and enunciations. In order to give tradition its due, however, we shall still speak at first of the "didactic poem" of Parmenides. (*GA* 54, 4/3)

Heidegger offers a philosophical promise here. He prepares the conceptual ground for the essential contrast between Parmenides' original dictum and the "abstract" "didactic" content Plato elicits from what is known of Parmenides' views. But you must bear in mind that, broadly speaking, we *have* the "whole" of Plato's discussion, and we can never have the "whole" of Parmenides' poem. This yields at once the sense in which the hermeneutical purpose of Heidegger's analysis *can* only function as a carefully prepared piece of theater *for introducing Heidegger's own dictum and philosophical rationale*—or, against all odds, as a philosophical challenge in favor of a fresh reading of Parmenides' dictum if and only if Heidegger is able to provide its rationale. But *you must decide* whether Heidegger ever really intends to advance such an argument—or ever does. I confess I don't find the *argument;* I do find the *dictum.*

I think it fair to say, without suspicion of prejudice, that, apart from the essays collected in *Wegmarken* (*GA* 9), which includes the Plato piece, all the essays collected in *The Question Concerning Technology and Other Essays, What Is Called Thinking?* (particularly part 2), and *Basic Writings* (particularly "The End of Philosophy and the Task of Thinking" [1966]) would show that Heidegger expressly denies that he and the pre-Socratics *ever* meant to advance a metaphysics or epistemology *in Plato's or the post-Platonic sense.*

That kind of metaphysics, he explains, could never be what philosophical "thinking" finally signifies—in Parmenides' time or (more urgently) in ours. You see this very clearly in the adventurous "interpretation" of the most central and provocative of Parmenides' sentences, which Heidegger brings to bear against both Kant's and Hegel's theories (in what he takes to be his own *and* Parmenides' sense) and which (taken from fragment 8) reads as follows:

> For it is the same thing to think and to be.

Here, Heidegger fiddles with the phrase *to auto* ("the same"), *which he must at all costs replace,* offering instead the term *homoion* ("identical," that is, "similar," *not* "the same"). "Indeed," Heidegger asks, "how can thinking and being ever be identical [that is, the same]? They are precisely what is different: presence of what is present, and taking-to-heart."[5] In context, this contention is meant to confirm that to understand Parmenides' "whole" dictum is to understand that it is *not* captured by propositional claims at all! In proclaiming that "it is" (*that* "Being is"), Parmenides, Heidegger advises, "speaks neither of the 'existence' nor of the 'essence' of being" (*WCT,* 2:5, 172):

> But in the meantime we have learned to see [Heidegger reassures us, bringing the lectures to a close] that the essential nature of thinking is determined by what there is to be thought about: the presence of what is present, the Being of beings. Thinking is thinking only when it *recalls* in thought [what is] unspoken, tacitly [recalled]. And that is the duality of beings and Being. (*WCT,* 2:11, 244)

(Heidegger regularly slights what Parmenides says about the One, which *is,* after all, a "metaphysics" of the propositional sort.)

Elsewhere he adds: "Thinking is the most precursory of all precursory activities," by which he means to forestall the reduction of genuinely philosophical "thinking" to that kind of thought that favors the propositional sense of truth; hence his words expose the false impression he is bent on combating, that is, that philosophical "thinking" betrays a certain "weakness" of its own, since it "fails" to meet the fashionable opinion of "our era" that favors the hegemony of calculative reason. If we grasp all that aright, it will do no harm to admit (with Heidegger) that:

1. Thinking [in the sense Heidegger privileges] does not bring knowledge as do the sciences.
2. Thinking does not produce usable practical wisdom.
3. Thinking solves no cosmic riddles.
4. Thinking does not endow us directly with the power to act. (*WCT,* 2:11, 244)

As a consequence, Heidegger will claim (in "Plato's Theory of Truth") that Plato himself is responsible for the essential misstep that ushers in the great decline that we now know as metaphysics! Fantastic argument. Yet beware: for *we really don't know what all this means, and are never told*!

Everything Heidegger says here is admirably clear, except for the niggling fact that *he* must finally explain why it is that Parmenides does *not* and could never rightly maintain that thought and Being are "the same" (*auto*), or why Parmenides never really speaks of the existence or essence of Being though he seems to have done both! In any event, the question cannot be merely philological or hermeneutical: Heidegger obviously holds that there is some very deep philosophical barrier against the apparent identity. Is that a contradiction of the "precursory" nature of thinking, or is it the philosophical fruit of actually "thinking"? How does Heidegger know? Can he explain it convincingly to *us*? There's a dilemma there that exposes the inevitable vacuity of Heidegger's instruction.

Why, for instance—apart from Heidegger's say-so, speaking in his own and Parmenides' behalf—couldn't metaphysics and propositional truth *be* an appropriate continuation of "thinking" (in Parmenides' sense, if not in his own) proceeding *through* Plato *down* to our own day? I don't see the argument, though of course we have the dictum. Isn't Parmenides advancing some metaphysical claims—propositional truths, if you please—when he explicates the supposed dictum "What It Is" in fragment 8:

Being has no coming-into-being and no destruction; for it is whole of limb, without motion, and without end. And it never Was, nor Will Be, because it Is now, a Whole all together, One, continuous; for what creation of it will you look for? (Freeman 1948, 43)

I don't see how any of Parmenides' passages *can* be enough to advise us of what is "lost" (overcome by "oblivion"), if Heidegger cannot tell us how to recover what is missing. On Heidegger's advice, I make the effort to *think of* the "difference" between Being and beings and *I find nothing there* besides a purely verbal distinction! (It's a bit like being unaware of being in original sin and never quite knowing how to find out whether it's really true or not.) Nevertheless, *from* Heidegger's privileged vantage, we are given at least two philosophical corrections (the ones just mentioned), which, if valid, would—must—make sense within our fallen metaphysics. (After all, Heidegger *is* addressing us!)

But there's more that Heidegger claims about Parmenides' teaching—and there's more that we might claim (as Aristotle does) about the doubtfulness of Parmenides' doctrine. I hesitate to say . . . "Parmenides' metaphysics," but that is what it comes to. Well, I no longer know whether I'm deceiving myself in confessing not to have grasped Heidegger's distinction regarding "the duality of beings and Being." That, presumably, is the secret Heidegger has penetrated. I understand it verbally all right—up to a point—but I don't know what I've grasped! It is the decisive theme, I'm convinced, of the whole of the "later" Heidegger's account of Plato's theory of truth, which, I'm also convinced, holds the key to the entire mystery of the *Kehre*. We had better have the text in hand:

> Why and in what way is thinking directed and called into its own essential nature by the Being of beings? [That is Heidegger's supreme question.] *That* it is so, Parmenides states unequivocally in fragments 5 and 8, 34/36 [i.e., in the sentence we have already read: "For it is the same thing to think and to be"; and in another: "for not separately from the presence of what is present can you find out the taking-to-heart"]. Parmenides, it is true, does not speak of the call. However, he does say: in the presence of what is present there speaks the call that calls us into thinking, the call that calls thinking into its own nature in this way, that it directs *noein* [thinking] into *einai* [Being]. (*WCT,* 2:11, 242)

The clue, if that is what it is, is simply this: that, prior to language, prior to "languaged" thought, the "primordial" thinking Heidegger features and claims Parmenides is explaining is "*called*" into play by Being itself—"present" as the "Being of beings." This means that thinking (the "thinking" that is *not* yet propositional) is first "called" into play by the "presence" of Being. (That *is* indeed what Heidegger means by the *Kehre*. But what does it finally mean?) It is said to be what metaphysics "forgets." Well, perhaps. But the same fragment 8 goes on to make its own "propositional" claims about Being (cited in the foregoing extract), which, at the very least, *is inseparable from the other.* There you have a very real possibility

Heidegger nowhere broaches, unless to insist on the priority of the "alethic" conception of the truth of Being over the "propositional." But the text does not support any such disjunction.

I venture a leap here. Plato goes wrong (according to Heidegger)— and in going wrong begins the descent into the whole of Western metaphysics—by "transforming" the alethic conception of truth (which has yet to be explained) by the propositional account. That means that there is a deep "thinking," deeper than language, that is called into play by encountering the Being of beings, which then informs (and itself calls into play) our discourse about plural beings (*Seiende*). I confess I cannot see how the distinction between "Being" and "beings" is not a mere artifact of language read back into the analysis of "what is." There is no separation in Parmenides: *there couldn't be,* if we accept the "metaphysical" reading of the "One." That affords at least one clear source of deception in Heidegger's "later" thought.

It's in this same passage, in *What Is Called Thinking?* that Heidegger draws out his devilishly clever exposé of Kant and Hegel. He takes both Kant and Hegel to be offering one or another "variation of Parmenides' statement," per the oblivion of the Being of beings. He cites, from Kant's First *Critique* (A158/B197) the following: "The conditions of the possibility of experience in general are at the same time conditions of the possibility of the objects of experience," and expressly notes that the expression "'at the same time' is Kant's [own] interpretation of *to auto,* 'the same,'" the expression Heidegger frets over (the expression in Parmenides). (Fabulous argument!) Heidegger then goes on to remark that Hegel "transposes and transmutes Kant's principle into the Absolute, when he says in the Preface to the *Phenomenology* 'that "Being is Thinking,"'" which of course subsumes Hegel (like Kant) under the distinct lessons Heidegger assigns to a reading of Plato and Parmenides (*WCT,* 2:11, 243).

Both the *Parmenides* and the piece on Plato's theory of truth are primarily philological and hermeneutical exercises—that is, inadequate for our needs. They do have philosophical pretensions, I admit. But neither, as far as I can see, advances compelling philosophical arguments *for the theory of truth* Heidegger plainly favors in his close examination of Parmenides' and Plato's views. I cannot judge Heidegger's philological expertise, though I am impressed (I admit) by the testimony that appears to confirm the increasingly strengthened reception of Heidegger's reading of *The Republic* among the philologists (see, e.g., the summary in Bernasconi 1985, ch. 2). On the hermeneutical side, I find that Heidegger's ingenuity cuts both ways: Heidegger seems to have uncovered (on his own say-so) what remains hidden from the modern world, what the history of metaphysics has made us "oblivious" of. That is the point, apparently, of the conclusion of the essay on Plato's theory of truth:

> The story recounted in the "allegory of the cave" provides [Heidegger says] a glimpse of what is really happening in the history of Western humanity, both now and in the future. Taking the essence of truth as the correctness of the representation, one thinks of all beings according to "ideas" and evaluates all reality according to "values." That which alone and first of all is decisive is not which ideas and which values are posited, but rather the fact that the real is interpreted according to "ideas" at all, that the "world" is weighted according to "ideas" at all.
>
> Meanwhile we have recollected the original essence of truth. [Notice the idiom: How have we penetrated the "oblivion"?] Unhiddenness reveals itself to this recollection as the fundamental trait of beings themselves. Nonetheless, recollection of the original essence of truth must think this essence more originally. Therefore, such recollection can never take over unhiddenness merely in Plato's sense, namely, as yoked under the *idea.* . . . What is first required is an appreciation of the "positive" in the "privative" essence of *alêtheia.* The positive must first be experienced as the fundamental trait of being itself. . . . Because this exigency stands before us, the original essence of truth still lies in its hidden origin. ("PDT," 182)

(You must ask yourself here: What kind of investigation, what kind of "thinking," is Heidegger pursuing? Can it be taught?) The explication offered in the *Parmenides* more than confirms how risky Heidegger's hermeneutics is. Heidegger scrupulously challenges the reliability of his own penetration of the pre-Socratic ontology. And so he should! Yet, at the most telling moment, he also brings his analysis of Parmenides' poem under the lesson of his reading of Plato's allegory of the cave, which, of course, "transforms" a philological analysis into a supposedly authoritative clue about the Parmenidean ontology (see for instance *GA* 54, the second part). But surely the hermeneutical judgment cannot be more than a draft of *Heidegger's* own ontology cast in the form of what he calls *a dictum,* which is to say, a philosophy affirmed but not demonstrated— a doctrine that cannot possibly be demonstrated.

We are still dealing with preliminaries here. Yet, certain conclusions seem unavoidable. For one thing, *if,* as seems obvious, the most salient and rigorous part of the treatment of the ontological question in the *Parmenides,* in part 2 of *What Is Called Thinking?* and in "Plato's Doctrine of Truth" is chiefly philological or hermeneutical, then the textual analysis could not possibly establish the remarkable philosophical claim that is being advanced. It certainly conveys the double thesis of Heidegger's own "dictum": namely, the "duality of Being and beings" and the oblivion that has eclipsed memory with the advent of Western metaphysics. At best, there is next to nothing in these texts that could reasonably count ("methodologically") as supporting Heidegger's "dictum."

I trust I may take a page from Heidegger's own challenge to the adequacy of Hegel's account of "science" offered in the *Phenomenology*—which, without adjustment, applies by analogy (and with equal force) to the "dictum" so cleverly advanced in "Plato's Doctrine of Truth." Ponder the force of the following passage, for instance, which reports no more than what Hegel himself affirms:

> It is incumbent upon science alone [this is Heidegger speaking in Hegel's behalf] to establish the meaning of the words "the Absolute," "knowledge," "truth," "objective," and "subjective." To do so, however, science must have entered from its very start into the *parousia* of the Absolute—it must be with its absoluteness. Else it would not be science. If this is right, then it is against the very nature of science even to become involved with any doubts and considerations that remain outside the realm and beneath the level of truth. If science thus keeps clear of unfitting critical doubts, it will nonetheless remain under the suspicion that it asserts itself absolutely as absolute knowledge, but fails to produce its credentials. It thus violates most flagrantly that very claim of certainty which it pretends to meet to pure perfection.[6]

One need hardly agree with Heidegger's critique to agree with the justice of insisting that Hegel produce the requisite "credentials." Yet I find no evidence that *Heidegger* obeys his own scruple. *In* the sense in which he speaks of "beings" in metaphysical terms answering to ordinary discourse, Heidegger produces no "credentials" that show the "truth" (or the plausibility) of holding to the duality of Being and beings. I see no "oblivion" there—among those who understand perfectly well what Heidegger is driving at!

Second, if you turn back to the passage cited from the essay on Plato's theory of truth, you will not fail to notice that, in what amounts to the distinction between the "propositional" account of truth (correspondence, *orthotês:* "correctness of representation") and the "alethic" account ("unhiddenness" of Being), the first is treated relationally and the second is not—it is (rather) assigned primarily to Being itself (to the very "Being of beings") to which the deeper kind of "thinking" responds, to Being *alone.* Now, *that* calls for supporting "credentials" *and,* in doing so, affords a toehold for Heidegger's opponents.

To advance the argument efficiently from here, I now suggest, however, an unlikely detour and a recapitulation.

Heidegger claims to have wrested a "forgotten" truth from the pre-Socratics—preeminently from Parmenides: namely, that of the duality of Being and beings and the oblivion of Being itself (the oblivion of the "Being of beings"), which he pointedly takes note of in his account of Plato's "transformation" of the meaning (or essence) of truth. This allegedly marks the beginning of the decline (and resultant danger) that *is* the very tradition we call metaphysics, which courses down to our own time and has now overtaken us in what—in one of Heidegger's most successful essays, "The Age of the World Picture"—signifies the triumph of metaphysics restricted to the methodology of science ("the world picture"), the primacy of the propositional over the alethic, the rise of the "subjective" role of the human as the originating "measure" of Being (*metron*, as Protagoras has it) over the alethic, the loss therefore of the pre-Socratic ontology that features the "call" to "thinking" to conform to the "presence" of Being itself, and the growing hegemony of the *metaphysical* "world picture" that humans *construct* according to their "idea" of (*their*) representing "What Is." (Heidegger's rhetoric is almost unbearable here.)

There is, however, no convincing evidence that Parmenides favors anything like Heidegger's notion of the "duality of Being and beings." On the contrary, Parmenides appears to be claiming that "What Is" not only *is*, but is, necessarily and changelessly, One. He is obviously asserting what he takes to be propositionally and metaphysically true. If so, then Parmenides cannot be said to support Heidegger's "dictum," for he himself rightly stands at the head of the metaphysical tradition! And if that is so, then Plato's theory of truth *cannot* be the "transformation" Heidegger alleges it is. More likely, it is a perfectly respectable further step in a declension of metaphysics initiated by Parmenides himself, colored by the bold contrast between the views of Parmenides and Heraclitus at least. Furthermore, it is precisely the logic of Parmenides' conflating What Is (Being) and what exists without change (Being)—in effect, what must be indivisibly One—that Aristotle corrects in order to "save" the Being of the changing world we know. *Not Being*, we may say (that is, *Nothing*, in Parmenides' sense), is hardly the same as *Non-Being* (the power, in things, to undergo change): that is Aristotle's contribution. *If* Parmenides may be rightly "corrected" here—and why should he not?—then Heidegger must be completely mistaken.

Keep in mind the beginning of Parmenides' poem and ask yourself whether it actually affirms, or lends itself to affirming, what Heidegger imputes:

> Come now [the goddess who instructs Parmenides begins], and I will tell
> you (and you must carry my account away with you when you have heard
> it) the only ways of enquiry that are to be thought of. The one, that [it]
> is and that it is impossible for [it] not to be, is the path of Persuasion
> (for she attends upon Truth); the other, that [it] is not and that it is
> needful that [it] not be, that I declare to you is an altogether indiscern-
> ible track: for you could not know what is not—that cannot be done—
> nor indicate it.
>
> What is there to be said and thought must needs be, for it is there
> for being, but nothing is not.[7]

I see no way of denying that a strong "propositional" sense of truth is operating here, a sense that affirms what Heidegger says Parmenides never
affirms (regarding the essence and existence of Being) and that also justifies Aristotle's well-known distinction between there being nothing at all
and there being something that changes.[8]

I take this to expose what has gone dreadfully awry in Heidegger's
analysis of Parmenides' "dictum." Heidegger plainly believes he has shown
us just how Parmenides' intuition was so completely and misguidedly re-
versed—because of Plato's mediation—by the time we reach our "new
age," the "age of the world picture":

> That which is [Heidegger affirms] does not come into being at all
> through the fact that man first looks upon it, in the sense of a represent-
> ing that has the character of subjective perception. Rather, man is the
> one who is looked upon by that which is; he is the one who is—in com-
> pany with itself—gathered toward presencing, by that which opens itself.
> To be beheld by what is, to be included and maintained with its open-
> ness and in that way to be borne along by it, to be driven about by its
> oppositions and marked by its discord—that is the essence of man in the
> great age of the Greeks. . . . Greek man is as the one who apprehends
> [der Vernehmer] that which is, and this is why in the age of the Greeks the
> world cannot become picture. Yet, on the other hand, that the beingness
> of whatever is, is defined for Plato as eidos [aspect, view] is the presuppo-
> sition, destined far in advance and long ruling indirectly in concealment,
> for the world's having to become picture.[9]

Either Heidegger must mean that Parmenides is right (by way of alêtheia:
unconcealment) in denying the reality of what may change as well as
Being's being indissolubly One, or Aristotle is right in holding that Parmenides is wrong to deny change. In either case, Heidegger cannot justify
his own reading: He cannot consistently disjoin the alethic and proposi-

tional senses of truth and he cannot assign any prior privilege to *alêtheia* free of propositional challenge.

You see how Heidegger bends the sense of fragment 8 and ignores Parmenides' "propositional" claims. Parmenides—and therefore Plato—is made to yield to an alien ontology. Heidegger is evidently older than the pre-Socratics! More than that, you glimpse here the essential nerve of Heidegger's fantastic campaign to undermine the achievement of both Kant and Hegel: *They* have obviously "forgotten" the Being of beings. That is the point of the tortured phrasing, "To be beheld by what is . . .": It obviates at a stroke the entire language of subjective representations (*Vorstellungen*) and subjective presentations (*Erscheinungen*). Brilliant, no doubt, but surely crazy.

What, after all, is it to be "beheld" or "called" by Being? It's no more than a mesmerizing word for some instant magic. If you see all this, you see as well the sense in which Aristotle's famous account of truth, precisely because of its being an informative tautology, fits (without the least adjustment) the work of the entire philosophical company, including Parmenides, Protagoras, Plato, Aristotle, the medievals, Descartes, Kant, Hegel, Nietzsche, and Heidegger himself, as well as the champions of the "world picture" whom Heidegger so strenuously opposes.

Consider Aristotle:

> To say [says Aristotle] of what is that it is not, or of what is not that it is, is false, while to say of what is that it is, and of what is not that it is not, is true. (*Metaphysics* 1011b25–27)

(Aristotle, you realize, is the master of the informative tautology.) You have only to read the formula without philosophical guile—without favoring, say, Aristotle's or Heidegger's philosophical program—to see how protean, how near and how far from Parmenides, the formula actually is. It's true that analytic philosophers read Aristotle's formula as the "first expression of the *correspondence theory* of truth," hence propositionally (see, e.g., Blackburn and Simmons 1999, 1). But they ignore the fact that the "correspondence theory" need not be restricted in any criterial way and may accommodate many different senses of "correspondence." Heidegger nowhere explains just why Parmenides' affirmation that Being Is and is necessarily One is *not* itself a correspondentist claim. *Why* is it not?

We are now ready for the announced detour. Consider Wittgenstein. Wittgenstein offers, in the *Tractatus*, quite unintentionally, an intriguing alternative to Heidegger's account of *alêtheia*, which Heidegger would never willingly endorse and which Wittgenstein implicitly rejects in *Philosophical Investigations*. I myself have no wish to endorse Wittgenstein's alternative, although it shows a remarkable flexibility regarding the "propositional" approach, which Heidegger nowhere rightly anticipates. (The matter bears directly on Heidegger's reading of Plato.) Strange though it may seem, Wittgenstein introduces a number of terms that intuitively provide "propositional" analogues of what Heidegger has in mind in the "alethic" account of truth intended to trump the propositional. Wittgenstein does indeed offer a correspondence theory of truth—in fact, a "picture" or representational theory—which, read as such, must count as instantiating what Heidegger assigns to the "age of the world picture": It *is* indeed a picture theory of truth in the double sense. Furthermore, it never pretends to offer a metaphysics or an epistemology but "only" what Heidegger might call "the essence of truth," as the world shifts from *alêtheia* to *idea.*

Here, at any rate, is what Wittgenstein (1972) offers in the *Tractatus:*

> Pictorial form is the possibility that things are related to one another in the same way as the elements of the picture. (2.151)

> There must be something identical in a picture and what it depicts, to enable the one to be a picture of the other at all. (2.161)

> A picture cannot, however, depict its pictorial form: it displays it [*es weist sich auf*]. (2.172)

> A proposition is a picture of reality. (4.01)

> A proposition *shows* [*zeigt*] its sense. (4.022)

> A proposition *shows* how things stand *if* it is true, and it *says* [*sagt*] *that* they do so stand. (4.022)

I find quite splendid the ease with which Wittgenstein's idiom accommodates what Parmenides says as well as what Heidegger says, despite the fact that Wittgenstein clearly speaks in the idiom of what Heidegger identifies (in a derogatory way) as the "propositional" conception of truth. Here, now, for the sake of a close comparison, is Heidegger's summary of Plato's "errancy" in transforming the theory of truth:

> When [Heidegger explains] Plato says of the *idea* that she is the mistress that allows unhiddenness, he points to something unsaid, namely, that henceforth the essence of truth does not, as the essence of unhidden-

ness, unfold from its proper and essential fulness but rather shifts to the essence of the *idéa*. The essence of truth gives up its fundamental trait of unhiddenness. ("PDT," 176)

What Heidegger has in mind is this: that Plato, like Descartes after him, is very nearly a crypto- or proto-Kantian or post-Kantian! Certainly Heidegger means to draw attention to the fact that—for reasons akin to those of the Parmenides he invents—he eludes the corrupting "subjectivism" and "constructivism" of the propositional approach to truth. *Alêtheia,* you remember, belongs to Being *alone, not* to any *relationship* initiated by (and including) the human subject who construes reality (as does Plato supremely) under his *idea.* (In the limit, in our own "age," this means, under the terms of the "world picture.") The doctrine of *alêtheia,* you see, is utterly incompatible with the tradition of metaphysics—Kantian and post-Kantian thinking in particular. But that is just what, unwittingly, Wittgenstein's alternative so effectively places in jeopardy!

How so? you ask. Well, Wittgenstein is plainly elucidating—as are all the other philosophers mentioned—the essential "relation" between "Being and thinking": what, prejudicially, Heidegger calls "presencing" and what, more naturally, is the essential theme of realism. Wittgenstein has of course his own theory, which happens to apotheosize what Heidegger calls "the world picture." But the most intriguing lesson to be gained here is simply that Wittgenstein provides a completely plausible analogue of "unconcealed" Being (*alêtheia*) *within* the bounds of the propositional conception of truth itself. Now, does Wittgenstein capture "enough" of the alethic within the propositional or does he not? If he does, Heidegger's entire argument shatters at a stroke; if he does not, then we are being asked (by Heidegger) to choose disjunctively between one or another ultimate intuition regarding the relationship between "Being and thinking"—which, according to Heidegger himself, is utterly "concealed," utterly subject to oblivion![10]

How could we possibly overturn twenty-five hundred years of Western thought this way? The sheer arrogance and arbitrariness—and crazy brilliance—of Heidegger's *Kehre* cannot, I fear, be recovered. For, what we now see, if I may put my finding in a sly way, is that the alethic conception of truth is itself a construction according to the *idea* of toppling the "world picture" as the sign of the "unconcealment" of another "age" beyond our own! That is surely the prophecy of "The Question Concerning Technology" and "The End of Philosophy and the Task of Thinking." But it is *not* a vision that *can* be freed in any way from the propositional conception it abhors and opposes: It is itself a rebel part of that same conception. Of course, if that is so, then Heidegger has simply misread the lesson of Plato's theory of truth. What Plato says is hardly "unhidden" in any way.

I have been speaking of Heidegger's conception of Plato's theory of truth from the start. But you may not have noticed. You have only to reread the very beginning of Heidegger's essay to get your bearings. It opens this way, a little obliquely:

> The knowledge that comes from the sciences usually is expressed is propositions and is laid before us in the form of conclusions that we can grasp and put to use. But the "doctrine" [the "dictum"] of a thinker is that which, within what is said, remains unsaid, that to which we are exposed so that we might expend ourselves on it. . . . What remains unsaid in Plato's thinking is a change in what determines the essence of truth. The fact that this change does take place, what it consists in, and what gets grounded through the transformation of the essence of truth—all of that can be clarified by an interpretation of the "allegory of the cave." ("PDT," 155)

What follows is indeed Heidegger's rendering of the meaning of the allegory along the lines I have been tracking. But you surely see that the matter is not a philological or hermeneutical question of the sort Heidegger ventures in *Parmenides* and in *What Is Called Thinking?* or even in the textual summary of the cave allegory in the Plato essay. Hence all of *these* discussions are no more than a kind of scaffolding, not at all suitably "grounded" in either metaphysics (in the narrow sense) or, more profoundly, in the intuitions of the pre-Socratics said (by Heidegger) to settle for *alêtheia* alone.

Heidegger's charge is that it was Plato who, in the *Republic*, first betrays the priority of *alêtheia* (unconcealment) in yielding to the doctrine of *orthotês* (correctness), that is, what is made to accord with the *idea* of the age—propositionally, by way of correspondence or similarity (*homoiôsis*) between what is affirmed and the states of affairs (or facts, in Wittgenstein's sense), which one finds in the phenomena of the world. That *is* precisely what Wittgenstein intended in distinguishing between *sagt* and *zeicht*, though he speaks in the offending way—"post-Platonically," so to say. Nevertheless, what he offers fits remarkably well *all* the formulations produced during the twenty-five hundred years that have elapsed since Parmenides wrote his poem and Plato his *Republic*.

More than that, the correction needed beyond the *Tractatus*, which Wittgenstein knew was needed, leads us even deeper into the "propositional" mode—well beyond the supposed advantage of Heidegger's "alethic" invention. In fact, in *Philosophical Investigations,* Wittgenstein provides, again unwittingly, an absolutely stunning and unanswerable challenge to Heidegger's alethic conception. For there, in a famous remark, Wittgenstein (1953, vol. 1, sec. 242) observes: "If language is to be a means of communication there must be agreement not only in definition but also (queer as this may sound) in judgments." Of course, Wittgenstein is right. But that means, in effect, that the "unconcealment" of Being cannot issue from Being itself, or issue in any way apart from the orienting beliefs and judgments of human subjects or in any way independent of the relationship between knower and known. Although it is perfectly true that, by the time he writes the *Investigations,* Wittgenstein has effectively rejected the *Tractatus,* nevertheless what he says (here) spells out what he may have had in mind by *zeicht,* namely, that it is encumbered by the propositional mode of truth.

I have in effect been signaling that we are not likely to find Heidegger's intuition in either Parmenides or Plato. It cannot be reclaimed from the ancient texts. To be sure, Heidegger has in mind the recovery of an ancient *paideia* (see, e.g., "PDT," 166–67); but it has proved to be no more than a fevered prophecy. You must read the Plato essay with "The Age of the World Picture" in mind. There, the would-be argument is presented in its own voice, though it does show us how to "transform" the Parmenidean and Platonic texts into the Heideggerean *Bildung.* (It's Heidegger rather than Plato who betrays us.) You have only to compare the opening passage of "The Age" with the opening passage of "Plato's Doctrine" (cited a moment ago):

> In metaphysics [it begins] reflection is accomplished concerning the essence of what is and a decision takes place regarding the essence of truth. Metaphysics grounds an age, in that through a specific interpretation of what is and through a specific comprehension of truth it gives to that age the basis upon which it is essentially formed. This basis holds complete domain over all the phenomena that distinguish the age. Conversely, in order that there may be an adequate reflection upon these phenomena themselves, the metaphysical basis for them must let itself be apprehended in them.[11]

Heidegger then launches into his familiar exposé of the dangers of "the modern age." But what is of particular interest here is the privileged prophecy he reserves for himself by the so-called alethic reading of the ancient texts. What, in a devilishly clever way, he manages to do is "transform" *alêtheia* into a historically necessary disclosure of the metaphysics of our own age. He thereby invokes a magical substitute for a Kantian or a

Husserlian, or even a Hegelian, transcendentalism: a seer's discovery of What Is—which evidently needs no "credentials" beyond its own rhetoric.

I cannot spare more than the briefest glimpse of how this particular story plays out:

> One of the essential phenomena of the modern age [Heidegger offers] is its science. A phenomenon of no less importance is machine technology. . . . If we succeed in reaching the metaphysical ground that provides the foundation for science as a modern phenomenon, then the entire essence of the modern age will have to let itself be apprehended from out of that ground. . . . the methodology of the science becomes circumscribed by means of its results. More and more the methodology adapts itself to the possibilities of procedure opened up through itself. . . . modern science is beginning to enter upon the decisive phase of its history. Only now is it beginning to take possession of its own complete essence.[12]

The entire essay supplies the sense in which the metaphysical essence of the age proves to be the necessary ground of all of its characteristic phenomena, that is, of all those that are thereupon permitted to count as the "unconcealment of Being"!

Its necessity is ideally asymptotic and equilibratory, as perhaps Kant and Husserl and Hegel themselves intended. Heidegger has simply found a braver and brasher and far quicker way of arriving at the "essence of Being"—a fortiori, at the "essence of truth"—without any transcendental scruple at all. But you will have noticed that *what,* of Being, *alêtheia* allows to be "disclosed" is always constructed and reconstructed by a sort of *epoché* from the side of the would-be *idea* of one's own age. It cannot otherwise be "unconcealed," "presenced"; but then it cannot supply any supporting "credentials" except within the indissoluble "relationship" that holds between Being and thinking. It cannot issue from Being alone, except as a figurative compliment. There, at one stroke, you have the fatal weakness and self-betrayal of the *Kehre* and the vindication of Plato's supposed "transformation" of the essence of truth.

I don't deny that contemporary "analytic" theories of truth are also a disaster. But Heidegger's line of thinking cannot "save us." *Alêtheia* can have no prior or separable power over the propositional; it is itself inseparable from the method of *orthotês*. I see no "transformation" of the essence of truth in the gathering tradition, only a better sense of the difficulty of fathoming what best to mean by the "relation" between Being and thinking.

Notes

1. For a sense of the puzzles that currently occupy the analytic discussion of truth, see Davidson 1999.

2. For a sense of this so-called "pragmatist" critique of a purely linguistic treatment of truth sketched very interestingly by the young British philosopher Frank Ramsey, who appears to have influenced Wittgenstein both with regard to the *Tractatus* and in the later direction pursued in *Philosophical Investigations,* see Nils-Eric Sahlin, *The Philosophy of F. P. Ramsey* (Cambridge: Cambridge University Press, 1990), particularly ch. 2.

3. See Pattison 2000, esp. ch. 6, for an unusually clear impression of the impact of the later Heidegger's influence—in an introductory text that is surely much more than that.

4. For a brief assessment of the current analytic literature on truth, see Margolis 2003, ch. 3.

5. See, for instance, Martin Heidegger, *What Is Called Thinking?* trans. J. Glenn Gray (New York: Harper and Row, 1968), 240–41—in Lecture 11, the final lecture of part 2 of the collection. [Hereafter, references to this work will be cited as *WCT,* with part, lecture, and page numbers.]

6. Martin Heidegger, *Hegel's Concept of Experience* (New York: Harper and Row, 1989), 40–41.

7. These lines (marked as citations 291 and 293) are from Proclus and Simplicius, in Kirk, Raven, and Schofield 1983, 245, 247.

8. Thus Aristotle affirms, in *Metaphysics,* bk. 2: "becoming is between being and not being, so that what is becoming is always between that which is and that which is not" (994a27–28). The translation is by W. D. Ross (1984). Cf. also, Aristotle, *Physics,* 1.8.191b13. Aristotle seems to be pointedly answering Parmenides.

9. Martin Heidegger, "The Age of the World Picture" (1938), *The Question Concerning Technology and Other Essays,* trans. William Lovitt (New York: Harper and Row, 1977), 131.

10. For a sense of Heidegger's complex view of "oblivion," see Heidegger, *GA* 54, the first part.

11. Heidegger, "Age of World Picture," 115–16.

12. Heidegger, "Age of World Picture," 116, 124–25.

With Plato into the *Kairos* before the *Kehre:* On Heidegger's Different Interpretations of Plato

Johannes Fritsche

For a volume in honor of Heidegger's sixtieth birthday in 1949, Ernst Jünger contributed an essay entitled "Über die Linie." When, six years later, Jünger himself reached this age, Heidegger reciprocated with an essay of the same title except that he put *die Linie* in quotation marks (*GA* 9, 385/291).[1] Jünger's title is ambiguous. It can announce the line as the topic under discussion ("[An Inquiry] Concerning the Line") but it can also mean "Over the Line" in the sense that someone steps over, or crosses, the line. The quotation marks in Heidegger's title confine it to the first meaning. As he says right at the beginning of his return present, in Jünger's essay the preposition *über* means "across [*hinüber*], *trans, meta*" (386/292), whereas he himself uses it "only in the sense of *de, peri*" (386/292). For the old warhorse and author of novels and other texts on World Wars I and II, Ernst Jünger, his own title was second nature, so to speak. Still, it hit precisely the aspirations of the recipient of his gift. After all, Heidegger had always conceived of himself as breaking "new grounds." In addition, at the latest from the middle of the 1930s on, he had maintained that thinking had to step beyond the science that carried in its title the word "meta" as prefix—the science of metaphysics—to actually achieve what, for him, metaphysics had always only promised, namely, to step over the line that separated physical things from what was beyond them. Whether it is language's wisdom or its *Treppenwitz*[2]—according to Heidegger, the only ones who managed to do so were some of those Greeks who used as the title of their writings the—in this respect—modest preposition *peri* and the noun that, in metaphysics, stands for what metaphysical philosophers have to transcend, namely, *phusis* (nature) as in Heraclitus's and Parmenides' title *Peri phuseôs* (*On Nature*).

The metaphor of the line occurs at a prominent place in a promi-

nent text of Plato's, namely, the *Republic.* The idea of the good as the ultimate end of knowledge (504a4–6d5) can be compared to the sun (506d6–
9b10). The simile of the sun is followed by the simile of the divided line
(509c1–11e5), which in turn is followed by the simile of the cave (514a1–
19d7). In each of the latter two similes, Plato lays out a topography of different realms of reality, divided by lines, and a way that crosses these lines.
The idea of the good and the simile of the cave were particularly important for Heidegger in the first half of the 1930s. He lectured on them and
on Plato's *Theaetetus* twice, namely, in the winter semesters 1931–32 and
1933–34—one year before and one year after Hitler's seizure of power in
January 1933. The two lecture courses mark a watershed in Heidegger's
understanding of Plato as well as in his own self-understanding. Before
them and even in the 1931–32 lecture itself, Plato was for Heidegger the
sort of phenomenologist as which Heidegger understood himself during
this time. Shortly afterward, however, their ways had parted inasmuch as
both Heidegger himself and Heidegger's Plato had changed dramatically.
For, already in the 1933–34 lecture and thereafter, Heidegger was the historian of the history of being, and Plato the beginning of metaphysics, or
precisely that form of philosophy which both phenomenology in the early
Heidegger and thinking in the later Heidegger had to overcome.

I discuss this change with reference to Heidegger's notions of truth
(*alêtheia*) and of revolution, that is, the establishment of a new state of affairs, in *Being and Time* called "historicality." For this purpose, in the first
section I lay out the notion of historicality, Heidegger's understanding of
the task of the history of philosophy in the 1920s, and his interpretation
of truth in Plato and the Greeks at that time, and in the second section his
interpretation of Plato and truth in the lecture course from summer 1935,
Introduction to Metaphysics. In the third section, I present the two lecture
courses on the *Republic* and the *Theaetetus* and relate them to Heidegger
before 1931–32 and in 1935. In the final section, I suggest that Heidegger's *Kehre* (turn) did not take place, as one might be led to gather from
the first three sections, between 1931–32 and 1933–34 but rather only
after *Introduction to Metaphysics,* and that the drama of historicality—or,
more general, politics—was indeed very important for it. As one can
already see from the number of texts and topics envisaged here, I sketch
a trajectory or a map, with only few areas and links drawn out more in detail while the other ones are to be treated on other occasions.

Historicality, History of Philosophy, Truth, and the Greeks in the 1920s

Is *Being and Time* a book in the spirit of modernity? In his *Demythologizing Heidegger,* Caputo (1993) answers this question emphatically in the affirmative. *Being and Time* is the consummation of modern philosophy, of Kantian and neo-Kantian transcendentalism. Correspondingly, Heidegger's project of a destruction of the history of ontology in *Being and Time* is "far from being *post*-modern or *anti*-modern" (11). Rather, it "is formulated precisely from the standpoint of the advantages of modernity" (11) as its "aim is to loosen the grip of ancient ideas on modern ones" (11). As Caputo concludes, since *Being and Time* is distinctively modern, it cannot be the cause of two of Heidegger's features in the 1930s, namely, his Nazism and his preoccupation with the Greeks (as the origin from which we have fallen away and which we have to retrieve) (1, 16, 36ff.).

Being and Time contains two kinds of investigations. Heidegger discovers the transcendental structures, the phenomena, or existentialia, that make it possible for a human being, a Dasein, to be in a world and to approach and experience beings in specific ways. He assumes that each of these existentialia is omnipresent in the sense that, whenever and wherever a Dasein is, these existentialia have always already been at work. However, a Dasein can actualize these existentialia either in a genuine or in a fallen way, and this difference prepares the way for the second kind of investigation, namely, the issue of authenticity, which culminates in the discussion of historicality in sections 72–77, the most primordial level of *Being and Time* (*BT,* 372/424). As I have shown elsewhere (see the summary in Fritsche 1999b, 124–42; see also Fritsche 2003), here Heidegger is indeed resolutely antimodern. Authenticity and historicality are not, as most American interpreters assume (Fritsche 1999b, 207–15 passim), about individual Dasein, each of which distances itself from everything to achieve its unique singularity. Rather, like the other conservatives and right-wingers at the time, Heidegger regards the development of modern *Gesellschaft* (society) as a falling and downward plunge (with liberalism, social welfare, socialism, and, finally, communism as its steps; see Fritsche 1999b, 68ff., 274ff.; see also Fritsche 2003). At some point in this downward plunge, *Geschick* (destiny) raises its voice and calls upon the Dasein. Inauthentic Dasein try to ignore, or fight, the call while authentic Dasein comply with it. The call calls upon the Dasein to cancel society and to replace it with a revitalization of *Gemeinschaft* (community), which has been pushed aside by society. Other right-wingers wanted to revitalize the Christian love community or some other sort of community. Heidegger, however, sides with the National Socialists and their call for the revitalization of the *Volksgemeinschaft* (community of the people). In what follows, I refer to Heidegger's analyses of omnipresent existentialia as "structural analyses" and to his notion of historicality (which I will spell out in more detail) as the "drama of historicality." Heidegger interprets Plato in the light of both of these two kinds of investigations only in the two lecture courses from 1931 to 1932 and 1933 to 1934.

The revitalization of community against society concerns only the authentic and inauthentic modes of several or even all existentialia—in the first place, "being-with" (*BT,* 117ff./153ff.) and "historicality" (372ff./424ff.)—but not these existentialia themselves. Thus, even if, in *Being and Time,* Heidegger proposes the most radical version of antimodern politics, he might still maintain that, in comparison to the ancient philosophers, the modern ones have advanced much further toward the discovery of the existentialia themselves. However, Caputo is wrong also regarding Heidegger's project of a destruction of the history of philosophy. For in the lecture courses related to the project of *Being and Time,* Heidegger assumed that the Greek philosophers since Thales indeed made progress regarding the task of philosophy to discover the omnipresent phenomena or existentialia. Plato advanced further than Parmenides, and Aristotle further than Plato. Still, because of certain self-evident and deep-seated orientations among the Greek philosophers, even Plato and Aristotle, in all their achievements, did not manage to fully break through. However, after Aristotle a decline set in, and philosophy got back onto the right track only in Husserl and Heidegger himself.[3]

If philosophy after Aristotle is a downward plunge, "no other way is open to us than the one the Greeks traveled, namely to come to philosophy by philosophizing" (*GA* 19, 257/177), as he says in the lecture course on Plato's *Sophist* in the winter semester 1924–25. Pointing to the paradigmatic character of Plato's research (413/285) Heidegger dismisses a romanticism, widespread not the least in phenomenology itself, "which believes that it can step directly into the open space, that one can, so to speak, make oneself free of history by a leap" (413/286). For, philosophical questioning is

> not concerned with freeing us from the past [*Vergangenheit*] but, on the contrary, with *making the past free for us, with liberating the past from the tradition* [*frei zu lösen aus der Tradition*], and especially from the ungenuine tradition. For the latter has the peculiar characteristic that in giving, in *tradere*, in transmitting, it distorts the gifts themselves. . . . Ruthlessness

toward the tradition is reverence toward the past, and it is genuine only in an appropriation of the latter (the past) out of a *destruction* [*Destruktion*] of the former (the tradition). (*GA* 19, 413f./286)

This approach to the history of philosophy is structurally identical with the drama of historicality. We have to repeat and revive something—here called the "past [*Vergangenheit*],"[4] Greek philosophy, in particular Plato and Aristotle—by destroying the tradition between the Greeks and us since this tradition has distorted the past. The approach differs from the drama of historicality "only" inasmuch as Heidegger here at no point suggests that something or someone—Plato or Aristotle—calls upon us to destroy the tradition and to revive the Greeks. The same attitude is explicitly at work in *Being and Time*, for instance, in Heidegger's treatment of truth. According to the tradition in which the moderns self-evidently live, truth is nothing but a character of judgments and consists in agreement between judgments and facts. However, according to Heidegger, this notion covers up what he regards as primordial truth, namely, truth as uncovering (*BT*, 212ff./256ff.). As he suggests rhetorically, this act of "eliminating [*ausschalten*] the idea of agreement from the conception of truth" (219/262) and of "plunging the 'good' old tradition [of truth as agreement] into nullity [*in die Nichtigkeit stoßen*]" (219/262) seems highly arbitrary. However, his own definition of truth as uncovering "contains only the *necessary* interpretation of what was primordially surmised in the *oldest* tradition of ancient philosophy" (219/262). In other words, philosophy has to revitalize the Greek notion of truth by destroying the later tradition as the latter has covered up the Greek notion with something that is derivative, if it is at all.

Immediately after *Being and Time*, Heidegger rethought his agenda in terms of the vocabulary of transcendence and freedom, as is shown, for instance, in the 1929 text, *On the Essence of Ground*.[5] However, despite his emphasis on Kant in this context, this reorientation did not fundamentally change his attitude toward the history of philosophy.

What was it that made the Greek philosophers possible? In the lecture on the *Sophist*, Heidegger speaks of the "field of investigation out of which the basic concepts of Greek philosophy grew" (*GA* 19, 321/223). The world in which Greek Dasein finds itself is "at first disclosed only within certain limits. Man lives in his surrounding world, which is disclosed only within certain limits" (13/9). It is the drive of Greek Dasein to uncover the world beyond these limits that determines its experience of truth. Heidegger points out that—in contrast to the German expression for truth, *Wahrheit*—the Greek word, *alêtheia*, contains an alpha privative (15/10). For the Greeks "*alêtheia* means: to be hidden no longer, to be uncovered" (16/11). The privative expression indicates that the Greeks were aware "that the uncoveredness of the world must be wrested [*errungen*], that it is initially and for the most part not available [*verfügbar*]" (16/11). In *Being and Time*, Heidegger uses the formula that truth as uncoveredness "must always first be wrested [*abgerungen*] from entities" (*BT*, 222/265) and that the "factical uncoveredness of anything is always, as it were, a kind of *robbery* [*gleichsam immer ein Raub*]" (222/265). One wrests [*erringt*] something only against the resistance of its owner, as it were. A robber approaches and attacks the owner of the desired good only because the latter does not want to give it away voluntarily. The qualification "as it were" points into either of two directions. It could indicate that Heidegger takes into account the motif of hubris in ancient Greek culture. Just as in the case of a victim of a robbery, there is something in the beings that does not want them and itself to be uncovered. In that case, Heidegger would assume that the Greeks experienced in the beings something comparable to intentions of human beings, and the phrase "as it were" would remind one of the difference between this something and human intentions. However, at no point in the lecture course or in *Being and Time* does Heidegger consider the possibility that the Greeks experienced any internal and intentional resistance, so to speak, on the part of the beings and of being against their being uncovered. Thus, the qualification "as it were" most probably rules out that, like a victim of a robbery, beings and being don't want to be robbed or uncovered. Cultivation of land, colonization, or seafaring is difficult, laborious, time-consuming, and dangerous, and one has to overcome many obstacles, but none of these hindrances indicates an internal resistance on the part of the beings against their being uncovered.

However, the beings and being also don't want to unconceal themselves, for they themselves are neutral toward this distinction. Unconcealedness does not belong to the beings themselves, since they exist even if they are not unconcealed (*GA* 19, 17/11), and disclosure is "itself a mode of Being, and indeed not of the beings which are first disclosed—those of the world—but, instead, of the beings we call human Dasein" (17/12). Neither does concealedness belong to beings themselves or being: "For all of Dasein's strivings toward knowledge must maintain themselves against the concealedness of beings, which is of a threefold character: (1) ignorance, (2) prevailing opinion, (3) error" (23/16). Greek Dasein experiences concealedness of beings exclusively as a contingent state of itself, of its position relative to the beings; a contingent state that it can overcome. No one calls upon Dasein to do so. Rather, Dasein approaches beings and being "by itself [*von sich aus*]" (23/16) in order to unconceal them. Dasein is the master of truth and of true beings: "To be true, to be in the truth, as a determination of Dasein, means that Dasein has at its disposal [*Verfügung*], as unconcealed, the beings with which Dasein is dealing in its everyday life [*Umgang pflegt*]" (23/see 16). According to Heidegger, both Plato and Aristotle perceived this notion of truth, Aristotle "in a more precise way" (23/16) than Plato. The notion of truth applies not only to facts and things but also to their causes and principles. Dasein presupposes that there are causes and principles of facts and things, and it presupposes that knowledge of empirical relations leads to knowledge of principles (77/53). Knowledge of principles, in turn, is necessary for Dasein's power to dispose of beings (43, 77/30, 53), and wisdom and knowledge are in the first place a matter of production (38/27). The meaning of being for the Greeks is production for the sake of the usage of beings in everyday life (269/186), and "to conduct into being means therefore: to con-duce into availability for everyday life, in short: to produce. . . . Being thus means to be produced" (269f./186).

Plato and Truth in *Introduction to Metaphysics*

The lecture course in summer 1935, *Introduction to Metaphysics,* consists of four parts. Heidegger develops the understanding of being as *phusis* and *alêtheia* in the pre-Socratic Greeks (*GA* 40, 3–99/1–92/1–97),[6] interprets fragments of Parmenides and Heraclitus (100–55/93–146/98–155) and the first chorus in Sophocles's *Antigone* (155–73/146–65/155–76) and returns to Parmenides and Heraclitus to develop the difference between the pre-Socratics and metaphysics (174ff./165ff./176ff.). The course is much like a *matryoshka,* a Russian doll containing several smaller reproductions of itself. Heidegger talks about three actors in three plays, namely, the Germans, the Greek tragic heroes, and the pre-Socratic philosophers. Proceeding from the first to the other ones, one realizes that each performs the drama of historicality.[7]

The drama of historicality consists of two larger parts, namely, the move out of *Gesellschaft* and the return into *Gesellschaft* to replace it with a revitalization of *Gemeinschaft.* More in detail, it consists of seven elements:

1. a description of society at the beginning of the drama making clear that society is a downward plunge in which the authentic possibilities are covered up (see Fritsche 1999b, 29ff., 43ff., 129ff.; see also Fritsche 2003);

2. the call of destiny raising its voice and coming to the fore (see

Fritsche 1999b, 7ff., 22ff., 57ff., 125ff., 129ff.; see also Fritsche 2003, 90ff.);

3. the move of authentic Dasein out of society in obedience to the call (see Fritsche 1999b, 43ff., 129ff.; see also Fritsche 2003);

4. authentic Dasein's recognition of the difference between society and the authentic possibilities (see Fritsche 1999b, 49ff., 55ff., 129ff.);

5. authentic Dasein taking over the task destiny bestows upon it (see Fritsche 1999b, 21ff., 50ff., 62ff., 129ff.);

6. authentic Dasein fighting in the name of community against society to replace society with community (see Fritsche 1999b, 21ff., 63ff., 129ff.); and

7. the recognition that this fight is a revitalization of community (see Fritsche 1999b, 17ff., 21ff., 59ff., 129ff.).

As I pointed out, in the 1920s Heidegger's notions of the history of philosophy as well as of the Greeks were similar to the drama of historicality, but also different from it. The destruction of the history of philosophy shares with the drama of historicality the general structure of revitalization through destruction, but it lacks element 2, the call. The Greeks in the 1920s, however, do not only not answer to any call, but, in addition, they do not aim at any revitalization. Acknowledging no authority above him and being concerned—as any other authentic and, in a way, even ordinary Greek Dasein—with the increase of his power of disposal of beings and their principles, the Greek philosopher is pretty much the opposite of authentic Dasein in *Being and Time* as the latter submits itself to the call and instrumentalizes itself for the revitalization of a past world. Thus, when in 1935 Heidegger finds the drama of historicality also in the Greeks, these Greeks have come a long way, so to speak. Nonetheless, Heidegger does not present his new notion of the Greeks as a break with his old one but rather, implicitly, as a result of progress of insight in which the elements of the old notion are preserved in the new one—or, sublated by perversion, so to speak.

At the beginning of the second part, Heidegger lays out four distinctions, the ones between being and becoming, being and *Schein* (*GA* 40, 100/93 ["appearance"]/98 ["seeming"]), being and thinking, and being and the ought (100ff./93ff./98ff.). As to the second one, taking over his results of the first part, he maintains that the Greeks experienced being, *phusis,* as consisting in "appearing [*Erscheinen*], in the offering of a look [*Aussehen*] and of views [*Ansichten*]" (111/see 104/110), and this experience opens up the difference between an appearing in which the beings appear as they are in truth and an appearing into a "look that precisely covers over and conceals what beings are in truth—that is, in unconcealment" (112/ see 104/110). Heidegger labels this second kind of appearing *"seeming in the sense of semblance [Anschein]"* (112/see 104/110) and continues:

> Where there is unconcealment of beings, there is the possibility of seeming [as semblance, my comment], and conversely: where beings stand in seeming, and take a prolonged and secure stand there, seeming can break apart and fall away. (*GA* 40, 112/see 104/see 110)

As one already sees (see also Fritsche 1999b, 194ff., Fritsche 1999a), this is an abstract scheme of the entire drama of historicality with seeming (as semblance) functioning in it like society does in the drama of historicality in *Being and Time*. At some point, beings are present as they are in truth, and thereafter the condition described in element 1 emerges, the downward plunge and its result. However, this seeming will at some point disappear, as is promised in the drama of historicality from elements 4 and 5 onward, at the latest. In the lecture course on the *Sophist*, concealedness was exclusively a matter of Dasein not being in the right position toward the beings through ignorance, prevailing opinion, and error. Heidegger mentions these three factors here in 1935 (*GA* 40, 111/104/109f.). However, here in 1935 concealedness, seeming and deception are a matter of being itself (116/108f./114), and seeming covers itself up as seeming and presents itself as being (116/108f./114). Deception as a human phenomenon is possible only because deception is in being and the appearance of beings (116/108f./114f.).

In 1924, Greek Dasein ventures out and uncovers beings. Here in 1935, Heidegger emphasizes this aspect more than ever, in particular in his interpretation and very colorful paraphrases of the first chorus of the *Antigone* (*GA* 40, 157ff., 169f./148ff., 160f./158ff., 172f.). However, Greek Dasein's dangerous and polemical activities are instrumental to being. Dasein ventures out because it has been called upon by being. In *Being and Time*, inauthentic Dasein tries to evade the call of conscience "by slinking away from that thin wall by which the 'they' is separated, as it were, from the uncanniness of its Being [Unheimlichkeit seines Seins]" (*BT*, 278/ 323). The metaphor of the line occurs frequently in *Introduction to Metaphysics*, and Heidegger stages the drama of historicality as a happening centered around a line or, more precisely, a front line, a trench.[8] Heidegger maintains that Greek "man . . . oversteps the limits of the homely" (*GA* 40, 160/see 151/see 161), and "using violence [*Gewalt*] is the basic trait not just of his doing but of his Dasein" (159/see 150/160). Ordinary and inauthentic Dasein live below the line, in a realm that Heidegger characterizes in the same way in which he has characterized society and liberalism already in *Being and Time* (see Fritsche 1999b, 133, 142ff., 274, 280). For, if one regards this violence performed by authentic Dasein as brutal and arbitrary, one looks upon it from the perspective of ordinary and inauthentic Dasein, who live in the

> domain in which the agreement upon compensation, compromise, and mutual supply [*Verabredung auf Ausgleich und gegenseitige Versorgung*] sets [*abgibt*] the standard for Dasein, and accordingly all violence is necessarily deemed only a disturbance and offense. (*GA* 40, 159/see 150/see 160)

Inauthentic Dasein remains in this realm. Authentic Dasein, however, moves toward the limit and beyond, and it does so because being calls upon it to do so, for being uses authentic Dasein as the breach through which it enters the realm below the line. The being-here of historical man means:

> Being-posited as the breach [*Bresche*] into which the preponderant violence of Being breaks in its appearing. . . . Being itself throws man into the course of this tearing-away, which forces man beyond himself, as the one who marches out, to Being, in order to set Being into the work. (*GA* 40, 172/see 163/see 174)

Being the breach historical man is

> an *in-cident*, the incident in which the violent powers of the released preponderant violence of Being suddenly come forth and enter into the work as history. (*GA* 40, 172/see 164/see 174)

These quotes contain elements 2 and 3 of the drama of historicality, and they are already a short formulation of elements 4 through 7. Heidegger leaves no doubt that he is not talking about theoretical activities. Rather, historical man—the poets, the thinkers, and the statesmen (*GA* 40, 66, 161f., 166/62, 152, 157/65, 163, 167)—demolishes the world of seeming and establishes a new world; one in which being and beings appear as they are in truth. By leaving the realm under the line, society, historical man is no longer bound by any laws valid in society because he establishes new laws. The creators are "without statute and limit, without structure and order, because they themselves *as* creators must first establish all this in each case" (162/see 152f./see 163), and in contrast to the equality and compromise in the realm of seeming, the new world contains "rank and domination" (141/133/see 141; see also 49f., 66, 182f./46, 62, 174/48, 65, 185f.). Heidegger claims that *noein* in Parmenides does not mean thinking in the modern sense but rather an act in which being calls upon Dasein and demands that Dasein realize the new world. Apprehension "is the happening [*Geschehnis*] that has man" (150/141/see 150), and man "has to transform into history the Being that has disclosed itself to him" (152/see 143/see 153; see also, e.g., 178f., 184, 187/169f., 175, 178/181, 187, 190). These are elements 2 through 5 and already element 6 of the drama of historicality. Thus, in element 6, authentic Dasein is called into the "battle [*Kampf*] between Being and seeming" (113/see 105/see 111; see also 66, 112ff., 146f., 201/61f., 105ff., 138, 192/65, 111ff., 147, 205), the battle as "*de-cision for Being against* [the seeming, which from the viewpoint of being and authentic Dasein has become, my comment] Nothing [since being demands the destruction of seeming, my comment]" (177/168/179). A summary of the entire drama can be found in Heidegger's summary of his Parmenides interpretation in *Introduction to Metaphysics:*

> *Logos* here stands in the closest connection with *krinein*, separating as deciding, in the execution of the gathering toward the gatheredness of Being. The *selecting* "gleaning" [*das* auslesende *"Lesen"*] grounds and sustains the pursuit of Being and the rejection of seeming. The meaning of *krinein* includes: to select, to bring into relief, to set the measure that determines rank. (*GA* 40, 182/see 174/see 185)

As I pointed out elsewhere (Fritsche 1999b, 200ff.), if one replaces the relevant terms here with the ones used in *Being and Time,* one has an excellent abstract of the drama of historicality in *Being and Time* and a summary of its decisive passage in section 74. Being collects itself, puts itself together to come out and demand its re-realization (Fritsche 1999b, 55ff., 129ff., 200ff.). Authentic Dasein takes over the task to realize being and *liest aus,* that is, throws out (Fritsche 1999b, 67, 134, 202, 316f.) the basic features of the world of seeming and replaces them with a proper manifestation of being, the new world. As to element 7, Heidegger inserts into his narrative here and there a "re-" or "back again/to."[9]

As was already indicated, in the last part of *Introduction to Metaphysics,* Heidegger claims that Plato and Aristotle are the beginning of metaphysics (*GA* 40, 183ff./175ff./186ff.). In Plato, being and *phusis* is conceived as idea, and this means that look and view as idea now dominate the coming forth—an upheaval in which "an essential consequence is falsified into the essence itself" (192/see 183/195). Truth is no longer experienced as the happening that captures the authentic Dasein and forces them to revolutionize the world but has become the correctness of judgment (194/186/199). Logos is no longer apprehension as in Parmenides but, as judgment, has established itself as "*the* standard-setting domain" (196/187/200), the starting point of modern reason's domination over being and beings (194f.185f./197f.). This change has "its inner ground in a transformation of the essence of truth into truth as correctness" (198/see 190/203). Heidegger describes this process as a "fall-down and secession [*Abfall*]" (193/see 185/see 197) and as the "breakdown of unconcealment" (199/191/see 204) to add that this formula has to be properly understood. For, as he surmises, the "inception, as incipient, must, in a certain way, leave itself behind. (In this way, it necessarily conceals itself, but this self-concealing is not nothing)" (199f./see 191/204). In this way, the inception sets the stage for the Germans (see, e.g., 40ff./ 37ff./40ff.) as actors in the drama of historicality. The lecture abounds with pertinent phrases. In short, today "man, peoples . . . have long since fallen out of Being, without knowing it" (40/see 37/see 39). However, the Germans have to "restore the historical Dasein of man—and this also means our own-most future Dasein, in the whole of the history that is allotted to us—back to the power of Being that is to be opened up originally/as it was originally [*ursprünglich*]" (45/see 41f./see 44). This is the "historical mission of our people" (53/see 50/52) and the "directive of the inception" (214/205/219).

The Lecture Courses on the *Republic* and the *Theaetetus* in 1931–32 and 1933–34

In his book *Heidegger's Philosophy of Being*, Herman Philipse (1998) identifies several themes in the notion of being in *Being and Time* (67ff.), and he sees—like many other interpreters—a neo-Hegelian theme, formulated in nine theses, only in the later Heidegger (151ff.). Still, according to Philipse, the neo-Hegelianism does not come out of the blue. Rather, it results willingly-unwillingly, as it were, from the fact that, in *Being and Time*, "the transcendental solution for the tension between historicism and essentialism is . . . unstable" and "tends to degenerate into Neo-Hegelianism" (169). However, the drama of historicality is certainly a variation of Neo-Hegelianism or reverted Hegelianism.[10] Regarding this reverted Hegelianism, the relation between *Being and Time* and the later Heidegger is much more direct than Philipse assumes, for the "reverted" Hegelianism of *Introduction to Metaphysics* is "just" an expansion of the "reverted" Hegelianism of the drama of historicality in *Being and Time*. In *Being and Time*, Heidegger applies the drama of historicality only to the German people; in *Introduction to Metaphysics*, however, to the German people and to the pre-metaphysical Greeks as well, and these Greeks present the authentic experience of being (e.g., *GA* 40, 65ff., 108ff., 180ff./61ff., 99ff., 171ff./64ff., 105ff., 182ff.). In a way, this application is in no way surprising. In *Being and Time*, the drama of historicality marks authentic Dasein at the deepest level of investigation and existence, and the community of the German people as destiny calls Dasein into its authentic existence. Already in *Being and Time* and related lectures, philosophy has to repeat the Greeks. By applying the drama of historicality also onto the Greeks themselves, Heidegger forges a "manly" bond between the Germans and the Greeks—the people with the most powerful and spiritual languages (*GA* 40, 61/57/60), whose "tribalty [*Stammesart*] and language [are of] the same origin [*Herkunft*]" [*GA* 36/7, 6]—and makes the pre-Socratic Greeks do in the first happening of the inception what the German people do in the return of the inception. The revolution of the Germans would be illusionary if the inception had not been, and the inception would not be what it is if the Germans did not repeat it. As he says in the 1931–32 lecture course on the *Republic* and the *Theaetetus,* if we are still resolved to exist from out of an understanding of beings,

> *alêtheia* must occur. For, that it did *once* [namely, in the Greeks, my comment] occur is the abiding origin of our existence, so long as this existence itself, not that of the individual but *our* history, lasts. (*GA* 34, 122/ see 88f.)

In order "that *alêtheia* might still *remain* an occurrence [*Geschehen*]" (*GA* 34, 122/89) we have to ask for it as this is the only way "in which we can really bind *alêtheia* to our own Dasein" (122/89). As these quotations already indicate, the lecture courses on Plato mark important steps on the itinerary of the expansion of *Being and Time*'s drama of historicality onto the pre-Socratics.

At the beginning of the 1931–32 lecture course, Heidegger lays out the history of the notion of truth and the need to go back to Greek *alêtheia* ("what has been torn away from hiddenness [*Verborgenheit*] and, as it were, been robbed of its hiddenness" [*GA* 34, 10/7; see also 13/8f.]) by and large in the same way as he did in the course on the *Sophist,* and he chooses Plato's simile of the cave (1–19/1–13).[11] In other words, it is the drama of historicality without the call even though, right at the end of the introduction, Heidegger inserts, in a formulation as undetermined as it is precise, the call and the need of a proper response (19/13).[12] The simile of the cave has certainly always been significant to philosophy and its history. In the 1920s and 1930s, however, it gained specific importance for some philosophers and philologists in Germany who, in reaction against neo-

Kantianism as well as against the Weimar Republic, focused on Plato's political philosophy and propagated their version of Heidegger's drama of historicality. The people in the cave are the Weimar Republic, and Hitler repeats Plato by replacing a democracy with a totalitarian state.[13] Heidegger interprets the simile of the cave as the drama of historicality as well and thus joins those philosophers, not without indicating, however, that they have not realized the depth of the issue (115f./83f.).

Heidegger divides the simile of the cave into four parts, 514a2–15c3, 515c4–15e5, 515e5–16e2, and 516e3–17a6. In the first part, he finds element 1 of the drama of historicality (*GA 34*, 22–30/18–23), and in part 2 elements 2, 3 (37/28f.), and 4 ("beings separate out into those that are more and those that are less *beingful*" [33/26; see also, e.g., 91/66]) (31–38/23–29). Interpreting part 3 (38–79/29–58), he develops Plato's notion of ideas (47–60/35–44) as not caught up in the modern split between subject and object (64–79/48–58; see also 111/80f.), develops element 5 ("projective *binding of* oneself [ein entwerfendes *Sich-binden*] . . . I can acquire power by *binding* myself. . . . Such binding is not a loss of power, but a taking into one's possession" [59f./44]; "becoming free as binding oneself to the ideas, as letting *being* [*Sein*] give the lead" [73, 96/54, 69f.]), and gives three examples of element 6, namely, the revolutions in natural science, science of history, and poetry (60–64/45–48).

The fourth part, the one on the return into the cave, is very short and seems not to contribute anything substantial, especially since the words *alêtheia/alêthês* are not used. Heidegger points out this absence as a serious objection against his interpretation (*GA 40*, 80, 88/59, 64). However, one has to realize that, without being talked about, truth is "nevertheless what is *treated,* and indeed in a definite central sense" (88/64). Indeed, only in the return into the cave finds liberation its "fulfillment" (91/ see 67). As a matter of fact, Heidegger finds here element 6 of the drama of historicality. Having gained power through submission to being in part 3, the philosopher translates being into an "ultimate decision and lawgiving" (82/60) and "in advance of his age, produces this being [*Sein*], lets it originate" (82/see 60). Thus, in this situation, the beings and seeming "are *set over against each other,* because both do raise and *can* raise the *claim* to unhiddenness" (90/65). This is "a *primordial* struggle [*ursprünglicher Kampf*]" (92/67 and often), and the idea of the good as "*empowerment* [*Ermächtigung*]" empowers the philosopher to put the new laws, issued by being, and the battle against seeming to work (108ff./78ff.).[14]

The two parties that Plato pits against each other in the battle deserve and even require a more detailed discussion. First, on his way out of the cave, does the philosopher discover only ideas and the idea of the good, as the simile of the cave seems to suggest? The ideas must not, so to speak, hang in the air. They require a foundation. Second, what, precisely, is the condition of those against whom the philosopher launches the fight? In other words, how does seeming operate? Heidegger discusses both questions in the part on the *Theaetetus,* the first under the title of soul and the second under the title of untruth, the opposite of truth.

Regarding the first question, the different senses presuppose "a unitary region of perceivability" (*GA* 34, 175/127), which is provided by the soul. In fact, soul is "nothing else but precisely this relationship to the perceivable that holds up the region of possible perceivability, the region-opening and holding-open relationship to the perceivable" (176/128). Heidegger maintains that, as this relationship, soul in Plato is not caught up in the modern split between subject and object (178/129; see also 196/142 passim). Interpreting *Theaetetus* 185a8ff., he engages in an interpretation of what he provisionally calls "excess [*Mehrbestand*]" (*GA* 34, 186ff./133ff.). One always perceives more than what the senses perceive for one perceives that which is "*in common* [*gemein*]" (188/136) to all what one perceives through the senses. This excess has a structure and includes many ideas, and it is grounded in and put forth by soul. For Plato, soul is what Heidegger, interpreting also Plato's notion of *erôs* (love), calls "striving for being [*Seinserstrebnis*]" (203ff./147ff.). In striving for being, soul holds ahead of oneself these different ideas. Thus, the excess is actually a

> *pregiven* [*Vorgabe*] . . . it is *held up* in advance (*a priori*) for us in striving perceiving, as what must already be understood in order that something sensory can be perceived as a being. . . . That the soul is as such striving for being means that man as existing has always already stepped out beyond himself in his directedness to the all-embracing horizon of being [*Sein*]. (*GA* 34, 231f./165f.)

As is clear, Heidegger combines here two topics, the issue of the structure of being which has been with him since his habilitation and the notions of care in *Being and Time* and of transcendence in *On the Essence of Ground* and lectures related to it in the late 1920s.

Regarding the second question, the theory of soul also provides Heidegger with the means to give an account, starting with Plato's *sunapsis aisthêseôs pros dianoian* (*Tht.,* 195d1; *GA* 34, 311/220) of untruth. Everything perceived cannot but be perceived within the horizon of possible ideas, looks, that soul produces and holds ahead of oneself, as Heidegger illustrates by a drawing of a "*forking* [*Gabelung*]" (*GA* 34, 309ff./219ff.) as an image of the "essential construction" (314/222) of Dasein. If this is the case, it is possible that one identifies something as a look that is actually not displayed by the perceived thing. Theaetetus is approaching me from a distance. I perceive him under the horizon of all the looks that my soul holds ahead of myself, among them the looks of Theaetetus and of Socrates. Since Theaetetus and Socrates look similar, it can happen that I mistake Theaetetus for Socrates, a process that, according to Heidegger, is prior to predication (309–14, 315ff./219–22, 223ff.). Up to this issue, Heidegger has followed Plato in all that he reads in the *Theaetetus*. It is only here—in the exact explanation of the forking, right before the end of the entire lecture course—that Heidegger has "to go beyond" (291, 312/207, 221; see, however, also 71/52) Plato, for Plato finally misinterprets the phenomenon as "the un-correctness of the *logos,* of the preposition" (*GA* 34, 319/226). One might wonder what, beyond relatively simple acts of visual recognition, the relevance of this issue for the alleged fight might be. However, already in *Being and Time* rational thinking and predication are not the decisive factor but rather mood, as is also the case in 1931–32 (221, 238/158, 170). The resistance of those who live in seeming is seated deeper than the capacity of producing judgments.

As is obvious and as I already pointed out, the structure and content of *Introduction to Metaphysics* differ from the lectures related to the project of *Being and Time*. Without going into the details of both types, a lecture course related to the project of *Being and Time* has several or all of the following features each of which occurs in the part on the *Theaetetus* of the 1931–32 lecture:

1. Plato and Aristotle, as Heidegger himself does, investigate phenomena, and in particular they start with everyday phenomena. Also in 1931–32, Plato does not discuss, as the Marburg School maintains, theory of science and knowledge (*GA* 34, 151/110f.). Rather, *episthamai* means "the *mastering knowing-one's-way-around* [*beherrschende Sich-auskennen*] in something, familiarity in dealing with something" (153/see 112) in every kind of production and cultivation, craftsmanship, agriculture, warfare, etc. (153/111f.). Knowledge as seeing in the simile of the cave and knowledge as production and maintenance in the *Theaetetus* coincide in "*disposal* over the unhiddenness of beings" (161/117) (157–61/114–17), which is the same meaning of being as in the lecture on the *Sophist.* Thus, Plato investigates "the unprejudiced pre-scientific everyday self-understanding of man" (169/123).

2. Plato and Aristotle, as Heidegger himself tries to, investigate the phenomena without being caught up in the split between subject and object that is, according to Heidegger, characteristic of modern philosophy. In 1931–32, Heidegger stresses this aspect from the beginning on

(*GA* 34, 25/20) and develops it in particular with reference to Plato's notions of perception and fantasy (162ff./118ff.), soul (171ff./124ff.), and *doxa* (normally translated as "opinion"; Heidegger translates "view [*Ansicht;* 256/182f.]") (246ff./176ff.).

3. Plato and Aristotle, as Heidegger himself does, ground different phenomena in, or try to reach at, a superstructure, in *Being and Time* called *Sorge* (care), that is not caught up in the subject-object split. As was already indicated, in 1931–32 Heidegger redeems this feature by his interpretation of soul in Plato. He even credits Plato with getting into view what in *Being and Time* is called primordial temporality (*GA* 34, 226f./162f.).

4. Plato and Aristotle, as Heidegger himself does, approach the phenomena by breaking through the prejudgments of other philosophers. In 1931–32, Heidegger stresses this aspect especially in his interpretation of *Theaetetus,* 187d-191c (*GA* 34, 263–92/187–207).

5. Because of features 1–4, Plato and Aristotle are the most advanced Greek philosophers, and they are on the right track concerning the solution of the problems and the proper interpretation of the phenomena. For 1931–32, see *GA* 34, 194, 238, 241, 248f., 267, 276f., 283f., 286f., 290f., 292ff., 308, 314/140, 170, 172, 177f., 190, 196f., 201f., 204, 206f., 208ff., 218, 222, and also 34f./26f. (Plato is right concerning the two conceptions of truth and their relation).

6. Despite features 1–5, however, Plato and Aristotle don't manage to fully break through, for they share with the other Greeks some self-evident orientations—notably, an interpretation of speech as something present at hand (*BT,* 165/209) and the conception of the being of beings as "'presence' [*Anwesenheit*]" (*BT,* 25/47)—that obscure the proper approach to the phenomena. In 1931–32, this motif occurs in *GA* 34, 222.3–11, 225.21–26.3, 226.26–31, 234.6–16, 248.1, 249.6–11, 252.22–32, 263.20–25, 282.18–22, 283.32–35, 284.16–22, 320.13–24/159.10–16, 161.28–162.2, 162.22–26, 167.22–29, 177.12f., 178.3–7, 180.19–25, 187.31–88.4, 201.5–8, 202.4–6, 202.21–26, and 226.37–27.7.[15]

7. Heidegger locates the flaw in Plato or Aristotle. As was indicated, in 1931–32 he does so regarding Plato's interpretation of false *doxa.*

8. Because of features 6 and 7, Heidegger has to go beyond Plato and Aristotle and develop the proper account of the phenomenon. As was already shown, in 1931–32 Heidegger does so regarding the phenomenon of false *doxa* and the forking at the end of the lecture.

9. Since philosophy after Plato and Aristotle is a downward plunge (by taking *"alone"* [*GA* 34, 284/202] the aspect of Logos in *doxa;* see also 181/131), we have to repeat the Greeks (15ff., 111, 116, 119ff., 123ff., 182, 322/11ff., 80f., 84, 86ff., 89ff., 131f., 228).

10. This repetition is relevant not only to philosophy but to the entire current world (*GA* 34, 7ff., 45, 73f., 77f., 83, 86, 112ff., 119ff., 122, 145ff., 209, 213, 238ff./5ff., 34, 54f., 57f., 61, 62f., 81ff., 86ff., 88, 104ff., 150f., 153, 170ff.) as, for instance, it is an illusion to try to cure the current "external misery [through] the regulation of the international economy" (121f./88), as he says here in 1931–32, within a very severe economic crisis after the Wall Street crash in 1929.[16]

Also in 1933–34, Heidegger makes clear from the beginning on that we have to repeat the Greeks (*GA* 36/37, 88f.) since history after the Greeks is a downward plunge resulting in "Enlightenment and liberalism" (166), in which "all the powers to be fought against today have their roots" (166; see Marxism 147f., 151). At the end of his interpretation of the simile of the cave, he summarizes that we have seen that truth is unconcealing and the happening of history, and that this is not the history of theoretical thinking (*GA* 36/7, 225). Rather, it is "the totality of the history of one people as, in the Greeks, this history happens for us in advance, so to speak [*wie sie uns bei den Griechen gewissermaßen vorausgeschieht*]" (*GA* 36/7, 225),[17] and the Greeks are about the "*projection* of the world" (225). We on the other side of the inception are, even though Germans, for the most part just regular Dasein and even hostile toward National Socialism.[18] Thus, we need a leader (see also Fritsche 1999b, 85ff., 123f., 141f.). Heidegger continues:

> Today, the leader [*der Führer*] speaks again and again of the re-education [*Umerziehung*] toward the National Socialist world-view. This does not mean to adduce some or the other slogan, but rather to bring about a total change [*Gesamtwandel*], a projection of a world, from out of the bottom of which he educates the entire people. National Socialism is not some or the other system but rather the radical change [*Wandel von Grund aus*] of the German and, as we believe, also the European world. (*GA* 36/37, 225)

As I have shown, this belief in Hitler and National Socialism, far from having nothing to do with Heidegger's thinking, is the fulfillment of the notion of authentic existence and historicality in *Being and Time*. The alliance between Hitler and the Greeks has been virtually present already in *Being and Time* and has been worked out in the years after *Being and Time*.

Still, the 1933–34 lecture differs from the 1931–32 lecture in a way that is already indicated by the structure of both courses. In the 1931–32 lecture, the introduction takes 19 pages (*GA* 34, 1–19/1–13), the part on the simile of the cave 127 (21–147/15–106), and the part on the *Theaetetus* 174 (149–322/107–228). The 1933–34 lecture has one part more, and the proportions have changed. After a short introduction (*GA* 36/37, 83–89), a part on Heraclitus, language, and Plato takes 37 pages (89–125), the part on the simile of the cave 103 (127–229), and the part on the *Theaetetus* only 34 (231–64). In the first part, Heidegger makes three claims. First, in Plato one sees the "last fight [*letzte Kampf*]" (*GA* 36/37, 123) between truth as unconcealment and truth as correctness of statement for already in Plato himself and after Plato the latter prevails. Second, authentic truth is articulated, as in *Introduction to Metaphysics*, in Heraclitus's fragment on *polemos, Kampf* (battle, fight) (B 53), which Heidegger already here interprets as the drama of historicality, with special emphasis on element 6 (*GA* 36/37, 89ff.).[19] Third, as his fragment B 2 shows, Heraclitus articulates the authentic notion of language, namely, "*language is law-giving gathering* [*Sammlung*] *and thus disclosedness of the structure* [*Gefüges*] *of the beings*" (*GA* 36/37, 116). Heidegger raises here the alternative whether language is "in itself something primary, something that cannot be reduced to something else" (*GA* 36/37, 104) or whether it presupposes other structures of world-disclosure (100ff.). Historically, the latter view has become dominant since the times of Plato and Aristotle through the interpretation of speech as something present at hand (*GA* 36/37, 102ff.). Up to the early 1930s, Heidegger himself has not assumed the former. From that time on, however, he maintains that, as he puts it in *Introduction to Metaphysics*, "essence and Being speak in language" (*GA* 40, 58/see 53/57).[20] As already *Introduction to Metaphysics* shows, these three claims mark a turn in consequence of which one of the two kinds of investigations of *Being and Time* disappears and has already shrunken to 34 pages in 1933–34 from the 174 pages devoted to it in the 1931–32 lecture. The phenomena to be accounted for are no longer reduced to sempiternal existentialia discovered in structural analyses but rather to language and its changes in the history of being. The other kind of investigation, however, the drama of historicality, receives an even longer treatment than in 1931–32, especially since it already occurs in the part on Heraclitus. It does so because, as *Introduction to Metaphysics* shows, it remains vital to Heidegger.

Being and Time contains several references to philosophers in the history of philosophy as well as to history at large. I have focused on two, on the reference to the Greeks in the section on truth and on Heidegger's notion of historicality. The section on truth (*BT*, 212ff./256ff.) is placed right at the end of the last chapter of division 1 of *Being and Time,* the chapter in which Heidegger gathers all the existentialia in the structure of *Sorge* (care) (180ff./225ff.). In the preceding chapter, Heidegger develops several existentialia, first in general or in their ordinary instantiation (*BT,* 134ff./172ff.) and in a second step in their instantiation through fallen

Dasein or Dasein in the downward plunge (166ff./210ff.). This distinction indicates a notion of history as a downward plunge or falling in which at some point a crisis, a buzzing in the air, emerges to revert this downward plunge (see Fritsche 1999b, 29ff.; see also Fritsche 2003). In division 2, Heidegger lays out, along with the temporal interpretation of the existentialia developed in division 1, the structures and moves that enable Dasein to get out of its fallenness and downward plunge and become authentic. This discussion culminates in the notion of historicality (see Fritsche 1999b, 43ff., 124ff., and frequently). At the end of the downward plunge in division 1, the Greeks enter the stage as those whom we have to revitalize by stepping out of the tradition in which we live and by "plunging [that tradition] into nullity" (*BT,* 219/262) since it has covered up and distorted the Greeks. At the end of the same downward plunge retold in division 2, the community of the people, under the name of destiny, enters the stage and calls upon us to revitalize it by a "*disavowal* [*Widerruf*]" (*BT,* 386/438; see Fritsche 1999b, 21ff., 43ff., 66f., 83f., 101, 124f., 134f., 152f., 181f. passim) of society since society has toppled and covered up community. Regarding Heidegger's Greeks and Germans, in a way one just has to put 2 and 2 together.

Precisely because the chapter on historicality targets the deepest level of analysis and existence, Heidegger's discussions of the existentialia and of truth would perhaps not miss anything systematically significant if he had left out the chapter on historicality and the reference to the Greeks in the section on truth. The remaining references to the history of philosophy and history at large would probably not necessarily point to one single history. One could interpret the distinctions between ordinary and fallen Dasein and between inauthentic and authentic Dasein, as well as, say, Heidegger's interpretation of Descartes (*BT,* 89ff./122ff.), as possibilities that can be realized at any given time in history in different individuals or groups. Also, especially since in *Being and Time* and the lectures related to it, in contrast to the community of the people calling upon the Germans, neither the philosopher, when revitalizing the Greek way of philosophizing, nor these Greeks themselves, when unconcealing the beings, answered to any call; after *Being and Time* the Greeks and the community of the people might, in principle, have gone more or less their own ways, so to speak.

However, they did not do so. In the years to come, Heidegger explicitly tied together what, already in *Being and Time,* strongly leans toward each other. In 1931–32, he makes good on the legend of Plato in Syracuse and introduces the drama of historicality, as the key, into the structural analyses performed by the Greeks. The Greeks are no longer, as in the 1920s, just unconcealing phenomena, beings, their principles, and their being. Rather, in doing so, Plato discovers that the discovered structures contain the imperative to revolutionize the realm below the line, the cave, and Plato lays out the drama of historicality, which for Heidegger, up to that point, only the community of the German people has been performing. The expansion of the drama of historicality from the Germans in *Being and Time* onto the Germans and the Greeks in the 1931–32 lecture and later gives to history explicitly the unity of one single history within which, at the end of the drama of historicality, under the leadership of Hitler the Germans repeat the drama of historicality that the Greeks had performed in the beginning of the drama of historicality. The Greeks and the Germans work in a temporal tandem, so to speak, and Hitler is the agent of the revitalization of the Greek experience of being.

In 1931–32, the drama of historicality has already blossomed into the authentic experience of being in the Greeks and has explicitly become the structure governing the one single history of the "West," but it still takes place within the framework of existentialia, or side by side with them, even though, already at that point, the primacy of the existentialia over the drama of historicality might be seriously challenged or even voided. In any case, in 1933–34 the universalized drama of historicality quite openly sheds its subordination to omnipresent existentialia, and this process is completed in *Introduction to Metaphysics*.[21] From *Introduction to Metaphysics* onward, the drama of historicality unfolds itself as the different epochal ways of approaching beings, and it presupposes only the history of language and being but not omnipresent existentialia. Finally, in the course of this turn, Heidegger, as one would say in German, *wechselt die Pferde* (changes his horses). In 1931–32, Plato, along with Aristotle, was still the paradigmatic Greek to repeat for Heidegger. Thus, Heidegger went toward the anticipated National Socialist seizure of power with Plato as the revolutionary. From the 1933–34 lecture onward, Heraclitus and Parmenides were the Greeks to repeat. Thus, in 1933–34 and 1935, they are the revolutionaries.[22]

Heidegger's Drama of Historicality and His *Kehre*

Introduction to Metaphysics is the first text in which Heidegger's "reverted" Hegelianism is no longer grounded in omnipresent existentialia discovered in structural analyses. In addition, according to my presentation so far, it would be the first text in which Heidegger draws the consequences out of his very recent discovery that Plato and Aristotle are not the most advanced of the Greek philosophers but the beginning of a different epoch, the beginning of metaphysics. The interest in structural analyses and the assumption of Plato and Aristotle as the most advanced of the Greek philosophers went hand in hand in the 1920s and in the 1931–32 lecture, and both of these features were abandoned in the 1933–34 lecture. Thus, it is possible that their replacement with a history of being is indicative of the *Kehre* (turn) and that *Introduction to Metaphysics* is the first document of Heidegger after the *Kehre*. However, I have left out passages in the 1931–32 lecture in which Heidegger says that, already in Plato, there was a "waning of the fundamental experience" (*GA* 34, 120/87) of *alêtheia*. Still, these passages might be later additions by Heidegger.[23]

In any case, whether or not they are later additions, *Introduction to Metaphysics* is still prior to the *Kehre*. In the famous letter to Richardson from 1962 (see Richardson 1963, XVII), Heidegger dates the *Kehre* to around 1937. Habermas (1990, 156ff.) relied on this information when, in 1985, he interpreted the *Kehre* as a result of Heidegger's political disappointment with National Socialism and a rationalization, through the history of being, of his political engagement with it. Jean Grondin, however, in his 1987 book *Le tournant dans la pensée de Martin Heidegger*, located the *Kehre*—the thinking, answering the *Kehre* in Being itself, of radical finitude—already in 1928 (Grondin 1987, 76). In an article from 1991, he argues against Habermas and refers to section 262 of Heidegger's *Contributions to Philosophy*, written between 1936 and 1938, to defend his own interpretation (see Grondin 1991). However, Grondin turns this section upside down. To be sure, in that section Heidegger talks about an impasse of *Being and Time* and also about a new path he began in 1928. However, he does not say, as Grondin has it, that he continues pursuing this 1928 path. Rather, he lays out faults of both the path pursued in *Being and Time* and the 1928 path, and he concludes with directives for a new path that, he hopes, avoids the insurmountable impasses encountered on the path of *Being and Time* and the 1928 path.[24] In section 262, Heidegger does not use the word *Kehre*. However, when in 1962 he reflected upon his development, he certainly reserved the term *Kehre* for the third path, the one laid out for the future, and not for the 1928 path whose insurmountable difficulties he had recognized in 1936–38. Thus, being written between 1936 and 1938, section 262 confirms Heidegger's own information from 1962. If that is the case, *Introduction to Metaphysics* is still prior to the *Kehre*.[25]

In addition, section 262 of the *Contributions* also confirms Habermas's interpretation of the motivation for the *Kehre*. As, for the political left, for instance Horckheimer's famous essay "Traditional and Critical Theory" shows, in the *kairos* situation of the 1920s and 1930s in Germany and

Europe, several leftist and rightist theories, in all their differences (see Fritsche 1999b, 68ff., 148ff., 173ff.), shared one feature, namely, a peculiar mode of verification. A theory can fully be recognized as true only if in the future the new state of affairs that it anticipates as possible or even necessary, and which it helps to bring about—socialism, the community of the people, or some other community—has indeed become reality. As I have shown, the drama of historicality remains identical from *Being and Time* to *Introduction to Metaphysics*. In *Being and Time* and in 1931–32, it was Heidegger's anticipation of the National Socialist revolution; in 1933–34, his contribution to the proper execution of that revolution; and in 1935, his way to breathe new life into it as he, even in 1936 believing in Hitler (Fritsche 1999b, 217), feared that it was losing its momentum and in danger of relapsing into liberalism.[26] In the 1933–34 lecture, Heidegger speaks of a decision, more decisive than Plato's parricide in the *Sophist*, in which we stand today, and which has been expressed in *Being and Time* (*GA* 36/37, 255); a "radical change [*Wandlung von Grund aus*]" (255) of the understanding of being, which alone will provide the frame "for the spiritual history [*Geistesgeschichte*] of our people" (255).[27] This assumption "cannot be demonstrated but rather is a *belief* [*Glaube*] that must be vindicated through history" (255).

There are many ways of interpreting events that look like a refutation of a prognostic theory. When, in early Christianity, the widespread expectation of the imminent readvent of Jesus Christ was disappointed, the time horizon for expectation was expanded. Others give up the theory in question. After National Socialism and Stalinism, Adorno developed a theory of society and rationality that, in a way, carries the implication that it will be a sign of the truth of the theory that, sooner than later, hardly anyone will be able anymore to duplicate the notions of the theory and the motifs to develop it. On the political right, Max Scheler regarded World War I at its beginning as the decisive break with modernity and the beginning of the revitalization of community (Fritsche 1999b, 87ff.). After World War I, however, he viewed it as a further stage of modernity providing not the actuality but only the possibility of a step out of modernity (Fritsche 1999b, 274; before he abandoned any right-wing politics after Hitler had entered the political scene [Fritsche 1999b, 142ff.]). Regarding the issue of verification, several of Heidegger's later statements on the state of man and being certainly have the same ring as comparable ones in Adorno. More important, however, while in 1933–34 and even in 1935 Heidegger thought that National Socialism would lead us out of liberalism and Marxism, a remark on liberalism and the current state of affairs in section 262 of the *Contributions* (*GA* 65, 449/316) indicates that he acts here like Scheler after World War I and establishes the interpretation of National Socialism that would remain with him, namely, that National Socialism is the consummation of society, liberalism, and metaphysics with just the possibility of looking beyond metaphysics (see, e.g., Fritsche 1995). Most important, however, Heidegger reacts like many early Christians. As was mentioned, section 262 contains directives for the new path to pursue from 1937 on. Close to the beginning, Heidegger writes:

> Whoever ever wants to go under the eyes of the history of be-ing and wishes to experience how be-ing stays away [*ausbleibt*] in its own essential sphere and for a long time abandons this sphere to what is precisely not its ownmost . . . such a one must be able to grasp above all . . . (*GA* 65, 447/see 315)

One cannot avoid to relating this sentence to a very recent disillusionment on the part of Heidegger about Hitler and National Socialism. In 1936, he still believed in Hitler's capacity to be the agent of the rearrival of the authentic experience of being, though he had strong doubts concerning the empirical state of National Socialism (Fritsche 1999b, 217). In 1937, he seems to have given up his belief in Hitler and to have concluded that being continues to stay away from the sphere of seeming.[28] However, Heidegger does not give up his belief in being and his theory. Rather, he infers that he was wrong about the time horizon of his expectation, and he takes this error as a sign of flaws in the paths he has pursued up to that point. He also recognizes that these paths were, in Greek terms, hubristic. As he says at the end of section 262, one has to learn that

> the attempt at enthinking does not transgress its own historical measure and thus fall back into what has been up to now. (*GA* 65, 452/318)

Also because, in the same section 262, he maintains that the way in which he had approached the question of being on the path pursued in *Being and Time* was "necessarily" laid out that way (*GA* 65, 451/317), the hubristic aspect will refer—exclusively or in part, at least—to what was common to the path in *Being and Time* and the 1928 path, namely, the revolutionary ambitions of the drama of historicality, as the authentic experience of being, related to a figure and a political movement that was, as he thought to recognize in 1937, the consummation of "what has been up to now" (452/318) and not, as he had hoped up to then, the decisive break with the status quo. After the *Contributions*, Plato and Aristotle remain for Heidegger the beginning of metaphysics, and the pre-Socratics remain the inception the moderns have to repeat. In this sense, the drama of historicality stays firmly in place for the moderns. However, the necessity of the

Greeks to repeat and those who have to repeat them have changed through Heidegger's recognition of hubris; for after 1937, neither the pre-Socratics nor "we" nor anyone else will be the kind of violent revolutionary that Hitler, the German people, Plato, and the pre-Socratics were between 1927 and 1935. Furthermore, the time horizon for the expectation of the rearrival of being has changed. Consequently, in his 1955 return present to Jünger, Heidegger, in all friendship, makes clear that, just like Plato's notion of idea, Jünger's notion of *Gestalt* in his "revolutionary" 1932 book *Der Arbeiter* (*The Worker*), stems from *Ge-Stell*, that is, from metaphysics (*GA* 9, 400f./303); that, in general, Jünger is still caught up in metaphysical thinking (395/299 and often); and that we have not yet reached the line, let alone transgressed it (389ff., 405ff./294ff., 306ff.).[29]

Notes

1. M. Heidegger, "Zur Seinsfrage: Über 'Die Linie,'" in *GA* 9, 385–426. On the title of the volume in honor of Jünger, *Freundschaftliche Begegnungen* (*Friendly Encounters*), see Fritsche 1999b, 290–92, 323–25. Quotations in English not followed by a reference to an English edition are my own translation. If a reference to an English translation is preceded by "see," I have altered the English translation.

2. A *Treppenwitz* is a silly joke; quite literally, a *Witz* (joke) made in passing on the *Treppe* (stairways), the public realm that runs through the various layers of apartments or offices just as, in Plato's simile of the divided line, the vertical line runs through the various layers of reality.

3. This view does not exclude that, before Husserl and Heidegger, some other modern philosopher might have made moves into the right direction. In the second half of the 1920s, Heidegger praised Kant—not, however, as Caputo would have it, for liberating philosophy from the grip of the Greeks but rather for revitalizing their way of philosophizing. As he says in a lecture course in SS 1926 on the history of Greek philosophy from Thales to Aristotle (which operates on the model summarized above [see *GA* 22, 22, 32, 218, 313 passim]), "[After Aristotle] decay [*Verfall*] of Greek philosophy. Thereafter, this high level of research hasn't been achieved any more. In modernity [*Neuzeit*], Kant became the first Greek again [*ist Kant wieder der erste Grieche geworden*], though only for a short time" (313). In his Aristotle lecture in WS 1921–22, Heidegger uses, at least in the German original, a colloquial formula to lay out his program for the years to come: We have to confront ourselves with Greek philosophy, and it is quite possible "that, in this settlement of accounts, as much as we have progressed in the last two thousand years, we still come up short [*den Kürzeren ziehen*]" (*GA* 61, 170/128).

4. From *Being and Time* on, at the latest, Heidegger changes his vocabulary and labels a past that we have to repeat *Gewesenheit* and a past that should not be repeated *Vergangenheit* (see Fritsche 1999b, 284).

5. On this turn, see Görland 1981; Grondin 1987, 66ff., 71ff. (for whom this is Heidegger's famous *Kehre*, as will be discussed in the last section); Thomä 1990, 458ff.; Hackenesch 2001, 35ff.

6. He does so with reference to poems by Goethe and Matthias Claudius, two quotations from Nietzsche, etymologies of Indo-European words, and Greek and Latin grammatical terms, but without any quotation from Greek philosophers or other Greek texts (except the reference in passing to Aristotle's *Metaphysics* 4.1.1003a27 [*GA* 40, 17/16/17]). Only at the beginning of the last third of this first part does he quote a Greek text, namely, fragment B 53 of Heraclitus, the fragment on *polemos,* war (47/61f./64f.; see also, in later parts, 87, 107, 110/113, 140, 144/120, 149, 153; and *polemos* in fragment B 80 [127/166/177]). The fragment contains neither the word *phusis* nor the word *alêtheia*. In parts 2–4, Heidegger constantly refers back to part 1 and uses its results as premises in his interpretations, a method which, in light of the peculiar procedure in part 1, looks utterly circular.

Heidegger discusses the first two of the occurrences of *alêtheia* and *alêthês* in Parmenides (fragments B 1, ll. 29, 30; B 2, l. 4; B 8, ll. 15, 28, 39, and B 51; *GA* 40, 86/112/119) and none of the occurrences of *phusis* and *phuô* (fragments B 8, l. 10; B 10, ll. 1, 5, 6; B 16, l. 3; and B 19, l. 1). He discusses the two occurrences of *phusis* (fragments B 1 [*GA* 40, 97/127/134] and B 123 [*GA* 40, 87/114/121]) in Heraclitus but not the occurrence of *alêthês* (fragment B 112). He quotes a sentence with *phusis* in *Timaeus* (50e1–4) but for other purposes (*GA* 40, 50/66/70), quotes Pindar, *Olympian Odes* 9.100 (*GA* 40, 77/101/106), and interprets Sophocles' *Oedipus at Colonus,* ll. 1224f., along the line of his Heraclitus and Parmenides interpretation (*GA* 40, 135/177/189). The first chorus of the *Antigone* contains *phulon* (l. 342) and *phusis* (l. 345). Heidegger does not mention this but, in truly brilliant translations, makes the words fit his interpretation of *phusis* (*GA* 40, 112/147/156). He does not discuss, and does not even mention, any of the so-called natural philosophers among the pre-Socratics.

7. On the strategic function of Heidegger's *Antigone* interpretation for his interpretation of Heraclitus and Parmenides in 1935, see Fritsche 1999a, 10ff.

8. On the motif of trenches and lines in Heidegger, see Fritsche 1995; see also Fritsche 1999b, 1ff., 87ff., 224ff. passim.

9. See *GA* 40, 152, 173, 178, 180, 182, 192/143, 164, 169, 172, 174, 183/153, 175, 180, 183, 185, 195. Even if, or especially if, these occurrences of "re" do not mean the reoccurrence of a temporal past, they are meant to minimize the difference between the pre-Socratics in *Introduction to Metaphysics* and the Germans in *Being and Time* and in *Introduction to Metaphysics*. The repetition of the Greeks that the Germans have to perform looks more convincing if already the Greeks performed a revolution through repetition even though for Heidegger's purpose of an alliance between the German *Volksgemeinschaft* and the Greeks it was, in principle and as Heidegger's writings after 1942 show, not necessary that the Greeks perform a revolution, let alone a revolution through repetition. See note 14.

10. For Philipse, Heidegger's neo-Hegelianism is finally a "reversal of Hegel" (1998, 172) for "Heidegger's narrative of productionist metaphysics turns Hegel's optimism into pessimism" (172). In what follows, I use "reverted Hegelianism" in the following sense: In his *Science of Logic,* Hegel thinks manifestation as alien-

ation. Concretely, in the *Philosophy of Right,* this is the step of the disappearance of the Greek state and the emergence of the person, subjectivity, and (modern, capitalist) society. In Heidegger's drama of historicality in *Being and Time* and in rightwing thinking at his time in general, it is the disappearance of (the Greek, the Christian love, the *Volks-,* etc.) community and, as in Hegel, the emergence of society (see Fritsche 1999b, 68ff. passim; see also Fritsche 2003), and in the drama of historicality in the later Heidegger, it is the disappearance of the pre-Socratics and the beginning of metaphysics. In Hegel, however, manifestation as alienation is integrated into a logic of manifestation as development and sublation. Concretely, in the *Philosophy of Right,* Hegel recognizes the right of society and subjectivity, and he polemicizes against all efforts to go back to some or the other premodern state. Subjectivity and society must not be canceled but sublated. For Heidegger and other right-wingers at his time, however, the concept of society and subjectivity is of no inner value. Thus, it must be canceled and not sublated (see Fritsche 1999b, 21ff., 57ff., 68ff., 152ff., 173ff. passim). While romantic rightwingers wanted to re-realize community in its premodern state, revolutionary rightists—such as Hitler, Scheler (before his turn), and Heidegger—maintained that society was "just" a matter of mentality displayed in liberalism, parliamentarianism, unions, and social democracy, and that the revitalization of community could and should take over the capitalist mode of production and modern technology (see Fritsche 1999b, XII, 18ff., 68ff., 72ff., 114ff., 127ff., 134ff., 153ff., 180ff.; see also Fritsche 2003). The issue of optimism or pessimism is a different one, and in Heidegger pessimism, if one can label it that way, comes in only after his recognition that the National Socialist revolution did not bring about the return of the inception (see the last section).

11. On *GA* 34, 16–18/11–12 and similar passages, see note 23.

12. In the drama of historicality in *Being and Time,* Heidegger uses for the proper response of authentic Dasein to the call of destiny a sentence with the verb *erwidert* (*BT,* 386), which Macquarrie and Robinson have translated with "makes a *reciprocative rejoinder*" (*BT,* 386/438) and Stambaugh (1996, 352f.) with "*responds.*" While the verb *erwidern* in itself is indeed notoriously ambiguous, the context in Heidegger shows clearly that he means it in the sense of "to comply with a call for help/command" (Fritsche 1999b, 7–28 passim). Macquarrie and Robinson's translation (and Stambaugh's as well [Fritsche 1999b, 335f.]) promotes the "American" understanding of Heidegger, according to which authentic Dasein behaves like the prototypical USA-individual (Fritsche 1999b, 207–15; while in fact it is a *Held* [hero], the paradigmatic individual for conservatives and right-wingers in Germany at Heidegger's time [Fritsche 1999b, 323–27 passim]). Deconstructionism and postmodernism in the United States have managed to sell Heidegger, who until the end of his career has sermonized *Fügung in* (compliance with/ subjugation to) destiny and fate, as the first and epoch-making critic of these and other "metaphysical" notions.

13. For an introduction to the issue, see Orozco 1995, 32–90. Heidegger did not invent the drama of historicality but just picked up and raised to the height of authentic existence a theory of history that united many different right-wingers at the time (see my discussion of Adolf Hitler [Fritsche 1999b, 68–87] and Max

Scheler [87–124]); a theory of which left-wingers (e.g., Georg Lukács [149–73] and Paul Tillich [173–87]) as well as liberals (e.g., the late Scheler [142ff.]) recognized that it was the opposite of their theories.

14. In section 74 of *Being and Time,* the drama of historicality proper, Heidegger uses the term *Geschehen* several times, centered around the sentence in which he comments on the notion of destiny: ". . . destiny [*Geschick*]. This is how we designate the historizing [*Geschehen*] of the community, of the [*des*] people" (*BT,* 384/see 436; see Fritsche 1999b, 13 n. 17). Although he also used it in other ways, the term *Geschehen* has become his main shorthand for authentic history. In 1931–32, Heidegger uses the term's variants *geschehen, Geschehen, Geschehnis* constantly from the beginning of his interpretation of part 2 of the simile of the cave on (*GA* 34, 31/24) and, in fact, from the beginning of the entire course on (15ff./11ff.) as the "occurrence [*Geschehen*] of *alêtheia* [is the] genuine content of the allegory" (87/64) of the cave. As I cannot show here, by the usage of *Geschehen,* Heidegger is able to find in particular elements 2 and 7 of the drama of historicality in Plato's simile of the cave. His effort is not very convincing. This unconvincingness, in turn, just shows how eager he obviously was to align his drama of historicality and Plato and to minimize as much as possible remaining differences (see previous note 9).

15. Because of the issue discussed later (see note 23), I quote at least one of these passages. Heidegger points out the different kinds of characters included in the excess (*GA* 34, 219ff./157ff.), among them characters thematized in Plato's *Sophist.* In his interpretation of the *Sophist* in 1924–25, Heidegger had discussed them (*GA* 19, 500ff./346ff.), and he had emphasized the two limits of the Greeks mentioned earlier (e.g., *GA* 19, 225/155). In 1931–32, Heidegger continues pointing out how much the later Plato "struggled [*damit gerungen hat*]" (*GA* 34, 221/159) to clarify these things, and finally he says: "It is another question whether Plato really succeeded in demonstrating the inner connection between the various characters of being [*Sein*]. No more than Aristotle, and later Kant, did Plato find his way through this problem [*mit dem Problem nicht durchgekommen*]. The reasons for this already lie hidden at the beginning of ancient philosophy; Plato himself was no longer able to master them. The superior strength of what had already determined the direction of the understanding of being [*Sein*] remained in force" (*GA* 34, 222/159; on Kant in such contexts, see previous note 3). The Heidegger of the history of being was no longer interested in the problem at stake, and he no longer used the language of *ringen mit* and *mit einem Problem durchkommen.* The phrase "no longer" obviously does not mean that others before Plato had managed to solve the problem at hand but that Plato was no longer able to do so. Rather, it means that Plato achieved many things but failed or no longer managed to achieve also the solution of this problem. The reason why he could not solve this problem is not that with him a new epoch began that separated him from the earlier philosophers who could solve the problem since, at their time, the space of authentic truth had not yet collapsed. Rather, the reason is an understanding of being that did not establish itself in Plato but had been there already since the beginning of antique philosophy. Though Plato broke the power of several preconceptions (esp. *GA* 34, 263–92/187–207), even he could not break the under-

standing of being that had been with the Greek philosophers from the beginning on. Thus, not being broken, this understanding of Being and its superior strength did not come into existence with Plato but "remained in force" in him.

16. Heidegger was always very elitist, and so, he says, were the Greeks (e.g., *GA* 34, 32/25). Modernity and modern liberalism are, in the first place, a loss of Being: "But this staking of the authentic Self, and the stance arising therefrom, are not immediately available to every arbitrary human being, nor to all in the same way. The Greeks knew better than anyone else before and after them that every existence has its own law and rank. All leveling [*Gleichmacherei*] is at bottom an *impoverishment* of Dasein—not of these or those possessions and goods, but of being [*Sein*] as such" (238f./170).

17. Note *geschieht* (see previous note 14). Close to the beginning of the lecture, Heidegger says that to listen to the inception "does not mean to return to antiquity and declare it to be the rigid [*starr*] yardstick of all Dasein [but rather] that this great inception is projected beyond and ahead of ourselves as that which we have to catch up with—again, not in order to bring Hellenism [*Griechentum*] to completion, but in order to fully employ and bring to domination the fundamental possibilities of the proto-Germanic tribalty [*um die Grundmöglichkeiten des urgermanischen Stammeswesens auszuschöpfen und zur Herrschaft zu bringen*]. . . . If we, in this way, with the primordial courage of our Dasein, directed forward, listen back to the voices of the great inception—not in order to become Greeks and Greek but in order to perceive the elemental laws of our German tribalty in their most simple forcefulness and greatness and to expose ourselves to this greatness as a trial for proving ourselves [*um die Urgesetze unseres germanischen Menschenstammes in der einfachsten Eindringlichkeit und Größe zu vernehmen und uns selbst dieser Größe zur Prüfung und Bewährung*]—then we hear . . ." (*GA* 36/37, 89; the "tribalty [*Stammesart*] and language [of the Greeks] shares with us the same origin [*Herkunft*]" [GA 36/37, 6]). As also the entire quote itself and the adjective "rigid" show, formulas such as "not in order to become Greeks and Greek but" do not, as they are often read in American literature, demand the destruction of every past, including the Greeks, but are the polemical statement of a revolutionary rightist against romantic rightists (see previous note 10).

Heidegger's drama of historicality calls for a revitalization—or "repetition" (*BT*, 386/438; see Fritsche 1999b, 13ff., 57ff. passim)—of a past, and so does his concept of destruction of the history of philosophy in the 1920s. In both cases, it is not a matter of simple repetition, as it were, because a repetition of the past community exactly the way it was—that is, without modern technology and capitalist mode of production—would not succeed. Similarly, an exact copy of Greek philosophy would end up in the same difficulties in which Greek philosophy had ended. To use modern technology in the fight against society redeems and sublates at best modern technology, but not society (see note 10). To analyze modern philosophy as a downward plunge in order to become a "Greek again" (*GA* 22, 313) and to recognize and overcome the limits of the Greeks is not a sublation of modern philosophy, let alone, as Caputo has it, modern philosophy itself. In the 1950s and later, Heidegger used in his theory on modern technology formulas that are not that dissimilar to formulas of sublation. It is not impossible that the phrase in *Introduction to Metaphysics* that I quoted earlier—the "inception, as incipient, must, in a certain way, leave itself behind. (In this way, it necessarily conceals itself, but this self-concealing is not nothing)" (*GA* 40, 199f.; see 191/204)—is the first of such gestures toward an integration of elements of sublation. The fact that it would occur in the first text of Heidegger as the historian of the history of being would not speak against this possibility. When, in the 1920s, interpreting Plato and Aristotle and not so much the pre-Socratics, he developed the notion of being as being produced (see end of first section), the notion of Greek or, in general, handicraft production was for Heidegger polemical against modern subjectivity and technology and had utopian qualities in his fight against society (and he criticized in Plato and Aristotle only that they interpreted also other phenomena in light of being as being produced). To integrate elements of sublation would be one possible way of saving and redeeming a hope that was so dear to Heidegger within a framework in which production was no longer the Greek experience of Being but had become the beginning of metaphysics.

18. See notes 16 and 28.

19. In his comments, written shortly after 1945, on his *Rectoral Address,* Heidegger fends off criticism of this speech and maintains that he used the notion of *Kampf* (battle) not in the sense of "war" but rather in the sense of *polemos* in Heraclitus's fragment B 53, which, in turn, means what *erôs* in Heraclitus means ("*SGU,*" 28/20f.). His comment is as true as it is beside the point. In 1931–32, in his interpretation of the philosopher as liberator Heidegger maintains that, according to Plato, the liberator—Socrates!—does not talk to the people in the cave but proceeds—like the creators in *Introduction to Metaphysics*—"by laying hold of them violently and dragging them away" (*GA* 34, 85/62), and Heidegger immediately applies this model to the situation at his time (86/63). In his comments on *polemos* in Heraclitus's fragment B 53 in 1933–34, he maintains that *polemos* does not mean "*agôn*, contest, in which two friendly opponents compete with each other" (*GA* 36/37, 90), and that the opponent "is not a partner" (90) but, in the language of Carl Schmitt's *The Concept of the Political* from 1932, the "foe [*Feind*]" (*GA* 36/37, 90). Again, he immediately applies this notion to his time. A foe is the one "who is the source of an essential threat to the Dasein of the people and its individual members" (90f.). Having settled in the innermost root of the Dasein of a people and acting against the essence of that people, the foe within a people is much more dangerous than a foe outside of the people (91). Thus, one has to spot that foe and "to launch the attack on a long-term basis with the goal of the total annihilation [*völligen Vernichtung*] of the foe" (91). In 1933–34, Heidegger was professor of philosophy and dean of the university of Freiburg. Such a person could hardly launch a more brutal threat against possible or actual dissidents of National Socialism.

20. See Christina Lafont (1994) on Heidegger's theory of language in *Being and Time* (29ff.; her critique of Tugendhat 80ff.) and from the middle of the 1930s on (117ff.).

21. In 1936–38, Heidegger refers to the beginning of this emancipation of the drama of historicality from its subordination to existentialia thus: "Thinking became increasingly historical, i.e., the differentiation between an historical view

and a systematic view became increasingly untenable and inappropriate. Be-ing itself announced its historical essential sway" (*GA* 65, 451/317f.; see also note 24).

22. The fact that, in 1933–34, Plato is no longer the paradigmatic Greek is no reason not to analyze the drama with reference to him. Later on, after Plato and Aristotle have become the beginning of metaphysics, Heidegger finds traces of the pre-Socratics in them. Since, in 1933–34, Heidegger was dean of the university, he probably couldn't spend that much time on the preparation of his courses. The editor of the 1933–34 lecture comments that Heidegger wrote a manuscript only for the introduction and the first part, while for the parts on the *Republic* and the *Theaetetus* he used the manuscript of the 1931–32 lecture (*GA* 36/37, 129, n. 4). It is not that, in 1933–34, Heidegger says on the cave and the *Theaetetus* something substantially different from what he had said in 1931–32. Still, the change concerning Plato already leaves its mark. For instance, in the part on the cave, Heidegger sees Plato's theory of ideas at the beginning of a development that finally leads to Marxism and "mishmash [*Mischmasch*]" out of which National Socialism leads us (*GA* 36/37, 147f.). To get rid of Marxism requires a reckoning with the history of the theory of ideas (151). In the part on the *Theaetetus*, Heidegger drops completely the discussion of the excess, cuts off, so to speak, the edges of Plato's breaking through the prejudices of earlier philosophers, and drops completely the theme of the need to step beyond Plato regarding the proper interpretation of the phenomena. At the end, he has an interpretation of the forking as the condition of the possibility of the fight and a call for decision and the people (262ff.), which is, relatively, much too long and also arbitrary. Possibly, such an interpretation was already his intention in the 1931–32 lecture. In 1933–34, however, it just shows that he no longer has a genuine interest in his 1931–32 *Theaetetus* interpretation.

In the 1942 essay "Plato's Doctrine of Truth" ("Platons Lehre von der Wahrheit"), Heidegger does not even once use the key term of his interpretations in 1931–32 and 1933–34, *Geschehen* (see note 14); neither does he use the vocabulary of the philosopher as producing being, new law-giving, and so forth, and of the idea of the good as empowerment. He uses a word with the root *Geschehen* ("what is really happening [*das eigentlich Geschehende*]"; "PDT," 237/182) only once, as a term for the alleged epochal change that, in Plato, truth as correctness of judgment takes over. In other words, as in contrast to the 1931–32 and 1933–34 lectures, the Plato of 1942 does not lay out the drama of historicality. To be true, Heidegger refers to the fourth stage of the narrative in the simile of the cave, he uses the word "battle [*Kampf*]" ("PDT," 223/171), and he also says that the narrative is completed only in that fourth stage (223/171). However, while in 1931–32 and 1933–34 in this fourth stage the philosopher replaces the existing world with a new world, in 1942 he just leads the people upward so as to see being and to realize that the idea of the good grants the appearing of the visible form, and that "[t]hrough this granting, the being [*Seiende*] is held within being [*Sein*] and thus is 'saved' [*gerettet*]" (229/176). In terms of the line, the philosopher no longer crosses the line to return into the realm below the line in order, finally, to replace the latter with a different world; rather, he points toward the realm above the line to ennoble, as it were, the realm below the line and its inhabitants. Regarding the pre-

Socratics, Heidegger performs the same reinterpretation at the latest from his course on Parmenides in 1942–43 onward, shortly after the disastrous loss of huge German armies at Stalingrad, the turning point of World War II.

In his interpretation of the simile of the cave in SS 1926 (*GA* 22, 99–108), the way upward is a matter of making explicit the understanding of Being at work in the inhabitants of the cave (103). The dramatic peculiarities of his 1931–32 and 1933–34 interpretations are absent, and Heidegger does not even mention the fourth stage. Already in summer 1926, the interpretation of the simile of the cave is followed by an interpretation of the *Theaetetus* (109–39). Here, Heidegger is interested in the problems of becoming, nonbeing, and Logos, and he has not yet zoomed in on the problem of false *doxa* as a crucial aspect of seeming and its power of persistence. Independent of this issue, however, here in 1926 Heidegger is, as one sees immediately, still far away from the ingenuity and peculiar elegance of the part on the *Theaetetus* in the 1931–32 lecture. It is a pity that, to my knowledge, the later Heidegger never commented extensively on his lectures on Plato and Aristotle in the 1920s and early 1930s. As to their phenomenological core, so to speak, in principle he didn't need to retract anything substantial. He just had to acknowledge that he had misunderstood as the limit, unbreakable even for Plato and Aristotle, of the Greeks what, as he realized in 1933–34, was in fact the beginning of a new epoch in the history of being.

23. In his guidelines for the publication of his lectures, Heidegger requested that every editor produce a single continuous text out of Heidegger's manuscript of the lecture and the other materials related to it. The editor of the 1931–32 lecture, Hermann Mörchen, had available, in addition to Heidegger's manuscript and transcripts of the actual lecture, relatively much material that was written by Heidegger after the lecture (*GA* 34, 334f./237f.). Mörchen has inserted some of it (335f./239), and obviously quite a lot. With its 322 pages, the 1931–32 lecture is perhaps the longest one, even though Mörchen left out most of Heidegger's summaries of the previous session at the beginning of a new one (336/239). (For instance, though fully formulated texts, the 1921–22 lecture has only 160 pages and the 1933–34 lecture 181; even the lecture on the *Sophist,* conducted four hours per week, is shorter [610 pages].) It contains the following passages in which Heidegger says that Plato was no longer fully in the realm of the original experience of truth: *GA* 34, 16.8–18.7, 93.9–94.2, 120.5–20, 122.3–4, 123.13–25.20; probably also 13.22–14.20, 15.23, 16.3, 46.30–31, 58.1–4, 94.6–10, 106.16, 137.15–38.3 (or 138.25), and also 117.18–22 (or only 117.21), 142.16–44.12, and 146.1–12/11.10–12.26, 67.33–68.13, 87.12–24, 88.26–27, 89.15–91.1; probably also 9.22–10.7, 10.36, 11.6–7, 35.18–19, 43.11–13, 68.16–20, 77.9, 99.9–26 (or 100.6), and also 85.17–21 (or only 85.20), 102.33–4.3, and 105.16–18. These passages amount to between six and ten pages, and they are all in the part on the *Republic,* while all references to Plato's shortcoming in the part on the *Theaetetus* operate in the framework of Plato and Aristotle as the most advanced of the Greek philosophers (see previous note 15). On *GA* 34, 16.32–17.4/11.29–35, Heidegger announces a discussion of truth in the pre-Socratics, but he makes good on such a promise only in the 1933–34 and not in the 1931–32 lecture. As was mentioned, for the parts on the *Republic* and the *Theaetetus,* Heidegger used the manuscript of the 1931–32 lec-

ture (see *GA* 36/37, 129, n. 4). Thus, one can easily imagine that he added the passages in question to the manuscript of the 1931–32 lecture when he reread it for the preparation of the 1933–34 course. The additions would occur only in the part on the *Republic* because the drama of historicality remained vital to him whereas he had lost interest in structural analyses. (One of the aforementioned passages, which itself might contain later additions, displays very nicely the issue for Heidegger in those days: "The essence of *alêtheia* is not clarified, so that we come to suspect that Plato does not yet grasp it, or no longer grasps it, in a *primordial* manner. Yet was it *previously* grasped in such a way?" [*GA* 34, 93.9–12/67.33–35].)

There are several ways, some more probable than others, to account for the aforementioned passages, even the sentence on page 93.9–12/67.33–35 as it stands, as parts of the original lecture in 1931–32. If they were already delivered in 1931–32, it would show that the concerns and the framework of the 1933–34 lecture were already present in 1931–32. However, it would also show that, at that point of time, these concerns did not yet push aside, so to speak, the approach of the lectures in the 1920s. For the points of my paper it does not matter when Heidegger began considering the turn of 1933–34.

As to possible "re-inscriptions," so to speak, in the *Rectoral Address* (a further instantiation of the drama of historicality, see Fritsche 1999b, 216ff.) Heidegger does not mention Heraclitus's fragment, uses only three proper names—Aeschylus, Prometheus, and Carl von Clausewitz ("*SGU*," 11, 11, 18/7, 7, 12)—and finishes with a quote from Plato ("*SGU*," 19/13). Plato has a distinguished place in the speech (see Fritsche 1999b, 220ff.). In addition, Heidegger's reference to *energeia* as "human 'being-at-work'" ("*SGU*," 12/7) certainly stems from his lecture course on Aristotle in SS 1931, in which Aristotle is still the culmination of Greek philosophy (see on Heidegger's summary Fritsche 1999b, 344f.). Thus, given the 1931–32 lecture on Plato and battle, it is possible that, in the *Rectoral Address,* Heidegger thought (more, equally, or only) of Plato, and that, from the 1933–34 lecture on, Heraclitus's battle and, from the lecture course in WS 1942–43 on, the pre-Socratics as pious thinkers overshadowed Plato. The replacement of Plato with Heraclitus would also disassociate Heidegger from the reactionary Platonists (see previous note 13) and his own Plato interpretation at that time. (Heidegger sees in the usage of "being exposed [*Ausgesetztheit*]" in the *Rectoral Address* a clear indication that "battle [*Kampf*]" in the *Rectoral Address* refers to Heraclitus ["*SGU*," 28/21]; see, however, for instance "*given over* [*ausgesetzt*]" [*GA* 34, 77/56]). At any rate, Heidegger's later comment on his usage of *Kampf* (battle) in the *Rectoral Address—Kampf* as the "reciprocal recognition that exposes itself to what is essential [*das wechselseitige sich anerkennende Sichaussetzen dem Wesenhaften*]" ("*SGU*," 28/21)— is certainly a cynical euphemism for the threat of "total annihilation" (*GA* 36/37, 91) in the 1933–34 lecture (see previous note 19), a formula which is as blasphemic as is the "plunging . . . into nullity" (*BT,* 219/262) in *Being and Time.*

24. In section 262 of the *Contributions,* Heidegger sketches a history of being, addresses a difficulty thinking it—namely, representational thinking—and points out that even his usage of the distinction between the ontological and the ontic remains caught up in this difficulty (*GA* 65, 446–50/314–17). He continues, in Emad and Maly's correct translation:

1. By this approach be-ing itself is apparently still made into an object, and the most decisive opposite of that is attained which the run up of the question of be-ing has already opened up for itself. But *Being and Time* after all aims at demonstrating "time" as the domain for projecting-opening be-ing. Certainly, but if things had remained that way, then the question of being would never have been unfolded as *question* and thus as enthinking of what is most question-worthy.

2. Thus it **was** [*galt*] necessary to overcome, at the deciding juncture, the crisis of the question of being that **was** necessarily **initially** so laid out [*notwendig so zunächst angelegten*], and above all to avoid an objectification of be-ing—on the one hand by *holding back* the "temporal" interpretation of be-ing and at the same time by attempting besides to make the truth of be-ing "visible" independent of the issue of the "temporal" interpretation of be-ing (freedom unto the ground in *On the Essence of Ground,* and yet especially in the first part of this treatise the ontic-ontological schema is still thoroughly maintained). By merely thinking further in the direction that had been set forth by the question, the crisis **did** [*ließ*] not let itself be mastered. Rather, the multiple leap into the essential sway of be-ing itself **had** [*mußte*] to be ventured, which at the same time **required** [*forderte*] a **more originary** [*ursprünglichere*] enjoining into history [*Einfügung in die Geschichte*].

3. The relation to the inception, the attempt to clarify *alêtheia* as an essential character of beingness itself, the grounding of the distinction of being and a being. Thinking became increasingly historical, i.e., the differentiation between an historical view and a systematic view became increasingly untenable and inappropriate. Be-ing itself announced its historical essential sway.

4. However, there was and still continues to be a fundamental difficulty: Be-ing is to be projected open in its essential sway, but projecting-opening itself is the "essential sway" of be-ing, is projecting-opening as en-ownment.

5. Unfolding the question of being unto enthinking of be-ing must all the more unreservedly give up any representational approach, the more inabiding in be-ing this enthinking becomes; and this unfolding must come to know that . . . (*GA* 65, 451/see 317f.; italics Heidegger's; boldface and enumeration mine; none of my changes of Emad and Maly's translation is relevant to the issue of Grondin's rendering of the passage.)

Obviously, in points 1 and 2, Heidegger states one or more shortcomings of *Being and Time.* In points 2 and 3, he reports about a path he embarked on after *Being and Time* to avoid the latter's shortcoming(s). In the phrase in brackets in point 2, he obviously refers to *On the Essence of Ground* as representative of this path; since *On the Essence of Ground* was published in 1929, he embarked on the path in question between 1926–27 and 1929, say, 1928 (see previous note 5). In the same phrase in brackets, he says that also the path of 1928 suffers from a shortcoming. In point 4, he states a further shortcoming of the path of 1928. In point 5, switching from the imperfect tense to the present tense, he lays out criteria of a path that, he obviously hopes, avoids the shortcomings of *Being and Time* as well as of the 1928 path (on the continuation of the quotation see the remainder of the paper). Thus, in the entire passage, Heidegger talks about three paths, namely, *Being and Time,* the 1928 path, and a third one which he obviously begins in the years the *Contributions* were written, that is, between 1936 and 1938.

In his 1991 essay "Prolegomena to an Understanding of Heidegger's Turn," Grondin refers to point 1 (102) and quotes point 2 thus:

> In order to surmount, at a decisive moment, the crisis of the question of being (a question which **must** necessarily be set into motion in this manner); above all, in order to *avoid a reification of being* (*vor allem* eine Vergegenständlichung des Seyns zu vermeiden), we **must,** on the one hand, retain the "*temporal*" interpretation of being, and, on the other, attempt to render the truth of being "visible" independently of this perspective. . . . [Grondin's ellipses] The crisis **cannot** be mastered by simply thinking further in the direction of questioning already initiated. We **must** attempt a multiple leap into the essence of being itself, which **will** at the same time necessitate a **most original** penetration into history. (Grondin 1991, 102; italics Grondin's, boldface mine)

According to Grondin, Heidegger says here that, after *Being and Time,* there has been just one new path, the one of 1928, emerging out of the recognition of the essential flaw of *Being and Time;* between 1936 and 1938, Heidegger looks back to this path and affirms that he continues pursuing it; thus, the *Kehre* took place in 1928 (Grondin 1991, 102f.; according to Grondin, with *Introduction to Metaphysics,* Heidegger took up again the path of 1928 as, in the early 1930s, he had given up to pursue the "task of thinking" because he had succumbed to the "raving madness [*frénésie*]" [Grondin 1987, 76; see also 16, 125; *frénésie* also used for modern technology, 106] of Nazism).

As one sees, Grondin leaves out passages 3, 4, and 5; leaves out the sentence in brackets on *On the Essence of Ground* in passage 2; renders the imperfect tense of all the governing verbs in passage 2 as present or future tense; replaces the comparative "more originary" in passage 2 with the superlative "most original"; and leaves out "initially" in passage 2. As one easily recognizes, all these changes one would make if one intentionally wanted to find in the passage the content that Grondin sees in it. The maneuvers of Grondin, a Gadamer scholar and Gadamer biographer, are a stunning example of the power of prejudice in Gadamer's sense. Also, as one can already surmise from Emad and Maly's "enjoining," Grondin's "penetration into history" turns Heidegger's *Einfügung in die Geschichte* upside down.

While in, say, skiing a *Kehre* can be a matter of a split second, Heidegger's *Kehre* certainly required more time for its execution, if not its conception (see Richardson 1963, XVII). Thus, when in section 262 of the *Contributions* Heidegger lays out, in the present tense, criteria for a new path, it is not necessary that, in the *Contributions* themselves, he has already managed to produce texts that meet these criteria. One could even imagine that, in hindsight, Heidegger would not ac-knowledge any of his texts as a successful completion of the *Kehre*, and he would still be right in speaking of the *Kehre* and its beginning in 1937. For the same rea-son, however, it is not impossible that, in 1936–38, he had already been thinking for some time according to the criteria of section 262, at least in one line of his thinking. Thus, the *Kehre* might have begun earlier, maybe even shortly after the 1928 path. As to my knowledge, there is nothing in Heidegger's speeches and lec-tures in the first half of the 1930s that would entitle one to contradict his own rec-ollection in 1962. Besides, it would still be a matter of three paths and not, as in Grondin, of only two. See also note 25.

25. In his notes, obviously written during the time of the *Contributions* or later and published in 1983, to *Introduction to Metaphysics* Heidegger criticizes the lec-ture in the same vocabulary in which, in section 262 of the *Contributions,* he criti-cizes the paths before the *Kehre:* "All this without first saying the swaying [*Wesung*] itself in a primordial manner!" (*GA* 40, 217); "the lecture gets stuck half-way, not only because . . . but because, basically, it does not get out of the chain of its understanding of being. And it does not manage to do so because the question—even the basic question—in no way carries into the essential issue, namely, into the swaying [*Wesung*] of being itself" (*GA* 40, 219).

26. One can gather such an interpretation of *Introduction to Metaphysics,* which I suggested elsewhere (Fritsche 1999b, 200ff.; Fritsche 1999a, 9ff.), also from sec-tion 262 of the *Contributions* (see the remainder of the paper). In the light of the eminent role of the drama of historicality from *Being and Time* to *Introduction to Metaphysics* (after which Heidegger maintained it but not without an important modification; see the remainder of the paper) it is in no way idle to ask whether and, if so, in which way Heidegger's turn in 1928 and possible other turns before the *Kehre* were politically motivated. Their minimum political relevance is that they did not turn him away from his preoccupation with the drama of historical-ity and its anticipation and promotion of National Socialism.

27. For *Geist* in this context, see note 28.

28. As he continues the preceding quotation, one has "to grasp above all that projecting-openings are thrown into *that* which, thanks to their clearing, again be-comes a being and only tolerates be-ing as an addendum to it, an addendum that 'abstraction' had devised" (*GA* 65, 447/315). This is another of Heidegger's for-mulas for seeming, about whose power of persistence he has been thinking from 1931 on, at the latest, as he has been thinking about concealment in relation to the basic structures of Dasein and Being since 1928. Shortly after the National Social-ist seizure of power, Heidegger saw himself in a threefold pincer, as it were. He recognized many, even among the party members, who just pretended to be for National Socialism, or who did not even do that (*GA* 36/37, 14, 79). In addition, he saw in the politics of National Socialism itself a tendency to slow down and re-lapse into liberalism (*GA* 36/37, 119, 211). Finally, he had reservations concerning "the talk of blood and soil as much referred to forces" (*GA* 36/37, 263). In 1936–

38, he decided that these phenomena were part of the seeming that had began with the beginning of metaphysics, and that, for the time being, this seeming was too powerful.

As to blood and soil, Heidegger objects that "blood and soil are indeed powerful and necessary. However, they are *not the sufficient* condition of the Dasein of a people. Other conditions are *knowledge and spirit* [*Wissen und Geist*], and they don't come as an appendix. Rather, only knowledge brings the stream of the blood into a direction and a course, only knowledge brings the soil into the pregnancy of what it is capable of carrying. Knowledge provides nobility on the soil to the deliverance of what it is capable of carrying [*bringt erst den Boden in die Trächtigkeit dessen, was er zu tragen vermag; Wissen verschafft Adel auf dem Boden zum Austrag, was er zu tragen vermag*]" (*GA* 36/7, 263). In his 1916 work *Formalism in Ethics*, Scheler had developed a hierarchy of four types of large communities (as opposed to small communities, such as a family) with the (world-embracing) love-community (the Roman Catholic Church) at the top, followed by communities of culture (as, for instance, Western Europe) and the states. At the bottom of this hierarchy are the *Volksgemeinschaften*, the various communities each made up by one people. In this hierarchy, each higher community restricts and, so to speak, ennobles the ones below it (see Fritsche 1999b, 136ff.). Heidegger highly praised *Formalism in Ethics* (Fritsche 1999b, 146). Nonetheless, in *Being and Time* he abolished all the philosophical means available, say, to Scheler to distance oneself from National Socialism (Fritsche 1999b, 136ff., 145ff.), and he regarded the community of the German people to be the only relevant community (138ff.). Here in 1933–34, Heidegger demands that the German community of the people need something higher than blood and soil. That which he proposes occurs in Scheler's hierarchy but in a different way, and from the viewpoint of Scheler it is not necessarily higher than the community of the people. For, the "*knowledge and spirit*" relates of course to the people of the Greeks "whose tribalty [*Stammesart*] and language shares with us [Germans] the same origin [*Herkunft*]" (*GA* 36/7, 6).

The knowledge that Heidegger attributes to the philosopher places him above the *Führer*, above Hitler. In *Republic* book 6, Plato makes the famous claim that philosophers have to be appointed as the strictest guardians of the state (503b4f.). In 1933–34, Heidegger says that this thesis does not mean that professors of philosophy should become chancellors for "this would apriorily be a disaster" (*GA* 36/37, 194). This statement sounds jovial and modest, but it isn't, for, Plato's thesis "means that the humans that carry in themselves the rule of the state must be philosophizing humans. Philosophers qua philosophizing humans have the task and the function of *phulakes*, guardians. They have to take care that the rule and the order of the rule is permeated by philosophy; not, however, by one or the other philosophical system but rather by a knowledge that is the deepest and broadest knowledge of man and human being. . . . In a state, Plato says, there can be only *few* of such guardians" (*GA* 36/37, 194; see also Fritsche 1999b, 142).

Heidegger's language is full of conservative and reactionary modes of speech, and some of his notions even resonate with very specific phrases at the time. As I pointed out, in 1931–32 as well as in 1933–34 (see *GA* 36/7, 198ff.) Heidegger's key term of his interpretation of the idea of the good in Plato is *Ermächtig-*

ung (empowerment). The idea of the good as *Ermächtigung* empowers the philosopher to annihilate the existing laws and to replace them and their world with a new world. Since Heidegger interprets Plato in terms of the drama of historicality only in 1931–32 and 1933–34, in his Plato interpretations from 1926 and 1942 the term *Ermächtigung* is absent (see previous note 22). Having been appointed as chancellor of Germany on January 30, 1933, Hitler on March 23, 1933, made the parliament pass a law that granted him dictatorial power. This law was called the *Ermächtigungsgesetz*, the *Gesetz* (law) for Hitler's *Ermächtigung*. The discussions surrounding it are an example of the fight between being and seeming. For, several jurists—the guardians of the Weimar Constitution, so to speak—argued that, since the law was passed according to paragraph 76 of the Weimar Constitution, the Weimar Constitution remained in power and binding for Hitler's rule. Carl Schmitt (1934) argues that such is not the case. Rather, the law is a transitional constitution that disavows the Weimar Constitution and prepares the way for the new constitution of the National Socialist state, which in no way is any longer bound by the Weimar Constitution. The *Ermächtigungsgesetz* is, so to speak, the "breach into which the preponderant violence of being breaks in its appearing" (*GA* 40, 172/see 163/see 174). The guardians of the Weimar Constitution drag it down and interpret it in terms of the old state, in terms of seeming, so as to make being "become[s] a being" again and "an addendum to beings" (*GA* 65, 447/315). The authentic Dasein, however, understand the *Ermächtigungsgesetz* as the arrival of the new state which annihilates the old state.

29. On the latter motif and on Heidegger's production of *Kitsch* after 1945, see Fritsche 1995, where I also show that Heidegger tried "to silence Auschwitz silently" (155). What I label the drama of historicality Bambach labels Heidegger's "*Ursprungsphilosophie*" (Bambach 2003, 50 passim) (philosophy of origin), which Heidegger in the 1930s enacted in a "martial" (333) mode and after 1945 in a "pastoral" (333) one. In this perspective, Heidegger's history of being is "an expression of his own fiercely Germanocentric emphasis on autochthony in its most political form" (Bambach 2003, 176; on Heidegger and Plato see 180ff.). For Derrida and other deconstructionists, metaphysics is a type of thinking in terms of binary oppositions with the denunciation, or elimination, of one of the opposites. In this sense, Heidegger's "binary logic of inclusion and exclusion" (Bambach 2003, 211 and often) or the drama of historicality is metaphysics at its worst (Fritsche 1999b, 21ff., 29ff., and constantly).

Remarks on Heidegger's Plato

Stanley Rosen

Heidegger's attitude toward Plato varies from one period of his career to another, but in general, Platonism means for him the so-called theory of Ideas. I say "so-called" because the word "theory" conveys to modern philosophical ears the notion of a systematic explanation containing well-articulated principles and concepts from which the diverse phenomena being studied may be reduced to an underlying deductive unity that serves as the basis for the prediction of their future behavior. This is not true of Plato's "Ideas," which are described in the dialogues in various and incompatible ways, often in poetical or rhetorical idiom, and in terms that sound more like an advertisement for the fecundity of the hypothesis than a discursively precise explanation of the phenomena.

To say this in another way, Heidegger is famous for his central obsession with the question of being, and he takes the doctrine (as I shall refer to it) of Ideas to be the heart and soul of the Platonic response to that question. In this essay, I shall be concerned primarily with Heidegger's interpretation of Plato as what one could call an ontologist of production. On this view, the Ideas are projections or hypostases of how things look to the human thinker. Stated as simply as possible, Heidegger reverses the traditional interpretation of the Platonic Ideas as genuine, unchanging, and eternal entities that exist independent of the modifications of human cognition. In a way that shows the unmistakable influence of Nietzsche, Heidegger sees Plato as the originator of the modern doctrine of subjectivity. Genuine being (what Plato calls *ontôs on*) is on Heidegger's interpretation not an eternal paradigm of transient particulars but a kind of anticipation of the will to power, that is, of the concealment of being by the looks of beings, looks that constitute a human perspective with a view to utility and domination. This claim is also familiar to us as the accusation of the reification of being, which is not a thing, entity, or *res* but a process of manifestation, a partial emergence from darkness or chiaroscuro into the light. In short, to be is for Plato (as for Aristotle) to be something definite, in Aristotle's formulation, this thing here of such and such a kind. That is true of the Ideas as well. Heidegger rejects this account as the attempt by the human intelligence to gain mastery over being and to make it accessible to human manipulation.

The main purpose of this essay is to present a criticism of the interpretation of Plato as the originator of a productionist account of being. However diverse and rhetorical the various discussions of the Ideas may be, they point us in quite a different direction from the one indicated by Heidegger. Heidegger does not so much attribute to Plato a secret doctrine, the reverse of his stated hypothesis, as he gives a kind of psychoanalytical interpretation of the actual motives and significance of that hypothesis. On this reading, Plato is an unconscious instrument of the "errance" of being. One sees here something of the Hegelian conception of the partial presentation of the absolute through the instrumentality of world-historical thinkers, with the major difference that for Hegel, the process of presentation terminates in fulfillment, whereas for Heidegger, the predominant modes of presentation in the history of Western philosophy lead us to nihilism. Hence the need to find another way to the lighting up of being, unencumbered by the imaginary productions of the human will.

A second goal of this essay is to show how Heidegger assimilates Plato into the Aristotelian doctrine of being qua being. In order to carry out this goal, I shall suggest that there are two doctrines of being in Aristotle or, let us say more cautiously, two parts to Aristotle's doctrine, of which one, the doctrine of categories and predication, is either blended together with or entirely replaces the other, the doctrine of noetic intuition of pure form. The unifying thread of these two main points can be stated as follows. Heidegger interprets Aristotle's doctrine of predication as a kind of scientifically more precise version of Platonistic productionism, in which the true nature of being as the emergence process of beings is concealed by linguistic artifacts or discursive products of how beings look to human cognition. Instead of bespeaking being, Aristotle and his successors speak of this or that property of beings. As Heidegger puts it, the doctrine of predication, or saying "something about something" (*ti kata tinos*), refers to two "somethings" (*etwas als etwas*) or reifications of being. This interpretation carries with it the corollary that being is covered over by the view of its "look" to us as a this-something. Heidegger thus sees anthropocentrism at the very origin of the Western tradition, which he designates as Platonism. The thesis of the concealment of being by humanly produced beings is a revision of Nietzsche's doctrine of will to power, the culmination of Western metaphysics.

The revision is essentially as follows. Whereas for Nietzsche, the projections of the will to power are concealments of the intrinsic chaos of Becoming, and to that extent may exercise a salutary effect because they create the conditions necessary for human existence, for Heidegger, reification or concealment is the cause of our estrangement from being. Heidegger does not advocate the dissolution of these reifications, since that would be to return to primeval chaos. Instead, he mysteriously advocates a change in attitude toward human life, a change that is rooted in the apprehension of being, that is, of the lighting process rather than of the objects that are illuminated. The aforementioned process is more like Fichte's absolute ego, which conceals itself within its presentation as a finite determination or entity, than it is like Nietzsche's effulgence of chaos. In other words, Heidegger is closer to Fichte's theism than to Nietzsche's atheism.

One could also say that Heidegger adopts Aristotle's charge that Plato provides us with a dualism of eternal paradigms (or in Aristotle's language, essences) on the one hand and generated particulars on the other. But it is easy to see that this criticism can be applied to Aristotle's own doctrine of the two senses of *ousia* or essential being, namely, the *sunolon,* or concrete particular, and the *eidos,* or species-form. Whereas Heidegger in effect rejects both these versions of essentialism, he gives no alternative account, so far as I am aware, of the formal structure of intelligible beings. Platonic-Aristotelian dualism is replaced by a doctrine of the manifestation or lighting-up of being, a doctrine that curiously enough relies implicitly upon a faculty of noetic intuition, only now of the process of illumination (and concealment) rather than of the determinate beings that are rendered open and hidden by that process. It is true that those who are open to the manifestation of being are supposed to see beings or things in a new light. But how this process actually functions is described in a quasi-poetic, rhetorically congealed manner that eschews the analysis of formal structure on the one hand and the function of the vision of being on the other. In short, Heidegger avoids dualism by ignoring the problem of what it is to be anything at all or, if that is too extreme, by subordinating it to the antecedent and prerational exhibition of being. Differently stated, he places great emphasis upon the phenomenological description of moods and the practical affections of the spirit (which he calls Dasein in the period with which we are mainly concerned), as well as of the manner in which we apprehend the things of everyday experience, for example, as tools for the carrying out of one task or another. That is, he concentrates upon how we experience being rather than upon the principles and formal elements of beings. One consequence of this shift in emphasis is that to be *unterwegs zur Sprache* (on the way toward language) is frequently to be within the penumbra of silence. As Heidegger puts it in his Nietzsche seminars, genuine thinking proceeds "in the claim to the soundless voice of Being."[1]

Heidegger thus attributes to Plato the responsibility for initiating what seems rather to be the gradual historical deterioration of Platonism. This deterioration, stated briefly, is as follows. Plato's dualism is that of Ideas and the doctrine of Eros. The history of metaphysics can be regarded as the steady assimilation of the Ideas, which are originally (and contrary to Heidegger) understood as entirely independent of human cognition, into eros, known variously as *nous,* spirit, *Geist,* the *ego cogitans,* self-consciousness, *Streben,* will to power, and even care (*Sorge*), to include Heidegger himself in this historical process. The first step in the transformation, or rather, the attempted overcoming, of this "Platonist" dualism is Aristotle's attempt to unite forms with the material substrate of particular instances on the one hand and with the intellect on the other. This attempt at unification provides the basis for the subsequent disappearance of essences and the gradual emancipation of subjectivity, the two necessary presuppositions for the emergence of the various forms of metaphysical productionism that dominate in late modern and contemporary philosophy.

In my opinion, Heidegger's own rejection (or deconstruction) of Platonism is not as thorough as he seems to believe. Instead, Platonism is replaced by Neoplatonism (the emanation of beings from being) on the one hand and a kind of transcendental subjectivity (the immanent transcendence of Dasein) on the other. Heidegger certainly rejects the various productionist doctrines of Western metaphysics; it is not the human thinker who produces being but rather being that produces beings. But humanity constitutes the locus or residence of this production, and the exhibition of what is produced depends upon the appropriate determinations or attunements of the human spirit. For example, as just noted, we can see the continued presence of Platonic eros in the doctrine of *Sorge* ("care") that plays a central role in *Being and Time.* With all due allowance for the great differences, Heidegger is in this respect, and in this context, a residual Platonist, but not, of course, a Platonist in the sense that he rejects.

The same point can be illustrated by Heidegger's version of what Husserl calls "pre-predicative" awareness, that is, the prediscursive openness to being. Plato's Ideas, at least in some of his portraits, are not initially accessible to discursive intelligence. They must be intuited or seen by the nondiscursive intellectual power of the intellect in order to become available to discursive analysis. This is a point that Heidegger retains, albeit in a quite different context and set of terms. In what Heidegger calls "Platonism," however, intuition is replaced by production. That is to say, we intuit, or know, only what we ourselves make. The inaccessibility of God's knowledge of his creations is thus counterbalanced by our knowledge of what we create. Pagan thought succumbs to Christianity, which in turn collapses before the onslaught of the emancipated human will, of which the decisive step is the modern European Enlightenment. The Ideas or pure forms are thus replaced by the symbolic constructions or models of human imaginative intelligence, itself in the service of what Descartes calls "the passions of the soul." We thus arrive at the odd situation that Heidegger, who rebukes all of Western philosophy as Platonism, is himself in some ways closer to the original Plato than the so-called Platonists. This closeness is partially obscured by the distorted polemic against Plato.

Let me come back now to the relation between Aristotle and Plato, which serves as an indispensable backdrop to Heidegger's interpretation of Plato. The Aristotelian dualism consists in the aforementioned two doctrines of being. The first doctrine is that of noetic intuition of the form or essence. This intuition is pre-discursive or pre-predicative and has nothing to do with logical deduction. The key point here is that there is no predication with respect to essence. The essential properties must be grasped simultaneously as belonging together, with no one property the owner (i.e., subject) and the others what is owned (i.e., the properties). This initial grasp is the necessary basis for subsequent analytic discourse, that is, for predication on the basis of the categories. In other words, we cannot deduce the inner unity of an essence, which is either given to us or not. As Aristotle puts it elsewhere (*De Anima* 431b21ff.), the soul becomes "somehow" the beings it receives directly, without comment or analysis. In this sense, metaphysics, or the science of being qua being, is grounded in silence, not in Logos. On this point, it is correct to say that Aristotelianism is a continuation of Platonism. But there is no Platonic equivalent to the science of being qua being; the ostensible science of dialectic is as it were advertised in the dialogues but never actually exhibited in action (as I have shown in my various studies of Plato). As to the science of being qua being, it is about neither the Heideggerian "emergence process" nor the Platonic particular formal looks. It is rather the science of a discursive schema, a recipe for what is required of something in order to qualify as a being: namely, to possess an essence along with properties that are instances of one or another of the remaining categories. This is the formal structure that must be exhibited by any determinate being whatsoever. One element of that structure is the *eidos* or species-form (or what Aristotle calls *to ti ên einai*); and it is not given by the doctrine of predication but instead by noetic intuition.

Let me clarify a possible ambiguity at this point. The structure in question is ontological, not just linguistic. To be is to be an essence (*ousia* in the sense of species-form) together with various properties that instantiate one or more of the remaining categories. But the science of being qua being is a discursive analysis of a structure that is accessible if and only if the essence is itself antecedently accessible. And as we have seen, the essence is not accessible via discursive analysis or synthesis; it must be given to discourse by intuition. Therefore silence lies at the heart of the discursive science of being qua being. This silence leads us to attempt to cover it over with more discourse. The silent center of metaphysics threatens its discursive superstructure with dissolution. We attempt to meet this threat by filling the silence with words. More precisely, we take one of three paths. First, we say that the essence is invisible, then, unknowable, and finally, nonexistent. But this latter path leads directly to nihilism. Hence we modify our trajectory in one of two ways. Either we become nominalists and stipulate essence to the extent that is required for logical deduction—in other words, essence is redefined as syntax—or else we attempt to approximate to the invisible essence by an endless series of phenomenological descriptions of how it looks to us. But a pure syntax is talk about nothing, and it is hard to know how to verify phenomenological descriptions of the indescribable, for an essence is not a describable look but the unity of differences that presents itself as a describable look. In one last formulation, the description of a look is not the description of the essentiality of its structure.

To summarize the immediately preceding paragraphs, Aristotle makes two radical changes in the teaching of the Platonic dialogues. First, Aristotle retains the Platonistic notions of form and noetic intuition, but he eliminates Eros. One reason for doing so is no doubt his dislike of myths when used by philosophers. At least as important, however, is the fact that Eros is an expression of human incompleteness, more precisely, of our lack of a discursive grip on the elements of formal intelligibility. Aristotle situates the active form within the noetic intellect, no doubt in order to provide this grip as the foundation for the doctrine of categories and predication, more generally, for the science of being qua being. Whereas Aristotle is in no sense a "productionist," it would be fair to say that by attributing the actualization of the essence to the activity of pure noetic thinking, he comes a step closer to productionism than one finds in Plato. I believe that this view is of some importance for understanding the consequences of Heidegger's approach to Plato by way of Aristotle. Equally important is the fact that Eros represents the role played by the psyche in the "illumination" of the Ideas. It is thus closer to Heidegger than is the purely discursive or rationalist doctrine of being qua being that lies at the heart of Aristotle's most important work.

The second radical change is that Aristotle introduces a science of being qua being, which is not the science of *ousia* in the sense of species-forms, namely, the entities that take the place of the Platonic Ideas. Let us put to one side for a moment the differences between the Platonic Idea and the Aristotelian *ousia*. The main point of interest for us is that the *ousia qua* species-form is one element (albeit the most important) or category in the table of constituents of the *ousia* qua compound individual or separate substance. The doctrine of predication is about the categorial elements of separate substance, not about species-forms. There is no predicational knowledge of the species-form, according to Aristotle. The *ousia* in this sense is given by noetic intuition. Predication thus rests upon a substratum that is the necessary presupposition of analytic or discursive knowledge, but not itself a product of that knowledge. This characteristic of predication is the basis for the historical rejection of essences and the shift in attention to the doctrine of predication. That is, the history of Western metaphysics, in its rationalist or "Aristotelian" tradition, shifts to the pursuit of knowledge of separate substances. As is especially obvious in the modern epoch, and most of all in British empiricism, intuition is rejected, and its role is transferred to sense-perception. What one could call "metaphysics" is thus transformed into the philosophy of language. Stated as succinctly as possible, metaphysics in the Aristotelian sense is already a concealment of metaphysics in the Platonist sense. Aristotle is thus the first step in the repudiation of Platonism, not the crucial stage of its transformation into the history of Western philosophy.

Let us now look more carefully at Heidegger's interpretation of Plato, in order to have a broader selection of evidence for reflecting upon the tendency to Aristotelianize him. There are four main points in Heidegger's interpretation of Plato. I have already discussed the first point in the opening section of this essay; the second point is treated at length in my book *The Question of Being*. I shall be primarily concerned in what follows with the third and the fourth points.

Point 1: Plato initiates a shift in Greek thought from the primacy of *phusis,* understood as growth, emergence into the light, self-manifestation as a process, to the particular and determinate look of what emerges or manifests itself. The Platonic idea is the decisive step in the reification of being. Sometimes Heidegger emphasizes the inevitability of this shift in attention or self-concealment of being, which can show itself only in the determinate beings that are the manifestation of its activity. At other times, however, and especially in his later thought, Heidegger treats the original Greek thinking of *phusis* as already a falling away from being. This view is part of his most extreme doctrine, the need to return to the origin of Western thought, not to reduplicate it in an ontologically reconstituted manner but in order to find another way, a way of thinking altogether other than that of the Greeks, and one that is associated with other gods.

Point 2: In Platonism, the openness to *phusis,* which we can call a pure theoretical reception of what happens or gives itself, is replaced by an anthropocentric or utilitarian validation of the goodness of being (the Idea of the good), which is manifested in the utility of beings to serve as tools for the carrying out of human purposes or, more radically, for the satisfaction of the will. Heidegger thus discerns the origin of Nietzsche's doctrine of the will to power in the shift from emanation or process to things, as well as the emphasis upon technology that defines European metaphysics and culminates in the replacement of Platonic Ideas by machines, the direct extension of the human will to dominate.

Point 3: Ideas are conceived as blueprints, themselves produced by the divine craftsman, in accord with which he makes the material copies or natural things of genesis and which in turn are copied by human craftsmen by means of *technê.* Heidegger constructs this interpretation largely on the basis of the discussion in book 10 of the *Republic* of the Idea of the bed.[2] This is the source of considerable confusion in Heidegger's analysis. First, he pays no attention to the dubious status in Socrates' own doctrine of an Idea of an artifact. The main point here is the denigration of the poets, whom Socrates wishes to subordinate to the craftsmen for political purposes, namely, as part of his refutation of their authority over human beings.

Second, Heidegger misreads the actual text, according to which the creator of the cosmos is called a gardener (*phutourgos*), not a carpenter. In other words, Socrates' account is actually in inner accord with Heidegger in that it interprets the being-process as one of growth and emergence. Furthermore, it is not all human beings, but only the craftsmen who copy the original in technical production. And there is also a difference between producing a copy of an Idea and making an image, for example, in a painting, of the produced copy. Heidegger overlooks this aspect of Socrates' account and assimilates all three stages into the activity of production. The natural status of the Ideas in the garden of the divine creator is suppressed and identified instead as ontologically the same as the production process of the technician. Similarly, the difference between the imitator and the craftsman is ignored. Heidegger claims that the same Idea is manifested in the physical bed and its painted copy. But Socrates says nothing about the presence of the Idea in the painting. If Heidegger's account were correct, then it would be superfluous to attempt to see the Ideas themselves. One could simply study them in their more accessible form as artifacts or imitations.

In this interpretation of Plato, Heidegger transforms the Ideas into products of the imagination, that is, tools invented by human beings to facilitate the manipulation of nature in a utilitarian manner. Growth is transformed into manufacture. The Ideas are seen as products of the perspective of the agent of cognition rather than as original manifestations of the being-process. An Idea is a look, that is, how something looks to me. As perspectivist imaginings, the Ideas are brought into being, which is to say that they are initially possibilities rather than actualities. This view is a reversal of the classical view; for both Plato and Aristotle, actuality is higher than possibility. Heidegger distorts the ancient doctrines in order to see in them the prototype of modern productionist metaphysics, with its preference for possibility and progressive mastery.

Point 4: In the same period during which Heidegger was developing his interpretation of Platonic metaphysics as productionism, he also propounded the thesis that the Platonist (and so Western European) doctrine of being is a general conception, an "average" conception of what is common to beings of different types. The first point to be made about this thesis is that Heidegger clearly regards Aristotelian species-forms as ontologically the same as Plato's Ideas. But the concept of "average" or "general" being cannot be applied in either case. As it happens, this point can be brought out rather easily. I begin with a distinction between artifacts like beds and natural beings like horses or persons. If god makes the Idea of a natural being, he also makes those beings, because the Ideas, like the species-forms, are coordinated to their instances. Not every instance of a given form need exist simultaneously, but there are no forms of nonexistent entities. What Plato calls the "genuine being" (*ontôs on*) and Aristotle calls "actuality" (*energeia*) refers not to the being of a possible kind of entity but to the actual presence (as Heidegger himself insists) of the fullest sense of the "being" of any existing spatiotemporal particular. If that were not so, the potentiality of the uninstantiated Idea or form would be at the same "ontological" level as the actual Idea or form of existing instances. To say this in another way, imaginary Ideas would become ontologically equal to eternal or genuinely apprehended Ideas. Ideas, like forms, are discovered through the mediation of their instances and not simply by speculation on what might be.

Since "genuine" Ideas or forms are Ideas or forms of space-time particulars, there cannot be Ideas or forms of artifacts. So far as I know, neither Plato nor Aristotle says so explicitly, but it follows from the doctrine of actuality. The entire discussion of the Idea of the bed, which serves Heidegger as a paradigmatic text for his analysis, is therefore rendered ambiguous. But even if we take it seriously, there is still an important point to be made. In the case of both natural and artificial particulars, the being of each kind is not homogeneous with the being of any other kind. To be a bed is quite different from being a horse. Otherwise stated, the Idea or form of a horse exhibits not simply the being but the way of being a horse. And ways of being are not general. It might be argued that all Ideas or forms have themselves a general structure that is common to all ways of being. This is what Aristotle seems to mean by "being qua being," namely, the structure of the *sunolon* or compound substance, as described in the doctrine of the categories. But, as I have already emphasized, the structure of the compound substance is not the same as the structure of the species-form or simple substance, and it is this substance that exemplifies the primary sense of being as *ousia*. Furthermore, just as in the case of the Platonic Ideas, each species-form exhibits a way of being, not just the general or average property of being.

Heidegger would have been much closer to the truth had he argued that there is no general sense of "being" (and certainly none of "being") in either Plato or Aristotle. It will be helpful to remind ourselves of the various kinds of Ideas that appear in the Platonic dialogues. First, there are Ideas of the particular look of a thing, for example, the look of a cow, a tree, or a man. The look is the original of which the particular cow, tree, or man is a copy. This is not the same as an Aristotelian *eidos*, contrary to Heidegger's reductive interpretation. A man is not a copy of the essence "man." Second, there are Ideas of moral qualities, abstract relations, and various concepts that lack a determinate look, many of which can scarcely be defined with precision. The outstanding example is that of the soul, which Socrates says in the *Phaedrus* cannot be described by humans in a Logos, but only in myths. The Idea of justice is a more accessible example. Contrary to the ostensible dogmatism of Plato in the *Republic,* justice is defined as "minding one's own business," which is itself so vague as to be meaningless. In order to know what my business is, I must know who I am, and the attempt to discover that leads us, of course, to philosophy, or knowledge of ignorance. Much the same can be said of the Idea of beauty, which is said to be beautiful but can hardly be described in a technically precise and exhaustive manner. Third, there are the "greatest genera" discussed in the *Sophist* and their analogues in dialogues like the *Parmenides* and *Philebus.* I refer to being, same, other, rest, change, one, many, and so on. It is clear that they are radically different from the first two kinds of Ideas and also that they are not Aristotelian species or genera.

This brief review is enough to show that there is no single, uniform, general doctrine of being in Plato, and certainly no doctrine of being as production or manufacture. Plato does not equate nature, *technê*, and imitation as Heidegger claims, thanks to an inaccurate reading of the tenth book of the *Republic*, which is for more than one reason a poor choice of proof-texts. The error Heidegger makes is easily stated. By making the Idea of the cow, God also makes cows. But by making the Idea of the bed, if there is such an Idea, God does not also make beds. So there is a difference between gardening and carpentering, not to mention painting. To

STANLEY ROSEN

the previous reflections on this topic, I add one more remark. In the *Introduction to Metaphysics,* Heidegger argues explicitly that there is no one sense of "being" that is common to the senses of the participle, the infinitive, and the copulative use of the term. One could not arrive at a general conception of being without having ignored or "forgotten" this fact. Such a forgetfulness may indeed characterize later stages of Western metaphysics, but there is no reason to attribute it to Plato and Aristotle.

The plurality of conceptions of being in Plato is thus shown by the different senses given to words like "Ideas" and "greatest genera," whereas in Aristotle, the crucial example of this pluralism is the difference between the compound and the simple substance, that is, the subject and the essence. There is a community of things of a certain kind, where "kind" exhibits the Idea or species-form. But this is not the same as a so-called general doctrine of being. Heidegger himself seems to move from community to generality in his interpretation of the founding fathers of Platonism. And he thereby assimilates Plato into Aristotle, or treats Aristotle as a more developed version of Plato. This point is most easily illustrated by the following passage from the *Introduction to Metaphysics:*

> *Phusis* becomes Idea (*paradeigma*); truth becomes correctness. The *Logos* becomes a proposition, it becomes the place of truth as correctness, the origin of the categories, the fundamental proposition about the possibilities of being. "Idea" and "category" are in the future the two titles under which Western thinking, doing, and estimating existence in its entirety stand. The last part of this assertion may very well be true, but what Heidegger blurs, not to say ignores, is that "Idea" and "category" belong to two separate dimensions of what we can call the Platonist tradition. We cannot capture the unity of this or that particular essential configuration by predicative discourse, for two reasons. First, unity is unspeakable. Second, in order to give a predicative or discursive account of an essence, we would have to be able to distinguish the essential from the accidental properties. But we cannot make this distinction unless we already know the essence. I remind the reader that the impossibility of demonstrating a necessary connection is at the basis of Hume's empiricism and leads directly to Kant and modern constructive philosophy. This process takes place because Hume and Kant both reject intellectual intuition, which is not rehabilitated until Husserl.[3]

Let me now summarize the consequences of Aristotle's conception of the antepredicative structure of the essence or species-form. A separate substance is the owner of its properties. It certainly looks as if one of those properties is a species-form of such and such a kind (after all, primary *ou-*

sia is the first in the list of categories). Furthermore, one could argue that it is perfectly possible to analyze essences into their separate components. To take an example, "rational" and "animal," it might be held, are the properties of the essence "human animal." In fact, however, this is not a case of predication but synonymy; the expression "rational animal" is the same as "human animal," because all humans, and only humans, are rational. So "rational" is identical with "human." Otherwise put, "rational" differentiates the genus "animal," but it is not an essential property of the genus because it is false to say that "animals are rational." This is enough to show that we cannot know what a human animal is unless we know what it is to be rational.

It is persons like Socrates who are called "rational animal," not the genus "animal" or the species-form "human being." But we cannot arrive at this essence by predicating one property of an owner. The owner is in this case the unity "rational animal," and not, say, "animal" with the property of rationality. The latter would yield "animals are rational," which is of course (usually) wrong. In sum, we can analyze an essence that we already know, but not into owner and property. No one part of the essence "stands beneath" or is "thrown" or "built" beneath the others to serve as their support. Sentences describing essences are, so to speak, phenomenological descriptions rather than predicative propositions. And the forms of phenomenological description are given to cognition, not constructed by it. It follows that the science of being qua being is not the science of being in its highest sense (*ousia* as species-form or essence).

The question arises whether the intellectual apprehension of pure forms is a mode of ontological production. A complete analysis of this question would take us altogether beyond the limits of a short essay. But I must say a few words on this topic. The key to Aristotle's argument is the subject-predicate structure of the scientific proposition, or what I am calling the owner-property structure. Aristotle's doctrine is complicated by the fact that he allows scientific statements about separate substances but not about what we call "being" in the highest sense. It is self-evident that individuals like "Socrates" or "this particular horse" cannot be the answer to the question "What is being?" If there is an answer to this question, it must explain the fundamental properties of essences. But essences are themselves particular, for example, rational animal; the essence of a family of particulars is general only in the sense that it underlies each particular in the family, but it is quite distinct from all other essences, for example, plant or horse.

The answer to the question "What is being?" requires an account of the properties that are essential to essences in general. But this process is circular. We first have to know what is essential before we can provide such an account, and we cannot learn the nature of necessity from an analysis that presupposes such knowledge. This conundrum is the ancestor of Hume's recognition that we cannot provide an analytic explanation or verification of a necessary connection. Note that such terms as "one," "being," "true," and so forth apply to substances as well as essences. In brief, even if we could identify properties that belong to every essence, how could we demonstrate that the properties are essential, without invoking the perception of essentiality, which is what we are looking for? But finally, even if every obstacle to the apprehension of essence in general could be overcome, that still would not provide us with a sufficiently general knowledge of being, and certainly not of Heidegger's *Sein* because not all beings are essences. Heidegger resolves this problem by turning away from beings to being, but he pays the price of not being able to say anything about it that is not already a determination or expression of a property. The fact that the determination takes the form of bad poetry rather than analytic discourse changes nothing. And why a poetic account of being should escape the charge of productionism is beyond my comprehension.

To come now to the conclusion of this series of reflections, let us grant that, despite his poetical thinking, Heidegger produces nothing but allows being to show itself to the human gaze. Since nothing can be said of being except in language, and inasmuch as language is predicative, or says something of something, Heidegger's triumph is in fact defeat; that is, philosophy is redefined, not just from Logos, but from speech to silence. In the Platonic-Aristotelian tradition, we begin from the looks of everyday appearances and proceed by analysis to the formal structure of beings. This formal structure is called an Idea or a form. As the etymology suggests, forms are, in the deepest sense of the phrase, how things look to us. But these looks provide the basis for all rational discourse, and of poetry as well. There is no direct proof that we have not produced these forms; the best we can do is to show by argument what would follow from the productionist thesis and how it differs from the consequences of orthodox Platonism. In order to account for the order and intelligibility of nature (or if you prefer, of experience), one would have to distinguish between essential and accidental production. But how could one do so without advance apprehension of essentiality? We are thus back in the circle of Aristotelian metaphysics, or, allowing for a moment Heidegger's generalization, of Platonism. We cannot emerge from the circle on the basis of the Heideggerian teaching without erasing it, and that is not fundamental ontology but ontological nihilism.

I conclude that the serious philosophical debate is not between Plato and Heidegger but rather between Plato and Kant. Heidegger is a decadent version of Kantianism; as such, he has great value in showing the dangerous consequences of the Kantian position. But the position is not thereby refuted. The argument continues.

Notes

1. M. Heidegger, *Nietzsche*, 2 vols. (Pfullingen: G. Neske, 1961), 2:484.

2. Heidegger, *Nietzsche*, 1:198–217.

3. M. Heidegger, *Einführung in die Metaphysik* (Tübingen: M. Niemeyer, 1953), 194 (my translation).

Heidegger's Uses of Plato and the History of Philosophy

Tom Rockmore

It is sobering to realize, since so much in philosophy depends on interpreting written texts, those of our contemporaries as well as those written by philosophers who on occasion lived long ago, that, after some two and a half thousand years of debate, there is still no generally accepted view about how to read and to appropriate philosophical writings. This theme is confused and confusing. We can distinguish rival claims about textual interpretation as subjective or objective according whether it is believed we can get it right about what the text really or in fact says. Those who think that textual interpretation is subjective hold that there is no hope of making an objective claim, since meanings are not discovered, uncovered, or revealed in the text but rather "imported" into it, that interpretation and the interpretive disciplines do not yield knowledge, or at least not rigorous knowledge, that there is no such thing as valid interpretation since all interpretations are "valid;" and that there is no way to bring the open-ended interpretive debate to an end.[1] On the contrary, those who think interpretation is objective believe that objective interpretive claims are routinely made, that meanings are discovered, uncovered, or revealed in the text but not "imported" into it, that under proper conditions interpretation and the interpretive disciplines do yield (rigorous) knowledge, that there are valid (and invalid) interpretations, and that the interpretive debate can be and in practice normally is brought to an end (see, e.g., Hirsch 1967).

The view that interpretation yields knowledge beyond the endless interpretive debate is widely held in the cognitive disciplines, including the various sciences but even in aesthetics. This issue cuts across doctrinal boundaries separating, for instance, continental and analytic philosophers. Within analytic philosophy, this point can be illustrated by a difference in perspective between W. V. Quine and Donald Davidson. Quine's view of the indeterminacy of translation, which yields the inference that interpretation is always indeterminate, hence not determinate (1960, 26–79), is opposed by Davidson's idea that through a process of triangulation we come ever closer to what is really there (2001, 123–34).

Those who hold that interpretation yields (rigorous) knowledge often take a strong, or metaphysical realist, line. The term "realism" is used in many different ways. By metaphysical realism I will understand the widespread view, with roots in early Greek philosophy, that there is a mind-independent external world which, under appropriate conditions, can be known as it is (see Devitt 1997). Stephen Weinberg, for instance, thinks that unless science uncovers the structure of the real world, it is not worth doing (1999, 49). Similarly, Monroe Beardsley (1982) holds that the aesthetic features of an artwork are independent of our perception of them.

Martin Heidegger holds a similarly metaphysical realist view of textual interpretation. His view separates him from his disciples Jacques Derrida and Hans-Georg Gadamer. Derrida apparently holds the extreme antisemantic view that, since any reference can always be "deconstructed," definite reference is never possible. Gadamer, like G. W. F. Hegel, holds the more moderate position that interpretation, while perspectival, depends on the views that prevail at a given time and place, hence on the historical moment. This comparison leads to the idea that we read texts differently at different times, but can never discover what is there beyond interpretation. Heidegger holds a more extreme view. He believes that under appropriate conditions, we can and indeed must go beyond whatever view is, so to speak, in the air at a given historical moment to determine meanings that are in the text in independence of what different readers say about it.

Heidegger offers an outstanding illustration of the metaphysical realist view of interpretation. The early Heidegger believes that interpretation yields valid claims to know in determining meanings independent of the interpreter. According to Heidegger, we can go back behind the later Western philosophical tradition to grasp the problem of the meaning of being as it was originally raised in ancient Greek philosophy. Yet it is not clear that we can reliably claim to grasp meanings that are in the text in independence of interpretation, nor that we can go back behind the interpretive tradition, nor even that we can recover problems, doctrines, theories, or ideas as they were originally raised at some earlier time. Accordingly, this paper will utilize Heidegger's different Plato interpretations as an example of the nature and limits of a metaphysical realist approach to the philosophical tradition. I will be arguing against Heidegger's goal of recovering the question of being as it was originally raised as implausible in principle and inconsistent in fact with his actual practice. I will further be arguing in favor of the plausibility of a very different, "constructivist" approach to the philosophical tradition.

ı

Reading the History of Philosophy

From the perspective of text interpretation, Heidegger is a remarkable philosophical figure. He stands out, even among German philosophers, through his deep grasp of selected portions of the philosophical tradition and through his complicated interweaving of systematic and historical themes in his writings. Few philosophers demonstrate as wide and as deep a grasp of the philosophical tradition as Heidegger does. In Germany during the period in which he was active, others with a similar grasp might be Cassirer and Gadamer. Yet more than anyone since Hegel, it would seem that Heidegger makes his philosophical theories depend on his reading of the history of the philosophical tradition. Hence, much is at stake in his readings of philosophical problems and figures as concerns his own views.

In discussing Heidegger's textual interpretation, we will need to distinguish what he says about it from his specific interpretive practice. It is almost a banal truism that even historians of philosophy have very little to say about what it means to interpret texts, particularly texts written many years ago. In other fields, such as theology, literary criticism, and so on, textual interpretation is frequently made an issue. Yet in philosophy, those who are frequently or even mainly concerned with textual interpretation in various ways, such as historians of philosophy, tend, with rare exceptions, to restrict reflection about their practices to occasional hints. To the best of my knowledge, the only philosopher who provides a historical account of philosophy and of its history is Hegel, whose view of the historicity of philosophy, perhaps because his theories belong to the philosophical tradition, is rarely discussed.[2]

In part, the relative disinterest in issues of interpretive theory derives from the relative disinterest in the history of philosophy, above all in English-speaking countries. Disinterest in this theme runs hand in hand with the simplistic idea that later is better. A general lack of philosophical culture, a failure to master the relevant languages and literatures, is particularly widespread in the United States, a relatively new country, one without a long history. A further reason emerges from American pragmatism, which, at least in its original formulations, was future-oriented, mainly concerned with discernable consequences, at least officially unconcerned with the past. None of the American pragmatists takes a historical view of knowledge.

Lack of attention to the history of philosophy, which is by no means confined to the English-language discussion, is a leading theme in the modern philosophical tradition. From Descartes through Kant to Husserl, there is a steady belief that, at least for cognitive purposes, the prior philosophical tradition does not matter other than as the very long and nearly equally dismal record of a great many mistaken views held by nearly as many philosophers over a long period of time, for at least two main reasons. On the one hand, a succession of important systematic philosophers (Descartes, Kant, Husserl) has consistently held that, despite extraordinary effort by many talented people, absolutely nothing of value has yet been accomplished. Such thinkers, who should not be confused with epistemological skeptics, accept the Cartesian view that we need to start over, from the beginning, in turning away from anything we thought we knew, in order finally to make a new beginning. On the other, very often the same philosophers follow the Cartesian view that acceptable claims to know are true now and forever, beyond time, in time but not of time, since they are certain, apodictic, unrevisable, unrelated to time and place, in short, utterly permanent.

A related view is widespread in Anglo-American analytic philosophy, whose representatives often accept versions of Quine's reported distinction between the history of philosophy and philosophy. There is a strong tendency among analytic philosophers to equate philosophy with analytic philosophy while taking an ahistorical perspective to the history of the discipline and disdaining dialogue with other philosophical approaches. Quine, who had a selective knowledge of some topics in the history of philosophy, typically disdained philosophical dialogue with continental philosophy (see Rorty 2001). Quine's followers, who, like Quine, are unconcerned to dialogue with other tendencies, are often largely unaware of the wider history of their discipline, which they so often treat as philosophically irrelevant, to be ignored rather than known, as not worthy of refutation or even of careful study.[3]

This disinterest manifests itself in such ways as a general concern to isolate systematic from historical considerations, for instance, in erecting a conceptual barrier between philosophy and its tradition, in a lack of awareness of even main aspects of important positions, and in a lack of caution, on occasion in a kind of eagerness, to make sweeping claims based on little discernable grasp of the texts. The same philosophers who demand the most rigorous standards for what in practice are often trivial claims exhibit little or even no hesitation in uninformed but sweeping comments. Rorty's suggestions that Dewey and Davidson are the paradigm pragmatists (1999, 24) and that Sellars and Brandom overcome the split between analytic and continental philosophy (1997, 11) tell us more about

Rorty than about either of these philosophers, pragmatism, or analytic and continental philosophy.

European philosophers are usually more interested in the history of philosophy, which they often regard as their main field of research. Heidegger, as noted earlier, differs from other philosophers in combining to an unusual degree, more than anyone since Hegel, systematic and historical elements within a single position. For Heidegger at least, the stakes are high since, to an unprecedented degree, his position directly depends on his reading of the prior philosophical tradition.

On Heidegger's Early Plato Interpretation

Interpretations of philosophical texts are never self-contained nor innocent. All of us read other people's writings, and all of us need, if challenged, to be able to justify why we approach philosophical texts as we do and not in some other way. Another way to put the point is to say that general strategies employed in textual interpretations of any kind need to be justified or legitimated, not merely applied. Issues might include why we are interested in some details but not others, whether presumed authorial intent is relevant, whether the opinions of other commentators need to be given a particular weight, whether the historical background is useful in shedding light on the writings in question, and so on.

In turning now to Heidegger's Plato interpretation, I am interested less in details of what he says about Plato—others in this volume are better equipped to offer expert judgments about the details of Heidegger's readings of Plato—than in the view of the interpretation of the history of philosophy presupposed in his remarks on Plato, other historical figures, and the history of philosophy in general, especially in his early writings, say, through *Being and Time.*

Heidegger addresses Plato in lectures from the mid-1920s, including the lectures on the *Sophist,* and directly in texts composed after the so-called but mysterious turning in his thought (*Kehre*), and after his turn away from Nazi politics, with which his later view of Plato may be related.[4] His later rejection of philosophy for thought (*Denken*) implies an abandonment of the earlier, radical effort to renew the problem of the meaning of being he presented in *Being and Time* as the main conceptual thread of Western philosophy.[5] Though he never gives up his interest in being, his displacement of the problem from its historical appearance in the heart of early Greek philosophy is a result of his turn away from philosophy. Readings of historical figures and doctrines after his self-described turning away from philosophy presumably have·a different function than before that period, when he still considered himself to be engaged in issues, problems, and themes central to Western philosophy.

I will be concerned with Heidegger's view of Plato during the period he was interested in Western philosophy, especially in *Being and Time* and other early writings where he presupposes a certain view of Plato (and of Plato within the Western philosophical tradition). Heidegger's remarks on Plato in *Being and Time* are mainly "strategic," intended to justify the orientation and specific shape of his own investigations but not more than incidentally concerned with Plato's own theories. As part of his concern with the problems, themes, and doctrines of Western philosophy, Heidegger consistently presupposes specific views of Plato and the Platonic tradition. Such views require textual interpretation to back them up. He provides detailed interpretation of Plato in his lectures but not in his writings during the period he was directly concerned with Plato, Western philosophy, and philosophy in general. It is then ironic that the detailed textual interpretation he needs to support his idiosyncratic readings of the history of philosophy appears only when he is in the process of turning away from it.

In *Being and Time,* Plato mainly functions for Heidegger as an important source of the principal problem or problems that allegedly neither he nor anyone else has solved (or resolved or perhaps even made a dent on). Heidegger's treatment of Plato here is superficially similar to the way Aristotle is later treated in the approach of the Tübingen school (Conrad Gaiser, Hans-Joachim Krämer) to Plato's so-called unwritten doctrine. In the same way as the Tübingen school turns to Aristotle to recover doctrines Plato allegedly communicated orally but did not record in written form, so Heidegger turns to Plato to recover a problem. In both cases, the competence of the philosophical source in question, for the Tübingen school Aristotle and for Heidegger Plato, is restricted to reporting on the issue (or issues) in question. In both cases, some of the greatest names in philosophy are reduced to a kind of routine journalistic function. The difference, of course, is that the Tübinger Platonists read Plato as far superior to Aristotle. This approach, which is carefully worked out by Gaiser, Krämer (1990), and others, assumes a caricatural form in still others. J. N. Findlay, who was never a member of this school, provides an extreme (and extremely improbable) version of this approach in which Aristotle appears as mentally subnormal (1978). For Heidegger, on the contrary, neither Plato nor Aristotle can make progress on the problem of being, but Plato is weaker than Aristotle.

Heidegger's interest in Plato for his own theories is suggested in the very short passage preceding the introduction to the book through a citation from a speech by the Eleatic Stranger in the *Sophist*. The Eleatic Stranger, who appears in the dialogue, is a pupil and critic of Parmenides and pupil of Zeno. The passage Heidegger cites occurs in the midst of de-tailed criticism of Eleatic doctrine (*Sph.*, 237b–49d) where the theme of nonbeing is being studied. The Eleatic Stranger suggests that the general question of specifying the meaning of nonbeing requires us to make sense of the terms we use, including the conceptually prior question of the meaning of being (243d). He then indicates problems in the use of the term, pointing to the difficulty of the question.

Heidegger begins the discussion in citing a passage where the Stranger states that no one knows precisely what "being" signifies (*Sph.*, 244a), before continuing on to direct criticism of Parmenides. Heidegger, who takes this passage as the "official" excuse for *Being and Time*, cites Plato's Greek, then (in the original) provides a German "translation" or paraphrase—the difference, which is not always clear, is compounded in translations of Heidegger's own "translation"—before observing that we are no closer to an answer now. This remark serves as the "official" excuse to again raise the question of the meaning of being.

In citing this passage, Heidegger draws attention to the (legitimate) distinction between interpreting Plato's writings as a main source of his theories and/or as a source of a philosophical problem, doctrine, or theme. Although the cited passage is drawn from one of Plato's texts, Heidegger is not interested in grasping any particular Platonic doctrine nor in Plato's general theories, but rather in identifying a theme, the meaning of being, that, Heidegger contends, runs as a leading thread throughout early Greek philosophy and the entire later Western philosophical tradition.

According to Heidegger, this single problem that has persisted un-changed for almost two and a half millennia, has still not yet been ade-quately studied, and in the meantime has receded into oblivion, where it has been forgotten. Heidegger believes that over the years, this problem has engaged some of the most important philosophical minds, that the prevailing view from Plato and Aristotle to Hegel has remained the same, and that the same problem that stimulated Plato and Aristotle remains even today unchanged as the main problem of Western philosophy. Since Heidegger takes it as a given that this problem concerns a struggle among giants, he implicitly suggests that in taking it up, he now takes his place as a true philosophical giant.

Philosophy is a historical discipline, which can never be isolated from the history of philosophy. Heidegger insists on so-called authentic historicity (*Geschichtlichkeit*). Yet this way of raising the question appears to be insensitive to the historical nature of the philosophical tradition. Hei-degger seems to be suggesting that views come and go but the problem that interests him is intrinsically timeless and has remained the same beyond the meanders of the philosophical debate. Yet if this problem, indeed any problem, depends on the positions, theories, debates, or other contexts in which they arise, it is implausible to suggest it remains or should remain unchanged, or again should or could plausibly be taken up as it originally arose. It would, for instance, be incorrect to believe that the problem of knowledge in Kant is the same as in Descartes. Kant was aware of, influenced by, and reacted against the views of Descartes. For Descartes, to know is to know the mind-independent external world as it is. But the author of the critical philosophy contends we cannot know we know cognitive objects we do not in some manner "construct." The point is that problems do not remain stable but change over time. Heidegger later makes an analogous point in pointing to the difference between *energeia* in Greek and *actus* in Latin to justify his view of the utter difference between earlier and later Western philosophy.[6] It is further unclear that the distinction Heidegger makes between beings and being as such is ever made in ancient Greek texts in the same or an analogous way. It seems as if Heidegger were reading a modern concern into texts that were written for other purposes. It is finally even unclear that the Greek term "to be" (*einai*) functions in the same way the German word "to be" (*sein*) or its close relatives do in German or in other modern European languages (see Kahn 2003).

This point can be generalized. Heidegger correctly calls attention to the need to think historically, that is, against the background of the historical tradition. But, perhaps because of his negative treatment of tradition as a central obstacle in getting clear about the problems in the texts, he does not seem to be sensitive to it in his interpretive practice. His treatment of the problem of being as a single problem from ancient Greek philosophy to Hegel presupposes there is one and only one problem, not more than one. This way of raising the question presupposes that, although there may indeed be differences among, say, Hegel, Plato, and Aristotle, they are finally not significant. Perhaps for that reason, here and elsewhere in his early writings, for instance, in his lectures on Plato's *Sophist* during the winter semester of 1924–25 (*GA* 19), Heidegger typically runs Plato and Aristotle together as if they were concerned with precisely the same themes or questions, as if there were no important differences between them, as if there were in fact a single identifiable ancient Greek approach to the problem of being. Heidegger further implausibly claims in section 82 of *Being and Time* that Hegel has the same basic view of time as do Plato and Aristotle. Yet in virtue of his historical perspective, Hegel differs from the great Greek philosophers who lack this perspective but who further differ among themselves.

TOM ROCKMORE

Interpretive Realism and Ontological Phenomenology

Earlier I suggested that Heidegger employs a recognizably metaphysical realist approach to reading the texts of the history of philosophy. Heidegger's strong realist approach to the texts derives from his realist view of interpretation. This view is illustrated in his famous (Nietzschean) example of the hammer. According to Heidegger, we understand things we encounter or with which we come in contact with respect to their possible uses, uses they objectively possess and which can be uncovered. In understanding, we do not "import" the use but rather find, uncover, or discover it as already there. For instance, we do not attribute the property of being useful for hammering to the hammer, which only functions in that way because it objectively possesses that particular property. "The hammering itself uncovers the specific 'manipulability' of the hammer. The kind of Being which equipment possesses—in which it manifests itself in its own right—we call "*readiness-to-hand*" (*BT*, 98).

I take Heidegger to be claiming in this and in similar passages that the hammer in fact "contains" or possesses a specific use, a use which is not projected onto it and which can only be uncovered since it is objectively possessed. Hammers are for hammering, and nothing else, say, the heel of a shoe, will do. Yet it seems fairly obvious that any claim about, say, a hammer and the uses to which it can be put depends on the fact that Heidegger contingently happened to live in a society in which there were such things as hammers. In a society in which there were no hammers, it seems unlikely that one could uncover this single allegedly correct usage when confronted with such an object. It further seems unlikely that the ordinary or even the unusual observer, one without contact with a society in which hammers were a usual or even an unusual occurrence, would accept the claim that hammers are for hammering and nothing else, for instance, to use as doorstops, paperweights, or for other purposes.

Heidegger's confidence about being able to uncover, say, hammering as intrinsic to hammers points to his relation to Husserlian phenomenology. Beginning in Husserl, phenomenology as it arose in the early twentieth century developed an essentialist approach to knowledge claims. According to this approach, which has deep roots in ancient Greek philosophy, especially Aristotle, essences, roughly what makes something what it is, can allegedly be differentiated from mere facts. Husserl's position changed from the period of the initial breakthrough to phenomenology at the turn of the twentieth century to a period slightly later when he came to believe that reduction was indispensable to phenomenology. Throughout this later period, Husserl (1962, sec. 2–3, pp. 46–50) steadily contends that sciences of experience are sciences of contingent fact, but essences are disclosed through pure intuition.

Husserl was not deeply interested in and rarely comments directly on the philosophical tradition. Much of his knowledge about specific positions seems to be derived from others. His early grasp of Kant, crucial for the position he developed in the early breakthrough to phenomenology in the *Logical Investigations,* was filtered through Natorp (see also Kern 1964). Starting with the second edition of *Ideas,* volume 1, Husserl insists that reduction is an indispensable methodological feature of phenomenology. Heidegger, who was unusually knowledgeable about the history of philosophy, applies phenomenology to interpretation while silently dropping the concept of reduction.

Essentialism, which is controversial, has been the topic of much discussion. Wittgenstein attacks the very idea of essentialism, which Husserl and then Heidegger uncritically adopt.[7] In Heidegger, phenomenological essentialism and interpetive metaphysical realism coincide. He features phenomenological readings of philosophical texts committed to uncovering what, beyond the mere play of appearances, is really in them, like the capacity to hammer that is supposedly innate to hammers but not, say, to chairs. Like metaphysical realist philosophers who claim to cognize the mind-independent real, going beyond the mere play of appearances, Heidegger claims to be able to determine problems, concepts, or ideas in philosophical texts that are allegedly hidden from view in virtue of the interpretations they have undergone in the philosophical discussion and the later direction of the philosophical debate.

Dasein, the History of Ontology, and Phenomenology

Husserlian reduction is a methodological device to focus in principle on what is directly given as it is given. In bracketing existence, Husserl puts out of play any claims about the reality of what is given. Heidegger, who gives up reduction, does not have this move available. As a direct result of dropping Husserlian reduction, there is for Heidegger no difference between essentialism and realism. Heideggerian essentialism is a form of realism, more precisely, a form of the traditional epistemological claim that to know requires a grasp of the mind-independent real as it is.

Heidegger deploys his essentialist realism in claiming to grasp the intrinsic meaning of particular objects, like hammers, in analyzing the average structures of Dasein and in reading philosophical texts. Since he never clearly describes his approach to texts, it will be necessary to reconstruct it from indications in his writings. Heidegger devotes detailed attention to a number of philosophers, in writings composed for publication especially after the so-called turning in his thought. But arguably the chief instance of Heidegger's textual interpretation is his sustained effort in *Being and Time*[8] and in many later writings to analyze the problem of the meaning of being he points out in the cited passage from Plato's *Sophist*.

This description is ironic since, in virtue of his distinction between beings and being as such, for Heidegger the problem of the meaning of being is hopelessly miscast as a question about things. The Greeks were not concerned with being as such as Heidegger understands it, but rather with beings, or at most the unity of a being. Thus in the *Metaphysics,* when Aristotle remarks that no one has spoken about what it means to be something or about what constitutes the being of things (988b34–35), that there is a science which concerns only being as such (1003a21–21), and when he surveys four main meanings of "being" (5.7), he has in mind beings, not being as such. Heidegger's professed aim is to go back behind the philosophical tradition to take up the problem as it was originally posed in ancient Greek philosophy. But we must ask ourselves: What sense can we make of the idea that problems can be recovered as they were originally raised? Why is the original way authentic, whereas other, later ways of raising the problem are inauthentic? Would it make sense to claim to read *Hamlet* in the way that Shakespeare intended it? Is a way of reading *Hamlet* that could be reliably attributed to Shakespeare the only authentic way to read this play? And we must further ask if we can approach the history of philosophy in a way that reveals what is really there as opposed to what appears to be there to different observers in different ways in different times and places?

Heidegger's demonstration of his claim comports successive accounts of Dasein, of destroying the history of ontology, and of the phenomenological method of investigation. The excuse for studying Dasein, or his situated conception of the subject, is that it is the "official" clue to the question of the meaning of being. Heidegger claims that Dasein must be investigated to begin with, since it possesses a preontological understanding of being (*BT,* 35). In section 5, the analytic of Dasein, he asserts that we need to bring out the being of Dasein in a preparatory fashion in its average everydayness in order to work out the meaning of being. He further claims that time is the horizon to understand being as well as Dasein that understands being (39).

It is not clear how this general assertion about implicit knowledge of being could be demonstrated. Heidegger seems to be relying on the fact that ordinary people use the word "being" in everyday language. Yet Heidegger's complex philosophical distinction between beings and being as such is certainly wholly unknown to the average person. It scarcely follows that in using the term, ordinary people are alluding, in even the most extended sense, to being as Heidegger understands it, or that the analysis of ordinary use of language can bring us closer to the goal of grasping being in general.

In section 6, called "The Task of destroying the history of ontology," he asserts that Dasein is its past, which may be hidden to it, but can also be discovered and studied (*BT,* 41). The relation to the past, which can be either positive or negative, is negative when what it transmits is concealed, hence inaccessible (43). If this occurs: "Dasein no longer understands the most elementary conditions which would alone enable it to go back to the past in a positive manner and make it productively its own" (43). Heidegger illustrates his claim through key references to Descartes, Kant, and the general problem of recovering the philosophical tradition.

It is clear that all of us depend to a greater or lesser extent on our past, by which we are influenced and which, if Freud is correct, is never wholly behind us, never wholly past. The Western philosophical tradition belongs to human culture, hence to the past of human beings. It is, however, very unclear how anyone could literally be the philosophical tradition. It is easier to believe that certain themes raised earlier in the Western philosophical tradition later became distorted or were simply forgotten. Heidegger attempts to demonstrate this further claim with respect to the question of the meaning of being through references to Descartes, Kant, and ancient Greek philosophy. His remarks on Descartes and Kant are intended to illustrate the more general claim that theories, concepts, problems, and ideas can be seamlessly later recovered as they were when they initially came into the discussion. In effect, this is to take the later discussion as a kind of false appearance behind which one can go to grasp what is being incorrectly depicted. If that is correct, then the problem of recovering the past, for instance, the original formulation of a philosophical concept, problem, or theory, consists in penetrating behind a false appearance, what for Marxism is a merely ideological representation, to the essence, to what really is.

Heidegger says that the problem of the meaning of being was inadequately formulated and later forgotten in pointing to Descartes and to Kant. According to Heidegger, Descartes conflates the problem with the world in failing to question the being of the *cogito,* or subject (*BT,* 44), and Kant, who was influenced by Descartes, lacks an ontological analysis of the subject (*BT,* 45). These specific interpretations of Descartes and Kant raise highly specialized issues that cannot be pursued here. Suffice it to say that I think Heidegger is right that Kant is influenced by Descartes.

This belief is important to note, since most commentators insist on Kant's relation to Hume, which Kant describes in the *Prolegomena*. On the contrary, I think that Heidegger's reading of the Cartesian *cogito* both here and in later writings, including the famous 1938 lecture,[9] is overly reductive, insensitive to the full view of the subject as both passive and active, spectator and actor, and simply misrepresents his French predecessor's view.

For present purposes, the more important issue is not whether Heidegger provides a plausible reading of either Descartes or Kant, but whether, in seeking to understand the question of being, we can "loosen up its history," so to speak, that is, to employ Heidegger's term, "destroy" it in order to "arrive at those primordial experiences in which we achieved our first ways of determining the nature of Being" (*BT*, 44). Ancient Greek ontology is oriented toward the world or nature in the sense of presence, which points toward the grammatical present (47). According to Heidegger, the high point in the ancient Greek study of ontology is reached in Aristotle, who, in abandoning Plato's dialectic, provides the first detailed interpretation of the temporal structure of being (48), which we can understand only after "destroying" the ontological tradition (49).

Heidegger's account here passes rapidly over three ideas he simply runs together: the specific interpretation of particular theories, say, those of Descartes or Kant; then the so-called destruction of the history of ontology, which is carried out through criticizing particular theories; and finally, coming back to allegedly primordial experiences through such criticism or in other ways. In one sense, it looks very much as if Heidegger is trying to disqualify later views of being in order to call attention to the merits of Aristotle's view. That is obviously an acceptable procedure. It is certainly plausible that numerous ideas in the tradition did not earlier receive the attention they deserve and would look better if the obvious alternatives were criticized. Yet it does not follow that in criticizing selected positions (in order to exhibit the merits of a prior alternative) we can ever return to what Heidegger, more than two thousand years later, takes to be "primordial experiences" in ancient Greek philosophy.

Heidegger's First View of Interpretation

Heidegger's view of destroying the ontological tradition yields two separate issues that can be stated as questions: How should we go about interpreting philosophical texts? How, as a result, can we recover the tradition, where "recover" means to uncover the tradition as it originally was before it was later covered up through the ensuing discussion? The two issues are related since it is only through textual interpretation, if at all, that we can recover the tradition. Heidegger offers two views of interpretation as yielding phenomenological truth. The first is phenomenological interpretation in a Husserlian mode, which, through phenomenological seeing, is intended simply to bring the debate to an end by seeing what is, by grasping essences. This approach is closely related to Gadamer's simplistic view that at a certain point, further debate in good faith is no longer possible and disagreement becomes disingenuous.[10] The second view is the idea of phenomenological interpretation as a circular process, which, as Derrida suggests, merely yields endless interpretation, or interpretation without end, in short, the usual open-ended philosophical debate, which cannot simply be brought to an end.[11]

Heidegger specifically links interpretation to phenomenology and truth. The question is whether any form of interpretation, including his own, is sufficient to make out his claim to recover the problem of the meaning of being as it was supposedly originally and authentically raised in ancient Greek philosophy. He seems to have two different, incompatible views of interpretation and truth. The first, lesser-known, stronger view of phenomenological interpretation allegedly yields phenomenological truth in a specifically Husserlian sense, or *veritas transcendentalis*. It is a version of the traditional philosophical claim to know in an unrevisable, apodictic manner. This view is difficult to defend since it has never been clear that there actually is any unrevisable knowledge. The second, better-known, weaker view of phenomenological interpretation is easier to defend but inadequate to make out the claim to recover the philosophical tradition through textual interpretation.

In section 7, in remarks on the phenomenological method of investigation, Heidegger repeats his intention of explaining being phenomenologically, where phenomenology is understood methodologically, meaning with respect to the things themselves (*BT*, 50). In the account of phenomenon, he claims that appearance is a not-showing itself (52). Appearance, which is distinguished from the phenomenon, is a not-showing itself and that which does the announcing, and the sense of phenomenon lies in showing itself (53). As concerns Logos, he claims that true does not mean agreement but rather the taking of entities in question out of their hiddenness (56).

This entire phase of the discussion gives the impression of being unfinished. It is best understood with respect to Kant's difficult effort to make sense of the distinction between phenomena and appearances, where the latter refer beyond themselves to something which appears. In his view, Heidegger seems to be presupposing a version of the neo-Kantian, causal reading of the thing-in-itself as self-manifesting, hence as a cause.

In the preliminary conception of phenomenology, he says that "phenomenology" means "to let that which shows itself be seen from itself in the very way in which it shows itself from itself." This statement is an explication of the (Husserlian) maxim "To the things themselves" (*BT*, 58). According to Heidegger, in a science of phenomena, everything must be exhibited or demonstrated directly. This claim is easier to understand when the object is visible. Yet since the being of entities remains hidden, and even forgotten (59), the sense of the claim is more difficult to understand. In practice, since the being of entities cannot be directly given, Heidegger can insist when it suits him that any particular instance of phenomenological seeing is incomplete. Certainly, one would not want to claim that each and every experience has been exhaustively mined, that nothing further could possibly be learned by still more experience of the same object. Yet Heidegger's suggestion would be more interesting if there were a way of distinguishing between full and incomplete forms of phenomenological seeing.

Heidegger further claims that "the meaning of phenomenological description lies in *interpretation*," (*BT*, 61), or hermeneutics (62), but phenomenological truth is *veritas transcendentalis* (62). These two claims are obviously inconsistent. He is conflating constatation, or determining what is the case, with interpretation, or weighing and evaluating different possible views of something. He describes phenomenology as interpretive while making claims for phenomenological truth that are incompatible with, and go beyond, interpretation of any kind. Interpretation always concerns the ways something appears, but Heidegger is suggesting we can go beyond mere interpretation in grasping something as it is, for instance, a hammer as a hammer.

Heidegger further muddies the interpretive waters in talking about transcendental truth. It is one thing to say that description of any kind is always and necessarily interpretive and something else to say that claims to know are transcendental. Since Kant, transcendental claims are usually understood as universal and necessary, unrevisable, beyond debate, hence beyond interpretation. In a word, a transcendental claim is not an interpretive claim, and an interpretive claim is never transcendental. Applied to the problem of the meaning of being, this view suggests that we could recover the original problem by going behind the succeeding discussion, that is, by returning back behind the ensuing tradition. Heidegger's claim that phenomenological truth discloses transcendent being (*BT*, 62) seems to mean that every being also points beyond itself to transcendent being. If, in knowing any particular thing, one also knows the being of beings, or being in general, then knowing any particular thing also provides access to transcendent being. It is difficult to know what

Heidegger is affirming here. His claim sounds almost Platonic, as if each individual thing, which can be known as it is, also shed light on being in general in which it "participated." Yet it does not follow that in knowing any particular thing, one therefore knows the problem of the meaning of being as it was originally posed.

Heidegger's Second View of Interpretation

Only the first, traditional form of interpretation is consistent with the idea of going back behind the philosophical tradition in order to interpret the meaning of being as the problem was originally raised. If there were such a thing as interpretation yielding transcendental truth, that is, truth about transcendent being, and if it could be applied to textual interpretation, then Heidegger could presumably claim to know in a way which could never later be called into doubt. Such an approach would at least in principle enable us to cut through interpretive disputes in grasping what is in the texts beyond all discussion about them.

That seems to be what Husserl has in mind in the concept of phenomenological seeing in transcendental phenomenology. Husserl is apparently claiming that under proper conditions specified with respect to phenomenological methodology, the observer can grasp what is being observed as it is. Husserl describes a complex method that when correctly applied is supposed to yield this result. It is clear that in working out his view of method, Husserl is making a determined effort to justify his conceptual claims. Like Descartes, Husserl thinks that proper method is the key to successful epistemology. One might not accept his view of method, especially his concept of reduction. It appears that no single later phenomenologist accepts reduction as Husserl understands it. Yet if we accept his view of method as justifying its claimed results, then we can in principle accept the proper application as justifying the uses to which Husserl puts transcendental phenomenology.

Heidegger proposes a theory of interpretation with epistemological intent. His intent is epistemological since he is intending to learn about being as the problem is depicted in certain philosophical texts. Interpretation is meant to yield phenomenological knowledge. Unlike Husserl, Heidegger does not employ a specifiable method that arguably justifies the claims made for it. He tells us how he understands interpretation, but he does not tell us how to engage in interpretation in a way that must, or is even likely to, produce reliable results. Heidegger makes claims he neither justifies nor even attempts to justify. Since he neither attempts to apply his view to interpreting texts nor to justify its cognitive claims, we can ignore it as a possible solution to the problem which interests him.

This leaves only the second, better-known, weaker view of hermeneutical interpretation, which Heidegger develops in accounts of understanding and interpretation (*BT*, sec. 32) and of truth as disclosure (sec. 44). This second view is generally consistent with his normative view of phenomenology as interpretive, but it is useless for the official goal of recovering the problem of the meaning of being as originally raised. Interpretation can promote one reading among others in weighing the advantages or disadvantages of a particular reading of one or more texts. One might, for instance, believe that Heidegger's innovative concept of truth as disclosure enables us to grasp the basic insight with respect to truth throughout ancient Greek philosophy. In that case, one could say that Heidegger's insight is not only seminal for his own position but also for understanding ancient Greek philosophy that is transformed when viewed from this new perspective. But for Heidegger's purposes, that would be insufficient, since no interpretation that anyone can put forward can ever guarantee we have finally reached the so-called primordial experience in which the problem that interests Heidegger was originally raised in ancient Greece.

In section 32, he contends that interpretation always arises from a prior understanding (*BT*, 188). It follows that there is not and cannot be anything like a pure given. This general point is frequently urged in the debate, for instance, in Neurath's (1959) critique of the early Carnap's idea of pure protocols and in Davidson's (1991) rejection of the empiricist distinction between form and content. At stake is the notion of pure givenness according to which something can be known without the interference of a conceptual framework. Kant, who denies immediate knowledge, claims we know only through the imposition of the categories of the understanding. Husserl's view of phenomenological seeing uncritically takes over Kant's conception of pure given with the aim of going back behind the forms of understanding to grasp what is as it is.

Heidegger's suggestion simply destroys Kant's distinction between sensation and the categories that are applied to them. Kant relies on the empiricist distinction between form and content in assuming that categories are applied to pure, unadulterated, but formless sensations. Husserl takes over a version of this empiricist idea in claiming to know essences as present in phenomenological seeing in a way wholly unprejudiced by any commitment, for instance, an ontological commitment to existence.

Here as elsewhere, despite his interest in phenomenology, Heidegger is closer to Kant than to Husserl. Heidegger's very Kantian point undermines his own claim to go back behind the tradition to understand the problem of being as it was originally raised as well as Husserl's conception of phenomenological seeing. It suggests, against Husserl, that there is no perception that is not already interpretive or innocent of presuppositions, that interpretation is always circular, and that we do not discover meanings in the texts but rather find only what we put there. An example might be the use for the hammer, which Heidegger also pretends to uncover as already there. Yet lacking is any account of how we become acquainted in the first place with what we only later, on the basis of prior acquaintance, are able to interpret. In suggesting that we know only what we in some sense construct, Heidegger further raises the issue of the objectivity of cognitive claims.

Heidegger comes back to this issue in section 44, where he develops his account of truth. According to Heidegger, the traditional view of truth associates truth and being (*BT*, 256) in understanding truth as assertion, whose essence lies in agreement of a judgment with the object, and truth as agreement (257). In rejecting this view, Heidegger contends that confirmation means that something shows itself as it is through so-called being uncovering (261). In adopting this conception of truth, Heidegger claims to return to the original ancient Greek view, which, if he were correct, would mean that he had at least recovered one ancient Greek doctrine by going back behind the tradition (262). According to Heidegger, truth is shown by uncovering (263), but disclosure must be authentic (264) to avoid semblance and disguise (265). Heidegger further contends that truth depends on Dasein and only is when Dasein is (269).

How do we know when we know? Heidegger makes everything depend on the subject and the object, on the former since, he claims, there is only truth when there is a subject, and on the object, since a claim for truth does not depend on a judgment about correspondence but rather on the fact that the object is discovered as it is. But how does the subject know when it knows the object? Heidegger's way of responding only postpones but does not resolve the question of interpetive error, which arises, in this account, in the injunction to accept only authentic disclosure that avoids, for instance, such obvious pitfalls as semblance and disguise, in brief taking mere appearance for what is.

This suggestion is clearly difficult with respect to recovering the authentic form of the problem of the meaning of being. Heidegger needs to have some reliable way, other than a mere injunction, to avoid conflating, say, gold with fool's gold. He claims that since ancient Greek philosophy commentators have been led astray in suggesting that there is an original, better, in fact correct view consisting in the way the problem was originally posed. Perhaps. Yet how, on the basis of Heidegger's theories of interpretation, can we know if there is no way to distinguish between what appears to be the case and what is the case, between an apparently correct interpretation of a text and a correct interpretation, between another reading and Heidegger's?

Heidegger has no way to justify his effort to provide the correct reading of the problem of the meaning of being by going back behind the tradition. He has no way to justify the very idea of getting it right about a particular text, idea, theory, or doctrine in independence of the discussion of it. His enthusiastic claim for the relative virtues of Aristotle's theory of time over those of another theory cannot be adjudicated through the supposed destruction of the history of ontology. It can only be adjudicated through the effort to show that this particular view, or this reading of a particular view, is more promising than the available alternatives. But Heidegger precisely wants to avoid opening a discussion of the issue on its merits, which is likely to lead to a debate which cannot easily be ended. I conclude there is no way to bring the debate to an end by allegedly grasping the correct, or authentic, interpretation of Aristotle's view of time, of the problem of the meaning of being as it was originally raised, or of any particular text, since an account of how that is possible has not and probably cannot be given. In a word, there is apparently no way to make sense of the very idea of authenticity as concerns interpretation.

Heidegger's Uses of Plato and Interpreting the History of Philosophy

This essay has examined Heidegger's uses of Plato to recover the problem of the meaning of being as it was originally and authentically raised in ancient Greek philosophy. I have argued that at least during the period when he was pursuing the supposedly main problem of Western philosophy, Heidegger was less interested in Plato's writings as a source of important philosophical doctrines than as a canonical source of the problem that concerned him. I have further argued that Heidegger has no account of how to recover the problem as it was originally raised. This difficulty is not minor but major since, to an unprecedented extent, more than anyone since Hegel, Heidegger's systematic position depends on his ability to read the philosophical tradition.

Earlier I noted that Heidegger's phenomenological reading of the history of philosophy is an essentialist form of strong, or metaphysical, realism. Like metaphysical realism of all kinds, Heidegger's position suffers from his inability to demonstrate that he in fact knows mind-independent reality as it is, in his case the ideas, problems, and concepts as they originally emerged in ancient Greek philosophy. There seems to be no reasonable alternative to concluding that Heidegger simply fails to make good on his claim to recover the problem of being as it was supposedly authentically raised in early Greek philosophy. Heidegger's failure in this regard derives from a deep tension between his phenomenological description of how we in fact interpret texts and the uses to which it is put. Interpretation does not and cannot grasp what is as it is in a way beyond further interpretation. Heidegger's theory of interpretation conflicts with his announced intention of recovering the problem of the meaning of being as it was supposedly originally and authentically raised in early Greek philosophy but later covered up and forgotten.

We always approach texts through conceptual frameworks or categorial schemes, rooted in the forms of life or historical moments we contingently happen to inhabit and on whose basis, through contact with the writings, we work out views about the texts we later test and develop through further textual study. Interpretation is an ongoing process, which can never be brought to an end, hence which can never claim to arrive at interpretive bedrock, the so-called primal experiences of ancient Greek philosophy. In fact, even that can only be a construction of what we, from the vantage point of our historical moment some two and a half millennia later, believe ancient Greek philosophy to be as the result of an interpretive process lasting centuries. It makes eminent good sense to intend to go behind later distortions to uncover or discover the text in its pristine newness unsullied by later misreadings or other accretions. But even this idea is no more than a rational construction, a regulative ideal that can never be constitutive. Heidegger suggests through his conception of Dasein that we take the subject seriously as rooted in the surrounding social context, but when we do that, we understand that the very idea of somehow going back behind the historical tradition is merely another form of the metaphysical realist self-delusion that knowledge means surpassing what we ourselves construct through the desirable but impossible task of finally knowing mind-independent reality as it really is.

Notes

1. Nietzsche famously holds that there is only interpretation all the way down. In our time, the main proponents of skepticism about textual interpretation are Richard Rorty, Jacques Derrida and Paul de Man. Rorty is skeptical about any

claim to get it right. His own approach to textual interpretation reflects a cavalier attitude that illustrates this view. Derrida consistently opposes anything like definite reference, which leads to the idea there is no way to show that words link up correctly with things. For de Man, who opposes even the distinction between history and fiction, it is not possible to separate fiction from nonfiction.

2. Heidegger significantly claims that Hegel's philosophical treatment of the history of philosophy is and will remain the only one until such time as philosophy learns to think historically. See Martin Heidegger, *Nietzsche,* 2 vols. (Pfullingen: Verlag Günter Neske, 1961), 1:450.

3. There are numerous counterexamples of analytic philosophers interested in the history of philosophy, such as Alberto Coffa, Michael Friedman, Hans Sluga, Michael Dummett, and John Passmore.

4. Heidegger's turning to Nazi politics was arguably in part motivated by the same kind of Platonism which also motivated Lukács's implication in Bolshevist and then in Stalinist politics. Heidegger's later rejection of philosophy for thought (*Denken*) is perhaps motivated by his awareness of the link between his decision to play an active part of National Socialism. For discussion, see Rockmore 1997.

5. For turn away from Western philosophy for thought, see "Letter on Humanism," in Martin Heidegger, *Basic Writings,* ed. David Krell (New York: Harper and Row, 1977), 189–242, esp. 239–42.

6. See Heidegger, *Nietzsche,* 2:413.

7. For criticism of Husserlian and neo-Husserlian phenomenological essentialism, see Rockmore 2000.

8. Throughout this essay, numbers in parentheses refer to the English translation at *BT* in the Abbreviations list.

9. See "The Age of the World Picture," in Martin Heidegger, *The Question Concerning Technology and Other Essays,* trans. and intro. William Lovitt (New York: Harper and Row, 1977), 3–35.

10. This problem runs throughout Gadamer's hermeneutics, which he sees as overcoming epistemology, although he does not see the need to justify claims to know which epistemology regards as central. See Gadamer 1988.

11. I take this to be one of the consequences of Derrida's deconstruction of the very idea of definite reference, which in turn makes it impossible to hook words up with things in any insightful way.

Appendix 1: Selected Platonic Loci and Issues Discussed or Referred to by Heidegger

What follows is a list of selected Platonic loci and issues discussed or referred to by Heidegger. The list is chronological and covers the period from 1918 to 1973. The *Gesamtausgabe* still has a long way to go toward its completion, and the published volumes do not have indexes; thus, any such list is so far bound to be selective.

1918–19

Plato (*GA* 60, 303)

1919

Plato, *Sophist*, 242 c 8 f. (*GA* 56/57, 19)
Plato, *Republic*, 533 c 7–d 4 (*GA* 56/57, 20)
Plato (*GA* 56/57, 210)

1919–20

Eidos (*GA* 58, 237–38)
Platonic *erôs* (*GA* 58, 263)

1920–21

Plato, ideas, *anamnêsis* (*GA* 60, 39–40)
Plato (*GA* 60, 45, 47, 49)

1921–22

Plato (*GA* 61, 47, 54, 72)
Republic, 521 c 5–8; 480 ff.; *Apology*, 28 e 4; *Phaedo*, 61 a 3 f. (*GA* 61, 48–52)

1923

Ion, 534 e, 535 a (*GA* 63, 9)
Theaetetus, 163 c, 209 a 5 (*GA* 63, 9)
Republic, 511 b, c (*GA* 63, 43)
Plato (*GA* 63, 45)

1924–25

Dialectic, sophistic, philosophy; *logos, noein, on, mê on, eidos, ousia, dunamis koinônias, kinêsis, stasis, tauton, heteron, phantasia;* a running commentary of the *Sophist* (*GA* 19, 189–306, 353–518, 521–610)
Logos, rhetoric, dialectic, *sunagôgê, diairêsis, anamnêsis; Phaedrus,* especially 259 e–274 a and 274 b–279 c (*GA* 19, 308–45, 347–52)
Logos, onoma, eidôlon; Seventh Letter, 342 a 7 ff., 344 c 1 ff., d 1 ff. (*GA* 19, 346–47)
Theaetetus, 197 b ff. (*GA* 19, 518–21)

1925

Plato, *Sophist,* 263 e (*GA* 20, 100)
Plato (*GA* 20, 102, 109)
Plato, *Parmenides* (*GA* 20, 184, 204)
Plato, *dialegesthai, eidos, idein* (*GA* 20, 201)

1925–26

Aisthêton, nous, noêton, methexis (*GA* 21, 52)
Idea, eidos, theôria, noèton, aisthêsis (*GA* 21, 56–57)
Plato's theory of ideas (*GA* 21, 67, 70–71)
Ousia, ontôs on, logos (*GA* 21, 71–72)
Falsehood (*GA* 21, 168–69)

1926

Plato's philosophy, Platonism, theory of ideas, ontology, dialectic, truth, idea of the good, *idea, logos, anamnêsis; Phaedrus,* 249 e 4 f., *Republic,* 507 e, 508 a, 508 b, 509 a, 510 a–b, d, 511 a, d, e, 517 c (*GA* 22, 94–108)
Aisthêsis, epistêmê, doxa, logos; Theaetetus, 142 a–143 c, 143 d–151 d, 151 d–161 b, 180 c–184 a, 184 a–187 b, 187 b–189 b (*GA* 22, 109–27)
Heteron, koinônia; Sophist, 255 b, c, e, 256 b, 257 b 10, d 10 f. (*GA* 22, 127–28)
Allodoxia, doxa, dianoia, logos; Theaetetus, 189 b–190 c, 190 c–200 d, 201 a–d, 201 e–210 b (*GA* 22, 128–39)
Ousia, agathon, idea, logos, kinêsis, psuchê, dunamis koinônias (*GA* 22, 140–43)

1927

Plato (*BT,* 1, 2, 3, 6, 10, 25, 32, 159, 244 n.1)
Sophist, 242 c (*BT,* 6)
Sophist, 244 a (*BT,* 1)
Parmenides (*BT,* 39)
Timaeus, 37 d 5–7 (*BT,* 423)
Idea, on; the *Republic,* 533 b 6 ff. (*GA* 24, 73–74)
Logos; the *Sophist* (*GA* 24, 295)
Allegory of the cave; light, sun and eye; idea of the good as *epekeina tês ousias; Republic,* 509 b 2–10, 517 b 8 f., 517 c 3 f. (*GA* 24, 400–5)
Anamnêsis; Phaedo, 72 e 5f., *Phaedrus,* 249 b 5–c 6 (*GA* 24, 464)

1927–28

Plato, *kathodos, anodos* (*GA* 25, 405)

1928

Idea of the good as *epekeina tês ousias; Republic,* 509 b 9, 511 b 7, 517 b 8 f.; 517 c 2, c 3, c 3–4 (*GA* 26, 143–44)
Psuchê, ousia, on, technê, praxis, legein, anamnesis; Phaedrus, 249 b-c; *Theaetetus,* 185 a ff., 155 e 4 ff. (*GA* 26, 180–87)
Idea of the good as *epekeina tês ousias* (*GA* 26, 237)
Methexis, metaxu (*GA* 26, 233)
Republic, 509 b 6–10 (*GA* 26, 284)

1928–29

Plato (*GA* 27, 1, 249, 317, 319)
Sophist, 261 d, *koinônia* (*GA* 27, 58)
Plato, *theôrein* (*GA* 27, 169)
Phaedrus, 249 e 4–5; *Sophist* (254 a 8–b 1) (*GA* 27, 215)
Phaedrus, 247 b; *Phaedo,* 79 d, 81 a; *Seventh Letter,* 341 c (*GA* 27, 220)
Ideenlehre, chôrismos, methexis, ontôs on (*GA* 27, 321)

1929

Idea of the good as *epekeina tês ousias, noein; Republic,* 509 a–b ("EG," 160–62)
Eidos ("WM," 119)
Dialegesthai (*GA* 28, 30)
Allegory of the cave, *paideia, eidos, idea, archê, phôs, opsis, idea tou agathou, alêtheia, gnôsis* (*GA* 28, 351–61)

1929–30

Plato's Academy, *oudeis ageômetrêtos eisitô* (*GA* 29/30, 23, 55)
Plato, *Republic,* 476 c, 520 c, 533 c (*GA* 29/30, 34)
Plato (*GA* 29/30, 439, 488)
Logos tinos (*GA* 29/30, 484)

1930

Plato (*GA* 31, 37, 115, 196)
Euthydemos, 300 e–301 a, *ousia, parousia* (*GA* 31, 63–65, 96)
Parousia (*GA* 31, 76)

1931

Plato (*GA* 33, 5, 27, 28, 30, 39, 43, 60, 98, 164–65, 198)
Theaitetos, 152 a (*GA* 33, 197)

1931–32

Alêtheia, idea, horan, noein, paideia, pseudos, lêthê, idea of the good as *epekeina tês ousias; Republic,* 506–11, 514 a–517 a, 521 c 5 ff. (*GA* 34, 1–147)
Sophist, 247 d–e; *Seventh Letter,* 342 a–b, 343 b, 344 b (*GA* 34, 110)
Seventh Letter, 344 b 3, 7–8 (*GA* 34, 112)
Phaedrus, 249 b 5 (*GA* 34, 114)
Alêtheia, aisthêsis, epistêmê, doxa, dianoia, logos, phantasia, pseudês doxa, alêthês doxa; Theaetetus, 184 b–d, 151 e, 152 c, 187–97 (*GA* 34, 149–322)

1933, 1934–35

Plato's philosophy, essence of truth, allegory of the cave, *muthos, logos* (*GA* 36/37, 123–25)
Alêtheia, dialegesthai, orthoteron, idea, ousia, theôria, phôs, ontôs on, eidôlon, sophos, noein, horan, opsis, dunamis, psuchês periagôgês, paideia, lêthê, pseudos, idea of the good, freedom; *Republic,* 506–11, 514 a 1 f., 514 a–517 e, 521 c 5; *Phaedrus,* 249 b 5 (*GA* 36/37, 127–229)
Epistêmê, alêtheia, pseudos, aisthêsis, phantasia, doxa, allodoxia, pseudês doxa, alêthês doxa, peras; Theaetetus, 143 e ff., 187 c–200 b, 188 b 6 ff., 190 c 2 f., 197 b 8 ff., 200 b–201 c (*GA* 36/37, 231–64)

1935

Onoma, rhêma, pragma, logos; Sophist, 261 e ff. (*GA* 40, 60–62)
Chôra, enklisis; Timaeus, 50 e (*GA* 40, 70–72)
Plato's philosophy (*GA* 40, 102, 188)
Plato, *chôrismos, idea* (*GA* 40, 113)
Plato's idealism (*GA* 40, 145)
Phusis, idea, eidos, ousia, paradeigma, ontôs on, mimêsis, mê on, homoiôsis (*GA* 40, 189–97)
Idea of the good, *eidos, dialegesthai* (*GA* 40, 205–6)

1935–36

Theaitetos, 174 a (*GA* 41, 2–3)
Meno, 85 d 4 (*GA* 41, 91)
Plato (*GA* 41, 99, 153, 155)

1936–37

Platonism and Plato; *idea, eidos, theôria, to ti estin, alêtheia, mê on, technê, poiêsis, polis, erôs, idea tou kalou, mimesis, demos, dêmiourgos, phusis, eidôlon, philosophia, logos, doxa, dikê, dikaiosunê, opsis, phronêsis,* art, god; Nietzsche's word: "My philosophy an *inverted Platonism*"; *Republic,* 437, 595 c, 596 a–d, 597 b, e, 598 b, 607 b; *Phaedrus,* 249 e, 248 a–b, 249 c, 250 a 5, b, d (*WPA,* 153–213)

1936–38

Nietzsche's Platonism as nihilism (*GA* 65, 115)
Idea (*GA* 65, 115, 126, 138, 191, 193, 214–15)
Western philosophy from Plato to Nietzsche (*GA* 65, 127)
Kinoumenon as *mê on* (*GA* 65, 194)
Platonism (*GA* 65, 196, 215)
Plato (*GA* 65, 198, 431)
Zugon (*GA* 65, 198)
Idea, koinon, aei (*GA* 65, 202, 206)
Idea, Platonism, idealism, koinon, agathon, homoiôsis, epekeina, chôrismos, alêtheia,
ousia, ontôs on (*GA* 65, 208–24)
Idea, ousia, ontôs on (*GA* 65, 271–73)
Idea, koinon, ousia, epekeina (*GA* 65, 286–89)
Idea, alêtheia, homoiôsis, zugon, phôs (*GA* 65, 329–35)
Idea, alêtheia (*GA* 65, 359–60)
Idea, phusis, ousia (*GA* 65, 433)
Idea, anamnêsis (*GA* 65, 453)
Noein, dialegesthai (*GA* 65, 457)

1937–38

Plato, *koinon, idea, eidos, ousia* (*GA* 45, 60–71)
Idea, eidos (*GA* 45, 74–75, 95, 97)
Plato, *ontôs on, idea* (*GA* 45, 84–85)
Plato (*GA* 45, 92, 99, 101, 111, 117, 121, 138, 222–23)
Theaetetus, 155 d 2 ff. (*GA* 45, 155)
Plato, *Republic, paideia* (*GA* 45, 180)

1938–39

Idea, ontôs on, epekeina tês ousias (*GA* 66, 90)
Idea (*GA* 66, 299)
Alêtheia (*GA* 66, 109)
Plato (*GA* 66, 127, 389)
Platonismus (*GA* 66, 140)

1939

Eidos, idea, koinon, Plato ("ECP," 275)

1940

Idea, eidos, ousia, on, ontôs on, mê on, agathon, idea of the good *as epekeina tês*
ousias, alêtheia, noein; das Apriori; history of Western philosophy from Plato to
Nietzsche as metaphysics; Plato and Platonism; *Phaedo,* 74–76 (*EN,* 190–215)

1941–42

Plato, metaphysics, technology (*GA* 52, 91)

1942

Allegory of the cave, *idea, eidos, agathon, paideia, alêtheia, noein, nous, homoiôsis, sophia, philosophia, theion, logos, orthotês; Republic,* 509 b, 514 a–517 c, 518 a 2, c 9 ("PDT," 203–38)
Plato, *Phaidros,* 246 ff. (*GA* 53, 140–43)

1942–43

Platonic dialogue; *Phaedrus* (*GA* 54, 131–32)
Polis, polos, alêtheia, Dikê, muthos, politeia, psuchê, pseudos, daimonion, idea, lêthê, theaô, theion, aisthêsis. Phronêsis, technê, anamnêsis, Platonism; *Republic,* 614 a 6, 614 b 2–621 b 7 (*GA* 54, 132–93)

1943–44

Plato (*GA* 55, 35, 56, 73–74, 76, 83, 227, 364)
Eidos, logos (*GA* 55, 251–58)

1946

Plato ("ANAX," 322, 344; "LH," 348, 354)
Idea ("ANAX," 334, 371; "LH," 331)

1953

Symposium, 205 b ("QCT," 12)

1955–56

Plato, *hupothesis* (*GA* 10, 24–25)
Plato, *idea* (*GA* 10, 69)
Plato (*GA* 10, 92, 95)

1958

Plato, *idea* ("HG," 434, 437)

1964

Plato's thought, history of philosophy, metaphysics, Nietzsche's "inverted Platonism" and Marx's reversal of metaphysics ("EP," 63, 78)

1968

Plato, *eidos* ("THOR68," 312)

1969

Plato, *idea, eidos, ousia, mê on, ontôs on* ("THOR69," 332–34, 336–37)

1973

Plato, *sehen* ("Z," 377–78)

Appendix 2: Further Reading

This list complements the extensive bibliography of Boutot 1987, 331–36, which includes works published up to 1987 on Heidegger's interpretation of pre-Socratics, Plato, Aristotle, and Greek philosophy as a whole. Only a few works listed in Boutot's bibliography have been included in this reference list; even fewer works published before 1987 and included in this reference list do not appear in Boutot's bibliography. This bibliography, however, is not comprehensive; it includes mainly recent articles written in English. (Full source citations appear in this volume's references list.)

Heidegger and Plato

Aubenque 1992
Barnes 1990
Bierwaltes 1992
Boutot 1987
Brogan 1997
Courtine 1990
Dostal 1985
Figal 2000
Gadamer 1983b
Galston 1982
Geiman 1995
Gonzales 1997, 2002
Hyland 1995, 1997
Kisiel 1993b
Peperzak 1997
Proimos 2001
Rojcewicz 1997
Rosen 1988, 1993
Schüssler 1996
Warnek 1997
Webb 2000
Wolz 1981
Zimmerman 1990
Zuckert 1996

Heidegger and Aristotle

Bernasconi 1986, 1989
Berti 1990
Brague 1984
Brogan 1989, 1990, 1994, 2000
Chanter 2000
Courtine 1992
Ellis 2000
Geiman 1995
Hatab 2000
Kisiel 1993a
Schurmann 1982
Sheehan 1988
Taminiaux 1989
Volpi 1984, 1988, 1994, 1996

Gadamer's versus Heidegger's Interpretation of Plato

Dostal 1997
Pöggeler 1997
Renaud 1999
Riedel 1990
Wachterhauser 1999
Zuckert 1996

Heidegger and the Presocratic Philosophers

Courtine 1993
Dastur 2000
De Gennaro 2000
Jacobs 1999
Maly and Emad 1986
Seidel 1964
Zarader 1990

Heidegger and Greek Philosophy

Gadamer 1983a
Guignon 2001
Maly 1993
Schoenbohm 2001

Heidegger and Neoplatonism

Beierwaltes 1980
Charles-Saget 1990

Kremer 1989
Narbonne 1999, 2001

Heidegger and the History of Philosophy

Gadamer 1981
Haar 1987
Kolb 1981
Krell 1981
Magnus 1981
Moran 1994
Okrent 1981
Sheehan 1981
Volpi 2000
White 1981

References

This list contains all sources cited parenthetically in the text that do not correspond to the abbreviations list in the front of the book.

Arendt, H. 1961. *Freedom and Serfdom: An Anthology of Western Thought*, ed. Albert Hunold, 191–217. Dordrecht: Riedel.

———. 1968. "What is Freedom?" *Between Past and Future: Eight Exercises in Political Thought*, 143–71. New York: Viking.

———. 1999. *Martin Heidegger, Briefe. 1925–1975*, ed. U. Ludz, 147–48. Frankfurt am Main: V. Klostermann.

Aubenque, P. 1992. "Oui et non." In *Nos grecs et leur modernes*, ed. B. Cassin, 17–36. Paris: Seuil.

Bambach, C. 2003. *Heidegger's Roots: Nietzsche, National Socialism, and the Greeks.* Ithaca: Cornell University Press.

Barnes, J. 1990. "Heidegger spéléologue." *Revue de Métaphysique et de morale* 2: 173–95.

Beardsley, M. 1982. *The Aesthetic Point of View*, ed. Micheal Wreen and Donald Callen. Ithaca, N.Y.: Cornell University Press

Beierwaltes, W. 1980. *Indentität und Differenz*. Frankfurt am Main: V. Klostermann.

———. 1992. "EPEKEINA: Eine Anmerkung zu Heideggers Platon-Rezeption." In *Transzendenz: Zu einem Grundwort der klassischen Metaphysik*, ed. L. Honnefelder and W. Schüßler. Paderborn, Germany: F. Schöningh.

Bernasconi, R. 1985. *The Question of Language in Heidegger's History of Being.* Atlantic Highlands, N.J.: Humanities Press International.

———. 1986. "The Fate of the Distinction between *Praxis* and *Poiesis*." *Heidegger Studies* 2:111–39. Repr. in R. Bernasconi, *Heidegger in Question: The Art of Existing.* New Jersey: Humanities Press, 1993, 2–24.

———. 1989. "Heidegger's Destruction of *Phronesis*." *Southern Journal of Philosophy* 28:S127–47.

Berti, E. 1990. "Heidegger e il concetto aristotelico di verita." In *Herméneutique et Phénoménologie: Hommage à P. Aubenque*, ed. R. Brague and J.-F. Courtine, 97–120. Paris: PUF.

———. 1997. "Heideggers Auseinandersetzung mit der Platonisch-Aristotelischen Wahrheitsverständnis." In *Die Frage nach der Wahrheit*, ed. E. Richter, 89–105. Frankfurt am Main: V. Klostermann.

———. 2000. "I luoghi della verità secondo Aristotele: a confronto con Heidegger." In *I luoghi del comprendere*, ed. V. Melchiorre, 3–27. Milan: Vita e Pensiero.

Blackburn, S., and K. Simmons, eds. 1999. *Truth*. Oxford: Oxford University Press.

Bonitz, H. 1849. *Aristotelis Metaphysica. Commentarius*. Repr., Hildesheim: Olms, 1960.

Boutot, A. 1987. *Heidegger et Platon*. Paris: PUF.

Brague, R. 1984. "La phénoménologie comme voie d'accès au monde grec: Note sur la critique de la *Vorhandenheit* comme modèle ontologique dans la lecture heideggérienne d'Aristote." In *Phénoménologie et Métaphysique*, ed. J.-L. Marion and G. Planty-Bonjour, 247–73. Paris: PUF.

———. 1988. *Aristote et la question du monde*. Paris: P.U.F.

Brogan, W. 1989. "A Response to Robert Bernasconi's 'Heidegger's Destruction of Phronesis.'" *Southern Journal of Philosophy* 28:S149–53.

———. 1990. "Heidegger and Aristotle: Dasein and the Question of Practical Life." In *Crises in Continental Philosophy*, ed. A. B. Dallery and C. E. Scott, 137–46. Albany: SUNY Press.

———. 1994. "The Place of Aristotle in the Development of Heidegger's Phenomenology." In *Reading Heidegger from the Start*, ed. T. Kisiel and J. van Buren, 213–27. Albany: SUNY Press.

———. 1997. "Plato's Dialectical Soul: Heidegger on Plato's Ambiguous Relationship to Rhetoric." *Research in Phenomenology* 27:3–15.

———. 2000. "Heidegger's Interpretation of Aristotle on the Privative Character of Force and the Twofoldness of Being." In *Interrogating the Tradition: Hermeneutics and the History of Philosophy*, ed. C. E. Scott and J. Sallis, 111–30. Albany: SUNY Press.

Caputo, J. D. 1993. *Demythologizing Heidegger*. Bloomington: Indiana University Press.

Chanter, T. 2000. "Heidegger's Understanding of the Aristotelian Concept of Time." In *Interrogating the Tradition: Hermeneutics and the History of Philosophy*, ed. C. E. Scott and J. Sallis, 131–57. Albany: SUNY Press.

Charles-Saget, A. 1990. "*Aphairesis et Gelassenheit, Heidegger et Plotin*." In *Herméneutique et Phénoménologie: Hommage à P. Aubenque*, ed. R. Brague and J.-F. Courtine, 323–44. Paris: PUF.

Cornford, F. M. 1937. *Plato's Cosmology. The* Timacus *of Plato*, translated with a running commentary by Francis Macdonald Cornford. London: Kegan Paul, Trench, Trubner and Co. Ltd.

Courtine, J.-F. 1990. "Le Platonisme de Heidegger." In *Heidegger et la phénoménologie*, 129–60. Paris: Vrin.

———. 1992. "Une difficile transaction: Heideger, entre Aristote et Luther." In *Nos grecs et leur modernes*, ed. B. Cassins, 337–62. Paris: Seuil.

———. 1993. "Phenomenology and/or Tautology." In *Reading Heidegger*, ed. J. Sallis, 241–57. Bloomington: Indiana University Press.

Dahlstrom, D. O. 1994. "Heidegger's Critique of Husserl." In *Reading Heidegger from the Start*, ed. T. Kisiel and J. Van Buren. Albany: SUNY Press.

Dastur, F. 2000. "Heidegger and Anaximander: Being and Justice." In *Interrogating the Tradition: Hermeneutics and the History of Philosophy*, ed. C. E. Scott and J. Sallis, 179–90. Albany: SUNY Press.

Davidson, D. 1991. "On the Very Idea of a Conceptual Scheme." In *Inquiries into Truth and Interpretation*. Oxford: Clarendon Press.

———. 1999. "A Coherence Theory of Truth and Knowledge." In *Subjective, Inter subjective, Objective*. Oxford: Oxford University Press.

———. 2001. "The Emergence of Thought." In *Subjective, Intersubjective, Objective*. Oxford: Clarendon Press.

De Gennaro, I. 2000. "Heidegger und die Griechen." *Heidegger Studies* 16:87–113.

Derrida, J. 1982. "*Ousia* and *Gramme*." In *The Margins of Philosophy*, trans. A. Bass, 29–67. Chicago: University of Chicago Press.

———. 1994. "L'oreille de Heidegger: Philopolémologie (*Geschlecht* IV)." In *Politiques de l'amitié*, 341–419. Paris: Galilée.

Devitt, M. 1997. *Realism and Truth*. Princeton, N.J.: Princeton University Press.

Dostal, R. J. 1985. "Beyond Being: Heidegger's Plato." *Journal of the History of Philosophy* 23 (1): 71–98. Repr. *Martin Heidegger: Critical Assessments*, vol. 2, ed. C. Macann, 61–89. London and New York: Routledge, 1992.

———. 1997. "Gadamer's Continuous Challenge: Heidegger's Plato Interpretation." In *The Philosophy of Hans-Georg Gadamer*, ed. L. E. Hahn, 289–307. Chicago: Open Court.

Ellis, J. 2000. "Heidegger, Aristotle and Time in *Basic Problems* § 19." In *Interrogating the Tradition: Hermeneutics and the History of Philosophy*, ed. C. E. Scott and J. Sallis, 179–90. Albany: SUNY Press.

Figal, G. 1988. *Martin Heidegger: Phänomenologie der Freiheit*. Frankfurt am Main: Athenäum.

———. 2000. "Refraining from Dialectic: Heidegger's Interpretation of Plato in the *Sophist* Lecture." In *Interrogating the Tradition: Hermeneutics and the History of Philosophy*, ed. C. E. Scott and J. Sallis, 95–109. Albany: SUNY Press.

Findlay, J. N. 1978. *Plato and Platonism*. New York: Times Books.

Freeman, K. 1948. *Ancilla to the Pre-Socratic Philosophers*. Oxford: Basil Blackwell.

Fritsche, J. 1995. "On Brinks and Bridges in Heidegger." *Graduate Faculty Philosophy Journal* 18 (1): 111–86.

———. 1999a. "Heidegger in the *Kairos* of 'The Occident.'" *Graduate Faculty Philosophy Journal* 21 (2): 3–19.

———. 1999b. *Historical Destiny and National Socialism in Heidegger's "Being and Time."* Berkeley: University of California Press.

———. 2003. "Competition and Conformity: Heidegger on Distantiality and the 'They' in *Being and Time*." *Graduate Faculty Philosophy Journal* 24 (2): 75–109.

Gadamer, H.-G. 1980. *Dialogue and Dialectic: Eight Hermeneutical Studies on Plato*, trans. P. Christopher Smith. New Haven, Conn.: Yale University Press.

———. 1981. "Heidegger and the History of Philosophy." *Monist* 64 (4): 434–44.

———. 1983a. "Die Griechen." In *Heideggers Wege: Stududien zum Spätwerk*, 117–28. Tübingen: Mohr. Translated by J. W. Stanley as "The Greeks," in H.-G. Gadamer, *Heidegger's Ways* (Albany: SUNY Press, 1993), 139–52.

———. 1983b. "Plato." In *Heideggers Wege: Stududien zum Spätwerk*, 70–80. Tübingen: Mohr. Translated by J. W. Stanley as "Plato," in H.-G. Gadamer, *Heidegger's Ways* (Albany: SUNY Press, 1993), 81–93.

REFERENCES

————. 1985. *Gesammelte Werke*. Vol. 5, *Griechische Philosophie I.* Tübingen: Mohr [Siebeck].

————. 1987. "Der eine Weg Martin Heideggers." In *Gesammelte Werke*, vol. 2, 417–30. Tübingen: J. C. B. Mohr [P. Siebeck]. Translated into English by P. Ch. Smith as "Martin Heidegger's One Path," in *Reading Heidegger from the Start*, ed. T. Kisiel and J. Van Buren (Albany: SUNY Press, 1994), 27.

————. 1988. *Truth and Method*, trans. and edit. Garrett Barden and John Cumming. New York: Crossroad.

Galston, A. 1982. "Heidegger's Plato: A Critique of *Plato's Doctrine of Truth.*" *Philosophical Forum* 13:371–84.

Geiman, C. P. 1995. "From the Metaphysics of Production to Questioning Empowering: Heidegger's Critical Interpretation of the Platonic and Aristotelian Good." *Heidegger Studies* 11:95–121.

Gillespie, M. A. 2000. "Martin Heidegger's Aristotelian National Socialism," *Political Theory* 28 (April): 140–66.

Gonzales, F. J. 1997. "On the Way to *Sophia:* Heidegger on Plato's Dialectic, Ethics, and *Sophist.*" *Research in Phenomenology* 27:16–60.

————. 2002. "Dialectic as 'Philosophical Embarrassment': Heidegger's Critique of Plato's Method." *Journal of the History of Philosophy* 40 (3): 361–89.

Görland, I. 1981. *Transzendenz und Selbst: Eine Phase in Heideggers Denken*. Frankfurt: Klostermann.

Grondin, J. 1987. *Le tournant dans la pensée de Martin Heidegger*. Paris: Presses Universitaires de France.

————. 1991. "Prolegomena to an Understanding of Heidegger's Turn." *Graduate Faculty Philosophy Journal* 14 (2)–15 (1): 85–108.

Guignon, C. 2001. "Being as Appearing: Retrieving the Greek Experience of *Phusis.*" In *A Companion to Heidegger's "Introduction to Metaphysics,"* ed. R. Polt and G. Fried, 34–56. New Haven and London: Yale University Press.

Haar, M. 1987. "L'Histoire de l'être et son modèle hégélien." In *Le chant de la terre*, 141–60. Paris: l'Herne, 1987. Repr. in *Endings: Questions of Memory in Hegel and Heidegger*, ed. R. Comay and J. McCumber (Evanston, Ill.: Northwestern University Press, 1999), 45–56. Translated by R. Lilly as "The History of Being and Its Hegelian Model," in *The Song of the Earth* (Bloomington: Indiana University Press, 1993), 67–77.

Habermas, J. 1990. *The Philosophical Discourse of Modernity*, trans. F. G. Lawrence. Cambridge: MIT Press. (Original German edition published in 1985.)

Hackenesch, C. 2001. *Selbst und Welt: Zur Metaphysik des Selbst bei Heidegger und Cassirer.* Hamburg: Meiner.

Hamilton, E., and H. Cairns, eds. 1989. *The Collected Dialogues of Plato*. Princeton, N.J.: Princeton University Press.

Hatab, L. J. 2000. "Heidegger and Aristotle." In *Ethics and Finitude: Heideggerian Contributions to Moral Philosophy*, 99–115. Lanham, Md.: Rowman and Littlefield.

Hegel, G. W. F. 1942. *Philosophy of Right*, tr. T. M. Knox. Oxford: Clarendon Press.

————. 1977. *The Phenomenology of Spirit*, tr. A. V. Miller. Oxford: Oxford University Press.

REFERENCES

Hirsch, E. D. Jr. 1967. *Validity in Interpretation*. New Haven: Yale University Press.
Holz, H. G. 1981. *Plato and Heidegger*. London and Toronto: Associated University Presses.
Husserl, E. 1954. *Die Krisis der europäischen Wissenschaften und die transzendentale Phänomenologie*, Husserliana 6. The Hague: M. Nihjoff.
———. 1962. *Ideas: General Introduction to Pure Phenomenology*, trans. W. R. Boyce Gibson. New York: Collier.
———. 1984. *Logische Untersuchungen I, II*, Husserliana 18 and 19. The Hague: M. Nihjoff.
———. 1989. *Notes sur Heidegger*. Paris: Les Éditions de Minuit.
Hyland, D. A. 1995. "Truth and Finitude: On Heidegger's Reading of Plato." In *Finitute and Transcendence in the Platonic Dialogues*, 139–63. Albany: SUNY Press.
———. 1997. "Caring for Myth: Heidegger, Plato, and the Myth of Cura." *Research in Phenomenology* 27:90–102.
Inwood, M. 1999a. "Does the Nothing Noth?" In *German Philosophy Since Kant*, ed. A. O'Hear. Cambridge: Cambridge University Press.
———. 1999b. *A Heidegger Dictionary*. Oxford: Blackwell.
Jacobs, D. C., ed. 1999. *The Presocratics after Heidegger*. Albany: SUNY Press.
Jaeger, W. 1912. *Studien zur Entstehungsgeschichte der Metaphysik des Aristoteles*. Berlin: Weidmann.
———. 1923. *Aristoteles. Grundlegung einer Geschichte seiner Entwicklung*, 1st ed. Berlin: Weidmann.
Kahn, C. 1998. *Plato and the Socratic Dialogue*. Cambridge: Cambridge University Press.
Kahn, C. H. 2003. *The Verb "Be" in Ancient Greek*. Indianapolis: Hackett.
Kant, I. 1996. *Critique of Pure Reason*, trans. W. S. Pluhar. Indianapolis: Hackett.
Kern, I. 1964. *Husserl und Kant: Eine Untersuchung über Husserls Verhältnis zu Kant und zum Neukantianismus*. The Hague: M. Nijhoff.
Kirk, G. S., J. E. Raven, and M. Schofield. 1983. *The Presocratic Philosophers*, 2d ed. Cambridge: Cambridge University Press.
Kisiel, T. 1993a. *The Genesis of Heidegger's "Being and Time."* Berkeley and Los Angeles: University of California Press.
———. 1993b. "WS 1924–25: Interpretation of Platonic Dialogues." In *The Genesis of Heidegger's "Being and Time,"* 301–8. Berkeley and Los Angeles: University of California Press.
———. 1994. "Heidegger (1920–21) on Becoming a Christian: A Conceptual Picture Show." In *Reading Heidegger from the Start: Essays in His Earliest Thought*, ed. Theodore Kisiel and John van Buren, 175–92. Albany: SUNY Press.
———. 1996. "The Genesis of *Being and Time:* The Primal Leap." In *Phenomenology, Interpretation, and Community*, ed. L. Langsdorf and S. H. Watson, with E. M. Bower, 29–50. Albany: SUNY Press.
———. 2002. "In the Middle of Heidegger's Three Concepts of the Political." In *Heidegger and Practical Philosophy*, ed. François Raffoul and David Pettigrew, 135–57. Albany: SUNY Press.
Kolb, D. A. 1981. "Hegel and Heidegger as Critics." *Monist* 64 (4): 481–99.

Krämer, H. J. 1990. *Plato and the Foundations of Metaphysics: A Work on the Theory of the Principles and Unwritten Doctrines of Plato with a Collection of the Fundamental Documents*, ed. and trans. John R. Caton. Albany: SUNY Press.

Krell, D. F. 1981. "Results." *Monist* 64 (4): 467–80.

Kremer, K. 1989. "Zur Ontologischen Differenz: Plotin und Heidegger." *Zeitschrift für philosophische Forschung* 43:673–94.

Lacoue-Labarthe, P. 1980. *Typography: Mimesis, Philosophy, Politics*, ed. Christopher Fynsk. Cambridge, Mass.: Harvard University Press.

————. 1990. *Heidegger, Art and Politics: The Fiction of the Political*, trans. Chris Turner. London: Basil Blackwell.

Lacoue-Labarthe, P., and J.-L. Nancy. 1997. *Retreating the Political*, ed. Simon Sparks. London and New York: Routledge.

Lafont, C. 1994. *Sprache und Welterschließung: Zur linguistischen Wende der Hermeneutik Heideggers*. Frankfurt: Suhrkamp.

Lübbe, H. 1963. *Politische Philosophie in Deutschland: Sttudien zu ihrer Geschichte*. Basel and Stuttgart: Benno Schwabe.

Magnus, B. 1981. "Heidegger's Metahistory of Philosophy Revisited." *Monist* 64 (4): 445–66.

Maier, H. 1896. *Die Syllogistik des Aristoteles*, pt. 1. Tübingen: Laupp.

Maly, K. 1993. "Reading and Thinking: Heidegger and the Hinting Greeks." In *Reading Heidegger*, ed. J. Sallis, 221–40. Bloomington: Indiana University Press. Repr. in C. Macann, ed., *Martin Heidegger: Critical Assessments*, vol. 2 (London and New York: Routledge, 1992), 37–60.

Maly, K., and P. Emad, eds. 1986. *Heidegger on Heraclitus: A New Reading*. Lewiston, N.Y.: Edwin Mellen Press.

Margolis, J. 2003. *The Unraveling of Scientism: American Philosophy at the End of the Twentieth Century*. Ithaca, N.Y.: Cornell University Press.

Marion, J. L. 1989. *Réduction et donation: Recherches sur Husserl, Heidegger et la phénoménologie*. Paris: PUF.

Moran, D. 1994. "The Destruction of the Destruction: Heidegger's Versions of the History of Philosophy." In *Martin Heidegger: Politics, Art, and Technology*, ed. K. Harries and C. Jamme, 175–96. New York: Holmes and Meier. Translated as "Die Destruktion der Destruktion: Heideggers Versionen der Geschichte der Philosophie," in *Kunst - Politik - Technik: Martin Heidegger*, ed. C. Jamme and K. Harries (Munich: Wilhelm Fink Verlag, 1991), 295–318.

Narbonne, J.-M. 1999. "*Henôsis* et *Ereignis*: Remarques sur une interpretation heideggérienne de l'Un plotinien." *Les Etudes Philosophiques*, January–March, 105–21. Repr. in *La métaphysique de Plotin* (Paris: Vrin, 2001), 149–66.

————. 2001. *Hénologie, ontologie et Ereignis*. Paris: Les Belles Lettres.

Natorp, P. 1907. *Gesammelte Abhandlungen zur Sozialpädagogik: Erste Abteilung, Historisches*. Stuttgart: Fr. Frommanns Verlag [E. Hauff].

————. 1918. *Deutscher Weltberuf: Geschichtsphilosophische Richtlinien*. Vol. 1, *Die Weltalter des Geistes*. Vol. 2, *Die Seele des Deutschen*. Jena: Eugen Diederichs.

————. 1921. *Platos Ideenlehre: Eine Einführung in den Idealismus*. Leipzig: Meiner.

Neurath, O. 1959. "Protocol Sentences." In *Logical Positivism*, ed. A. J. Ayer, 199–208. New York: Free Press.

Nietzsche, F. 1988. "Der griechische Staat." In *Die Geburt der Tragödie: Unzeitgemäße Betrachtungen I-IV, Nachgelassene Schriften 1870–1873,* ed. G. Colli and M. Montinari. Munich: Deutscher Taschenbuch Verlag and de Gruyter.

Okrent, M. B. 1981. "The Truth of Being and the History of Philosophy." *Monist* 64 (4): 500–17.

Orozco, T. 1995. *Platonische Gewalt: Gadamers politische Hermeneutik der NS-Zeit.* Hamburg: Argument-Verlag.

Papenfuus, D., and O. Pöggeler, eds. 1990. *Zur philosophischen Aktualität Heideggers,* vol. 2, *Im Gespräch der Zeit.* Frankfurt am Main: V. Klostermann.

Partenie, C. 1998. "The 'Productionist' Framework of the *Timaeus.*" *Dionysius* 16:29–34.

Pattison, G. 2000. *The Later Heidegger.* London: Routledge.

Peperzak, A. T. 1997. "Did Heidegger Understand Plato's Idea of Truth?" In *Platonic Transformations: With and after Hegel, Heidegger, and Levinas,* 57–111. Lanham, Md.: Rowman and Littlefield. A shortened version of this text was published under the title "Heidegger and Plato's Idea of the Good," in *Reading Heidegger,* ed. J. Sallis (Bloomington: Indiana University Press, 1993), 258–85.

Philipse, H. 1998. *Heidegger's Philosophy of Being: A Critical Interpretation.* Princeton, N.J.: Princeton University Press.

Picht, G. 1977. "Die Macht des Denkens." In *Erinnerung an Martin Heidegger,* ed. G. Neske, 197–205. Pfullingen: Neske.

Pöggeler, O. 1963. *Der Denkweg Martin Heideggers.* Neske: Pfullingen.

———. 1997. "Ein Streit um Platon: Heidegger und Gadamer." In *Platon in der Abendländischen Geistesgeschichte: Neue Forschungen zum Platonismus,* ed. T. Kobusch and T. Mojsisch, 241–54. Darmstadt: Wissenschaftliche Buchgesellschaft.

Proimos, C. 2001. "Martin Heidegger on Mimesis in Plato and Platonism." In *Neoplatonism and Western Aesthetics,* ed. A. Alexandrakis, 153–63. Albany: SUNY Press.

Quine, W. V. 1960. *Word and Object.* Cambridge, Mass.: MIT Press.

Renaud, F. 1999. *Die Resokratisierung Platons: Die Platonische Hermeneutik Hans-Georg Gadamers.* Saint Augustin: Academia.

Richardson, W. J, S.J. 1963. *Heidegger: Through Phenomenology to Thought.* The Hague: Nijhoff.

Riedel, M. 1990. "Hermeneutik und Gesprächsdialektik: Gadamers Auseinandersetzung mit Heidegger." In *Hören auf die Sprache,* 96–130. Frankfurt am Main: Suhrkamp.

Ringer, F. 1969. *The Decline of the German Mandarins: The German Academic Community, 1890–1933.* Cambridge: Harvard University Press.

Robinson, R. 1953. *Plato's Earlier Dialectic.* Oxford: Clarendon Press.

Rockmore, T. 1997. *On Heidegger's Nazism and Philosophy.* Berkeley and Los Angeles: University of California Press.

———. 2000. "Essentialism, Phenomenology, and Historical Cognition." In *The Empirical and the Transcendental: A Fusion of Horizons,* ed. Bina Gupta, 49–60. Lanham, Md.: Rowman and Littlefield.

REFERENCES

Rojcewicz, R. 1997. "Platonic Love: Dasein's Urge toward Being." *Research in Phenomenology* 27:103–20.

Rorty, R. 1997. Introduction to *Empiricism and the Philosophy of Mind,* by Robert Brandom. Cambridge: Harvard University Press.

———. 1999. *Philosophy and Social Hope.* London: Penguin.

———. 2001. "An Imaginative Philosopher: The Legacy of W. V. Quine." *Chronicle of Higher Education,* 2 February, B7–9.

Rosen, S. 1988. "Heidegger's Interpretation of Plato." In *The Quarrel between Philosophy and Poetry,* 127–47. New York and London: Routledge.

———. 1993. "Platonism Is Aristotelianism." In *The Question of Being: A Reversal of Heidegger,* 3–45. New Haven and London: Yale University Press.

Ross, W. D. 1924. *Aristotle's Metaphysics: A Revised Text with Introduction and Commentary.* Oxford: Clarendon Press.

———. 1984. *The Complete Works of Aristotle.* Vol. 2. Revised Oxford Translation, ed. Jonathan Barnes. Princeton, N.J.: Princeton University Press.

Safranski, R. 1998. *Martin Heidegger: Between Good and Evil,* trans. E. Osers. Cambridge, Mass.: Harvard University Press.

Sallis, J. 1994. "The truth that is not knowledge." In *Reading Heidegger from the Start,* ed. T. Kisiel and J. Van Buren. Albany: SUNY Press.

Sallis, J., and K. Maly, eds. 1980. *Heraclitean Fragments: A Companion Volume to the Heidegger/Fink Seminar on Heraclitus.* University, Ala.: University of Alabama Press.

Schmitt, C. 1934. *Staat, Bewegung, Volk.* Hamburg: Hanseatische Verlagsanstalt.

Schoenbohm, S. 2001. "Heidegger's Interpretation of *Phusis* in *Introduction to Metaphysics.*" In *A Companion to Heidegger's "Introduction to Metaphysics,"* ed. R. Polt and G. Fried, 143–60. New Haven and London: Yale University Press.

Schurmann, R. 1982. *Le principe d'anarchie.* Paris: Seuil. Translated by C.-M. Gros as *Heidegger on Being and Acting* (Bloomington: Indiana University Press, 1987).

Schüssler, I. 1996. "Le *Sophiste* de Platon dans l'intepétation de Martin Heidegger." In *Heidegger 1919–1929: De l'herméneutique de la facticité à la métaphysique du Dasein,* ed. J.-F. Courtine, 91–111. Paris: Jean Vrin.

Seidel, G. J. 1964. *Martin Heidegger and the Pre-Socratics.* Lincoln: University of Nebraska Press.

Sheehan, T. 1981. "On Movement and the Destruction of Ontology." *Monist* 64 (4): 534–42.

———. 1988. "*Hermeneia* and *Apophansis:* The Early Heidegger on Aristotle." In *Heidegger et l'Idée de la phénoménologie,* ed. F. Volpi, 67–80. Dordrecht: Kluwer.

Stambaugh, J. 1996. *Being and Time: A Translation of "Sein und Zeit."* Albany: SUNY Press.

Taminiaux, J. 1989. "La réappropriation de l'*Ethique à Nichomaque: poiêsis* et *praxis* dans l'articulation de l'ontologie fondamentale." In *Lectures de l'ontologie fondamentale: Essais sur Heidegger,* 147–89. Grenoble: J. Millon. Repr. in *Hei-*

degger et l'Idée de la phénoménologie, ed. F. Volpi (Dordrecht: Kluwer, 1988), 107–25. Translated as *"Poiesis* and *Praxis* in Fundamental Ontology," *Research in Phenomenology* 17 (1987): 137–69.

———. 1994. "The Husserlian Heritage in Heidegger's Notion of the Self." In *Reading Heidegger from the Start: Essays in His Earliest Thought*, ed. Theodore Kisiel and John van Buren, 269–90. Albany: SUNY Press.

———. 1997. *The Thracian Maid and the Professional Thinker: Arendt and Heidegger*, trans. Michael Gendre. Albany: SUNY Press.

Thomä, D. 1990. *Die Zeit des Selbst und die Zeit danach: Zur Kritik der Textgeschichte Martin Heideggers 1910–1976*. Frankfurt: Suhrkamp.

Tugendhat, E. 1969. "Heideggers Idee von Wahrheit." In *Martin Heidegger, Perspektiven zur Deutung seines Werkes*, ed. O. Pöggeler. Köln: Kiepenheuer and Witsch.

———. 1970. *Wahrheitsbegriff bei Husserl und Heidegger*. Berlin: W. De Gruyter.

Van Buren, J. 1994a. "Martin Heidegger, Martin Luther." In *Reading Heidegger from the Start: Essays in His Earliest Thought*, ed. Theodore Kisiel and John van Buren, 159–74. Albany: SUNY Press.

———. 1994b. *The Young Heidegger: Rumor of the Hidden King*. Bloomington and Indianapolis: Indiana University Press.

Volpi, F. 1984. *Heidegger e Aristotele*. Padua: Daphne.

———. 1988. *"Dasein* comme praxis: L'assimilation et la radicalisation heideggérienne de la philosophie pratique d'Aristote." In *Heidegger et l'Idée de la phénoménologie*, 1–41. Dordrecht: Kluwer.

———. 1989. "Der Bezug zu Platon und zu Aristotles in Heideggers Fundamentalverständnis der Technik." In *Kunst und Technik: Gedenkschrift für Martin Heidegger zum 100. Geburtstag*, ed. W. Biemel and F.-W. von Herrmann, 67–91. Frankfurt am Main: V. Klostermann.

———. 1994. *"Being and Time:* A 'Translation' of the Nichomachean Ethics?" In *Reading Heidegger from the Start: Essays in His Earliest Thought*, ed. T. Kisiel and J. van Buren, 195–211. Albany: SUNY Press.

———. 1996. "La question du *logos* dans l'articulation de la facticité chez le jeune Heidegger lecteur d'Aristote." In J.-F. Courtine, *Heidegger 1919–1929: De l'hermeneutique de la facticité à la métaphysique du Dasein*, ed. J.-F. Courtine, 33–65. Paris: J. Vrin.

———. 2000. "Phenomenology as Possibility: The 'Phenomenological' Appropriation of the History of Philosophy in the Young Heidegger." *Research in Phenomenology* 30:120–45.

Wachterhauser, B. R. 1999. *Beyond Being: Gadamer's Post-Platonic Hermeneutical Ontology*. Evanston, Ill.: Northwestern University Press.

Warnek, P. 1997. "Reading Plato before Platonism (after Heidegger)." *Research in Phenomenology* 27:61–89.

Webb, D. 2000. "Continuity and Difference in Heidegger's *Sophist.*" *Southern Journal of Philosophy* 38:145–69.

Weinberg, S. 1999. Letter to the editor. *New York Review of Books* 46, no. 3 (February 18): 49.

White, D. A. 1981. "On Historicism and Heidegger's Notion of Ontological Difference." *Monist* 64 (4): 518–33.

Wilpert, P. 1940. "Zum aristotelischen Wahrheitsbegriff," *Philosophisches Jahrbuch der Görresgesellschaft* 53:3–16. Reprinted in F.-P. Hager, ed., *Logik und Erkenntnislehre des Aristotles* (Darmstadt: Wiss. Buchges., 1972), 106–21.

Wittgenstein, L. 1953. *Philosophical Investigations,* trans. G. E. M. Anscombe. Oxford: Basil Blackwell.

———. 1972. *Tractatus Logico-Philosophicus,* 2d ed., trans. (with corrections) D. F. Pears and B. F. McGuinness. London: Routledge and Kegan Paul.

Wolz, H. G. 1981. *Plato and Heidegger.* London and Toronto: Associated University Presses.

Zarader, M. 1990. *Heidegger et les paroles de l'origine.* Paris: Vrin.

Zeyl, D. J. 1997. *Timaeus,* translated by D. J. Zeyl, in J. M. Cooper and D. S. Hutchinson, eds., *Plato's Complete Works* (Indianapolis/Cambridge: Hackett, 1997).

Zimmerman, M. E. 1990. *Heidegger's Confrontation with Modernity.* Bloomington and Indianapolis: Indiana University Press.

Zuckert, C. H. 1996. *Postmodern Platos.* Chicago: University of Chicago Press.

Contributors

Enrico Berti is an associate professor of philosophy at the Universita di Padova. He is the author of *La filosofia del primo Aristotele, Il pensiero politico di Aristotele,* and *L'unita del sapere in Aristotele.*

Johannes Fritsche taught at the TU Berlin (Germany), the New School for Social Research (New York City), and Pennsylvania State University (University Park). He is the author of a book on Aristotle and of *Historical Destiny and National Socialism in Heidegger's "Being and Time."*

Michael Inwood is fellow of Trinity College, Oxford. He is the author of *A Heidegger Dictionary, Heidegger,* and *A Hegel Dictionary.* He is also the editor of *Hegel: Introductory Lectures on Aesthetics* and *Hegel: Selections.*

Theodore Kisiel is Presidential Research Professor at Northern Illinois University. He translated into English Heidegger's *Prolegomena zur Geschichte des Zeitbegriffs* and is the author of *The Genesis of Heidegger's "Being and Time"* and coeditor of *Reading Heidegger from the Start.*

Joseph Margolis is Laura H. Carnell Professor of Philosophy at Temple University and is the author of numerous books, including *What, After All, Is a Work of Art? Historied Thought, Constructed World,* and *The Flux of History and the Flux of Science.*

María del Carmen Paredes is a professor of philosophy at the University of Salamanca. She is the editor of *Mente, Conciencia y Conocimiento, Política y Religión en Hegel,* and *Subjetividad y pensamiento: Cuestiones en torno a Hegel* and coeditor of *Razón, Libertad y Estado en Hegel.*

Catalin Partenie is a fellow of the University of Québec at Montréal. He is the editor of *Plato, Selected Myths* and coeditor of Plato's *Complete Works* in Romanian. He translated into Romanian Plato's *Timaeus* (in collaboration), *Critias* and *Menexenus,* and Aristotle's *Protrepticus* (in collaboration).

Tom Rockmore is a professor of philosophy at Duquesne University and the author of many books, including *On Heidegger's Nazism and Philosophy, Cognition: An Introduction to Hegel's Phenomenology of Spirit, New Perspectives on Fichte* (edited with

Daniel Breazeale), *Heidegger and French Philosophy: Humanism, Antihumanism and Being,* and *Before and after Hegel: A Historical Introduction.*

Stanley Rosen is Borden Parker Bowne Professor of Philosophy at Boston University. He is the author of numerous books, including *The Question of Being: A Reversal of Heidegger, The Ancients and the Moderns, Plato's "Statesman," Plato's "Symposium,"* and *Plato's "Sophist."*

Jacques Taminiaux is Adelmann Professor of Philosophy at Boston College and the former director of the Centre for Phenomenological Studies at the Université de Louvain-la-Neuve. He translated into French Heidegger's *Die Frage nach dem Ding* and Hegel's *System der Sittlichkeit.* His books include *La fille de Thrace et le penseur professionnel: Arendt et Heidegger, Lectures de l'ontologie fondamentale: essais sur Heidegger,* and *La nostalgie de la Grèce à l'aube de l'idéalisme allemand.* He took part in Heidegger's last private seminar at Zähringen.